The Modern Baseball Card Investor

By Jeff Hwang

April 2014

The Modern Baseball Card Investor

For Luke, Bryce, Liam, Trystan, and the next generation of collectors.

About the Author

Jeff Hwang is a gaming industry consultant and the best-selling author of *Pot-Limit Omaha Poker: The Big Play Strategy* and the three-volume *Advanced Pot-Limit Omaha* series. A graduate of Washington University in St. Louis with degrees in both finance and management, Jeff is also an investment writer/analyst and a long-time contributor to The Motley Fool/Fool.com, a multi-media financial services company.

Jeff holds an MBA and MS in Hotel Administration from the University of Nevada Las Vegas.

Jeff has been an advantage player since 1999, when he took an interest in blackjack and started hitting up the cruise ships off the coast of Florida near his hometown of Ft. Lauderdale. Shortly after graduating from college in 2003, Jeff began covering the gaming industry stocks for The Motley Fool, where his highly regarded work on the gaming industry in general and the regional gaming markets in particular has led to references in *Cigar Aficionado*, as well as in business publications as geographically diverse as the *Las Vegas Business Press, Macau Business*, and the *Baton Rouge Business Report*. At the same time, Jeff also picked up poker, and began playing regularly on the riverboats in his adopted home of St. Louis.

Jeff's interest in blackjack, poker, and the gaming industry has led him to visit virtually every commercial casino in the United States, and has given him an intimate knowledge of the riverboat casinos unrivaled in the financial media. Meanwhile, the time spent playing poker primarily on the riverboats of Missouri, Mississippi, and Indiana provided the impetus for Jeff's first book, *Pot-Limit Omaha Poker: The Big Play Strategy*, which was released in December 2007.

Pot-Limit Omaha Poker has since become the best-selling book on Omaha poker ever written, and remains the standard text for Texas hold'em players looking to pick up the game.

In March 2008, Jeff was enlisted by *Card Player* magazine to write a regular column on Omaha poker, and – given his background as an investment analyst – bankroll management as well. And thanks in large part to the success of both the column and the book, Jeff quickly established himself as the world's leading authority on Omaha poker.

In August 2008, in an effort to dive deeper into the gaming industry, Jeff made the move to Las Vegas and enrolled in the dual MBA/MS in Hotel Administration program at the University of Nevada, Las Vegas.

In November of that year, in a partnership of mutual interests with North Carolina-based PokerTek, Jeff began hosting a regular small-stakes PLO game on PokerTek's PokerPro electronic poker tables in the fully-automated poker room at the Excalibur Hotel and Casino on the Las Vegas Strip. And on November 20th, 2008, Jeff hosted the official kickoff event at Excalibur with a lineup featuring Lyle Berman – a 3-time World Series of Poker gold bracelet winner, as well as Chairman of PokerTek, Lakes Entertainment, and World Poker Tour Enterprises – and David Sklansky, a 3-time WSOP bracelet winner, as well as perhaps the most influential poker author ever.

In June 2009, Jeff released his second book, *Advanced Pot-Limit Omaha: Small Ball and Short-Handed Play*.

In July 2009, in concert with poker room management at The Venetian, Jeff brought small-stakes live PLO to fruition in Las Vegas by starting a regular $1-$2 blind game with a $5 bring-in and $500 max buy-in. That game has since become the longest-running PLO game in Las Vegas in the post-Moneymaker era.

In October 2010, *Advanced Pot-Limit Omaha Volume II: LAG Play* and *Advanced Pot-Limit Omaha Volume III: The Short-Handed Workbook* were released simultaneously. Later that year, Jeff was contracted by PokerTracker to participate as a consultant on the development of PokerTracker 4.

In May 2011, Jeff and his friend Steven McLoughlin worked with poker room management at Aria to establish a $1-$3 PLO game with a $200-min/$500-max buy-in, while setting the structures for the $2-$5 and $5-$10 blind PLO games as well. The PLO games at Aria have run on a consistent basis ever since, while the $1-$3 blind game has been the most reliable small stakes PLO game in Las Vegas.

Jeff completed his MBA and MS in Hotel Administration at University of Nevada Las Vegas in May 2011.

In July 2011, Jeff was enlisted by HVS in helping conduct a market feasibility study on the Las Vegas Sands Spain project. The consulting project was one of the largest of its kind ever undertaken in the industry, and involved the cooperation of HVS offices in San Francisco, Las Vegas, Chicago, London, and Madrid. Jeff created the model designed to project gaming revenues from local and regional patrons, and participated in a two-week field study of the European gaming markets, ranging from London to Monte Carlo, Paris, Barcelona, and Madrid.

Upon completing his work on the project, Jeff returned to work as a consultant on the development of PokerTracker 4, the premier stat-tracking software for online poker players. PokerTracker 4 was released in the fall of 2012.

Acknowledgments

First and foremost, I'd like to thank my publisher, Matthew Hilger and Dimat Enterprises, for having an open mind about this project. This is our fourth book together, but the previous three – as are all of the previous books under the Dimat publishing label – were all poker books. When I broached the idea for a baseball card book a little over a year ago, Matthew was naturally skeptical, as anybody else would be who hadn't seen a baseball card in about two decades. But Matthew kept an open mind, and let me make my case; and here we are.

Matthew and I have a pretty unique working relationship, and there is no one I trust more in this business. This book was more or less written on a verbal agreement; sometimes a verbal agreement with the right person is more reliable than a written agreement.

Dan Hitt and Beckett Media

Frankly speaking, this book would not have been possible without the availability of Beckett's consistent, reliable pricing data. In that regard, I am greatly in debt to Dan Hitt and Beckett Media for granting permission to use their proprietary pricing data – they could very easily have said "No" and stopped this project dead in its tracks.

I'd also like to thank Dan for taking the time to review this text, giving me confidence that I would not embarrass myself with this text.

Brian Richards and the Motley Fool

I'd like to thank Brian Richards and the Motley Fool for publishing a series of articles I wrote on baseball (and football) cards in early-mid 2013 on Fool. com, allowing me to establish certain key ideas and test the market. I've been a contributor to Fool.com going back to my days as an intern in the summer of 2002, but baseball cards are a bit more alternative than my usual contributions regarding casino industry stocks. And again, Brian and the Motley Fool could easily have said "No;"and without those articles and the resulting feedback, it's quite possible that this book never gets written.

Mike Simmons

Mike was the sales rep at Beckett Grading Services who picked up my case when I inquired about bulk grading rates back in January 2013. In addition to being helpful with any questions I had about the BGS grading system, Mike was also responsible for passing me along to Dan Hitt when I inquired about referencing Beckett's proprietary online price guide data when I wrote the first of those articles for Fool.com.

Kristin Long, Samantha Krerowicz, and Greg Schneider

Props for the cover of this book go to Kristin Long and Samantha Krerowicz. Kristin is the master photographer responsible for the background photos spanning the cover of this book. You can check out more of her work at kristinlongphotography. com. Samantha is responsible for the design and layout, and can be found at krevichconsulting.com.

Some years ago, my friend Greg Schneider took the timeless profile pic that appears on the back cover; that photo now graces the cover of four books.

Coach Nick Garritano and the College of Southern Nevada

Last but not least, I'd like to thank Coach Nick Garritano and the College of Southern Nevada for letting us shoot the cover shot at their home field, William R. Morse Stadium.

Contents

Preface: Have Baseball Card Values Risen in 20-25 Years? Actually...

"By the '80s, baseball card values were rising beyond the average hobbyist's means. As prices continued to climb, baseball cards were touted as a legitimate investment alternative to stocks, with the Wall Street Journal referring to them as sound 'inflation hedges' and 'nostalgia futures.' Newspapers started running feature stories with headlines such as 'Turning Cardboard Into Cash' (the Washington Post), 'A Grand Slam Profit May Be in the Cards' (the New York Times), and 'Cards Put Gold, Stocks to Shame as Investment' (the Orange County Register)."

– Dave Jamieson, Author of *Mint Condition* (2010)

Indeed, the great baseball card bubble of the late 1980s and early 1990s would burst in spectacular fashion. By 1993, vast oversupply created by a combination of an influx of new competition (Score in 1988 and Upper Deck in 1989 would join Topps, Fleer, and Donruss to make the "Big 3" a "Big 5"), multiple manufacturers with multiple baseball card products (too many to name), and print runs thought to be in the millions, would render all but the new high-end issues such as 1989 Upper Deck, 1990 Leaf, 1992 Bowman, 1993 Topps Finest, and 1993 Upper Deck SP worthless.

With single-pack prices of such high-end issues in the multiple-dollar range and everything else worthless, the casual mass market collector (i.e. kids) would be chased from the baseball card market, and pushed towards more practical hobbies like video games, pogs, and AOL. Of those collectors that stuck around, many were finished off by the 1994 baseball strike.

And by the time the dust settled from the great home run chases of 1998 (Mark McGwire and Sammy Sosa) and 2001 (Barry Bonds' 73 HR season) through 2007 (the year Bonds passed Hank Aaron for the career HR record) – along with the ensuing steroid scandals – baseball card industry sales had dropped from $1.5 billion in 1992[1] down to $200 million by 2008,[2] where it reportedly still sat as of April 2012.[3]

---

[1] "Upper Deck Shakes Up Trading-Card Industry," by Richard Sandomir, New York Times, October 4, 1993

[2] www.forbes.com/2009/08/28/baseball-cards-economy-inflation-opinions-columnists-john-tamny.html

[3] www.nytimes.com/2012/04/09/business/media/apps-take-positions-in-the-topps-baseball-lineup.html?pagewanted=all&_r=2&

Where there were once an estimated 10,000-plus baseball card shops in America,[4] recent issues of Beckett Baseball magazine list fewer than 200 such brick-and-mortar hobby dealers in its directory. Hobby sales of new sealed boxes or whole cases are now dominated by a few such dealers with a large online presence and competitive prices – most notably Blowout Cards, whose online site also includes the largest online forum dedicated to sports cards – and dealers who operate on eBay and/or Amazon.com. Meanwhile, where baseball cards were once readily available at drugstores, grocery stores, and Kay Bee Toys stores (remember those?) across America, brick-and-mortar retail sales are now restricted largely to big box retailers Wal-Mart and Target.

The prices of unopened boxes of cards from the late 1980s and early 1990s have fallen dramatically over the last 20-25 years or so, reflecting a general widespread devaluation of cards printed during that time period. Nowadays, unopened wax boxes of 1988 Donruss can be had for $6 or $7 a box on eBay, or about half what a box would have cost at retail back in 1988 – or well less than half if you account for inflation. And where packs of 1990 Leaf Series II once went for $12 a pack in search of Frank Thomas rookie cards (RCs) worth $70 each back in early 1993,[5] whole sealed boxes with 36 unopened packs and an average of about two $20 1990 Leaf Frank Thomas RCs per box can now be had for $70 to $80 per box on eBay.

Not surprisingly, going back to a February 6, 1993 article in The Economist (US) entitled "Throw in the Cards," virtually every article that has been written about baseball cards over the past two decades has focused on these very details. And in the last twenty years, few – if any – industry outsiders have dared to relate baseball cards as investments.

But seemingly as a rule, these articles tend to overlook at least three key details:

1. **Graded cards.** High-grade examples of professionally-graded cards from Beckett Grading Services (BGS) and Professional Sports Authenticator (PSA) warrant premium valuations, often well in excess of ungraded book value. That said, Gem Mint condition (BGS 9.5 or PSA 10) graded rookie cards of premium (typically Hall of Fame-caliber) players from the 1980s and early 1990s have largely either held up well, or in some cases have actually *appreciated* considerably, maintaining valuations far beyond those ever achieved by ungraded examples of the same cards.

---

[4] www.slate.com/articles/sports/sports_nut/2010/03/the_great_baseball_card_bubble.single.html
[5] Source: "Throw in the Cards," *The Economist (US)*, February 6, 1993

2. **A card removal effect due to the presence of graded cards.** The presence of graded cards means that the highest-quality cards have been removed from the pool of ungraded cards on the market, thus resulting in lower overall values of ungraded cards. Consequently, focusing exclusively on ungraded values will understate card values by default.

3. **The investment profile of newer issues has improved dramatically over the last 20 years.** In addition to the premiums afforded to Gem Mint condition graded cards, the presence of a clear best product every year, smaller print runs, short-printed rookie cards and serialized parallels, autographed rookie cards, and an enhanced baseball prospect game have lead to a more exciting hobby with a better product and better economics. Meanwhile, graded cards and eBay in particular have brought enhanced liquidity to the cardboard stock market.

We'll talk about the newer issues in a minute. But first, let's start by examining card values of key rookie cards from the 1980s and early 1990s.

Historical Ungraded Card Values

If you only look at the prices of ungraded cards – as most casual onlookers tend to do – you'd get the impression that card values have taken a nosedive over the last 20 years (and of course they have). Moreover, you'd get the impression that even the best RCs of the best players would have made horrible investments.

Below is a table with historical ungraded prices of the key rookie cards from the 1980s and early 1990s. Prices are taken from the April issues of Beckett Baseball and Beckett Baseball Card Monthly magazines in five-year intervals starting in 1990, plus April 1993 to give us another reference point, and ending with December 2013 prices from Beckett.com.

Notable RCs from 1982-1994: Historical Ungraded Pricing

Card	#	April 1990	April 1993	April 1995	April 2000	April 2005	April 2010	Dec. 2013
1982 Topps Traded Cal Ripken Jr. RC	98T	$12.50	$275	$225	$200	$120	$150	$120
1983 Topps Tony Gwynn RC	482	20	40	32	60	25	20	25
1983 Topps Wade Boggs RC	498	35	35	20	25	15	15	15
1983 Topps Ryne Sandberg RC	83	12	60	32	20	15	20	20
1984 Donruss Don Mattingly RC*	248	65	45	55	30	40	25	40
1984 Donruss Joe Carter RC	41	15	45	70	12	8	8	8
1984 Donruss Darryl Strawberry RC	68	36	45	10	8	8	8	8
1984 Fleer Update Roger Clemens XRC	27	85	450	300	200	225	120	120
1984 Fleer Update Kirby Puckett XRC	92	120	375	325	80	60	80	100
1985 Topps Mark McGwire RC	401	18	30	8	175	40	30	20
1986 Donruss Jose Canseco RC*	38	50	60	30	30	10	10	12
1986 Donruss Fred McGriff RC	28	15	28	30	8	8	8	8
1987 Fleer Barry Bonds RC	604	1.50	20	35	40	60	15	12
1987 Fleer Barry Larkin RC	204	3.50	7	4	5	3	3	8
1987 Donruss Greg Maddux RC	36	1.50	6	8	20	10	10	10
1989 Upper Deck Ken Griffey Jr. RC	1	9	55	75	150	50	40	40
1990 Leaf Frank Thomas RC	300	–	60	85	40	20	12	20
1990 Leaf Sammy Sosa RC	220	–	0.90	5	80	40	12	12
1992 Bowman Mariano Rivera RC	302	–	0.20	0.30	8	15	40	60
1992 Bowman Mike Piazza RC	461	–	1.50	35	60	40	20	20
1993 SP Derek Jeter RC	279	–	–	7.50	100	60	100	150
1994 SP Alex Rodriguez RC	15	–	–	12	85	80	80	40

Sources: Beckett Baseball Card Monthly/Beckett Baseball magazines dated April 1990, 1993, 1995, 200, 2005, and 2013; Dec. 2013 pricing taken from Beckett.com, with permission

*The 1986 Donruss Jose Canseco RC hit $105 in April 1991 and $75 in April 1992, while the 1984 Donruss Don Mattingly reached $85 in April 1991.

However, the practice of looking only at ungraded values produces flawed arguments by excluding the values of the highest-quality, highest-value cards – the mint condition ones – by default.

Graded Cards

Professional Sports Authenticator (PSA) – a division of **Collectors Universe** (Nasdaq: CLCT) – launched in 1991, applying its experience as an authentication/grading service in the coin market to establish the first relatively objective 3rd-party authentication and grading service for trading cards. Beckett – the established market leader with its monthly price guide magazines – would later follow in 1999 with its own Beckett Grading Services (BGS). These two companies are the established leaders in this space; and while there are other competitors, PSA- and BGS-graded cards warrant by far the highest premiums due to these companies' strong brands and tough grading standards.

PSA grades cards with a single grade on a 10-pt. scale, with the highest grade being PSA10 Gem Mint (labeled GEM-MT 10 by PSA) – a basically perfect, at least reasonably well-centered card with sharp corners and edges, and a clean surface. The next-highest grade is PSA 9 Mint (MINT 9), which allows for one slight physical blemish (whether it be slight corner wear or a surface stain or scratch, or minor chipping on the edges), along with a higher tolerance for centering. The PSA grading scale was strictly in whole number increments until February 2008, when the company introduced grading in half-point increments (i.e. 7, 7.5, 8, 8.5, etc.) with the exception of a 9.5 score.

BGS similarly grades on a 10-pt. scale but in half-point increments, and with a final grade that is a weighted composite of four separate subgrades for centering, corners, edges, and surface. While a BGS 9 Mint grade is effectively equivalent to a PSA 9 Mint grade, a BGS 9.5 Gem Mint is essentially a perfect card and effectively equivalent to a PSA 10 Gem Mint, though BGS technically does have another level in the rare BGS 10 Pristine grade reserved for the best of the best. In addition, for autographed cards, Beckett includes an additional, separate grade for the autograph on a 10-pt. whole number increment scale, whereas PSA does not.

However, while effectively equivalent, it should be noted that BGS and PSA have different definitions for Gem Mint and Mint grades (and down the line) that represent differences in grading philosophies: As we will see later, PSA's grade definitions place a greater emphasis on the physical card with a greater tolerance for centering, while BGS places a greater emphasis on centering as a key attribute of a card's overall condition, while allowing a slightly greater tolerance for corners. As a consequence, a PSA 10 Gem Mint grade may be tougher to attain than a BGS 9.5 Gem Mint grade on issues where corners are often a concern (like vintage or 1980s issues), while a BGS 9.5 Gem Mint grade may be tougher to attain on issues where centering is more of a concern but corners aren't.

For the most part, a BGS 9.5 Gem Mint and PSA 10 Gem Mint example of the same card will carry roughly the same valuation in Chrome Era modern issues (c.1993/1996-present), though there are some discrepancies favoring certain PSA 10s in earlier modern issues (1981-c.1995), and others favoring the BGS 9.5s – particularly certain autographed cards with 10 Auto grades – in more recent issues.

That said, there is no question that the BGS 10 Pristine grade sits atop the graded value scale.

The table below shows the current graded book values for each of the cards in the previous table, along with the adjusted multiple. The **adjusted multiple** is simply the graded book value multiple to ungraded book value, adjusted for the cost of getting a card graded, which for our purposes is assumed to be $10 (the actual cost may vary by order size and desired turnaround time, but $10 is a good proxy). In other words:

Adj. Multiple = Graded BV / (Ungraded BV + $10)

Notable RCs from 1982-1994: Current Graded Card Pricing and Adjusted Multiples

Card	#	Ungraded BV	BGS 9.5	Adj. Multiple*	BGS 10	Adj. Multiple*
1982 Topps Traded Cal Ripken Jr. RC	98T	$120	$1,200	9.2x	–	–
1983 Topps Tony Gwynn RC	482	$25	$500	14.3x	–	–
1983 Topps Wade Boggs RC	498	$15	$400	16.0x	–	–
1983 Topps Ryne Sandberg RC	83	$20	$300	10.0x	–	–
1984 Donruss Don Mattingly RC	248	$40	$500	10.0x	–	–
1984 Donruss Joe Carter RC	41	$8	$120	6.7x	–	–
1984 Donruss Darryl Strawberry RC	68	$8	$60	3.3x	–	–
1984 Fleer Update Roger Clemens XRC	27	$120	$600	4.6x	–	–
1984 Fleer Update Kirby Puckett XRC	92	$100	$500	4.6x	–	–
1985 Topps Mark McGwire RC	401	$20	$400	13.3x	–	–
1986 Donruss Jose Canseco RC	38	$12	$100	4.6x	–	–
1986 Donruss Fred McGriff RC	28	$8	$60	3.3x	–	–
1987 Fleer Barry Bonds RC	604	$12	$120	5.5x	–	–
1987 Fleer Barry Larkin RC	204	$8	$60	3.3x	–	–
1987 Donruss Greg Maddux RC	36	$10	$100	5.0x	–	–

Card	#	Ungraded BV	BGS 9.5	Adj. Multiple*	BGS 10	Adj. Multiple*
1989 Upper Deck Ken Griffey Jr. RC	1	$40	$300	6.0x	$1,400	28.0x
1990 Leaf Frank Thomas RC	300	$20	$100	3.3x	–	–
1990 Leaf Sammy Sosa RC	220	$12	$40	1.8x	–	–
1992 Bowman Mariano Rivera RC	302	$60	$250	3.6x	–	–
1992 Bowman Mike Piazza RC	461	$20	$80	2.7x	–	–
1993 SP Derek Jeter FOIL RC	279	$150	$2,000**	12.5x	–	–
1994 SP Alex Rodriguez FOIL RC	15	$40	$400	8.0x	–	–

Source: Beckett.com, Dec. 2013, with permission
*Adjusted multiple represents the value of a graded card of a given grade divided by the ungraded book value, adjusted for the cost of having a card graded, assumed to be $10.
**PSA 10 valued at $28,500 by PSAcard.com; two PSA 10 copies sold in December 2013 for $32,500

The first thing you'll notice is that the BGS 9.5 graded cards in the table warrant healthy and sometimes massive premiums to ungraded book value. For example, a BGS 9.5 1993 SP Derek Jeter RC carries a book value of $2,000, for an adjusted multiple of 12.5x ungraded book value – well beyond its current peak ungraded valuation – while a BGS 9.5 1983 Wade Boggs RC carries a book value of $400, or a whopping 16.0x adjusted multiple to ungraded book, and also well in excess of peak ungraded value, which has never reached triple digits.

In addition to demand, the biggest reason these cards warrant such premiums is condition/grade scarcity: Of the nearly 11,000 1993 SP Derek Jeter RCs graded by BGS, for example, only 139 have been graded BGS 9.5, while only *12* of the nearly 11,000 cards graded by PSA have graded PSA 10 Gem Mint. Likewise, of the nearly 12,000 1994 SP Alex Rodriguez RCs submitted to BGS for grading, only 132 have been graded BGS 9.5, while only 40 of the over 14,000 such cards graded by PSA have graded PSA 10 Gem Mint.[6]

In fact, the PSA 10 grade on the 1993 SP Jeter in particular is so rare that, in December 2013, two such PSA 10 copies sold for $32,500.

---

[6] The discrepancy in Gem Mint frequency between BGS and PSA copies of the 1993 SP Derek Jeter RC and 1994 SP Alex Rodriguez RC is likely due to differences in each company's definition of Gem Mint that appear to affect this particular card issue, where centering does not appear to be a concern, but chipping and bad corners are a major issue. We'll discuss the 1993 SP Derek Jeter and differences in BGS and PSA grading standards in Part I in our discussion of some of the top modern card sales of 2013, and we will compare BGS and PSA grading standards directly in Part VII.

The graded values of the steroid bunch – Mark McGwire, Roger Clemens, Barry Bonds, Jose Canseco, and Sammy Sosa, and later Alex Rodriguez – have for the most part held up well compared to their *ungraded* book values.[7] The one notable exception is Sammy Sosa, whose 1990 Leaf RC's current graded value of $40 is well below its April 2000 peak ungraded value of $80. A BGS 9.5 1985 Topps Mark McGwire RC carries a 13.3x adjusted multiple and a valuation well in excess of peak ungraded book value, while the $600 graded book value of the 1984 Fleer Update Roger Clemens XRC still trumps its peak 1993 ungraded value of $450.

And while the 1987 Fleer Barry Larkin RC might seem like an odd inclusion considering its ungraded pricing has never reached double digits, a BGS 9.5 example carries a book value of $60.

The other thing you'll notice is the 1989 Upper Deck Ken Griffey Jr. RC, which is the only one that has pricing for a BGS 10 Pristine grade with a $1,400 book value and a 28.0x adjusted multiple. And the reason it is the only card in this group to have pricing is because BGS 10 Pristine examples of the other cards either don't exist, or are otherwise too rare to price.

Out of the over 30,000 Upper Deck Griffey RCs graded by BGS, 1,863 have been graded BGS 9.5 Gem Mint, while only 79 have gotten the BGS 10 Pristine grade. In contrast, there are exactly zero 1993 SP Derek Jeter BGS 10s, and zero 1994 SP Alex Rodriguez BGS 10s.

So have the value of baseball cards risen in the last 20 years?

The answer depends on the question you're really asking. If you're asking whether the cards from the 1980s and early '90s you have stuffed in binders or shoeboxes are worth anything, I would say you could probably go ahead and stuff them in a trash can and not be giving up much in terms of monetary value. Only the sharpest examples can attain a BGS 9.5 or PSA 10 grade; moreover, these cards need to be well-centered as well in order to attain such grades, and this is not an easy hurdle to pass – even for the cards that were printed in 2013, much less 1983.

But if you're asking whether the values of the key rookie cards of baseball's biggest stars have risen in the last 20 years or so, I would say that the answer is clearly yes, once you factor the Gem Mint condition, professionally graded cards by BGS and PSA.

---

[7] …though not to previous graded values, which were all much, much higher – as were the graded cards of most of the other players – during a graded card bubble of the late 1990s-early 2000s, coinciding with the stock market bubble of the same period.

Certainly there have been disappointments – Darryl Strawberry's career fell off a cliff at his age 30 season in 1992, and he was later suspended in 1995 for cocaine-related reasons; while Jose Canseco, Roger Clemens, Barry Bonds, Mark McGwire, and Sammy Sosa have seen their cardboard stocks hammered for steroid-related reasons. More recently, Alex Rodriguez's 1994 SP RC carried a BGS 9.5 valuation of $2,500 into 2013 before Rodriguez was implicated in the Biogenesis PED scandal, and ultimately suspended for the 2014 season. And clearly valuation is always a valid concern, as it is with stocks: You can't overpay and expect to generate a sufficient return on investment.

But much like the stocks of premium companies warrant premium valuations and tend to outperform their peers, the key rookie cards of baseball's biggest stars have tended to outperform the rookie cards of their peers, while the highest-quality, BGS 9.5 and PSA 10 Gem Mint graded examples of these cards have *vastly* outperformed the lesser-quality, ungraded versions of the same cards, and in some cases have appreciated considerably over the last 20-25 years or so.

And here's the key: If this is true of the key cards from a period of extreme oversupply, what does it say about the investment potential of more recently issued cards featuring better product printed in smaller numbers?

Introduction

In the past 20 years, the investment profile of newer baseball card issues has improved dramatically, and for at least eight good reasons:

1. Graded cards and multiple expansion

2. Smaller print runs yielding upside leverage

3. Short-printed RCs, limited print serialized parallels, and autographed prospect and rookie cards

4. The high end

5. An enhanced baseball prospecting game

6. Enhanced liquidity due to the presence of eBay and graded cards, as well as the presence of new online trading sites like COMC.com

7. A half-generation of current untapped potential demand, and

8. Fantasy sports, sports betting and untapped re-demand from former collectors who quit the hobby two decades ago.

Graded Cards and Multiple Expansion

As with the older cards from the 1980s and early 1990s, professionally graded cards of more recent issues in Gem Mint condition (BGS 9.5 or PSA 10) carry premiums over ungraded cards. Below is a table with current ungraded and graded BGS 9.5 values of some of the key Bowman Chrome RC or prospect autographed cards from 2001-2011 as of December 2013, along with their adjusted multiples.[8]

---

[8] As presented in the Preface, the adjusted multiple represents the graded value premium over ungraded value, adjusted for the cost of getting a card graded, which is assumed to be $10

Key Bowman Chrome Prospect/RC Autos: 2001-2011

Card	#	Ungraded BV	BGS 9.5	Adj. Multiple
2001 Bowman Chrome Albert Pujols Auto RC	340	$3,000	$9,000	3.0x
2002 Bowman Chrome Joe Mauer Auto RC	391	$150	$400	2.5x
2002 Bowman Chrome David Wright Auto RC	385	$120	$250	1.9x
2003 Bowman Chrome Hanley Ramirez Auto RC	334	$80	$150	1.7x
2004 Bowman Chrome Felix Hernandez Auto RC	345	$120	$250	1.9x
2005 Bowman Chrome Justin Verlander Auto RC	331	$120	$300	2.3x
2005 Bowman Chrome Matt Kemp Auto RC	349	$120	$250	1.9x
2005 Bowman Chrome Draft Ryan Braun Auto RC	168	$60	$300	4.3x
2006 Bowman Chrome Prospects Justin Upton Auto	BC223	$80	$200	2.2x
2006 Bowman Chrome Draft Draft Picks Evan Longoria Auto	66	$120	$250	1.9x
2006 Bowman Chrome Draft Draft Picks Clayton Kershaw Auto	84	$250	$300	1.2x
2007 Bowman Chrome Prospects Tim Lincecum Auto	BC238	$120	$200	1.5x
2008 Bowman Chrome Draft Prospects Michael Stanton Auto	BDPP115	$150	$250	1.6x
2008 Bowman Chrome Draft Prospects Buster Posey Auto	BDPP128	$200	$250	1.2x
2009 Bowman Chrome Draft Prospects Mike Trout Auto	BDPP89	$500	$800	1.6x
2010 Bowman Chrome Stephen Strasburg Auto RC	205B	$150	$350	2.2x
2011 Bowman Chrome Prospects Bryce Harper Auto	BCP111B	$350	$500	1.4x

Source: Beckett.com, December 2013 with permission

You'll notice that while the BGS 9.5-to-ungraded BV multiples are much smaller for these issues compared to the multiples for the cards from 1982 to 1994, the multiples do appear to expand over time within this sample as well. While the multiples for cards from 2007-2011 are generally in 1.2x to 1.6x range, the multiples for the cards from 2001-2006 are generally in the 1.7x to 2.5x range.

The 2010 Bowman Chrome Stephen Strasburg Auto RC appears to be an outlier with a 2.2x multiple, though one possible explanation may be that its ungraded book value recently dropped, while the graded BGS 9.5 value hasn't and may be due for a drop in the book. This is certainly the case with the 2005 Bowman Chrome Draft Ryan Braun Auto RC at 4.3x, which saw its ungraded book value drop from $150 in early 2013 down to $60 by the end of the year in the wake of the Biogenesis PED scandal and Braun's subsequent 65-game suspension,[9] while its graded BGS 9.5 book value remains unchanged from $300 but is probably due for a similar drop.

The 2006 Bowman Chrome Draft Clayton Kershaw auto may also be an outlier in the opposite direction: Its ungraded value has gotten a bump over the past year from $120 up to $250, and while its BGS 9.5 Gem Mint book value has gotten a bump from $200 to $300 over the same time period. That said, the more likely explanation for the relatively small 1.2x multiple is that either the BGS 9.5 Gem Mint value is due for another bump (given recent sales as high as $350), or that its ungraded value of $250 is overstated.

Smaller Print Runs and Upside Leverage

Print runs have fallen dramatically over the past twenty years, when print runs were thought to be in the millions.

According to Dave Jamieson in *Mint Condition: How Baseball Cards Became an American Obsession*, there were over a *million* 1989 Upper Deck Ken Griffey Jr. RCs printed, and yet the card still carries an ungraded book value of $40 today, along with a graded BGS 9.5 Gem Mint book value of $300 (6.0x adj. multiple) and a BGS 10 Pristine book value of $1,400 (28.0x adj. multiple). In comparison, the 1993 Stadium Club Murphy Derek Jeter RC was a relative short print – according to Beckett.com, the card had a print run of 128,000, and has enough demand for the card to carry a $100 ungraded book value and graded BGS 9.5 value of $350 (3.2x adj. multiple).

But in stark contrast, the key new issues feature far smaller print numbers: Unless my math is wrong or Topps is lying about their odds on their wrappers, the print run on the 2012 Bowman Chrome Draft Baseball cards was less than 15,000, and closer to 11,000 base cards excluding refractors.[10]

---

[9] http://sports.yahoo.com/news/brewers–ryan-braun-agrees-to-65-game-suspension-mlb-arod-220004864.html

[10] Based on two Rookie Autograph Superfractors in the set – Bryce Harper and Yu Darvish; and 1,251,400 packs of Hobby with two chrome cards per pack, and 75,816 packs of Jumbo with six chrome cards per pack, for a total of just under 3 million chrome cards before backing out autos, inserts, and printing plates. With 220 RCs and Draft Pick cards in the set, I get a print run around 13,000 including refractors, or closer to ~11,300 chrome base cards excluding refractors.

Think about it: If over a million 1989 Upper Deck Ken Griffey Jr. RCs can have a book value of $40 and 128,000 1993 Stadium Club Murphy Derek Jeter RCs can carry an ungraded book value of $100, what does that say about the potential value of future stars in the 2012 Bowman Chrome Draft cards with total print numbers about 1/10th that of the 1993 Stadium Club Murphy set?

And what about parallels or high end sets with print runs in the hundreds or less?

Short-Printed RCs, Limited Print Serialized Parallels, and Autographed Prospect and Rookie Cards

Manufacturers nowadays have enhanced the value of the classic rookie card through a variety of methods, whether it be short-printed RCs, limited print serialized parallels, autographed prospect and rookie cards, or some combination of the above.

Year in and year out, the key rookie cards in hockey are the Young Guns cards in the regular Upper Deck sets. These cards are deliberately short printed, and included as inserts to the tune of about one in every four packs. And because virtually every rookie in the Upper Deck set is in the Young Guns subset, trying to obtain a certain key rookie card of a certain player by opening packs is an extraordinarily difficult (futile for most) task, thus leading to relatively extraordinary valuations for non-autographed base cards.

Upper Deck Hockey Young Guns: Top RCs 2005-06 through 2011-12

Card	#	Pos.	Ungraded BV	BGS 9.5	Adj. Multiple
2005-06 Upper Deck Sidney Crosby YG RC	201	C	$300	$600	1.9x
2005-06 Upper Deck Alexander Ovechkin YG RC	443	LW	$100	$150	1.4x
2006-07 Upper Deck Evgeni Malkin YG RC	486	C	$120	$175	1.3x
2007-08 Upper Deck Jonathan Toews YG RC	462	C	$80	$150	1.7x
2007-08 Upper Deck Patrick Kane YG RC	210	RW	$50	$100	1.7x
2007-08 Upper Deck Carey Price YG RC	227	G	$50	$100	1.7x
2008-09 Upper Deck Steven Stamkos YG RC	245	C	$80	$150	1.7x
2009-10 Upper Deck John Tavares YG RC	201	C	$60	$150	2.1x
2010-11 Upper Deck Tyler Seguin YG RC	456	C	$80	$120	1.3x
2010-11 Upper Deck Taylor Hall YG RC	219	LW	$60	$100	1.4x
2010-11 Upper Deck Jordan Eberle YG RC	220	RW	$50	$100	1.7x
2011-12 Upper Deck Ryan Nugent-Hopkins YG RC	214	C	$60	$120	1.7x

Source: Beckett.com, January 2014

A more common approach is the use of limited print, serialized parallels, which both create a hierarchy of cards for any given player, and also carry premium valuations over the base cards. For example, the 2010 Bowman Chrome 18U USA Baseball Bryce Harper – Harper's first Bowman Chrome card, which is generally any player's key non-autographed card – carries an ungraded book value of $60; meanwhile, the Refractor parallel numbered to 777 carries a book value of $125, while the Blue Refractor #'d/150 is valued at $300, and the Gold Refractor #'d/50 books for $600, or a full 10x the value of the base card. Further up the hierarchy are Orange Refractors #'d/25, Red Refractors #'d/5, and a 1/1 Superfractor – each worth progressively more, and all too rare for Beckett to price.

In fact, the 2010 Bowman Chrome 18U USA Baseball Bryce Harper 1/1 Superfractor sold for $12,500 in September 2010, despite having a raised edge and being essentially ungradable.[11]

And where a common card in the 2012 Bowman Chrome Draft Draft Picks set carries a book value of $0.60, a Gold Refractor #'d/50 of the same player carries a book value of $15. Consequently, every baseball prospect of some minimal merit to be included in these sets has a card worth collecting on some level.

But the real key card for most baseball players is his first Bowman Chrome autographed card, which is generally a Bowman Chrome Prospects auto, or Bowman Chrome Draft Draft Picks auto. These cards themselves are relatively short-printed, with print runs generally in the 1,000-2,000 range. And like the non-autos, these cards also have limited print, serialized parallels which generally warrant large premiums over the base cards.

The table below shows some of the key Bowman Chrome autos, along with the values of their respective Blue Refractors #'d/150 and Gold Refractors #'d/50. The Gold Refractor #/50 autos first appeared in 2002, while the Blue Refractor #/150 auto first appeared in 2005. Once again, the Orange Refractors #'d/25, Red Refractors #'d/5, and 1/1 Superfractors are considered too rare for Beckett to price.

---

[11] www.beckett.com/news/2010/09/bryce-harper-superfractor-sale-confirmed-at-12500

Key Bowman Chrome Prospect/RC Autos: Gold Refractors #'d/50 vs. Base

Card	#	Base	Blue #/150	Gold #/50	Gold-Base Multiple
2002 Bowman Chrome Joe Mauer Auto RC	391	$150	–	$2,000	13.3x
2002 Bowman Chrome David Wright Auto RC	385	$120	–	$1,500	12.5x
2003 Bowman Chrome Hanley Ramirez Auto RC	334	$80	–	$500	6.3x
2004 Bowman Chrome Felix Hernandez Auto RC	345	$120	–	$800	6.7x
2005 Bowman Chrome Justin Verlander Auto RC	331	$120	$300	$1,000	8.3x
2005 Bowman Chrome Matt Kemp Auto RC	349	$120	$300	$900	7.5x
2005 Bowman Chrome Draft Ryan Braun Auto RC	168	$60	$150	$600	10.0x
2006 Bowman Chrome Prospects Justin Upton Auto	BC223	$80	$200	$500	6.3x
2006 Bowman Chrome Draft Draft Picks Evan Longoria Auto	66	$120	$250	$800	6.7x
2006 Bowman Chrome Draft Draft Picks Clayton Kershaw Auto	84	$250	$600	$1,200	4.8x
2007 Bowman Chrome Prospects Tim Lincecum Auto	BC238	$120	$300	$1,000	8.3x
2008 Bowman Chrome Draft Prospects Michael Stanton Auto	BDPP115	$150	$400	$800	5.3x
2008 Bowman Chrome Draft Prospects Buster Posey Auto	BDPP128	$200	$700	$1,200	6.0x
2009 Bowman Chrome Draft Prospects Mike Trout Auto	BDPP89	$500	$1,200	$3,000	6.0x
2010 Bowman Chrome Stephen Strasburg Auto RC	205B	$150	$300	$600	4.0x
2011 Bowman Chrome Prospects Bryce Harper Auto	BCP111B	$350	$1,000	$2,000	5.7x

Source: Beckett.com, December 2013

Interestingly, as is the case with graded cards, the value of the Gold Refractors #'d/50 appears to benefit from multiple expansion over the base cards over time as well.

The High End

Upper Deck redefined the term "high end" when it introduced 2003-04 Exquisite Collection Basketball at $500 per box, with one five-card pack per box. Bypassing the concept of busting boxes full of commons in search of hits, each five-card box was a box of hits. Like the football version that would come later, Exquisite Collection basketball was a memorabilia-driven set featuring a variety of limited print, serialized patch cards with on-card autos of rookies and stars – including Michael Jordan, an Upper Deck exclusive player.

The 2003-04 Exquisite Collection is perhaps quite easily the most valuable modern set ever produced, aided in large part by the now-legendary 2003 NBA Draft class. While the rest of the 78-card base set was #'d/225, the base RC patch autos of the top five picks in the draft – LeBron James, Darko Milicic, Carmelo Anthony, Chris Bosh, and Dwyane Wade – were all #'d/99. As far as base cards go, the LeBron James RC patch auto #'d/99 tops the list of all modern sports cards with an ungraded book value of $12,000, and sports a graded BGS 9.5 book value of $15,000.

These RC patches also have Rookie Patch Parallels #'d to each player's jersey number – which in the case of LeBron James means that there are only 23 such copies, while Carmelo Anthony only has 15 such cards. An *ungraded* copy of the LeBron James Rookie Patch parallel #'d/23 sold for roughly $25,000 on eBay in November 2013.

And through the 2008-09 NBA season, the Exquisite Collection RC patch auto was the most highly valued rookie card for basketball's biggest stars.

Exquisite Collection Basketball RC Patch Autos: 2003-04 through 2008-09

Card	#	Ungraded BV	BGS 9.5	Adj. Multiple
2003-04 LeBron James RC Jsy Auto #/99	78	$12,000	$15,000	1.2x
2003-04 Dwyane Wade RC Jsy Auto #/99	74	$4,000	–	–
2003-04 Carmelo Anthony RC Jsy Auto #/99	76	$3,000	–	–
2003-04 Chris Bosh RC Jsy Auto #/99	75	$1,900	$2,500	1.3x

Card	#	Ungraded BV	BGS 9.5	Adj. Multiple
2004-05 Dwight Howard RC Jsy Auto #/99	90	$2,600	$3,200	1.2x
2005-06 Chris Paul RC Jsy Auto #/99	46	$2,000	$3,500	1.7x
2007-08 Kevin Durant RC Jsy Auto #/99	94	$4,500	–	–
2008-09 Derrick Rose RC Jsy Auto #/99	92	$3,800	–	–
2008-09 Russell Westbrook RC Jsy Auto #/225	93	$1,100	–	–

Source: Beckett.com, January 2014

In January 2009, Italian collectibles publisher Panini Group gained an exclusive license to produce NBA trading cards, shutting Upper Deck and Topps out of the NBA market. And then in March 2009, Panini acquired Donruss Playoff, renaming the company Panini America.

Though Upper Deck would continue to produce the Exquisite Collection, it did so in 2009-10 without the RC patch autos, instead going with plain RC autos without NBA patches, while featuring the rookies in their college uniforms. And in 2009-10, Panini's Playoff National Treasures set – based on its football series, which similarly followed Upper Deck's Exquisite Collection to the market – essentially picked up where Exquisite left off, producing the most desired RC patch autos of the NBA's top rookies #'d/99.

Playoff National Treasures would be renamed Panini National Treasures in 2012-13.

Panini/Playoff National Treasures Basketball RC Patch Autos: 2009-10 through 2012-13

Card	#	Ungraded BV	BGS 9.5	Adj. Multiple
2009-10 Blake Griffin RC Jsy Auto #/99	201	$2,800	–	–
2009-10 Stephen Curry RC Jsy Auto #/99	206	$1,000	–	–
2009-10 James Harden RC Jsy Auto #/99	203	$800	$2,000	2.5x
2010-11 John Wall RC Jsy Auto #/99	201	$2,000	$2,600	1.3x
2012-13 Kyrie Irving RC Jsy Auto #/199	101	$1,500	–	–
2012-13 Anthony Davis RC Jsy Auto #/199	151	$1,200	–	–

Source: Beckett.com, January 2014
*2009-10 and 2010-11 Playoff National Treasures, and 2012-13 Panini National Treasures

Panini would push the envelope further, introducing the 2012-13 Panini Flawless basketball set in October 2013. Panini Flawless was released with an initial price point of $1,250 per 10-card pack/box; each box came in a *briefcase*, and included seven autos, two jumbo memorabilia cards, and a base card. Every card was #'d/25 or less, while base cards were *diamond-encrusted* and #'d/20.

Flawless was an immediate hit, with box prices exceeding $2,000 by November 2013. Among the most notable sales, a Kyrie Irving RC auto 1/1 sold for $9,200 on eBay in November 2013, while an Irving RC patch auto 1/1 sold for $10,000 on eBay in December 2013.

An Enhanced Baseball Prospecting Game

In 1992, Topps changed the rookie card game forever by including cards of prospects who had yet to play a game in the big leagues – and were often pictured in street clothes – in its landmark 1992 Bowman set. As this practice continued, the prospect cards included in Bowman sets were considered to be a player's rookie card until 2006, when only players who had been placed on a team's 25-man roster could have an "official" rookie card featuring the official MLBPA Rookie Card or RC logo issued that year (late season call-ups have generally been eligible to have official RCs issued the following season).

However, Topps was grandfathered into the practice of including minor league prospects in its major league sets, and continues to include prospect cards as "inserts" in its Bowman-branded sets (the term "insert" is used loosely here, as draft picks make up 165 of the 220 base cards found in packs of 2012 Bowman Draft, for example, while "official" rookie cards make up the other 55 cards). And official designations aside, collectors still recognize a player's first Bowman card – labeled "1st Bowman Card" and "1st Bowman Chrome Card" for the chrome versions (a discontinued practice for 2013-year cards) – as a player's true effective rookie card, whether it is included in the Bowman, Bowman Chrome, or Bowman Draft packs.

Whether or not this is good for the hobby is a source of debate. On the one hand, there is no question that the "official" RC vs. 1st Bowman Chrome Card problem – along with the fact that Topps includes the 1st Bowman Chrome Cards in three different sets each year – can be quite confusing to new collectors, or anybody who hasn't bought a baseball card in the last decade or two. Moreover, most of the 1st Bowman Chrome Cards are of players who are several years away from playing in the majors if at all, and with an extremely high washout rate; contrast this to a sport like hockey, where at least a player must actually play in the NHL before having a rookie card; or football, where every player who plays in the NFL and has a rookie card has generally played three or four years of college before turning pro.

As a consequence, baseball cards are generally far more speculative upon initial release than their football, hockey, and basketball counterparts.

On the other hand, we know where to find the key cards every year – the 1st Bowman Chrome Card or auto, or a limited print, serialized refractor parallel of the card, as released in Bowman, Bowman Chrome, and Bowman Draft packs. This is in stark contrast to the sets of the 1980s and early '90s, in which the key set changed every year. And as a pure game of identifying baseball's brightest prospects before they become baseball's biggest stars, there is no question in my mind that this prospecting game is a lot more exciting than it might be under different circumstances.

Enhanced Liquidity

In general, eBay has brought liquidity to the secondary baseball card market by providing a default meeting place for buyers and sellers. If a prospective buyer is looking for a particular card, he no longer has to go to a card show (which don't exist with the same size and frequency as they did 20 years ago anyway) to try to look for it – the buyer most likely only needs to look on eBay. And while eBay and PayPal fees are quite hefty, if you're a seller, eBay is generally the easiest place to find a buyer.

The presence of cards professionally graded by PSA and BGS has also helped enhance liquidity by effectively eliminating both the information and skill gaps between the buyer and seller; with graded cards, the buyer has full knowledge of a given graded card's condition and value without having to either see the card in person, or otherwise having to have the expertise to gauge a card's condition and thus its value.

Online forums – which didn't really exist to this extent 20 years ago – also help to enhance liquidity on the secondary market, while other trading sites have popped up as well.

The online consignment site COMC.com has further enhanced liquidity of lower priced cards by creating a centralized online exchange where all of the cards listed online are in one physical location, and can be traded multiple times without being shipped multiple times. Launched in 2007 as CheckOutMyCards.com,

COMC.com allows users to submit cards to the company's warehouse in Seattle, where the cards are scanned front and back and listed online for a small fee, as little as 25 cents per card.

In contrast to eBay, where a seller typically incurs both eBay and PayPal fees for every transaction made, a seller on COMC instead receives store credit for the full amount of the sale, and pays a further cash-out fee only upon cash out – similar to the way a stock investor only pays a capital gains tax upon selling a stock, and not while holding. Meanwhile, a buyer only pays shipping if/when he wants to have the item physically shipped; he can turn around and relist the item without incurring a shipping cost (the card is already located in COMC's warehouse), or can otherwise save on shipping costs by waiting until he has acquired multiple cards.

As such, users can flip cards for profit on COMC.com without ever physically being in possession of an actual card, the same way a stock investor can trade stocks online without ever physically being in possession of a stock certificate. But more importantly, the site dramatically improves the liquidity of low-priced cards by lowering the otherwise prohibitive transaction costs associated with them – most notably shipping costs, as well as the time it takes to list and sell and then ship such cards.

At the sports card and gaming collectibles Industry Summit in Las Vegas in March 2013, the company announced that it had listed its 10 millionth card, and had to that point shipped 3.6 million cards to 75 countries.

A Half a Generation of Untapped Demand Potential

I have a buddy named Randy Ohel, a 28-year-old professional poker player who won the $2,500 buy-in Triple Draw Lowball event and bracelet at the 2012 World Series of Poker in Las Vegas (Randy also final-tabled the $3,000 Pot-Limit Omaha Hi-Low Split event that year as well). Now Randy is the type of guy who will bet on anything if he thinks there is value in it; he is also equally adept at wearing a sports jersey with his favorite team on it on one day, and a Super Mario Bros. t-shirt on the next. And so if there was anybody I know who I thought for sure would have a stash of baseball cards, it was Randy.

Except when I told Randy about my little baseball card experiment, he looked at me like I was crazy. "I thought baseball cards aren't worth anything?" he said.

At first, I thought he thought that simply because that is the general perception of baseball cards these days, as it has been for the past 20 years. But then I had another thought: *Randy is not old enough to have been around when baseball cards were thought to have been worth anything!*

You see, I bought my first pack of baseball cards back in 1987, when I was six. I stopped collecting around 1993 or 1994 – and not because of the 1994 baseball strike, but rather because collecting was *futile*. The cards I could buy weren't worth anything, and the ones that had any value – 1992 Bowman, 1993 Upper Deck SP, 1993 Topps Finest, etc. – were too expensive.

But at five years older than Randy, I am just old enough to have been around when baseball cards had perceived value.

Think about it: What this means is that there is, quite literally, a half a generation or so of people aged 18-28 who are old enough to be in the workforce, but not old enough to have bought into the baseball card bubble. Incidentally, this half-generation also has significantly more experience playing poker and other gambling games at this age than did the half-generation that came before it.

Which brings me to the next point.

Fantasy Sports, Sports Betting, and Untapped Re-Demand Potential

I'll put it this way:

1. Do people like to gamble?

2. Do people like sports?

3. Do people like to gamble on sports?

Yes, yes, and of course.

As I mentioned earlier, the baseball card industry has seen primary sales fall from $1.5 billion in 1992, down to its current levels around $200 million. It's generally accepted that kids moved on from baseball cards to such things as video games and pogs; however, kids aren't responsible for the bubble bursting.

For starters, it wasn't kids who were hoarding whole cases of 1988 Donruss – it was adults. *Kids don't have money.* Moreover, viewed from the reverse angle, the baseball card industry grew to $1.5 billion in 1992 from about $500 million in 1989. If kids were responsible for the bubble bursting, then kids were also responsible for the bubble. And if kids were responsible for the bubble, then how did they get an extra $1 billion in discretionary income to spend on baseball cards?

The answer is they didn't. Kids don't have discretionary income; they have *allowances*.

The probability is that the growth in the industry was due largely to grown adults hoarding sealed cases of cards in a period of extreme oversupply. And whether they were investing or gambling – or thought they were investing but were actually gambling (as is often the case whether in the stock market or at the poker table) – they did this because they thought they saw value in doing so. And if kids got an extra billion dollars from their parents to buy baseball cards, it's because their *parents* saw potential value in buying baseball cards (and if there's another explanation other than value as for why kids would get a billion dollars to buy baseball cards, then we're screwed as a species). And if it was adults that stopped buying baseball cards by the case, then the biggest reason they stopped was because it became clear by the early 1990s that there was no value in it.

But then the next question is, if adults were responsible for the bubble bursting and the industry market size dropping from $1.5 billion in 1992 to $200 million today, then where did they go?

It's interesting to note that in the time that the baseball card industry has shrunk from a $1.5 billion market to a $200 million market, that fantasy sports – in which players draft teams and compete for prize money based on player stats – has grown from virtually nothing to become an estimated $3.6 billion industry in 2013, according to the Fantasy Sports Trade Association (FTSA). That figure includes $1.7 billion in entry fees and prizes, and another $1.9 billion in direct related spending including website hosting fees and subscriptions to magazines and websites catering to fantasy players.[12]

So people didn't stop gambling on sports when the baseball card bubble burst; they just started gambling on fantasy sports online. This is to say nothing of online sports betting, which itself generated $4.29 billion in revenue in 2005, up from $1.7 billion in 2001 according to Christiansen Capital Advisors (Fantasy sports, interestingly enough, got a carve out from the Unlawful Internet Gambling Enforcement Act of 2006). Moreover, the National Gambling Impact Study Commission (NGISC) estimated that, in addition to the $3.45 billion legally wagered in Nevada sports books in 2012, there was another $380 billion in illegal wagers (note that amount

---

[12] www.fsta.org/industry_demographics; Jan 2014

wagered is different from revenue or amount spent, which is likely some single-digit percentage of amount wagered).[13]

And so, if there are – as the FSTA says – nearly 37 million people in North America playing fantasy sports and already spending $3.6 billion and vast amounts of time betting on and researching players and prospects across a variety of sports, and there is another $380 billion-plus being wagered on sports either legally or (mostly) illegally, does it not stand to reason that some of these same people who had previously left the baseball card market in the last 20 years might re-divert some of their expenditures – and wagers – back towards baseball cards if they thought there might be value in it?

A Fascinating Game, and a Market Primed for a Potential Mass Revaluation

I hadn't bought a baseball card in nearly 20 years. But in the past couple of years since I've started re-examining the baseball card market, I've learned a lot about markets in general, about consumer and investor psychology, and about the value of scarcity.

In the fall of 2012, I acquired a 2012 Bowman Chrome Yu Darvish RC Auto graded BGS 9.5 with a 10 auto for $350 on eBay. The card had gone at least as high as $950 raw (ungraded) when the 2012 Bowman set was released earlier in the year,[14] and at the time had an ungraded book value of $600 (currently at $200 as of the end of 2013 – these things are volatile, and there was another unforeseen factor at play which we'll discuss later in this book). And, as the card was the only one of its kind in that grade on eBay, I figured I could just buy it and relist it at book value.

When the card arrived, I immediately listed the card on eBay for $650 with the Buy It Now and Best Offer features; and, as it was the only one listed at the time, I had some pricing power. A week later, another 2012 Bowman Chrome Yu Darvish RC Auto BGS 9.5/10 appeared on eBay in a straight auction, which took away my pricing power for the duration of the auction; a week later, I won that auction too for $350, thus once again clearing the market.

And a week after that, I sold the first one for $650.

The market for baseball cards is relatively liquid in the sense that if you want to sell

---

[13] www.americangaming.org/industry-resources/research/fact-sheets/sports-wagering, retrieved March 2014

[14] www.cardboardconnection.com/hottest-cards-in-2012-bowman-baseball

something of value quickly, it's not too difficult to find a buyer, though you may not get what you want for it. But it seems that the market for the scarcer, higher-end cards is quite illiquid, and consequently can be inefficient and potentially quite exploitable.

I tend to see it as a game, much like poker is a game, and the stock market is a game. Players make mistakes: People buy into bubbles, and panic sell on the downturn. People make valuation errors. People set up straight auctions for premium, relatively scarce cards into dry markets where nobody is looking, enabling values to be found. People sell premium cards at sub-premium prices because they need money quickly, also enabling values to be found. But at the same time, there is a lot of potential pricing power in the scarce, higher-end cards.

But on a macro level, I see a collectibles real estate market with favorable economics, with quite literally a half a generation of untapped current demand and another fantasy sports and legal/illegal sports betting market of potential re-demand, along with additional former collectors who don't play fantasy sports (like myself). And with recent supply levels geared towards a $200 million market – combined with a general perception that baseball cards are worthless – it may be time to consider the possibility that the modern baseball card market may be primed for a mass revaluation.

The Modern Baseball Card Investor

What follows is a book describing how an investment-minded collector and value-minded investor would analyze the baseball card market – and the greater sports card market – and approach the game.

Baseball cards are merely pieces of cardboard, and are not cash generating assets. And yet, seemingly absurd amounts of money still exchange hands for pieces of cardboard. So what is it that potentially makes a baseball card valuable?

We'll begin by discussing the concept of leverage and examining The Value of Scarcity in Part I.

Every player has one key card that stands out among the rest. In Part II: Key Cards and Multiple Expansion, we will examine some of the notable rookie cards from the 1980s and early 1990s, in order to: (a) demonstrate unequivocally that a player's key card in Gem Mint condition tends to benefit from multiple expansion far more than a player's secondary cards, or than identical cards in lesser condition; and (b) be able to identify a player's key card regardless of the often confusing rookie card definitions being used, regardless of the structure of a player's rookie cards, and regardless of the number of rookie cards a player has.

In 2006, the MLBPA changed the definition of a rookie card such that minor league prospects can no longer have an officially-recognized RC in a MLB-licensed set without having reached the major league level first. However, Topps was grandfathered into the practice of including prospects in its MLB-licensed products, which it does as "inserts" in its Bowman-branded products. In Part III: Prospect-RC Structures (2006-Present), we will apply the key card concept under the new prospect-RC structure, factoring the impact of rare parallels and autographed prospect and RC cards.

In Part IV: The Baseball Prospecting Game, we will observe the upside and the pitfalls of investing (or – more often – speculating) in minor league prospects, and present the Expected Value Comparison (EV Comp) approach to valuing prospects.

In Part V: Value Investing and the Gem Mint Game, we will discuss our approach to baseball cards within the value investing construct. We will examine card valuation by way of appraisal, as well as the limitations of having to rely on a series of relative valuations. We will also discuss more broadly the concept of multiple expansion, as well as the threat of overvaluation and multiple contraction, before identifying value opportunities.

In Part VI: The Supply Chain and the Value Cycle, we'll take a look at bigger picture issues. The game is ripe with many potential pitfalls, and from all directions – not just from dealers and other collectors, but from the manufacturers themselves. We will map out the supply chain – including the emergence of the case breaker as a recognized player in the supply chain – which will be important as we get to the topic of purchasing ungraded cards with the intent of building gems in Part VIII; we will also discuss the Value Cycle and explain how secondary market values affect box value, affecting future demand and then future supply, and then affecting future secondary market values and back again.

In Part VII: Grade Scarcity, Card Removal, and the BGS Grading System, we will examine the BGS grading system and its grading standards, and compare the BGS and PSA grading standards. We will also discuss the concepts of grade scarcity and card removal in greater depth.

In Part VIII: Building Gems, we will discuss the relatively advanced strategy of acquiring ungraded cards in order to build BGS 9.5 Gem Mint-or-better cards. The first two to four weeks following the initial release of a new card issue on the market are prime time for collector-investors looking to acquire ungraded cards in order to build BGS 9.5 Gem Mint or BGS 10 Pristine graded cards. During this time, a flood of new supply often hits the market in an exceptionally short period of time as case breakers bust much of the supply of a given issue. Rare, premium color parallels are readily available such that pricing pressure is present on the high end during this window.

But in order to build gems with any efficiency, we must identify and understand the strategies of the other players in the marketplace in order to figure out what types of sellers are most likely to sell ungraded potential gems, and what types of sellers are completely unlikely to do so. We will discuss the four basic types of ungraded strategies, and what types of cards, sellers, and listings we should avoid. We will discuss higher probability options and what to look for when examining cards over the Internet.

We will debate the relative merits of redemption cards. We will also discuss value plays and buying strategies which become more important when dealing with ungraded cards. We will also examine the value of case break player auctions, where you can bid on all of the cards or all of the autos of a given player.

We will also discuss submitting your cards for grading, including BGS' "min-grade" or "no-grade" option, as well as looking for group submissions in order to get the lowest bulk rate on your grading orders. We will also talk about what supplies you will need, and which cards you should grade.

And finally, in Part IX: Other Sports, we will examine the landscape of modern football, basketball, and hockey cards.

This book is for anybody who has ever bought a baseball card or plans on buying one. And whether you plan on buying one card or a million, I have little doubt that this book is for you.

Notes on Beckett Pricings, eBay/Terapeak Data, and BGS vs. PSA

Throughout this book, we will continually refer to Beckett pricings in the form of ungraded book values (BV) or BGS 9 Mint, BGS 9.5 Gem Mint, or BGS 10 Pristine book values. In fact, going back to the 1980s, the widespread use of the term "book value" has always generally referred to the prices used in the Beckett price guides.

It's important to realize what Beckett book value (now termed "Beckett Value" by Beckett) is and isn't. For starters, the term "book value" is a bit of a misnomer, as Beckett pricing is not actually meant to be an appraisal of underlying value, but rather a reflection of the price of recent market trades (investors will note the difference between "market price" and "intrinsic value"). That said, Beckett book values are meant to reflect the "Hi" end of the reasonable market price range, excluding outliers. As such, most trades occur at a discount to book value *by default* – and often significantly so in the case of ungraded cards, whether due to relative condition, or merely the uncertainty of condition that comes with dealing in ungraded cards, particularly over the Internet.

The most common complaint that collectors have about Beckett BV is that it tends to overstate actual market value, but this is missing the point. My view is that Beckett pricing practices are generally consistent, and that the availability of consistent pricing practices make Beckett pricings an invaluable tool for analytical purposes.

It's also important to note that the use of Beckett pricings is intended to be used for conceptual discussion only, and that this book is not meant to be used as a price guide. For the most up-to-date pricings, I strongly recommend that you visit Beckett.com.

eBay and Terapeak Data

It is important to use all of the available tools we have at our disposal, and while Beckett's pricings are invaluable, they represent only one data point for a given card. Moreover, Beckett does not include pricings for many of the rarer parallels.

As such, we will also often refer to actual eBay sales data throughout this book, often in conjunction with Beckett book values. Actual sales over the past 90 days can be found by going to "Advanced Search" on eBay and running a search including "Sold listings." In addition, much of the eBay sales data in this book was gathered from Terapeak.com, a subscription service which records eBay sales for up to the past 12 months.

On BGS vs. PSA Pricing

As the first player into the graded card market in 1991, PSA has gained a dominant advantage in vintage (pre-1981) issues in particular, and also maintains a healthy advantage over BGS in 1980s issues in terms of total cards graded and slabbed. PSA provides many of its own pricings for PSA-graded cards (no ungraded values) on its website PSAcard.com and in its Sports Market Report magazine. And to the limited extent that vintage (pre-1981) issues are discussed in this book, PSA graded pricings are used for graded cards from this time period.

But for both philosophical and practical reasons, we standardize on both BGS grading standards and Beckett's BGS graded pricing in this book. For starters, though PSA is clearly dominant in vintage and 1980s issues, BGS is clearly dominant in modern Chrome Era issues, particularly from the mid-2000s to present – through March 7, 2014, BGS had graded and slabbed 898,325 combined baseball/ football/basketball/hockey cards issued from 2001-2005, compared to 658,596 for PSA, for a little under a 1.4:1 advantage. For cards issued from 2006-2009, BGS had graded 467,737 cards, compared to 272,754 cards for PSA, for a wider 1.7:1 advantage. And for cards issued from 2010-2013, BGS had graded 391,532 cards, compared to 157,687 for PSA, for a widening 2.4:1 advantage.

If I had to venture three reasons why this spread is widening for modern issues, I would point to the presence of the BGS 10 Pristine grade allowing for increasingly high card values; BGS' separate auto grade; and BGS' more attractive slabbing (this last point being purely subjective).

This is not intended to discourage readers from using PSA given personal preference. In fact, for vintage card issues in particular for which BGS 10 Pristine grades are uncommon (or actually BVG 10 Pristine grades, as pre-1981 issues are graded by Beckett Vintage Grading), from when certified pack-inserted autos did not exist, and where demand is squarely fixated on PSA-slabbed cards, I strongly recommend using PSA. But because the focus of this book is on modern baseball cards, it makes sense to standardize around BGS the grading company, and thus also BGS pricing for these issues.

And then as a practical matter, Beckett.com provides significantly more graded pricing data for modern Chrome Era issues than does PSA. As such, with the availability of comparable ungraded and BGS graded pricing data, we also use BGS graded pricings for baseball cards from 1981-present as a default.

The Value of Scarcity: Key Concepts

Key Concept #1: For any given card at any given time, the presence of like or superior (scarcer) versions of the same card in equal or better condition on the market creates pricing pressure.

Key Concept #2: For any given card at any given time, the best available (scarcest) version of a card in the best condition has the greatest pricing power.

Key Concept #3: Over time, the demand for a Hall of Fame-caliber, star player's key cards tends to rise, while the supply of such cards in premium condition remains static. This static supply creates leverage.

Key Concept #4: The scarcer the card, the greater the leverage.

Key Concept #5: Over time, a combination of pricing power and scarcity-induced leverage creates the potential for outsized returns for scarce, high-demand collectibles.

Part I: The Value of Scarcity

The economics of the high end scarce are fundamentally different.

"My philosophy was, if you buy something that is absolutely the best in the world, you'd be okay because there is always another buyer for something at the top end."

– Bruce McNall, former co-owner of the Gretzky T206 Wagner

The famed Australian landscape photographer Peter Lik has sold hundreds of millions of dollars of his artwork through his 14 galleries located across the globe, including four galleries on the Las Vegas Strip. Lik specializes in large, brilliant, breathtaking images, which are serialized and printed to demand with a maximum print run of 950 copies each. The prices of his photographs rise in tiers as copies of each particular photograph are sold; for example, prices might start at around $4,000 (depending on the size) at the beginning of a print run, and reach prices over $100,000 as a photograph approaches the end of the print run.

In addition to the regular editions numbered to 950, each photograph also has another limited run of 45 artist's proofs, which have a higher starting price point.

In 2011, Lik made a splash when he announced the sale of a special 1/1 photograph entitled *One* (2010) for a whopping $1 million in a private sale. *One* was shot on the banks of the Androscoggin River in New Hampshire, the entire photo purely a reflection of the bright, colorful nearby trees in the water and shot to resemble an Impressionist painting.

However, Lik is far from the only photographer playing the scarcity game – in fact, with typical edition sizes of 950 copies, his photographs aren't particularly rare. Nor is his $1 million sale a record for a living photographer – that record belongs to the German Andreas Gursky, whose *Rhein II* (1999) sold for $4.3 million in a November 8, 2011 auction at Christie's New York.

Rhein II is perhaps brilliant in its bland simplicity. Tate.org.uk – the website of the Tate Galleries in the U.K. – describes the photograph as depicting a stretch of the Rhine River outside Düsseldorf, "immediately legible as a view of a straight stretch of water," but also "an abstract configuration of horizontal bands of colour of varying widths."[15] Or more crudely put, there is green grass with a walking path along the bottom, topped by a wide contrasting band that is the Rhine River, topped by a thin layer of green grass further off in the distance, and topped by overcast

---

[15] www.tate.org.uk/art/artworks/gursky-the-rhine-ii-p78372/text-summary

skies covering the top half of the picture, with no other identifying features or distractions.

Part of the appeal of the photo is that straight lines do not occur in a nature, and in fact are not quite natural in *Rhein II*, either: The walking path along the bottom is manmade, while the photo was digitally edited to remove such things as people walking dogs and a factory building. Another key element is Gursky's decision to place the horizon smack in the middle of the picture, ignoring the "Rule of Thirds."[16]

Nevertheless, Gursky holds claim as author of four of the eight most expensive photographs ever sold. And like much of Gursky's work, the print run on *Rhein II* was limited to only six copies – the $4.3 million copy was the largest of the six – including two artist's proofs. Meanwhile, miniscule print runs are a commonality among the most expensive photographs ever sold.

The 10 Most Expensive Photographs

	Photographer	Piece	Print Run	Sale Price	Date of Sale
1.	Andreas Gursky	*Rhein II (1999)*	6	$4,338,500	November 2011
2.	Cindy Sherman	*Untitled #96 (1981)*	10	$3,890,500	May 2011
3.	Jeff Wall	*Dead Troops Talk (1992)*	2	$3,666,500	May 2012
4.	Andreas Gursky	*99 Cent II Diptychon (2001)*	6	$3,346,456	February 2007
5.	Andreas Gursky	*Chicago Board of Trade III (1999)*	6	$3,298,755	June 2013
6.	Edward Steichen	*The Pond – Moonlight (1904)*	3	$2,928,000	February 2006
7.	Cindy Sherman	*Untitled #153 (1985)*	6	$2,700,000	November 2010
8.	Andreas Gursky	*Chicago Board of Trade (1997)*	6	$2,355,597	June 2013
9.	Unknown	*Billy the Kid (1879-80)*	1	$2,300,000	June 2011
10.	Dmitry Medvedev	*Tobolsk Kremlin (2009)*	1	$1,750,000	January 2010

Sources: Wikipedia, CBC, SLRLounge.com

Miniscule print runs are also a commonality among the most expensive baseball cards as well.

---

[16] The Rule of Thirds is a guideline in photographic composition proposing that a photographer should break a frame down into nine equal parts using two equally spaced vertical lines and two equally spaced horizontal lines, and that important elements – such as the horizon – should be placed along these lines.

The 1909-11 T206 Honus Wagner

Anybody who's ever bought a baseball card is familiar with the 1909-11 T206 Honus Wagner, widely regarded as the "holy grail" of baseball cards. Issued in 1909 by the American Tobacco Company as part of its 1909-11 T206 set, it is thought that fewer than 200 copies of the Honus Wagner card were printed before Wagner declined the company's request to use his likeness, whether it was because "he did not care to have his picture in a package of cigarettes"[17] (as he would state later), or if it was because they weren't paying him enough.

The alternative theory is related to the fact that Wagner apparently had no such issue promoting cigar brands, and in fact chewed tobacco himself. Meanwhile, giving credence to the notion that Wagner had it in him to hold out for more money, Wagner had "retired" in December 1907 at age 33, before receiving a 100% raise in salary to a then-sizable $10,000 prior to start of the 1908 season.[18]

Whatever the reason, fewer than 60 examples of the card are known to have survived to present day, and none are more famous, more valuable, or more controversial than the one that has become known as the "Gretzky Wagner."

The Gretzky Wagner a.k.a. "The Card"

The Gretzky Wagner is known as such because it was once co-owned by the NHL great Wayne Gretzky, along with former Los Angeles Kings owner Bruce McNall. But its significance is far greater than that: With a grade of PSA 8 NM-MT (Near Mint-Mint), it is *by far* the highest graded T206 Wagner in existence. Moreover, it was the first baseball card to sell for over a $1 million, while its last sale of $2.8 million in September 2007 makes it the most expensive baseball card ever.

"The Card" – as it is referred to by Michael O'Keefe and Teri Thompson in their book *The Card: Collectors, Con Men, and The True Story of History's Most Desired Baseball Card* (2008) – is also notable for many, many other reasons.

In 1985, a sports memorabilia dealer named Bill Mastro acquired the Gretzky Wagner from a collector named Alan Ray for $25,000, in a deal brokered by Long Island card shop owner Bob Sevchuk and financed by Rob Lifson, Mastro's long-time friend and future rival in the sports memorabilia auction business. A couple of years later, in 1987, Mastro more than quadrupled his money when he sold the

---

[17] See *Mint Condition: How Baseball Cards Became an American Obsession* by Dave Jamieson, pg. 38

[18] See *The Card: Collectors, Con Men, and The True Story of History's Most Desired Baseball Card* by Michael O'Keeffe and Teri Thompson, pg. 37

card for $110,000 to Jim Copeland, the owner of a chain of California sporting goods stores.

That $110,000 price tag instantly and dramatically raised the bar for what a baseball card – and other sports memorabilia – could be worth, revitalizing interest in the hobby and adding fire to the great baseball card boom (and eventually bubble) of the late 1980s and early '90s.

A few years later, Copeland lost interest in the hobby and sought to move his 873-piece memorabilia collection – including the T206 Wagner – in a one-shot deal, and wanted Mastro's help. Realizing that finding a single buyer for what would be over $4 million worth of memorabilia would be impossible, Mastro brought the consignment to Sotheby's – the New York auction house – who designated Mastro special consultant to the auction. And on March 22, 1991, the T206 Wagner had multiplied in value again with a new record sale price of $451,000. The auction was won by a phone bidder, who turned out to be Wayne Gretzky, with the backing of L.A. Kings owner Bruce McNall.

In total, Copeland's collection brought in $4.6 million, also setting a new record for a sports memorabilia auction.[19]

Later in 1991, Professional Sports Authenticator (PSA) launched its new card grading service. The first baseball card PSA graded would be the Gretzky Wagner; once slabbed, the card's label would carry the serial number 00000001 and the words McNall/Gretzky, along with a grade of PSA 8 NM-MT (near mint-mint).

By the end of 1994, McNall – co-owner of the card – was bankrupt and in jail, having plead guilty to conspiracy, wire fraud, and two counts of bank fraud, after being charged with defrauding six banks out of more than $236 million over ten years. Gretzky bid $225,000 and acquired McNall's share of the card in a bankruptcy hearing, and later in 1995 sold the card for a little over $500,000 to Wal-Mart and trading-card distributor Treat Entertainment for use in a Wal-Mart national sales promotional contest.[20]

On February 24, 1996, a postal worker in Florida named Patricia Gibbs won the Gretzky Wagner in the Wal-Mart contest, as Larry King pulled her name out of trunk (a trunk previously used by Honus Wagner during his playing years) on national TV. Gibbs clearly couldn't care less about the card itself; nor could she

---

[19] Jamieson, pg. 200
[20] O'Keeffe and Thompson, pgs. 113-115

afford to pay the taxes for winning the $451,000 card. After receiving the prize at the local Wal-Mart where she had submitted her entry for the contest, Gibbs immediately announced her intention to consign the card to auction.

In November 1996, The Card was back up for auction, this time at Christie's. Noted collector Michael Gidwitz – who had been outbid by Gretzky and McNall in the 1991 auction – won the auction for $641,500, registering yet another record for the card.

By the year 2000, with the prices of sports memorabilia reaching new levels – perhaps not coincidentally coinciding with the height of the tech stock bubble – Gidwitz determined that it was time to sell. Gidwitz consigned the card to Rob Lifson and his company Robert Edward Auctions – a division of Bill Mastro's MastroNet – who put the Gretzky Wagner up on eBay in a special auction.

On July 15, 2000, the card sold for $1,265,000 to a California collector named Brian Seigel, making the Gretzky Wagner the first million dollar card.[21]

In February 2007, Seigel sold the card for a record $2,350,000 in a private sale to an anonymous buyer later revealed to be former major league pitcher Tom Candiotti. And in September 2007, the card would change hands in another private sale, this time for the current record $2,800,000 to an anonymous buyer later revealed to be Arizona Diamondbacks owner Ken Kendrick.[22]

Controversy

Though ownership of the card has ended with Kendrick (at least for the time being), the story has continued to evolve. The Gretzky Wagner has long been steeped in controversy, as many experts who had seen the card going back to before Gretzky and McNall acquired it had long believed the card to have been doctored. More specifically, they believe that the edges may have been trimmed, producing the unusually sharp edges that resulted in the PSA 8 NM-MT grade. Moreover, all signs pointed to Bill Mastro. An investigation into the origins of the Gretzky Wagner is the primary subject of O'Keeffe and Thompson's book *The Card*, published in 2008.

In July 2012, Mastro was indicted on charges related to shill bidding and selling fake memorabilia – including an 1869 Cincinnati Red Stockings trophy, as well as a lock of hair purportedly belonging to Elvis Presley – during the 2000s at the

---

[21] O'Keeffe and Thompson, pg. 188
[22] Wikipedia, cardboardconnection.com

former Mastro Auctions, the sports memorabilia auction company he owned until 2004, and with which he served as chairman and CEO until 2009. The FBI also alleged that Mastro had "failed to disclose that he had altered the Wagner T-206 card by cutting the sides in a manner that, if disclosed, would have significantly reduced the value of the card"[23] prior to selling the card to Jim Copeland in 1987. And in 2013, Mastro plead guilty and admitted to trimming The Card, thusly destroying the value of the $2.8 million card.

Or maybe not.

Oddly, some – including the card's owner Ken Kendrick, as well as Steve Levine of Goldin Auctions – believe the card might even be worth *more*.[24] After all, the card is still by far the highest quality T206 Honus Wagner in existence, and now carries the further distinction as being the card trimmed by Mastro. And while they are clearly biased in the matter, it is hard to disagree, as at this point the card's grade is just a number, while the card has become "The Card." Meanwhile, it only takes one person with the desire and the scrap to take that point of view in order to raise the price of poker.

The Other T206 Wagners

While the Gretzky Wagner is by far the most storied T206 Wagner, it is not the only one making waves, as less controversial copies have reached new heights. The next most valuable T206 Wagner is the PSA 5 (MC) Jumbo Wagner, so called (and carrying the MC designation for miscut) because it is oversized. The Jumbo Wagner sold for $1.6 million at auction in August 2008, and later sold for $2.1 million in April 2013 in an auction held by Goldin Auctions. That $2.1 million is a record for a card sold at auction[25] (the two higher sales of the Gretzky Wagner were private sales).

The site t206resource.com tracks the sales history of the T206 Wagner, and the trend is clear. Even the lowest-grade examples – the PSA 1 Poor and PSA A Authentic (essentially not gradable) – have been trading in the $200k to $300k range in recent years, while none had sold for above $100,000 prior to 2004. One notable PSA 1 – a copy once owned by actor Charlie Sheen, displayed and stolen from the All Star Café in New York and later recovered – sold for $402,900 at auction (Robert Edward Auctions) on May 18, 2013.[26]

---

[23] fbi.gov
[24] Yahoo! Sports, dailymail.co.uk
[25] ESPN.com
[26] robertedwardauctions.com

Further up the ladder, a pair of PSA 2 T206 Wagners sold in May 2012 – one for $651,750, and the other for $654,500 – while a PSA 4 VG-EX (Very Good-Excellent) and an SGC 40 (graded by the Sportscard Guaranty) have broken the $1 million mark.[27]

Below is a list of the most notable sales of the T206 Honus Wagner.

The 1909-11 T206 Honus Wagner: Most Notable Sales History

Date	Grade	Sale Price	Notes
4/5/2013	PSA 5(MC)	$2,105,770	The Jumbo Wagner
4/9/2012	SGC 40	$1,232,466	
1/30/2012	PSA 4	>$1.5 million (est.)	Private sale
7/1/2009	SGC 40	$925,000	Private sale
11/22/2008	SGC 40	$791,000	
8/1/2008	PSA 5(MC)	$1,620,000	The Jumbo Wagner
9/1/2007	PSA 8	$2,800,000	The Gretzky Wagner – private sale (Kendrick)
2/27/2007	PSA 8	$2,350,000	The Gretzky Wagner – private sale (Candiotti)
7/21/2000	PSA 8	$1,265,000	The Gretzky Wagner – eBay sale
9/21/1996	PSA 8	$641,500	The Gretzky Wagner – sold to Gidwitz
3/22/1991	PSA 8	$451,000	Gretzky/McNall purchase Wagner

Sources: T206resource.com, *The Card* by Michael O'Keeffe and Teri Thompson

---

[27] t206resource.com

Modern Sports Cards

The story of the T206 Honus Wagner is one everybody is familiar with on some level; it is also, for the most part, the *only* story that continues to be told in the mainstream media, as copies of the card register $1 million and $2 million sales. Meanwhile, in the wake of the great bubble of the late 1980s and early '90s – an era from which unopened boxes are still available in extremely large supply – the average person tends to think of baseball cards as being worthless, or that cards with non-zero values are strictly a vintage thing.

Completely lost on people outside the hobby is the advent of the modern baseball card featuring limited print, serialized cards – not dissimilar in principle to the high end, limited print fine art photography of Peter Lik and Andreas Gursky discussed at the beginning of this chapter. Moreover, many such cards trade at prices that would shock anybody who hasn't looked at a baseball card in 20 years.

The definition of the modern baseball card can be a fuzzy one. Some people think of vintage cards as being pre-1968, while others set the cutoff date as being 1981, the year Fleer and Donruss entered (or re-entered in the case of Fleer) the baseball card business. In fact, Beckett Grading Services (BGS) does this in segregating its grading services; cards dating from 1981-present are graded by BGS, while cards dating before 1981 are graded by Beckett Vintage Grading (BVG).

Still others place the cutoff between vintage and modern at 1990.

However, it's important to realize that some of these definitions are over 20 years old, and that baseball cards have changed considerably over the past 20 years. Clearly, there is a huge difference between the cards of the 1980s and the cards of the 2000s. Moreover, setting the cutoff at 1981 is strictly a baseball-centric definition, as cards from other sports have followed different paths.

This demands new categorization.

Baseball-Specific Eras

For baseball specifically, I think it makes sense to set the cutoff between Vintage and Modern cards at 1981, with the term Vintage Era referring to any card issued prior to 1981.

- **Vintage (Pre-1981):** Purely PSA-dominated territory. PSA 9s warrant premium and often extraordinary values – in fact, PSA does not provide PSA 10 values for cards issued prior to 1973. PSA 10 Gem Mint grades are exceedingly rare.

The Modern Era for baseball cards specifically can be split into three distinct stages:

- **Vintage Modern/1980s (1981-1988):** Characterized by the presence of multiple manufacturers, as well as extreme overproduction towards the end of the decade. PSA is still dominant in terms of total slabs, though an unending supply of new boxes has allowed BGS to become competitive and establish a meaningful presence in this space. Card values are such that PSA 9 and BGS 9 Mint grades are often value neutral or value destructive (more on this in Part II). PSA 10 and BGS 9.5 Gem Mint grades are standard investment grade. BGS 10 Pristine grades are rare, particularly for cards issued in the early part of decade.

- **Modern Transition (1989-1996):** Transition period, characterized by extreme oversupply in the first few years, along with the emergence of the high-end issues and the use of minor league prospects in major league sets. 1989 Upper Deck represented the first step towards the high end, followed by 1990 Leaf. In 1990, Upper Deck introduced the first pack-inserted auto in the Reggie Jackson auto, hand numbered to 2,500 copies. The 1991 Donruss Elite inserts #'d/10,000 introduced the concept of foil-stamped, limited print, serialized cards. 1992 Bowman introduced the prospecting concept in full force.

1993 Finest took high end to a new level, introducing chromium-stock base cards and rare refractor parallels with an announced print run of 241 copies (though some are thought to be significantly shorter-printed).[28] 1993 SP represented Upper Deck's move to the high end, including a 20-card Premier Prospects all-foil subset including *the* Derek Jeter RC; this set would be the forerunner to later SP-branded products featuring limited-print, serialized base cards and parallels, autos, and memorabilia cards.

Topps Chrome was introduced in 1996, though its value was – and continues to be – preempted by minor league prospects previously appearing in other major league products. BGS and PSA are competitive, though PSA is still the clear leader in total slabs for this time period. BGS 10 Pristine grades are less rare, though no BGS 10 1993 SP Derek Jeter RCs or 1994 SP Alex Rodriguez RCs exist.

---

[28] Actually, according to Rich Klein of Sports Collectors Daily, the refractor print run of 241 copies was calculated by dealers, but simply never refuted by Topps (See www.sportscollectorsdaily.com/1993-topps-finest-baseball-broke-new-ground).

- **Bowman Chrome Era (1997-Present):** Bowman Chrome was introduced in 1997. With its combination of the Bowman prospecting brand representing "true" RCs, chromium stock cards, refractor parallels, and later the standard Bowman Chrome RC/prospect autos from 2001-present, Bowman Chrome has been the industry standard baseball brand ever since. Limited print, serialized parallels and autographed RC/prospect cards became standard fare in the industry at large. BGS gradually became dominant for new cards issued in this era, particularly for new card issues from the mid-2000s to present.

  The Bowman Chrome Era can also be split into a second stage. In 2005, Fleer ceased operations, and Major League Baseball declined to renew the license of Donruss Playoff, leaving Topps and Upper Deck as the only MLB-licensed card manufacturers. And then in 2006, the MLBPA changed the official definition of a "rookie card" such that effectively only players who had played in a game at the major league level ultimately could have an official rookie card carrying the new official "rookie card" logo (2006-2009) or RC logo (2010-present). Meanwhile, Topps was grandfathered into the practice of including minor league prospects in its MLB-licensed sets (albeit technically as "inserts"), effectively giving Topps a monopoly on a player's true key cards (more on this in Part III).

  Major League Baseball then made the monopoly official, giving Topps an exclusive MLB license in 2009, later extended in 2013 through the 2020 season.

Note that the preceding are very baseball-specific categorizations, as the Bowman Chrome brand does not have the same impact in other sports to the extent that it has been produced, while the introduction of the Topps Chrome brand in 1996 had significantly greater impact in basketball and football. Moreover, basketball and football have traditionally been far more competitive spaces.

Chrome Era Modern Sports Cards (1993/1996-Present)

Generally speaking, modern sports cards are characterized by a number of traits as distinct from vintage issues:

1. Chromes (chromium stock cards) and refractors
2. Premium products
3. Limited print, serialized cards and colored parallels
4. Prospect and RC autos, and other certified autographed cards
5. Memorabilia cards and patch autos

There isn't a defined cutoff date for modern sports cards, but rather more of a transition. The first truly modern cards arrived in 1993 with the introduction of the Finest chromium-stock brand in particular, as well as the SP brand; however, at this stage Finest and SP are the exception rather than the standard.

The Chrome Era kicked into high gear in 1996 with the introduction of the Topps Chrome brand to baseball, football, and basketball. Though Topps Chrome Baseball was – and continues to be – preempted and diminished by prospects previously appearing in other sets, Topps Chrome Football has been an industry standard ever since. But the Topps Chrome release with the biggest initial impact was the 1996-97 Topps Chrome Basketball set, including the Kobe Bryant RC (BV: $300; BGS 9.5: $800) and its key refractor parallel (BV: $2,500; BGS 9.5: $4,000).

The 1997-98 basketball sets would come with the proliferation of limited print, serialized parallels – many of which have attained absurd valuations – including the SkyBox Premium Star Rubies #'d/50 and SPx Grand Finale #'d/50, not to mention Fleer's E-X2001 Jambalaya (not numbered but similarly valuable). But most prominent are the Metal Universe Precious Metal Gems parallels #'d/100, split between green parallels (the first ten in the series) and red parallels (the last ninety in the series).

A red Michael Jordan graded BGS 9.5 sold for $17,400 in November 2013. The Cardboard Connection website regards the 1997-98 Metal Universe Precious Metal Gems Basketball (PMGs) set as "the parallel that started it all," noting that the PMGs "helped establish the market for colored parallels and serial numbered cards."[29]

These parallels in effect fulfilled the promise of the 1991 Donruss Elite inserts #'d/10,000 (hence the problem).

The first pack-inserted auto is thought to be the 1990 Upper Deck Reggie Jackson autos hand-numbered to 2,500 (BV: $150), but it was the 1994 Signature Rookies which provided the impetus for the autographed rookie/prospect craze by including an auto in every pack, hand #'d/8,650 (not a typo). However, the set was not MLB-licensed, and none of the cards are official RCs; as a consequence of that and the 8,650-set print run, the 50-card auto checklist is of mostly inconsequential impact value-wise, aside from the Derek Jeter auto which carries an ungraded BV of $150.

While Playoff Contenders Football dates back to 1993, it was in 1998 that Playoff introduced the longest current running line of standardized RC autos in the Playoff

---

[29] www.cardboardconnection.com/comprehensive-precious-metal-gems-card-guide

Contenders Rookie Ticket. The initial 1998 Playoff Contenders Rookie Ticket autos included the key RC auto of Peyton Manning (BV: $3,800; BGS 9.5: $5,500) with an announced print run of 200 copies. Playoff Contenders was renamed Panini Contenders in 2012, following the 2009 acquisition of Donruss Playoff by Panini; the Panini Contenders Rookie Ticket remains a solid bet as a football player's key auto.

The memorabilia card got its start when Press Pass included race-used tires in the Burning Rubber inserts in its January 1996 Press Pass NASCAR release. The company followed up later that year with the first cards including race-used sheet metal cards, race-used Dale Earnhardt fire-suit cards, and the first game-used jersey basketball cards.[30]

As noted in the Introduction, Upper Deck would build on these themes of serialized cards, patches, and autos, and ultimately raised the high-end bar with 2003-2004 Exquisite Collection Basketball. With five cards per pack and one pack per box at a then unheard of price of $500 per box, the set featuring RC patch autos of LeBron James, Dwyane Wade, Carmelo Anthony, and Chris Bosh (and Darko Milicic) #'d/99. Exquisite Collection would later be supplanted by Playoff National Treasures (renamed Panini National Treasures for 2012 Football and 2012-13 Basketball), and then raised once more by the 2012-13 Panini Flawless Basketball release, with an initial October 2013 price point of $1,250 per pack/ box/briefcase with 10 cards per pack.

That said, a baseball player's most desirable card is generally his first Bowman Chrome Auto Superfractor 1/1, first introduced in 2005. Meanwhile, at least since Topps moved to primarily on-card autos in 2011 Topps Chrome Football, a football player's most desirable card at the very top has generally been his Topps Chrome Auto Superfractor 1/1.

Notable Chrome Era Modern Sports Cards Sales in 2013

Below is a list of 15 of the most notable sales of modern sports cards in the 2013 calendar year. All of the sales took place on eBay, with the exception of the ungraded 2013 Bowman Chrome Prospects Yasiel Puig Auto Superfractor 1/1, which was listed on eBay at a Buy It Now or Best Offer price of $25,000 and subsequently sold off site for an undisclosed amount to Lomita, California-based dealer SBay Cards for use in a repackage product (more on this in a minute); this card later sold on eBay in a confirmed sale dated 1/8/14 as a BGS 9.5/10 for $17,999.

---

[30] www.presspassinc.com/who-we-are

Beside each card is its grade where applicable (autographed cards graded by BGS have two grades – one for the card, and a second for the auto), print run, and population (the number of cards given that same grade), along with the sale price and date of sale.

Chrome Era Modern Sports Cards: Notable eBay Sales 2013

	Card	Grade	Print Run	Population	Sale Price	Date
1.	1993 SP Derek Jeter RC	PSA 10	–	12	$32,500	12/21/13*
2.	2003-04 Upper Deck Exquisite Collection LeBron James RC Patch Auto #/23	Ungraded	23	–	$24,699	11/22/13
3.	2012 Topps Chrome Andrew Luck RC Auto Superfractor 1/1	BGS 9.5/10	1	1	$19,800**	10/18/13
4.	1997-98 Metal Universe Michael Jordan Precious Metal Gems #/100	BGS 9.5	100	2	$17,400	11/9/13
5.	1996-97 Topps Chrome Kobe Bryant RC Refractor	BGS 10	–	12	$16,250	8/16/13
6.	2013 Bowman Chrome Prospects Yasiel Puig Auto Superfractor 1/1	Ungraded	1	1	$10,000 - $15,000 (est.)***	9/28/13
7.	2012-13 Panini Flawless Kyrie Irving RC Patch Auto 1/1	Ungraded	1	1	$10,000	12/13/13
8.	2012 Finest Andrew Luck RC Auto Superfractor 1/1	PSA 10	1	1	$10,000	11/3/13
9.	1998 Bowman Chrome Derek Jeter Golden Anniversary Refractors #/5	BGS 9	5	1****	$9,961	9/10/13
10.	1998-99 Upper Deck Jordan Jersey Autographs Michael Jordan #/23	BGS 9.5/10	23	1	$9,730	10/20/13
11.	2012-13 Panini Flawless Kyrie Irving RC Auto 1/1	Ungraded	1	1	$9,200	11/4/13
12.	2009 Bowman Chrome Draft Mike Trout Orange Auto Refractor #/25	BGS 10/10	25	1	$8,500	1/24/13
13.	2010 Bowman Chrome Draft Matt Harvey Auto Superfractor 1/1	Ungraded	1	1	$8,200	4/23/13
14.	2013 Bowman Chrome Prospects Byron Buxton Auto Superfractor 1/1	Ungraded	1	1	$7,999	7/12/13
15.	2011 Topps Chrome Colin Kaepernick RC Auto Superfractor 1/1	BGS 9.5/10	1	1	$7,900	9/9/13

Sources: eBay, Terapeak.com, Beckett.com, PSAcard.com
*A second copy sold on 12/22/13, also for $32,500
**Price included 2012 Topps Chrome Andrew Luck RC Superfractor 1/1, graded BGS 9 Mint
***Sold as BGS 9.5/10 for $17,999 on 1/8/14
****The other four are graded PSA 9

Aside from the price tags, the one thing you notice about all of these cards is that they are, generally speaking, quite and absolutely rare. Eight of the 15 cards on this list are true 1/1s off the printer – the 2012 Topps Chrome Andrew Luck RC Auto Superfractor 1/1; the 2013 Bowman Chrome Prospects Yasiel Puig Auto Superfractor 1/1; the 2012-13 Panini Flawless Kyrie Irving Auto 1/1 and Patch Auto 1/1; 2012 Finest Andrew Luck Auto Superfractor 1/1; the 2010 Bowman Chrome Draft Matt Harvey Auto Superfractor 1/1; the 2013 Bowman Chrome Prospects Byron Buxton Auto Superfractor 1/1; and the 2011 Topps Chrome Colin Kaepernick RC Auto Superfractor 1/1.

Two others are 1/1s by virtue of grade – the 1998-99 Upper Deck Michael Jordan Jersey Autograph is the only one in graded BGS 9.5 Gem Mint condition with an accompanying 10 Auto grade, while the 2009 Bowman Chrome Draft Mike Trout Orange Refractor Auto #'d/25 is the only BGS 10 Pristine copy.

On the other hand, the 1998 Bowman Chrome Derek Jeter Golden Anniversary Refractor is the only BGS 9 Mint in the population report, but four others appear as PSA 9s in PSA's population report. Nonetheless, it is still a rare card with a print run of only five, making it rarer than Gursky's *Rhein II.*

Notes:

1. This is a fairly representative list, but not quite a list of the 15 highest recorded sales in 2013, nor the 15 most-valuable modern sports cards. For one thing, Michael Jordan cards could have populated about half the list, which would have defeated the purpose of making such a list. In addition, I did my best to weed out questionable sales, as not all sales are legitimate. One notable example is the 2012 Panini Contenders Andrew Luck Championship Ticket RC Auto 1/1, which according to Terapeak.com data recorded sales of $42,300 at auction on 2/20/13; $13,099 at auction on 3/6/13; and then finally $7,500 in a fixed-price listing on 3/15/13. Unfortunately, auction manipulation appears to be an ongoing concern, and few sales can be completely verified.

2. Notably, a second, distinct PSA 10 1993 SP Derek Jeter RC also sold for $32,500 on 12/22/13. That said, the PSA 10 1993 SP Derek Jeter RC likely highlights the difference in the definition of PSA 10 Gem Mint vs. BGS 9.5 Gem Mint in sort of a quirk that has – in this case – resulted in only 12 copies grading PSA 10 vs. 139 BGS 9.5s, and about a $30,000 difference in value.

The minimum standard for a BGS 9.5 Gem Mint grade is three 9.5 subgrades and one 9 subgrade (or three 10 subgrades with one 8.5 subgrade, which is much rarer). Essentially, this allows from one minor blemish – a card that is slightly off-center, or shows light corner wear in one corner, or a minor surface issue (like a light scratch), or a slightly rough edge. In contrast, PSA's definition of a PSA 10 Gem Mint grade shows a higher tolerance for centering and also allows for a "slight printing imperfection," but is quite explicit that the card has "four perfectly sharp corners," or presumably the BGS equivalent of 9.5 cornering or better.

As it turns out, the 1993 SP foil cards are notorious for chipping issues and thus bad corners. Meanwhile, centering does not seem to be a concern – a quick browse of the last several hundred 1993 SP Derek Jeter RCs in the BGS population report shows all 10s and 9.5 centering and only one card with 9 centering (slightly off-center), but a lot of really bad corner grades. Consequently, the most likely explanation for the discrepancy between the PSA and BGS Gem Mint populations is that BGS' definition of Gem Mint allows for 9 corners while PSA's definition does not – and *also* because centering is not an issue with this particular card.

Whether the PSA 10 Gem Mint grade is actually a tougher grade than a BGS 9.5 Gem Mint grade probably depends on the card set. It certainly seems to be the case with the 1993 SP Derek Jeter RC where corners are an issue but centering isn't. But I suspect that's not the case in some modern chrome sets where centering is an issue but corners are less of a concern; in fact, the PSA 10 grade appears to be slightly easier even on the 1993 Topps Derek Jeter RCs where centering is more of a concern: 1,180 of 12,213 (9.7%) 1993 Topps Derek Jeter RCs graded by PSA are PSA 10 Gem Mint, while only 743 out of 8,977 (8.3%) such cards graded by BGS have graded BGS 9.5 Gem Mint (there are six other BGS 10s).

We'll discuss the BGS grading system – and compare BGS' grading definitions to PSA's – in greater depth in Part VIII.

3. The price of the 2012 Topps Chrome Andrew Luck RC Auto Superfractor is probably overstated, as it was sold in a lot with Luck's 2012 Topps Chrome Superfractor 1/1 (non-auto) graded in BGS 9 Mint condition, which itself is probably a $4,000 to $5,000 card (maybe more) even as a BGS 9 Mint.

4. The 1997-98 Metal Universe Precious Metal Gems Michael Jordan BGS 9.5 Gem Mint is a true population of two, as PSA lists four PSA 9 Mint but no PSA 10 Gem Mint cards in its population report.

5. The 1996-97 Topps Chrome Basketball set was the first edition for the Topps Chrome brand, and the Kobe Bryant RC is the best card in the deck. Back then there were only base cards and refractors, in stark contrast to the sets of today with multiple levels of parallels and 1/1 superfractors. That said, the Kobe Bryant Refractor is truly the best card, and the twelve BGS 10 Pristine copies in Beckett's population report are the boss cards of them all.

6. As noted earlier, the 2013 Bowman Chrome Prospects Yasiel Puig Auto Superfractor 1/1 was listed on eBay with a Buy It Now or Best Offer price of $25,000, but ended with an offline sale to a buyer later revealed to be Lomita, California-based dealer South Bay Cards (SBay). SBay immediately sent the card to BGS to be graded, and with the announcement that the card had graded BGS 9.5 Gem Mint with a 10 Auto, the company revealed its intention to include the card in its Super Box offering, which is a high-end repackage product comprised of graded cards and memorabilia, as well as sketch cards specially made just for the product.[31]

The estimated $10k-$15k+ sale price of the Puig Superfractor auto is based on the sale price of one Puig 2013 Bowman Chrome Prospects Red Refractor auto #'d/5 at about $5,500 and the sale of three Purple Refractor autos #'d/10 in the $3,500-$4,100 range, as well as the sale price earlier in the summer of the 2013 Bowman Chrome Prospects Byron Buxton Auto Superfractor 1/1 for a tick under $8,000. That said, considering that the Buxton sold for about 3x-4x the $2,000-$2,500 range of his Red Refractor autos #'d/5, and that the roughly $15k+ price tag of the 2012 Topps Chrome Andrew Luck RC Auto Superfractor (excluding the value of the non-auto Superfractor included in the lot) is roughly 3x the value of his Red Refractor autos #'d/5, it's quite possible that the Puig Superfractor auto sold in the $15k-$20k range.

The card was later pulled in December 2013 by a Canadian collector named Adam Davidson, and sold on January 8, 2014 for $17,999.99.[32]

---

[31] Beckett.com

[32] www.sportscollectorsdaily.com/2013-bowman-chrome-superfractor-puig-hits-ebay-big-price-tag

Sidebar: Defining Vintage Eras for Other Sports

For baseball cards specifically, we generally use the term "vintage" to refer to any card issued prior to 1981, when Fleer and Donruss entered the market. However, it's not necessarily appropriate to apply this date to other sports.

In basketball, Topps was the only card manufacturer from 1969-79 through 1981-82. No cards were produced in 1982-83, and the only cards produced over the next three seasons were the Star issues sold in team bags at hobby shops. Fleer entered (re-entered) the market with the landmark 1986-87 Fleer set including the Michael Jordan RC (BV: $700; BGS 9.5: $6,000), and was the only game until 1989-90 Hoops and 1990-91 SkyBox, and then 1991-92 Upper Deck and 1992-93 Topps.

An argument can be made that the cutoff for vintage basketball cards should end with 1981-82 Topps; in fact, BGS also does this, with cards issued through 1981-82 Topps carrying the BVG (Beckett Vintage Grading) label, while the Star and Fleer issues that follow are graded by BGS. In football, cards issued from 1981-present are graded by BGS as they are in baseball, while hockey cards issued from 1981-82 and later are graded by BGS; earlier issues are graded and slabbed by BVG.

It's apparent that BGS has taken a baseball-centric approach in dividing the line between BGS and BVG for the purposes of its grading services. However, it's notable that the baseball-centric cutoff either coincides with or is attributable to the emergence of competition in 1981.

And based on the competition criteria, it can be argued that the vintage cutoff date for basketball, football, and hockey should end with 1988-89 Fleer Basketball, 1988 Topps Football, and 1989-90 Topps and O-Pee-Chee Hockey. In basketball, Hoops was introduced in 1989-90, providing competition to Fleer. In football, Topps was a monopoly card manufacturer from 1968 until 1989, with the introduction of 1989 Score and 1989 Pro Set. And in hockey, Topps and its Canadian partner O-Pee-Chee held a monopoly from 1964-65 through 1989-90, before Score, Pro Set, and Upper Deck sets all appear in 1990-91.

Absolute Scarcity and Relative Scarcity

By now, we know that scarcity has a lot to do with the ability of collectibles to command outsized prices and, in turn, generate outsized returns. But it turns out that there are really two kinds of scarcity:

1. Relative scarcity

2. Absolute scarcity

The distinction is very important, particularly as it relates to pricing power.

With regard to baseball cards, **relative scarcity** compares the scarcity of one card to another, or the scarcities of different parallels of the same card. For example, we know that a Bowman Chrome Orange Refractor #'d/25 is relatively scarce compared to a Gold Refractor #'d/50, which is relatively scarce compared to a Blue Refractor #'d/150 or #'d/250.

Generally speaking, rarer parallels are worth more than more common ones.

For the 2013 baseball card season, the two biggest cards were the 2013 Bowman Chrome Prospect autos of Minnesota Twins prospect OF Byron Buxton, and Los Angeles Dodgers OF Yasiel Puig. Buxton, the #2 overall pick in the 2012 MLB First-Year Player Draft, entered the 2013 season flashing all five tools and drawing comparisons to Pirates centerfielder and eventual 2013 NL MVP Andrew McCutchen; by the end of the season, after destroying low-A ball to the tune of a .341/.431/.559 (AVG/OBP/SLG) line including 32 stolen bases in 68 games, and doing similar damage in high-A ball with a .326/.415/.472 line with 23 stolen bases in 57 games as a 19 year-old, Buxton was drawing comparisons to Mike Trout.

The Cuban-born Puig, on the other hand, began the season in Double-A ball, but was called up to the major leagues after the star-studded Los Angeles Dodgers got off to a disappointing 23-32 start. Puig made his major league debut on June 3, and got off to a torrid start, hitting .437/.467/.713 for the month of June, helping spark a historic run for the Dodgers that saw the team go 69-38 to finish the season, win the division, and make the National League Championship Series, before losing to the St. Louis Cardinals.

Puig finished the year with a .319/.391/.534 line including 19 home runs in 104 games, and finished second in the National League Rookie of the Year (ROY) voting to Miami Marlins RHP Jose Fernandez.

The table below shows actual sales ranges for ungraded versions of the various parallels of Buxton's and Puig's Bowman Chrome Prospect autos on eBay in 2013. Buxton's cards were issued in 2013 Bowman packs released in May 2013, while Puig's cards were issued in 2013 Bowman Chrome packs released in September 2013. Once again, the Puig Superfractor price is an estimate, and could be understated. Meanwhile, it should be noted that Puig did not have a regular refractor (non-color) auto, and that his base auto (non-refractor) is thought to be a short print (SP).

Though there are some overlapping ranges, the general relationship between relative print run and relative value should be clear.

2013 Bowman Chrome Prospects Autos: Buxton and Puig

Color	Print Run	Byron Buxton	Yasiel Puig
Superfractor	1	$7,999	$10,000-$15,000+ (est.)
Red Refractor	5	$2,000-$2,500	$5,500
Purple Refractor	10	$1,000-$1,500	$2,900-$3,600
Orange Refractor	25	$900-$1,300	$1,500-$2,225
Gold Refractor	50	$700-$1,000	$650-$1,755
Blue Wave Refractor	50	$450-$600	$600-$1,200
Blue Refractor	150	$400-$500	$510-$1,000
Refractor	500	$200-$300	–
Base	–	$100-$200	$400-$650*

Sources: eBay, Cardboard Connection, Terapeak
*Short print (SP)

Key Concept: The rarer the parallel, the greater the value.

Absolute scarcity is scarcity in the truest sense, and with regard to baseball cards generally relates to the highest quality of the scarce. That is, relative condition is a relevant factor.

We know, for example, that the 1909-11 T206 Honus Wagner is generally scarce with fewer than 60 known copies in existence; but the Gretzky T206 Wagner is absolutely scarce, and is the boss card whether you think of it as the best condition example – with or without its PSA 8 NM-MT grade – or whether you think of it as the Gretzky Wagner or "The Card" with a one-of-a-kind story, trimmed or not. We also know that the 2012 Topps Chrome Andrew Luck RC Superfractor Auto and the 2013 Bowman Chrome Prospects Yasiel Puig and Byron Buxton Superfractors are 1/1s and are absolutely scarce. These cards have absolute pricing power over any like card of lesser condition or higher quantity.

Meanwhile, the 1996-97 Topps Chrome Kobe Bryant RC Refractor is Bryant's best RC, while the twelve BGS 10 Pristine copies are the boss cards and are absolutely scarce. These cards have near-absolute pricing power: They have absolute pricing power over any lesser condition copies of the 1996-97 Topps Chrome Kobe Bryant RC Refractor, as well as absolute pricing power over any of the base non-refractor versions of the card or any other Kobe Bryant RC. These cards cannot be trumped, and have absolute pricing power except in the case where there are two or more copies of the BGS 10 Pristine Refractors on the market at the same time.

We'll discuss the equivalent of the latter situation next.

Relative Scarcity and Pricing Power

Let's say for example that you have a 2009 Bowman Chrome Draft Mike Trout Gold Refractor Auto #'d/50, graded BGS 9.5 Gem Mint with a 10 Auto. You are considering selling your card on eBay, and ideally would like to get $4,000 for it.

Scenario #1: There's another identical 2009 Bowman Chrome Draft Mike Trout Gold Refractor Auto #'d/50, also graded BGS 9.5 Gem Mint with a 10 Auto. This one is listed with a Buy It Now price of $3,495. What's the most you can reasonably expect to sell yours for?

Answer: The answer is pretty simple. All else being equal (assuming the other seller has a good feedback score, for example), you can't reasonably expect to sell yours for more than $3,495 while the other one is on the market.

Scenario #2: The other competing Gold Refractor #'d/50 sold, but now there is a 2009 Bowman Chrome Draft Mike Trout Orange Refractor #'d/25, graded BGS 9.5 Gem Mint with a 10 Auto. This card is listed with a Buy it Now price of $3,995. What's the most you can reasonably expect to sell yours for?

Answer: Well, you are clearly not getting $3,995, as at that price anybody with $3,995 to spend would default to the Orange Refractor. And considering that the Orange Refractor is worth at least 25% to 50% more than the Gold Refractor – probably more, considering that the player in question is Mike Trout (leading to multiple expansion, which we'll get to later), and also considering that there were no Purple Refractors #'d/10 back in 2009 (putting the Orange Refractors #'d/25 higher up the ladder than in 2013 and more valuable relative to everything below it) – it is unlikely that you could get much more than $3,000 while a BGS 9.5/10 Orange Refractor #'d/25 is available for $3,995.

Scenario #3: The Orange Refractor #'d/25 has sold, and now the next best available variations of the 2009 Bowman Chrome Draft Mike Trout auto are a Gold Refractor #'d/50 graded BGS 9 Mint with a 10 auto, listed with a Buy It Now price of $2,795; and a Blue Refractor #'d/150 graded BGS 9.5 with a 10 auto, and with a Buy It Now price of $1,995. What's the most you can reasonably expect to sell yours for?

Answer: Now we're talking. You have the best available card, and as such are not subject to pricing pressure from the presence of like or superior cards on the market. You have absolute or near-absolute pricing power, and consequently have a much higher theoretical ceiling (to some extent, the *existence* of superior cards will generally place some theoretical limit on the price you can charge). As such, all you need is one buyer willing and able to pay a premium price for a premium card.

In the first scenario, we demonstrated that the presence of the other, *identical* Gold Refractor auto #'d/50 and graded BGS 9.5/10 created pricing pressure by placing a ceiling on the value of your card, as you cannot expect to sell yours for more than an identical card while the other one is still available. And in the second scenario, we demonstrated that the presence of a *superior* card created pricing pressure by placing a ceiling on the value of your card, as you cannot expect to sell your card for more than the price of a superior version of your card while the other one is still available.

Lastly, in the third scenario, we demonstrated that removing the identical Gold Refractor and superior Orange Refractor from the marketplace means that you have the best available card, and thus are no longer subject to pricing pressure. Consequently, the best available card has near-absolute pricing power with a much higher theoretical ceiling.

It's important to note that these principles of relative scarcity and pricing power do not apply only to high dollar amount cards – they apply for *any* card for which there are limited print parallels, whether we are talking about cards worth $100 or $10,000.

Key Concept: For any given card at any given time, the presence of like or superior variations of the card on the market in equal or better condition creates pricing pressure.

Key Concept: When you have the best available card on the market, you only have to sell to one person; but when there are other like or superior versions of the same card available on the market, you are generally forced to beat the market in order to sell the card.

Key Concept: The best available card on the market has the greatest pricing power.

Leverage

Over the long run, two key things happen that enable the value of scarce high-grade baseball cards to rise:

1. As the career of a true Hall of Fame-caliber star player progresses, the demand for the highest quality examples of that player's key cards will tend to grow, and

2. The supply of the highest quality examples of those key cards stops growing.

It's simple economics. If demand grows while supply stays the same, then prices will rise. That static supply creates **leverage** – that is, sensitivity to changes in demand, or the ability for card values to rise (or fall) and multiples to expand (or contract) along with changes in demand. Meanwhile, the scarcer the card, the more leverage the card has, and thus the more sensitive the card's value will be to changes in demand.

This – combined with pricing power – is the value of scarcity.

The problem for many of us who haven't looked at a baseball card in 20 years is that our frame of reference has been completely skewed. For many of us, our frame of reference is the baseball card bubble of the late 1980s and early 1990s, a period from which there were a zillion different overproduced card sets, and with unopened boxes which remain in endless supply. Consequently, leverage for most issues from this period is quite low, and our general perception of non-vintage baseball cards is quite weak.

But modern baseball cards are fundamentally different. For one thing, starting with the 2010 baseball season, there is only one licensed manufacturer of Major League Baseball cards – Topps – which in 2013 extended its exclusive licensing deal through 2020. Now there are only a handful of key sets issued every year, all of which are printed in numbers based on pre-order demand.

This doesn't mean that modern baseball cards aren't susceptible to bubble behavior – as we examine the supply chain and discuss the value cycle in Part VI, we'll see that Topps' policy of printing to pre-order demand comes with its own set of pitfalls. That said, modern card sets aren't printed in numbers such that there will be a zillion cases of unopened 2014-year boxes sitting in storage 20 years from now.

In fact, the autographed rookie and prospect card trend of the last decade or so virtually assures that there *won't* be a zillion cases of key issues from 2014 sitting in storage 20 years from now. For better or for worse, the proliferation of autographed cards has led to the widespread use of redemption cards, which carry an expiration date. As a result, redemption cards ultimately place an expiration date on the value of unopened boxes and cases.

Meanwhile, the advent of the limited print, serialized parallels means that even as the industry starts to grow again and supply along with it, there will generally be a subset of key cards for a given player with known static supply, and with high leverage among the rarest parallels.

Key Concept: The value of scarcity lies in a combination of upside leverage and pricing power.

Part II: Key Cards and Multiple Expansion

Every player has a key card that trumps all other cards of that player in terms of both recognition and value.

Stocks investors know that the stocks of premium companies – companies that tend to be the best players within a given industry, generally with the best brands and strong, sustainable competitive advantages – tend to command premium valuations relative to their peers in the form of higher price-to-earnings (P/E) ratios or EV/EBITDA (enterprise value/earnings before interest, taxes, depreciation, and amortization) ratios. Similarly, real estate investors know that premium real estate tends to warrant premium valuations in terms of higher prices per square foot compared to lesser like assets; moreover, the biggest gains to be had are often on the highest end, where the real estate is both most desirable and most scarce, and thus where pricing power is the greatest.

Baseball cards are similar to stocks to the extent that card values more or less track the popularity of a given player, and where the cardboard stocks of the game's biggest stars tend to command a premium over lesser stars and everybody else. Meanwhile, baseball cards are similar to real estate to the extent that much of a baseball card's excess value is derived from its relative scarcity among the more desirable collectibles, particularly on the high end of the hobby.

Owning a baseball card is, in effect, like owning a given player's collectible cardboard real estate.

As in both stocks and in real estate, baseball card collectors/investors pay the biggest premiums for the best assets – the best cards of the best players in the best condition. And over time, seemingly small advantages in value for the best assets tend to turn into large advantages and outsized returns.

Over time, the spread between the value of a BGS 9.5 or PSA 10 Gem Mint condition card and lesser graded and ungraded versions of the same card tends to widen. And over time, the spread between BGS 9.5 or PSA 10 Gem Mint condition versions of that player's key card and BGS 9.5 or PSA 10 Gem Mint condition versions of a player's second-best like cards (i.e. key RC vs. second-best RCs) also tends to widen.

This effect of widening spreads between the value of BGS 9.5 Gem Mint (or better) cards and the value of ungraded and lesser condition cards is (or should be) known as **multiple expansion**. And as we will see in a minute, this effect tends to benefit a given player's key card more than any other.

Key Cards

Every major league baseball player has a **key card** that tends to trump all other cards of that player in terms of both recognition and value. For cards issued from 1952 to 1980, identifying a player's key card is simple enough: If the player has an RC issued by Topps, then his Topps RC is his key card.

Everybody *knows*, for example, that the key Hank Aaron card is the 1954 Topps Hank Aaron RC, with an ungraded book value of $1,800 and a graded PSA 9 Mint book value of $28,000,[33] and that Roberto Clemente's key card is his 1955 Topps RC (BV: $2,200; PSA 9: $46,500). Everybody *knows* that Pete Rose's key card is his 1963 Topps RC shared with three other guys (BV: $1,000; PSA 9: $13,500), and that Nolan Ryan's key card is his 1968 Topps RC shared with Jerry Koosman (BV: $500; PSA 9: $8,000). And everybody *knows* that Ozzie Smith's key card is his 1979 Topps RC (BV: $60; PSA 10 Gem Mint: $14,000), and that Rickey Henderson's key card is his 1980 Topps RC (BV: $80; PSA 10: $9,000).

Before Topps gained monopoly status in 1956, players such as Don Larsen and Elston Oward had rookie cards issued in Bowman sets but not in Topps. Consequently, Don Larsen's key card is his 1954 Bowman RC (BV: $80; PSA 9: $650), and Elston Howard's key card is his 1955 Bowman RC (BV: $80; PSA 9: $775).

On the other hand, the most valuable card from this time period was not a rookie card at all: The iconic 1952 Topps Mickey Mantle (BV: $30,000; PSA 9: $425,000) from the landmark 1952 Topps set is the card that collectors most identify as Mantle's key card, and trumps his 1951 Bowman RC (BV: $8,000; PSA 9: $187,500).

But as we get to cards from the 1980s, identifying key cards starts to become a little bit trickier as multiple manufacturers join the fray, resulting in the presence of multiple RCs for most players. Moreover, the key sets were subject to change from year to year.

Modern Key Cards

For cards issued from 1981-present, a player's key card is typically either a player's rookie card (RC), an XRC (extended RC, a term used by Beckett to describe rookie or pre-rookie cards issued in extended or limited release sets from the years 1982

---

[33] PSA graded book values taken from PSAcard.com, January 2014; ungraded book values and BGS graded book values throughout book are courtesy of Beckett.com

to 1988), or a player's 1st Bowman Chrome Card (2006-present, though the 2013 issues do not carry the 1st Bowman Chrome Card label).

But regardless of the sometimes confusing definitions used to designate rookie cards, a player's key card is generally a player's first card issued as part of a major league set. And in cases where a player has multiple rookie or first year cards, there tends to be one boss card that trumps the others.

As we mentioned a moment ago, identifying a player's key card is important because the key card is the card most likely to benefit most from multiple expansion, and thus generate outsized returns. That said, because the "official" definition of rookie cards and related labels have changed over the past 30 years, the best way to demonstrate and examine these concepts is through case study.

Let's start by examining the varied rookie card structures of the 1980s.

1983 RC Comparison: Gwynn, Boggs, and Sandberg

Card	#	Ungraded BV	BGS 9 Mint	Adj. Multiple	BGS 9.5 Gem Mint	Adj. Multiple
1983 Topps Tony Gwynn RC	482	$25	$50	1.4x	$500	14.3x
1983 Fleer Tony Gwynn RC	360	$12	$25	1.1x	$120	5.5x
1983 Donruss Tony Gwynn RC	598	$15	$25	1.0x	$120	4.8x
1983 Topps Wade Boggs RC	498	$15	$30	1.2x	$400	16.0x
1983 Fleer Wade Boggs RC	179	$10	$20	1.0x	$60	3.0x
1983 Donruss Wade Boggs RC	586	$10	$20	1.0x	$60	3.0x
1983 Topps Ryne Sandberg RC	83	$20	$40	1.3x	$300	10.0x
1983 Fleer Ryne Sandberg RC	507	$10	$20	1.0x	$120	6.0x
1983 Donruss Ryne Sandberg RC	177	$10	$20	1.0x	$120	6.0x

Source: Beckett.com, Dec. 2013

The 1983 rookie card class featuring Hall of Famers Tony Gwynn, Wade Boggs, and Ryne Sandberg presents a simple, clear-cut example of these concepts. In 1983, the key issue was still the 1983 Topps set, which included the key RCs of all three players, with the Fleer and Donruss RCs of these players taking a clear backseat. In this case, the Topps RCs graded in BGS 9.5 Gem Mint condition also command an adjusted multiple to ungraded book that is far greater than that of the

Fleer and Donruss RCs. For example, the 1983 Topps Tony Gwynn RC in BGS 9.5 Gem Mint condition carries an adjusted multiple of 14.3x, or nearly triple that of the 1983 Fleer and 1983 Donruss Gwynn RCs.

Also note that the BGS 9 Mint condition cards from these sets carry little-to-no premium to ungraded book value. An adjusted multiple of 1.0x – as is the case with nearly all of the Fleer and Donruss RCs, with the exception of the 1983 Tony Gwynn RC (which is close enough at 1.1x) – means that if you send your card to get graded and have it come back a BGS 9, you are essentially breaking even. After all, if you have a card that carries an ungraded book value of $10, spend $10 to have it graded, and have it come back a BGS 9 Mint worth $20, you haven't made a profit.

Key Concept: The potential reward for holding a player's key card in Gem Mint condition or better is far greater than the potential reward for holding either lesser condition examples of the same card, or Gem Mint condition examples of a player's second-best cards.

1983 XRC, 1984 RC: Darryl Strawberry

Card	#	Ungraded BV	BGS 9 Mint	Adj. Multiple	BGS 9.5 Gem Mint	Adj. Multiple
1983 Topps Traded Darryl Strawberry XRC	108T	$25	$50	1.4x	$200	5.7x
1984 Donruss Darryl Strawberry RC	68	$8	$25	1.4x	$60	3.3x
1984 Fleer Darryl Strawberry RC	599	$5	$15	1.0x	$60	4.0x
1984 Topps Darryl Strawberry RC	182	$3	$25	1.9x	$50	3.8x
1984 Topps Tiffany Darryl Strawberry RC	182	$20	NA	–	NA	–

Source: Beckett.com, Dec. 2013

Darryl Strawberry presents a new structure of rookie card, as he was the first big star to have his first-year card come as part of an extended set in year one, and then have a full slate of RCs in year two.

In 1982, Topps issued its first Topps Traded set, including a combination of traded players and rookies from the 1982 season. That set included Cal Ripken's first Topps card by himself (his regular 1982 Topps RC is shared with two other players), as well as the first solo Topps cards of Steve Sax and Kent Hrbek (same story), along with the first card of Ozzie Smith in a St. Louis Cardinals uniform.

The 1982 Topps Traded set also included the first major league cards of Ron Washington, Eric Show, and an outfielder named Randy Johnson, all of which Beckett designated as XRCs because they appeared in an extended release rather than in the regular set.

Now this is where things get confusing. All three players have 1983-year cards. And by designating the 1982 Topps Traded cards as XRCs, Beckett is able to designate the 1983 cards as the official RCs. However, the explosion of Traded/Update/Rookies sets as the '80s progressed meant that the use of XRC designations was more arbitrary rather than being a practical definition, and Beckett discontinued use of the XRC designation in 1988.

Anyhow, the 1983 Topps Traded set included the XRC of Darryl Strawberry, which is his only first-year card. Though Strawberry's 1984 Donruss RC is widely considered to be his best official RC and can be argued as his key RC, the 1983 Topps Traded XRC is Strawberry's truest key card.

1984 Don Mattingly RCs: Premium Parallel

Card	#	Ungraded BV	BGS 9 Mint	Adj. Multiple	BGS 9.5 Gem Mint	Adj. Multiple
1984 Donruss Don Mattingly RC	248	$30	$80	2.0x	$500	12.5x
1984 Fleer Don Mattingly RC	131	$25	$40	1.1x	$150	4.3x
1984 Topps Don Mattingly RC	8	$25	$40	1.1x	$150	4.3x
1984 Topps Tiffany Don Mattingly RC	8	$60	$150	2.1x	$800	11.4x

Source: Beckett.com, December 2013

Don Mattingly's 1984 RCs present another interesting case. On the one hand, there's no question that Mattingly's 1984 Donruss RC is his key card: Despite the fact that there is relatively little difference in ungraded values among his regular release issues, the 1984 Donruss RC carries a BGS 9.5 adjusted multiple nearly triple that of Mattingly's Fleer and Topps RCs. But more interesting is the presence of the Topps Tiffany RC.

In 1984, Topps introduced the Topps Tiffany set, a premium version of the regular Topps issue using white stock rather than grey, and with a glossy finish on the front. This version was released as a complete set only, and in 1984 had a relatively low print run of 10,000 sets.[34]

The 1984 Topps Tiffany Don Mattingly RC carries both the highest ungraded and graded BGS 9.5 book values among Mattingly's RCs, and carries an adjusted multiple on par with that of the 1984 Donruss RC. Notably, the Topps Tiffany RC carries a significantly higher adjusted multiple compared to the regular Topps issue.

Key Concept: Premium, shorter print parallels carry premium valuations.

Note: Technically speaking, Beckett does not consider parallels to be rookie cards, and as such does not qualify cards from the Topps Tiffany sets or any other variations of cards (like gold variations, or limited print refractor parallels in modern issues) as RCs in its price guides. However, while this practice helps simplify the landscape for organizational (price guide) purposes, this is not a practical distinction – for practical purposes, any parallels of rookie cards *are* in fact rookie cards. Consequently, we will continue to label such cards as RCs throughout this book.

The Rare XRC: Clemens, Puckett, and Gooden

Card	#	Ungraded BV	BGS 9 Mint	Adj. Multiple	BGS 9.5 Gem Mint	Adj. Multiple
1984 Fleer Update Roger Clemens XRC	27	$120	$200	1.5x	$600	4.6x
1985 Fleer Roger Clemens RC	155	$20	$30	1.0x	$300	10.0x
1985 Topps Roger Clemens RC	181	$15	$30	1.2x	$150	6.0x
1985 Topps Tiffany Roger Clemens RC	181	$60	$100	1.4x	$800	11.4x
1985 Donruss Roger Clemens RC	273	$20	$25	0.8x	$120	4.0x
1984 Fleer Update Kirby Puckett XRC	93	$100	$150	1.4x	$500	4.6x
1985 Fleer Kirby Puckett RC	296	$15	$40	1.6x	$225	9.0x
1985 Topps Kirby Puckett RC	536	$12	$25	1.1x	$150	6.8x

[34] www.cardboardconnection.com/comprehensive-guide-to-topps-tiffany-baseball-cards

Card	#	Ungraded BV	BGS 9 Mint	Adj. Multiple	BGS 9.5 Gem Mint	Adj. Multiple
1985 Topps Tiffany Kirby Puckett RC	536	$40	$80	1.6x	$600	12.0x
1985 Donruss Kirby Puckett RC	438	$12	$25	1.1x	$120	5.5x
1984 Fleer Update Dwight Gooden XRC	43	$40	$80	1.6x	$400	8.0x
1984 Topps Traded Dwight Gooden XRC	42T	$12	$25	1.1x	$120	5.0x
1984 Topps Traded Tiffany Dwight Gooden	42T	$25	$36*	1.0x*	$350*	10.0x*
1985 Fleer Dwight Gooden RC	82	$3	–	–	–	–
1985 Topps Dwight Gooden RC	620	$2	$15	1.3x	$60	5.0x
1985 Topps Tiffany Dwight Gooden RC	620	$12	$35*	1.5x*	$550*	25.0x*
1985 Donruss Dwight Gooden RC	190	$3	$12	0.9x	$50	3.8x

Source: Beckett.com, December 2013
*PSA 9 Mint and PSA 10 Gem Mint pricing, PSAcard.com, 1/1/14

In 1984, Fleer joined the extended set fray with the introduction of Fleer Update, a landmark set which would be the most valuable set of the 1980s. The set included the only 1984-year cards of Roger Clemens and Kirby Puckett, as well as the key XRC of Dwight Gooden. Most collectors would identify the Fleer Update XRCs of all three players as their key cards.

Clemens, Puckett, and Gooden all have 1985-year RCs. Among the regularly issued 1985 RCs, the boss RCs for Clemens and Puckett are clearly their 1985 Fleer RCs, which carry by far the highest adjusted multiples. Beckett.com does not include graded pricing for the 1985 Fleer Dwight Gooden RC, but an educated guess might peg it at about $80-$100 (representing a 33% to 67% premium over his 1985 Topps RC, in line with the 50% premium for Kirby Puckett and 100% premium for Roger Clemens) or an adjusted multiple of about 7.7x ungraded book.

But again, the power goes to the parallel with the smaller print run, in this case the 1985 Topps Tiffany set with a print run of only 5,000 sets.

The graded pricings on the Dwight Gooden 1984 Topps Traded Tiffany XRC and 1985 Topps Tiffany RC present a unique scenario. As there is no BGS pricing, PSA pricing is used; but it should be noted first that BGS and PSA pricings may not be directly comparable due to differences in pricing methodology (PSA notes on PSAcard.com that its prices are meant to reflect average dealer prices, while Beckett's pricing are meant to reflect the high end of current reasonable sales ranges), while some differences in pricing are due to relative differences in graded population. That said, the PSA 10 value of the 1985 Topps Tiffany Dwight Gooden carries the highest graded value and highest multiple for any of the Gooden XRCs/ RCs, and is even higher than the PSA 10 value for Gooden's 1984 Topps Traded Tiffany XRC.

Why? Likely because there are a total of *zero* PSA 10 Gem Mint 1985 Topps Tiffany Dwight Gooden XRCs in PSA's population report (which begs the question how PSA has pricing for a card with zero population, unless BGS 9.5 sales are accounted for, or unless it is merely a projection), and there are only two BGS 9.5 Gem Mint copies. In contrast, there are thirteen PSA 10 and five BGS 9.5 Gem Mint copies of the 1984 Topps Traded Tiffany card in the PSA/BGS population reports, and there are 58 PSA 10s and 13 BGS 9.5 Gem Mint copies of the 1984 Fleer Update XRC.

Also interestingly, the 1984 Fleer Update XRCs of Clemens and Puckett carry lower adjusted multiples than the 1985 Fleer RCs, despite carrying a much higher price tag. That said, this is likely due to the relative scarcity of the 1984 Fleer Update set protecting the ungraded values of the XRCs, and not because the 1985 Fleer RCs are superior to the 1984 Fleer Update XRCs (they're not).

This is not a case without some basis for comparison. In Appendix B of *The Card* by Michael O'Keefe and Teri Thompson, Robert Lifson of Robert Edward Auctions presents a list of "The Most Valuable Baseball Cards in the World," entirely of vintage ilk. After presenting his list, Lifson notes that "the 'slope' of value plotted against grades is different for really rare cards than for more common cards."

Essentially, using the 1952 Topps Mickey Mantle and the "extremely rare" 1914 Baltimore News Babe Ruth as examples, Lifson says that relatively common cards (the Mantles) are far more condition sensitive than relatively rare ones (the Ruths). Lifson notes that whereas a 1952 Topps Mickey Mantle graded PSA 1 Poor-Fair[35] might fetch $1,000 to $2,000, a PSA 9 Mint example might run up $150,000+ or 75x

---

[35] Lifson's discussion was based on PSA's old whole-point grading scale; PSA's new half-point scale now separates Poor and Fair into PSA 1 Poor and PSA 1.5 Fair

to 150x the PSA 1 value. In contrast, while a 1914 Babe Ruth might be worth over $100,000 in PSA 1 condition, a PSA 4 VG-EX sold for $243,000 in 2005, while a PSA 7 or PSA 8 (none are known to exist) would be worth between $500,000 and $1 million, or only about 5x to 10x the PSA 1 value – a much narrower range.

Similarly, the relatively more common 1985 Fleer Clemens and Puckett RCs are more condition sensitive than their relatively rare 1984 Fleer Update XRCs.

Key Concept: Extremely rare cards are less condition sensitive than relatively more common ones.

Mark McGwire: 1985 Olympic RC, 1987 1st Card in MLB Uniform

Card	#	Ungraded BV	BGS 9 Mint	Adj. Multiple	BGS 9.5 Gem Mint	Adj. Multiple
1985 Topps Mark McGwire Oly RC	401	$20	$50	1.7x	$400	13.3x
1985 Topps Tiffany Mark McGwire Oly RC	401	$80	$150	1.7x	$900	10.0x
1987 Donruss Mark McGwire	46	$8	$20	1.1x	$30	1.7x
1987 Fleer Update Mark McGwire	76	$5	$10	0.7x	$25	1.7x
1987 Fleer Update Glossy Mark McGwire	76	$5	$15	1.0x	$20	1.3x
1987 Topps Mark McGwire	366	$4	$15	1.1x	$25	1.8x
1987 Topps Tiffany Mark McGwire	366	$12	$20	0.9x	$50	2.3x
1987 Donruss Rookies Mark McGwire	1	$10	$15	0.8x	$30	1.5x

Source: Beckett.com, December 2013

Though the 1985 Fleer set is generally the key set of that year, Topps got the jump on the competition by including Team USA Olympic cards in the 1985 Topps set; that set includes the most valuable card of the year in the 1985 Topps Mark McGwire RC, which is also McGwire's only rookie card, and thus his key card. The 1985 Topps RC carries a huge premium over McGwire's first cards in an Oakland A's uniform, which would come in the 1987 sets.

There are several items of note. First note the declining premium awarded to the Topps Tiffany sets along with a rise in print run: While only 5,000 Topps Tiffany sets were printed in 1985, 30,000 such Topps Tiffany sets were printed in 1987.[36] Secondly, while a big part of the spread between the 1985 Topps RC and the 1987 cards can be attributable to the fact that the 1985 card is the key card, it's important to note that print runs in general were also on the considerable rise by 1987. And because print numbers are considerably higher and unopened boxes of the 1987 issues still seem to be in virtually endless supply, by this point we start to see adjusted multiples fall considerably.

Lastly – and perhaps most importantly – it's important to note the structure of McGwire's rookie cards, because this pattern will be repeated as we get to more recent issues. McGwire has a 1985 RC, which is an RC by Beckett's definition because it appears in a regular issue set. As a consequence, McGwire's 1987 cards are not considered to be rookie cards by Beckett's official definition of the time.

Fast forward to 2010. Both Bryce Harper and Manny Machado have 2010 Bowman Chrome 18U USA Baseball cards issued in the 2010 Bowman packs. By this point, these cards are not considered RCs by official definition, but rather are defined as "inserts." Nevertheless, these are the first and truest key non-auto cards of both Harper and Machado.

Machado's first key card in an Orioles uniform would come later in the 2010 Bowman Chrome Draft set – itself issued as a draft pick "insert" in the 2010 Bowman Draft set by official definition – while Machado has 2013-year official RCs (more explanation in Part III). Harper, on the other hand, has 2011-year Bowman Chrome Prospects cards (issued as "inserts" in both 2011 Bowman and 2011 Bowman Chrome) as his first cards in a Nationals uniform, and has 2012-year official RC cards.

That the 1987 Fleer Update Glossy carries a lower graded BGS 9.5 book value than the regular issue is neither here nor there, and likely attributable to nothing other than price guide variance.

---

[36] cardboardconnection.com

1986 RC/XRC: Jose Canseco

Card	#	Ungraded BV	BGS 9 Mint	Adj. Multiple	BGS 9.5 Gem Mint	Adj. Multiple
1986 Donruss Jose Canseco RC	39	$12	$30	1.3x	$100	4.6x
1986 Fleer Jose Canseco RC	649	$8	$12	0.7x	$50	2.8x
1986 Topps Traded Jose Canseco XRC	20T	$4	$15	1.1x	$40	2.9x
1986 Topps Traded Tiffany Jose Canseco XRC	20T	$15	$20	0.8x	$100	4.0x
1986 Donruss Rookies Jose Canseco	22	$4	$8	0.6x	$25	1.8x
1986 Fleer Update Jose Canseco	20	$4	$12	0.9x	$40	2.9x

Source: Beckett.com, December 2013

In 1986, Donruss retook the throne with the key RC of Jose Canseco, as well as the lone RC of Fred McGriff (BV: $8; BGS 9.5: $60). Part of the appeal of the 1986 Donruss Jose Canseco RC over his 1986 Fleer RC is that the Donruss RC is a solo card, while Canseco's Fleer RC is shared with Eric Plunk. As Canseco did not have an RC in the regular 1986 Topps issue, the 1986 Topps Traded Jose Canseco is an unusual XRC by definition, despite appearing in the same year as his RCs.

That year, Donruss introduced its Donruss Rookies extended set including another 1986-year Canseco card, while the 1986 Fleer Update included Fleer's first solo card of Canseco. These cards are neither RCs nor XRCs by official designation. That said, my guess is that the Fleer Update Canseco maintains an adjusted multiple in line with the regular Fleer RC and Topps Traded XRC likely because it is his first Fleer solo card, while the Donruss Rookies version carries less weight because the original 1986 Donruss Canseco was already a solo card carrying the RC designation.

Note again the impact of the premium parallel: The 1986 Topps Traded Tiffany set had a print run of 5,000 sets, and the Topps Traded Tiffany Canseco XRC carries a valuation on par with the 1986 Donruss RC.

By this point, there is little-to-negative value in the BGS 9s.

Multiple 1986 XRCs: Barry Bonds

Card	#	Ungraded BV	BGS 9 Mint	Adj. Multiple	BGS 9.5 Gem Mint	Adj. Multiple
1986 Fleer Update Barry Bonds XRC	14	$12	$25	1.1x	$60	2.7x
1986 Donruss Rookies Barry Bonds XRC	11	$12	$25	1.1x	$60	2.7x
1986 Topps Traded Barry Bonds XRC	11T	$15	$25	1.0x	$60	2.4x
1986 Topps Traded Tiffany Barry Bonds XRC	11T	$100	$200	1.8x	$400	3.6x
1987 Fleer Barry Bonds RC	604	$12	$20	0.9x	$120	5.5x
1987 Fleer Glossy Barry Bonds RC	604	$12	$20	0.9x	$120	5.5x
1987 Donruss Barry Bonds RC	361	$12	$20	0.9x	$40	1.8x
1987 Topps Barry Bonds RC	230	$8	$15	0.8x	$30	1.7x
1987 Topps Tiffany Barry Bonds RC	230	$20	$30	1.0x	$80	2.7x

Source: Beckett.com, December 2013

By 1986, the Traded/Update/Rookies craze was in full force, and all three sets included the XRCs of Pittsburgh Pirates phenom Barry Bonds. Interestingly, while the market views the 1986 Fleer Update XRC as the key base XRC, the market also appears to view his 1987 Fleer RC as the true key card with the highest BGS 9.5 Gem Mint value and the highest adjusted multiple at 5.5x; the Fleer Glossy version carries an identical valuation.

The true boss card, however, is the 1986 Topps Traded Tiffany XRC with a relatively low print run of 5,000 copies and a BGS 9.5 book value of $400.

Note again the relative devaluation of the 1987 Topps Tiffany set, with 30,000 sets printed and a comparatively low adjusted multiple of 2.7x for the Bonds RC.

1987 RCs: Greg Maddux and Barry Larkin

Card	#	Ungraded BV	BGS 9 Mint	Adj. Multiple	BGS 9.5 Gem Mint	Adj. Multiple
1987 Donruss Greg Maddux RC	36	$10	$25	1.3x	$100	5.0x
1987 Fleer Update Greg Maddux XRC	68	$8	$15	0.8x	$60	3.3x
1987 Fleer Update Glossy Greg Maddux XRC	68	$8	$20	1.1x	$60	3.3x
1987 Topps Traded Greg Maddux XRC	70T	$10	$20	1.0x	$40	2.0x
1987 Topps Traded Tiffany Greg Maddux XRC	70T	$20	$40	1.3x	$150	5.0x
1987 Donruss Rookies Greg Maddux	52	$8	$25	1.4x	$100	5.6x
1987 Fleer Barry Larkin RC	204	$8	$25	1.4x	$60	3.3x
1987 Fleer Glossy Barry Larkin RC	204	$10	$25	1.3x	$150	7.5x
1987 Donruss Barry Larkin RC	492	$4	$20	1.4x	$40	2.9x
1987 Topps Barry Larkin RC	648	$2.50	$15	1.2x	$30	2.4x
1987 Topps Tiffany Barry Larkin RC	648	$20	$30	1.0x	$60	2.0x

Source: Beckett.com, December 2013

The 1987 Donruss Greg Maddux RC is Maddux's only official RC, and consequently is easily identifiable as the key card. But factoring parallels, the 1987 Topps Traded Tiffany Greg Maddux XRC carries both the highest graded and ungraded values, making it the most valuable of the Maddux RC/XRCs.

In stark contrast, Barry Larkin's 1987 Fleer RC is his key card among regular issues, but this time – in contrast to Maddux, McGwire, and Bonds – the 1987 Fleer Glossy parallel is the clear boss card, with a graded BGS 9.5 valuation 2.5x that of the regular Fleer RC, and carrying by far the highest adjusted multiple at 7.5x.

The 1987 Fleer Glossy sets were distributed as factory sets, and were hobby-only releases. But with a print run thought to be near 100,000 sets,[37] they don't carry

---

[37] www.psacardfacts.com/Hierarchy.aspx?c=2298

the same premiums as the Topps Tiffany sets. Why the Larkin Fleer Glossy RC carries a premium while the 1987 Fleer Update Glossy Maddux XRC, and 1987 Fleer Glossy McGwire and Bonds RC do not may (or may not) be attributable to the fact that the 1987 Fleer is Larkin's clear key card, where Bonds has 1986-year XRCs, McGwire has a 1985 RC, and Maddux's only RC is the Donruss RC. The other reasonable alternative is price guide variance.

1989-90 RCs: Ken Griffey Jr. and Frank Thomas

Card	#	Ungraded BV	BGS 9.5	Adj. Multiple
1989 Upper Deck Ken Griffey Jr. RC	1	$40	$300	6.0x
1989 Donruss Ken Griffey Jr. RC	33	$8	$60	3.3x
1989 Donruss Rookies Ken Griffey Jr.	3	$10	$50	2.5x
1989 Bowman Ken Griffey Jr. RC	220	$6	$80	5.0x
1989 Bowman Tiffany Ken Griffey Jr. RC	220	$80	$1,600	17.8x
1989 Fleer Ken Griffey Jr. RC	548	$10	$40	2.0x
1989 Fleer Glossy Ken Griffey Jr. RC	548	$30	$800	20.0x
1989 Topps Traded Ken Griffey Jr. RC	41T	$8	$30	1.7x
1989 Topps Traded Tiffany Ken Griffey Jr. RC	41T	$50	$300	5.0x
1989 Score Rookie/Traded Ken Griffey Jr. RC	130T	$6	$30	1.9x
1990 Leaf Frank Thomas RC	93	$20	$100	3.3x
1990 Topps Frank Thomas RC ERR NNOF	414A	$800	–	–
1990 Topps Frank Thomas RC	414B	$2	$50	4.2x
1990 Topps Tiffany Frank Thomas RC	414	$30	$400	10.0x
1990 Bowman Frank Thomas RC	320	$2	$40	3.3x
1990 Bowman Tiffany Frank Thomas RC	320	$20	$300	10.0x
1990 Fleer Update Frank Thomas RC	87	$2	$30	2.5x
1990 Score Frank Thomas RC	663	$2	$25	2.1x
1990 Score Rookie/Traded Frank Thomas	86T	$2	$30	2.5x

Source: Beckett.com, December 2013

There's no question that Ken Griffey Jr.'s key RC is his iconic 1989 Upper Deck RC. Despite not being particular rare with a print run thought to be over a million copies,[38] the Upper Deck RC carries the highest graded and ungraded book values

[38] see *Mint Condition* by Dave Jamieson, pg. 168

among regular issues, and with the highest BGS 9.5 adjusted multiple at 6.0x. It is also either the earliest or one of the earliest dated cards in the Beckett online price guide to include a value for the BGS 10 Pristine grade, which as of December 2013 was listed at $1,400. Meanwhile, actual sales in the second half of 2013 of the BGS 10 Pristine Upper Deck Griffey reached as high as $1,640, representing a 32.8x adjusted multiple to ungraded book.

In 1989, Topps reintroduced the Bowman brand, and produced a Bowman Tiffany set to go with its Topps Tiffany sets. The 1989 Topps Traded Tiffany set had a total print run of 15,000 sets, helping make the 1989 Topps Traded Tiffany Griffey about as valuable as the 1989 Upper Deck Griffey RC. But the print run on 1989 Bowman Tiffany totaled only 6,000 sets, resulting in both the highest graded and ungraded values among Griffey's RCs, and with a BGS 9.5 adjusted multiple of 17.8x – roughly triple that of the Upper Deck RC.

The 1989 Fleer Glossy set would be the last one, and would prove much more attractive with a print run of 30,000 sets, contributing to a graded BGS 9.5 value of $800. The Fleer Glossy RC is apparently quite condition sensitive, with a BGS 9.5 population of only 12 copies – hence the 20.0x multiple. By way of comparison, there are 57 BGS 9.5 copies of the Topps Traded Tiffany RC.

The 1990 Leaf Frank Thomas RC is generally considered to be Thomas' key RC, with both the highest graded and ungraded book values among regular issues. Interestingly, it does not command much of a premium multiple compared to his other regular RCs – probably hurt in large part due to a large print run (which include 655 BGS 9.5s and 1,904 PSA 10s, plus 15 BGS 10 Pristines) – though two BGS 10 copies sold for $1,500 each in January 2014 after Thomas was inducted into the Hall of Fame.

The relatively rare 1990 Topps Tiffany and Bowman Tiffany variations carry significant premiums. The 1990 Topps Tiffany set had a relatively modest print run of 15,000 sets, while the 1990 Bowman Tiffany set was limited to only 3,000 sets.

But by far the most valuable of Frank Thomas' rookie year cards is the 1990 Topps error which had no name on the front. Though the card has an ungraded book value of $800, several PSA 8 and BGS 8 NM-MT copies of the card sold in November 2013 roughly in the $1,400-$1,600 range.

Let's fast forward to 1993.

1993-94 RCs: Derek Jeter and Alex Rodriguez

Card	#	Ungraded BV	BGS 9.5	Adj. Multiple
1993 SP Derek Jeter Foil RC	279	$150	$2,000*	12.5x
1993 Topps Gold Derek Jeter RC	98	$25	$500	14.3x
1993 Topps Derek Jeter RC	98	$15	$120	4.8x
1993 Topps Micro Derek Jeter RC	98	$30	$750**	18.8x**
1993 Topps Inaugural Marlins/Rockies Derek Jeter RC	98	$120	$350**	2.7x**
1993 Stadium Club Murphy Derek Jeter RC	117	$100	$400	3.6x
1993 Pinnacle Derek Jeter RC	457	$25	$300	8.6x
1993 Bowman Derek Jeter RC	511	$25	$150	4.3x
1993 Select Derek Jeter RC	360	$15	$120	4.8x
1993 Upper Deck Derek Jeter RC	449	$15	$150	6.0x
1993 Upper Deck Gold Hologram Derek Jeter RC	449	$60	$900**	12.9x**
1993 Score Derek Jeter RC	489	$25	$120	3.4x
1994 SP Alex Rodriguez Foil RC	15	$40	$400	8.0x
1994 SP Die Cuts Alex Rodriguez Foil RC	15	$40	$300	6.0x
1994 SP Holoviews Alex Rodriguez RC	33	$30	$250	6.3x
1994 SP Holoviews Die Cuts Alex Rodriugez RC	33	$300	$1,000	3.2x
1994 Upper Deck Alex Rodriguez RC	24	$15	$50	2.0x
1994 Upper Deck Alex Rodriguez RC Auto	A198	$150	$300	1.9x
1994 Flair Alex Rodriguez RC	340	$20	$40	1.3x
1994 Collector's Choice Alex Rodriguez RC	647	$10	$80	4.0x
1994 Collector's Choice Silver Signature Alex Rodriguez RC	647	$15	$300**	12.0x**
1994 Collector's Choice Gold Signature Alex Rodriguez RC	647	$120	$850**	6.5x**
1994 Fleer Update Alex Rodriguez RC	86	$20	$30	1.0x

Source: Beckett.com, December 2013
*PSA 10 value listed at $28,500, PSAcard.com, 1/1/14
**PSA values from PSAcard.com, 1/1/14; PSA values reflect different methodology, intended to be "average dealer selling price" rather than Beckett "Hi" value

By 1993, we have a lot of new issues, particularly on the high end. There's no question the 1993 SP Derek Jeter Foil RC is the key card of the bunch, with the highest ungraded value and highest adjusted multiple to book. As we've noted, what makes the SP Jeter card especially interesting is that it is a very tough grade: Only 139 of the nearly 11,000 1993 SP Derek Jeter RCs graded by BGS are graded BGS 9.5 Gem Mint, while only 12 of the nearly 11,000 cards graded by PSA have graded PSA 10 Gem Mint.

And again, as a consequence of the unusual scarcity of the PSA 10 grade on this card in particular, the 1993 SP Jeter RC is listed with a PSA 10 value of $28,500, while two such copies sold on 12/21/13 and 12/22/13 for $32,500 each.[39]

The 1993 Topps Gold Derek Jeter RC is notable as a premium, shorter-printed parallel carrying very much a premium adjusted multiple at 14.3x – about triple that of the regular base Topps Jeter RC. The 1993 Topps Micro parallel does not have BGS pricing, but carries a PSA 10 price of $750 for an adjusted multiple of 18.8x, thanks to a miniscule PSA 10 population of only 13 copies (Note: Note again that PSA's pricing methodology is meant to reflect "average dealer selling prices" rather than Beckett's "Hi" value, and as such is by default more conservative, and thus the multiples slightly understated in relative terms).

In 1993, Topps also printed two foil-stamped sets commemorating the inaugural seasons of the Florida Marlins and Colorado Rockies – one for each team; though each team was given the option for up to 10,000 sets, only 5,000 Rockies sets and 4,000 Marlins sets were produced.[40] Due to the relatively small print numbers, the Rockies version of the Jeter RC carries an ungraded book value of $100, while the Marlins version carries an ungraded book value of $120; BGS does not post a graded value, but PSAcard.com lists a PSA 10 value for both at $350.[41]

Interestingly, the 1993 Pinnacle RC also carries a relatively high adjusted multiple, despite not being a particularly rare card; however, the Cardboard Connection notes that this card is "somewhat condition sensitive due to its black borders."[42]

The 1994 Alex Rodriguez RCs are more straightforward with RCs only in Upper Deck and Fleer product lines, but with more than a few parallels worthy of discussion. The boss card is the base 1994 SP Alex Rodriguez Foil RC, which sports an adjusted multiple of 8.0x – though its BGS 9.5 value of $400 as of the end of 2013 is a far cry from its $2,500 value entering 2013.

---

[39] A quick check confirms two distinct cards with different PSA serial numbers

[40] www.jetercards.com

[41] PSA makes no apparent distinction between the two sets, listing only "Inaugural" in its price guide

[42] www.cardboardconnection.com/player/derek-jeter-baseball-cards

The 1994 SP set also included a Die Cut parallel of the Rodriguez RC, as well as a Holoviews insert card (also known as Blue Holoviews) and a Die Cut Holoviews (also known as Red Holoviews) insert card. PSA pegs the value of a PSA 10 Gem Mint Die Cut parallel at $10,000, with the regular Foil RC at $900; and the Red Die Cut Holoview at $950 with the Blue Holoview at $130.

The $10,000 valuation of the PSA 10 Gem Mint 1994 SP Die Cut Holoview is overstated, as is the $1,000 BGS 9.5 valuation. One such PSA 10 copy (which PSA labels "Holoview Red" while BGS labels them "Holoviews Die Cuts") sold for $1,000 in a fixed price listing on 12/5/13, after another copy sold at auction for $386.78 on 11/2/13; a BGS 9.5 copy sold for $335 at auction on 12/9/13.

Clearly, the SP Die Cut Holoviews/Holoview Red is due for a downward correction in both the Beckett and PSA price guides.

The Upper Deck Collector's Choice RC has several parallels, including a Silver Signature, Gold Signature, White Letter Variation (BV: $30), and Silver Signature White Letter Variation. Of these, the Silver Signature White Letter Variation is the only one considered too rare to have an ungraded valuation, and has a BGS 9.5 Gem Mint population of 3. None of the parallels have graded BGS 9.5 book values, while the Silver Signature parallel has a PSA 10 book value of $300, and the Gold Signature is listed at a PSA 10 value of $850. One such PSA 10 Gold Signature card sold for $1,500 on 12/5/13. Also of note is the 1994 Upper Deck Alex Rodriguez RC Auto, which technically is not an RC by Beckett's definition, but for practical purposes is one of the earliest RC autos.

The Points of the Exercise

There are two main points of this exercise:

1. To demonstrate unequivocally that multiple expansion tends to benefit a player's key card or cards in graded Gem Mint condition far more than the same cards in lesser condition, and far more than that player's second-best cards in similar Gem Mint condition.

2. To be able to identify a player's key card regardless of the definitions of rookie cards being used, regardless of the structure of a player's rookie cards, and regardless of the number of rookie cards a player has.

Albert Pujols has 43 official 2001-year RCs listed in the Beckett Online Price Guide (OPG). Many of these cards are limited print, serialized base cards, and many of these have even more limited print, serialized parallels to go with them. Most are quite valuable relatively speaking, and yet the bulk of the cards are from product lines I had never heard of until I sat down to study them.

Everybody knows Bowman, Donruss, Fleer, Topps, and Upper Deck; and anybody who takes a minute to look at modern sports cards knows Bowman Chrome and Topps Chrome. Some will be familiar with Bowman's Best, Bowman Heritage, SP Authentic, Upper Deck's Ultimate Collection, Fleer's E-X, and Donruss Elite. But how many people know Absolute Memorabilia, Donruss Classics, Donruss Class of 2001, Donruss Signature, Fleer Authority, Fleer Focus, Fleer Futures, Fleer Game Time, Fleer Legacy, Fleer Platinum, Fleer Premium, Fleer Showcase, Fleer Tradition, Fleer Triple Crown, Leaf Certified Materials, Leaf Limited, Leaf Rookies and Stars, MLB Showdown Pennant Run, Sweet Spot, Topps Gallery, Topps Stars, Topps Reserve, UD Reserve, Upper Deck Evolution, or Upper Deck Gold Glove?

The answer is nobody who hasn't looked at a baseball card in 20 years, because none of these product lines existed 20 years ago, and most of these product lines no longer exist now.

But the better question is, do you *need* to know these brands? Well, unless you're really looking to invest in Albert Pujols, or unless you're interested in collecting Albert Pujols just because you're really interested in collecting Albert Pujols, the answer to that question is – for the most part – "Not really." You don't really need to know about all of these issues, because most of the people either in the hobby or coming back to the hobby won't know them either. Consequently, demand will continually gravitate towards the key cards from the brands that everybody knows: The 2001 Bowman Chrome Albert Pujols RC Auto, the 2001 Bowman RC – or better yet, the Gold parallel – and the Topps Chrome RC and its Retrofractor parallel (and also Topps Chrome Traded).

This gravitation towards key brands and thus key cards is what generates further multiple expansion.

By 2001, it is clear that Bowman Chrome is the industry standard brand, and the 2001 Bowman Chrome Albert Pujols RC Auto #'d/500 is the industry standard for a modern baseball rookie card. Because Albert Pujols does not have a Bowman Chrome non-auto, his regular Bowman RC gains value; and despite being among the least valuable of Pujols' RCs in ungraded form, the Bowman RC carries *by far* the highest adjusted multiple, with the Gold parallel carrying a premium value on top of that. And then on top of that, the Topps Chrome RC Retrofractor carries an ungraded book value of $200 and a PSA 10 value of $700, which are the highest values for non-serialized, non-auto parallels.

Beyond the key Bowman and Topps Chrome issues, there are many, many, many other Pujols cards of significant value, including many limited print, serialized cards.[43] Among the more notable non-autos are the SP Authentic RC #'d/1,250 and the high-end Ultimate Collection RC #'d/250 – both of which are Upper Deck products – as well as the E-X RC #'d/499 included in packs of 2001 Fleer Platinum XRC.[44]

I'll let you sort out the rest for yourself.

The tables below are fairly comprehensive lists of Albert Pujols RCs. The first table lists the three officially-recognized RC autos – Bowman Chrome, Donruss Signature, and SPx – as well as most of the others for which graded values are available (there are many others for which graded values are not available). Included in each table are the print run, and ungraded and graded BGS 9.5 book values from Beckett.com as of December 2013. Some cards don't have BGS 9.5 values listed on Beckett.com; for these cards, I have included the PSA 10 Gem Mint values from PSAcard.com where available, as of 1/1/14.

---

[43] ...and some not serialized, like the 2001 Donruss Career Stat Line Auto – itself a parallel of the limited print Donruss RC. PSA has the card listed as having a print run of 25, but it's unclear if anybody other than perhaps the manufacturer knows what the real number is.

[44] www.cardboardconnection.com/top-10-albert-pujols-rookie-cards

Albert Pujols: 2001 RC Autos

Card	#	Print Run	Ungraded BV	BGS 9.5	Adj. Multiple
2001 Bowman Chrome Albert Pujols RC Auto	340	500	$3,000	$9,000	3.0x
2001 Bowman Albert Pujols RC Auto	BAAP	–	$400	$600	1.5x
2001 Donruss Signature Albert Pujols RC Auto	151	330	$600	$1,350*	2.2x
2001 Donruss Career Stat Line Albert Pujols RC Auto	156	25?	–	$2,000*	–
2001 Donruss Class of 2001 Albert Pujols RC Auto	268	100	$600	$650*	1.1x
2001 Donruss Class of 2001 Crusade Albert Pujols RC Auto	C26	50	$700	$1,350*	1.9x
2001 SPx Albert Pujols YS RC Auto	206	1,500	$400	$700	1.7x
2001 Fleer Legacy Albert Pujols RC Auto	102AU	300	$200	$700*	3.3x
2001 Leaf Certified Materials Albert Pujols FF Hat RC Auto	158	75	$1,000	–	–
2001 Topps Reserve Albert Pujols RC Auto	TRA3	160	$800	$2,700*	3.3x

Source: Beckett.com, December 2013
*PSA 10 value from PSAcard.com, 1/1/14

The second table includes all of the non-auto RCs designated as such in the Beckett OPG, plus the Bowman Gold parallel and a few others. For more detail on the rest of the 2001-year Albert Pujols cards including other autos and limited print parallels, visit Beckett.com (a search on Beckett.com brings up a list of 203 2001-year Albert Pujols cards factoring all of these other cards).

Albert Pujols 2001 RCs: Non-Autos

Card	#	Print Run	Ungraded BV	BGS 9.5	Adj. Multiple
2001 Absolute Memorabilia Albert Pujols RPM RC	157	700	$60	$210*	3.0x
2001 Bowman's Best Albert Pujols RC	147	2,999	$150	$300	1.9x
2001 Bowman Albert Pujols RC	264	–	$30	$250	6.3x
2001 Bowman Albert Pujols Gold RC	264	–	$50	$400*	5.7x
2001 Bowman Heritage Albert Pujols RC	351	–	$50	$200	3.3x
2001 Donruss Albert Pujols RC	156	500	$150	$245*	1.5x

Card	#	Print Run	Ungraded BV	BGS 9.5	Adj. Multiple
2001 Donruss Career Stat Line Albert Pujols RC	156	154	$200	$750*	3.6x
2001 Donruss Classics Albert Pujols RC	108	585	$120	$250*	1.9x
2001 Donruss Class of 2001 Albert Pujols RC	268	525	$120	$315*	2.4x
2001 Donruss Elite Albert Pujols RC	156	900	$200	$500	2.4x
2001 E-X Albert Pujols RC	131	499	$250	$600	2.3x
2001 Fleer Authority Albert Pujols RC	102	2,001	$60	$120	1.7x
2001 Fleer Focus Albert Pujols RC	245	999	$60	$190*	2.7x
2001 Fleer Futures Albert Pujols RC	224	2,499	$50	$120*	2.0x
2001 Fleer Game Time Albert Pujols RC	121	2,000	$25	$165*	4.7x
2001 Fleer Legacy Albert Pujols RC	102	499	$80	$190*	2.1x
2001 Fleer Platinum Albert Pujols RC	301	1,500	$50	$120	2.0x
2001 Fleer Premium Albert Pujols RC	233	1,999	$80	$300	3.3x
2001 Fleer Showcase Albert Pujols RC	121	500	$150	$335*	2.2x
2001 Fleer Tradition Albert Pujols RC	451	–	$40	$100	2.0x
2001 Fleer Triple Crown Albert Pujols RC	309	2,999	$50	$165*	2.8x
2001 Leaf Certified Materials Albert Pujols FF Hat RC	158	200	$300	$650*	2.1x
2001 Leaf Limited Albert Pujols Jersey RC	367	250	$300	$575*	1.9x
2001 Leaf Rookies and Stars Albert Pujols RC	205	–	$120	$300	2.3x
2001 SP Authentic Albert Pujols FW RC	126	1,250	$250	$500	1.9x
2001 SP Game Bat Milestone Albert Pujols RC	92	–	$50	–	–
2001 SP Game Used Edition Albert Pujols RC	85	500	$150	$245*	1.5x
2001 Studio Albert Pujols ROO RC	191	700	$200	$300*	1.4x
2001 Sweet Spot Albert Pujols SB RC	121	1,500	$150	$250	1.6x
2001 Topps Chrome Albert Pujols RC	596	–	$30	$120	3.0x
2001 Topps Chrome Albert Pujols RC Retrofractor	596	–	$200	$700*	3.3x

Card	#	Print Run	Ungraded BV	BGS 9.5	Adj. Multiple
2001 Topps Chrome Traded Albert Pujols RC	T247	–	$40	$150	3.0x
2001 Topps Chrome Traded Albert Pujols RC Retrofractor	T247		$200	$275*	1.3x
2001 Topps Gallery Albert Pujols RC	135	–	$30	$80	2.0x
2001 Topps Reserve Albert Pujols RC	103	945	$80	$275*	3.1x
2001 Topps Stars Albert Pujols RC	198	–	$30	$120	3.0x
2001 Topps Traded Albert Pujols RC	T247	–	$25	$80	2.3x
2001 UD Reserve Albert Pujols SP RC	204	2,500	$80	$200	2.2x
2001 Ultimate Collection Albert Pujols T3 RC	111	250	$600	$1,250	2.0x
2001 Ultra Albert Pujols/Bud Smith RC	277	1,499	$60	$200	2.9x
2001 Upper Deck Albert Pujols SR RC	295	–	$25	$100	2.9x
2001 Upper Deck Evolution Albert Pujols RC	92	2,500	$30	–	–
2001 Upper Deck Gold Glove Albert Pujols GD RC	130	500	$100	$240	2.2x
2001 Upper Deck Pros and Prospects Albert Pujols JSY RC	137	500	$200	$200	1.0x

Source: Beckett.com, December 2013
*PSA 10 value from PSAcard.com

The ability to identify key cards in any situation will be key going forward, as it gives us a framework for thinking about the rookie card structures of more recent card sets. This will help us adapt to any changes in the industry, and as we examine other sports later on.

Part III: The Prospect-RC Structures (2006-Present)

The game has changed, and yet the game remains the same.

Several major developments occurred in the mid-to-late 2000s that have changed the competitive landscape of baseball cards. First in early 2005, Fleer ceased operations, citing poor sales and debts approaching $40 million;[45] Upper Deck acquired the rights to the Fleer brand later that summer at auction for $6.1 million.[46] That same year, Major League Baseball declined to renew the license of the company then known as Donruss Playoff, leaving Topps and Upper Deck as the only two MLB-licensed manufacturers of baseball cards.

Two more major developments occurred that have changed the game completely:

1. In 2006, the MLBPA changed the definition of a rookie card, and

2. In 2009, Major League Baseball granted Topps an exclusive license to produce MLB-licensed baseball cards using team names and logos, and in 2013 extended the exclusive license until 2020.

2006: MLBPA Changes RC Definitions

In 2006, the Major League Baseball Players Association (MLBPA) created a new set of rules regarding rookie card definitions. Starting in 2006, only players who are on a 25-man Major League active roster can have an official rookie card issued that year (late season call-ups typically have been eligible to have RCs issued the following season), designated by an official "Rookie Card" (2006-2009) or "RC" logo (2010-present).

This had a number of implications.

For one, it effectively granted Topps monopoly status on true rookie cards. Though officially the rules were created to keep minor league prospects out of major league sets, Topps was grandfathered into the practice of including prospects in its sets

---

[45] www.csmonitor.com/2005/0801/p11s01-alsp.html
[46] en.wikipedia.org/wiki/Fleer

by virtue of its contracts with the MLBPA. Baseballcardpedia.com notes that "As part of its long-standing agreement with the MLBPA, Topps is not bound to the Association's group licensing agreement."[47]

Essentially, only Topps could produce the first cards of minor league players as part of its major league sets.

From 2002-2005, Topps had designated its first cards of minor league prospects as "First Year" cards in both Bowman and Topps-branded products. From 2006-onward, Topps-branded cards would be reserved for RC-eligible and other major league player cards, while minor league players would be included as prospect "inserts" in Bowman-branded products, with their first cards from Bowman, Bowman Chrome, and Bowman Draft designated as "1st Bowman Card" or "1st Bowman Chrome Card;" the "1st Bowman Card" labeling practice was later discontinued for the 2013 issues.[48]

Another major implication of the new rules was the effective creation of a new – if often secondary – tier of key cards in the form of "Rookie Card" or RC-logo cards carrying the RC designation.

In the first few years under the new rules, this would be a source of confusion among collectors, as many of the players who had "Rookie Card" logos on their 2006-year cards had already had officially designated rookie cards in previous years. For example, Justin Verlander's 2005-year cards were already labeled "RCs" by Beckett's price guide definitions; as such, his 2006 Bowman Chrome "Rookie Card" is accompanied by an "(RC)" in the Beckett price guide, essentially labeling it a bastardization.

By 2010, the "(RCs)" would disappear, as the players who had officially-designated RCs prior to 2006 had by this point either made the major leagues and already had an (RC), or otherwise washed out and never made it. The "Rookie Card" logo would be replaced by an "RC" logo, and the new RC-logo cards would carry an official RC-designation in the Beckett price guides.

At this point, we start to see a slight re-valuation of the RC-logo card, though part of it is player dependent. San Francisco Giants C Buster Posey and Florida Marlins OF Mike Stanton (now known by his given name, Giancarlo Stanton) had 2008 Bowman Chrome Draft autos, but their first chrome non-autos would come in their

[47] www.baseballcardpedia.com/index.php/Rookie_Card
[48] The practice appears to have reemerged with the 2014 issues, with the label "1st Bowman."

2010 RC-year sets, and have legitimate value. Washington Nationals RHP Stephen Strasburg – the first overall pick in the 2009 MLB First Year Player Draft – would have his first Bowman Prospect and Bowman Chrome Prospect cards as part of the spring 2010 Bowman release, but would have his official RC cards later that same year in the 2010 Bowman Chrome and Bowman Chrome Draft sets, as well as many others; these RCs also have legitimate, if secondary, value.

Los Angeles Angels OF Mike Trout had a 2009 Bowman Chrome Draft auto, but did not have a chrome non-auto until his 2011-year RCs. Consequently, Trout's 2011 Finest, Bowman Chrome, and Bowman Chrome Draft RCs all have quite healthy ungraded book values in the $25-$30 range, while his 2011 Bowman Sterling RC carries an ungraded book value of $80.

On the other hand, Washington Nationals OF Bryce Harper – the first overall pick in the 2010 MLB First Year Player Draft – has a 2010 Bowman Chrome 18U USA Baseball card as his 1st Bowman Chrome card; but he also has two 2011-year Bowman Chrome Prospect cards plus a 2011 Bowman Chrome Prospects auto, as well as a 2012 Bowman Chrome Prospects card (issued in the spring Bowman release) before his 2012-year RCs show up. The 2010 Bowman Chrome card is worth more than the two 2011 Bowman Chrome non-autos, which are worth more than the 2012 Bowman Chrome cards. Interestingly, Harper's 2012 Bowman Chrome and Bowman Chrome Draft RCs are more highly valued than his 2012 Bowman Chrome Prospects card, while his 2012 Bowman Sterling RC is valued at $50 – or a healthy premium to the $30 valuation of his 2011 Bowman Sterling Prospects card.

Harper also has a 2012 Topps Five Star RC #'d/80 valued at $250 (the base cards in this initial 2012 Topps Five Star Baseball set were #'d/80), while his short-printed (SP) 2012 Topps RC is valued at $250, and his 2012 Topps Archives RC SP has an ungraded book value of $500.

So while the market still gravitates towards a player's 1st Bowman Chrome Card as his key card, we have to some extent seen the re-valuation of the "official" RC and the creation of another, secondary tier of key cards. Many of these RCs appear in higher-end issues with much smaller print runs than the Bowman Chromes. And this is before factoring RC-logo autographed cards or the premium, limited-print parallels, which add extra punch to the value of the RC-logo cards.

2009: Topps Gains Exclusive MLB Licensing Rights

In 2009, Topps essentially gained monopoly rights by securing an exclusive license to produce Major League Baseball-licensed cards. In 2013, the exclusive deal was extended through 2020.

Other companies still make baseball cards. Despite losing its MLB license in 2005, Donruss produced cards of prospects without using MLB team names, uniforms, or logos in its Donruss Elite Extra Edition sets from 2007 to 2009. In March 2009, Donruss Playoff was acquired by Italian collectibles manufacturer Panini, and subsequently renamed Panini America. Panini had acquired an exclusive license from the NBA in January 2009,[49] chasing the top players in Topps and Upper Deck from the market. Panini gained licensure with the NFL and NFLPA in the Donruss Playoff acquisition, and in 2010 acquired licenses with the NHL and NHLPA to create officially-licensed NHL trading cards, joining Upper Deck in that market.

In September 2011, Panini signed a deal with the MLBPA granting licensure[50] to use Major League Baseball Players – but not Major League Baseball team names or logos – in trading card products, starting with 2011 Donruss Elite Extra Edition. And in March 2013, Upper Deck was granted a similar license.[51]

That said, while other companies continue to make baseball cards and can technically make official rookie cards by the MLBPA definition, this has essentially become a one-player game, as nobody other than Topps can produce MLB-licensed cards with minor league prospects. This isn't to say that the other companies can't or don't make good or great products – both Panini and Upper Deck have developed reputations for creating high value products particularly in football and basketball, while Upper Deck remains the premier brand in NHL hockey cards – but for our purposes of focusing on key cards, we can safely ignore non-MLB-licensed brands for the time being.

Prospect-RC Structures: 2006-Present

As noted, the new RC rules have created a second tier of rookie cards of legitimate value in the form of official, RC-logo rookie cards. However, as we will see, the market still gravitates towards a player's 1st Bowman Chrome cards – particularly the auto, as well as premium parallels of the first non-autos – as a player's true

---

[49] en.wikipedia.org/wiki/Panini_Group
[50] paniniamerica.wordpress.com/2011/09/15/breaking-news-panini-america-inks-multi-year-trading-card-deal-with-mlbpa
[51] www.beckett.com/news/2013/03/mlbpa-grants-upper-deck-a-card-license

key cards. Let's examine the prospect-RC structures of some of the key players to appear after 2006. Namely:

1. Mike Trout

2. David Price

3. Stephen Strasburg

4. Bryce Harper

5. Yu Darvish

For the sake of simplicity, we will ignore inserts (not including the regular prospect cards, which are inserts only by technical definition). In addition, where a player like David Price has 26 2009-year RCs listed on Beckett.com – most of which have negligible differences in value – we will in some cases stick to the highlights.

Mike Trout

Los Angeles Angels OF Mike Trout – the 2012 AL Rookie of the Year – put up MVP-caliber numbers in his first two full seasons at the major league level, and many onlookers would argue that he deserved to win both the AL MVP award and the Rawlings Gold Glove award in both 2012 and 2013. We'll talk a bit more about Trout in Part IV: The Baseball Prospecting Game. That said, Trout is widely considered to be a generational talent, and his cardboard prices have set a new standard for card values across the board.

Trout is an interesting case study in that he has a Bowman Chrome Draft prospect auto but no Bowman Chrome Prospect non-auto. As a result, his 2011-year RCs benefit from a relatively direct path from prospect to RC, as his first chrome non-autos are also his official RCs.

Trout's true key card is the 2009 Bowman Chrome Draft Prospects auto. From that year, Trout also has a Bowman Sterling Prospects auto of secondary – though substantial – value.

Mike Trout: Prospect and RCs

Card	#	Ungraded BV	BGS 9.5	Adj. Multiple
2009 Bowman Chrome Draft Prospects Mike Trout Auto	BDPP89	$500	$800	1.6x
2009 Bowman Sterling Prospects Mike Trout Auto	MT	$350	$450	1.3x
2009 Donruss Elite Extra Edition Mike Trout Auto #/495	57	$350	$500	1.4x
2010 Bowman Platinum Mike Trout Refractor Auto	MT	$200	$300	1.4x
2010 Bowman Platinum Prospects Mike Trout	PP5	$20	$50	1.7x
RC Non-Autos				
2011 Finest Mike Trout RC	84	$30	$50	1.3x
2011 Bowman Chrome Mike Trout RC	175	$30	$80	2.0x
2011 Bowman Chrome Draft Mike Trout RC	101	$25	$80	2.3x
2011 Bowman Draft Mike Trout RC	101	$15	$40	1.6x
2011 Bowman Sterling Mike Trout RC	22	$80	$120	1.3x
2011 Topps Update Mike Trout RC	US175	$25	$80	2.3x
2011 Prime Cuts Mike Trout RC #/99	37	$120	–	–
2011 Playoff Contenders Mike Trout RC	17	$15	–	–

Card	#	Ungraded BV	BGS 9.5	Adj. Multiple
RC Autos				
2011 Finest Mike Trout RC Auto Refractor #/499	84	$250	–	–
2011 Bowman Sterling Mike Trout Auto Refractor RC #/109	19	$400	–	–

Source: Beckett.com, December 2013

Bowman Sterling is a hobby-only, high-end chrome-based set including only rookies (RCs) and prospects. Each box is a box of hits, and in 2009 included six packs per box, with two autographed cards, one relic, an RC and a prospect card per pack. Boxes of Bowman Sterling generally run about $250-$300 upon release.

Despite the higher price point for the boxes, Bowman Sterling autos generally go for less on the secondary market than do the Bowman Chrome autos. This is in part because the autos are easier to obtain, but also primarily because until 2012, the Bowman Sterling autos were strictly sticker autos (instead of signing the card directly, the player puts his signature on a sticker, which is later placed onto the card) rather than autos signed directly on the card.

Generally speaking, sticker autos are materially less valuable than on-card autos.

First introduced in 2010, Bowman Platinum is a secondary prospecting product that includes a mix of rookies and stars in its base set, plus a prospect insert set along the lines of Bowman Chrome. The 2010 Bowman Platinum Prospects Mike Trout is notable as Trout's first non-auto, though in 2010 the non-autos were strictly paper-based product rather than chrome-based. Trout also has an on-card auto refractor (chrome-based) from this set, though it carries less value as a second-year auto with the Platinum brand.

Trout has 2011-year RCs. Because Trout reached the majors mid-year, he does not have either a Topps paper or regular Bowman paper RC, as those are typically early-year releases (he does have a Topps Update RC, which is a paper card). Nor does he have a Topps Chrome RC, either.

Instead, Trout's first chrome-based non-autos are his 2011 Finest, Bowman Chrome, and Bowman Chrome Draft RCs. As Bowman Chrome Draft is released as part of the Bowman Draft paper set, Trout does have a 2011 Bowman Draft RC (paper) as well. Meanwhile, Trout's 2011 Bowman Sterling RC is his most valuable base non-auto RC (technically he does have a 2011 Playoff Prime Cuts RC #'d/99 listed at $120, though it is not an MLB-licensed product).

Trout's 2011 Finest RC autos are his only on-card RC autos, as his 2011 Bowman Sterling RC autos are sticker autos; note that there is no base Finest auto, as his base auto is a Refractor #'d/499. Moreover, Trout does not have a base 2011 Bowman Sterling auto, while his Refractor auto is short-printed at 109 cards (compared to a standard run for the set of 199 Refractors).

Now let's compare the Gold Refractor #/50 parallels.

Mike Trout: Gold Refractors

Card	#	Base	Gold #/50	Gold-Base Multiple
2009 Bowman Chrome Draft Prospects Mike Trout Auto	BDPP89	$500	$3,000	6.0x
2009 Bowman Sterling Prospects Mike Trout Auto	MT	$350	$1,000	2.9x
2009 Donruss Elite Extra Edition Mike Trout Auto #/495*	57	$350	$500	1.4x
RC Non-Autos				
2011 Finest Mike Trout RC	84	$30	$250	8.3x
2011 Bowman Chrome Mike Trout RC	175	$30	$250	8.3x
2011 Bowman Chrome Draft Mike Trout RC	101	$25	$300	12.0x
2011 Bowman Sterling Mike Trout RC	22	$80	$500	6.3x
2011 Topps Update Mike Trout RC**	US175	$25	$300	12.0x
RC Autos				
2011 Finest Mike Trout RC Auto Refractor #/499***	84	$250	$450	1.8x
2011 Bowman Sterling Mike Trout Auto Refractor RC #/109	19	$400	$400	1.0x

Source: Beckett.com, December 2013
*2009 Donruss Elite Extra Edition Signature Status parallel #'d/50
**2011 Topps Update Black is #'d/60
***2011 Finest Gold Refractor is #'d/75

Viewed this way, it is quite clear what the truest key card is, and how powerful it is to have the boss parallels of the boss card. There's no question that the 2009 Bowman Chrome Draft Mike Trout auto is his key card.

The 2011 Finest, Bowman Chrome, and Bowman Chrome Draft RCs are all close in value. That the Bowman Chrome Draft Gold Refractor carries a premium to the others is likely attributable to price guide variance, as I don't perceive any real difference in value between the Bowman Chrome Draft and Bowman Chrome RCs – if anything, both the Bowman Chrome and Bowman Chrome Draft Gold Refractors are worth a slight premium to the Finest Gold Refractor.

Note that the 2011 Finest Gold Refractor auto is #'d/75 rather than #'d/50, while the base auto is the Refractor auto #'d/499, thus the relatively small spread. Meanwhile, that the 2011 Bowman Sterling RC Gold Refractor auto #'d/50 is only $400 – equal to the Refractor #'d/109 – is likely a price guide error (these occasionally do occur); by way of comparison, the 2011 Bowman Sterling Prospects Bryce Harper Refractor auto #'d/109 carries an ungraded book value of $300, while the Gold Refractor #'d/50 books for $600.

The 2011 Topps Update card is paper, and there is no Gold Refractor #'d/50; rather, there is a Black parallel #'d/60. That said, its $300 value is probably also attributable to price guide variance, as I don't see it being worth a premium to the Finest or Bowman Chrome Gold Refractors #'d/50.

David Price

Tampa Bay Rays LHP David Price has a different structure. Price – the winner of the 2012 AL Cy Young Award – was made the No. 1 overall pick in the 2007 MLB First-Year Player Draft by the Tampa Bay Devil Rays (who shortened their name to the Tampa Bay Rays following the 2007 season). Price's first Bowman Chrome card was the 2007 Bowman Chrome Draft card issued in the 2007 Bowman Draft release, while he also has a 2007 Bowman Sterling Prospects auto.

In what would later become standard procedure with the No. 1 pick of the draft, Topps used Price's first Bowman Chrome Prospects auto to highlight the following year's spring Bowman release. Topps began including Bowman Chrome Prospects cards in its spring Bowman release starting in 2006; but the 2008 Bowman issue marked the first time that Bowman Chrome Prospects autos were included.

Price has 2009-year RCs. Because Topps did not gain its exclusive MLB license until 2010 – just before Trout's RC-year – Price has 26 RCs listed on Beckett.com, or more than triple that of Mike Trout. Only the highlights – the autos, and a few key base RCs – are listed below; Price also has various Topps, Bowman, Upper Deck, and SP-branded RCs with base card values primarily between about $1.00 and $2.50.

David Price: Prospect and RCs

Card	#	Ungraded BV	BGS 9.5	Adj. Multiple
2007 Bowman Chrome Draft David Price	BDPP55	$3	$20	1.5x
2007 Bowman Sterling Prospects David Price Auto	DPP	$40	$60	1.2x
2008 Bowman Chrome Prospects David Price Auto	BCP111	$50	$80	1.3x
RC Non-Autos				
2009 Bowman Chrome David Price RC	213	$4	–	–
2009 Bowman Sterling David Price RC	DP	$6	–	–
2009 Topps Sterling David Price RC #/250	13	$5	–	–
RC Autos				
2009 Topps Triple Threads David Price RC Jsy Auto #/99	132	$40	–	–
2009 Finest David Price RC Jsy Auto #/1425	164	$20	–	–
2009 SPx David Price RC Auto #/99	101	$50	–	–
2009 SP Authentic David Price RC Auto #/222	230	$25	–	–

Card	#	Ungraded BV	BGS 9.5	Adj. Multiple
2009 Upper Deck Spectrum David Price RC Auto	101	$30	–	–
2009 Upper Deck Ball Park Collection David Price RC Auto #/150	76	$25	–	–
2009 Upper Deck Signature Stars David Price RC Auto	201	$15	–	–
2009 Sweet Spot David Price RC Auto #/299	105	$30	–	–

Source: Beckett.com, December 2013

The first thing you notice is that Price's key card still appears to be the 2008 Bowman Chrome Prospects auto, despite the fact that he had a preceding 2007 Bowman Sterling Prospects auto, which is a sticker auto. But the other thing that stands out is that his 2009 Bowman Chrome RC appears to be more valuable than his 2007 Bowman Chrome Draft card.

But once we start looking at the value of the gold refractor parallels, it is clear that this is not the case.

David Price: Gold Refractors

Card	#	Base	Gold	Multiple
2007 Bowman Chrome Draft David Price Gold	BDPP55	$3	$80	26.7x
2008 Bowman Chrome Prospects David Price Auto	BCP111	$50	$350	7.0x
RC Non-Autos				
2009 Bowman Chrome David Price RC Gold Refractor	213	$4	$20	5.0x
2009 Bowman Sterling David Price RC Gold Refractor	DP	$6	$15	2.5x
2009 Upper Deck David Price RC*	401	$2.50	$30	12.0x
2009 UD A Piece of History David Price RC	101	$2.50	$6	2.4x
RC Autos				
2009 Finest David Price RC Jsy Auto	164	$20	$40	2.0x
2009 SP Authentic David Price RC Auto**	230	$25	$40	1.6x

Source: Beckett.com, December 2013
*2009 Upper Deck Gold parallel is #'d/99
**2009 SP Authentic card #'d/50 is the Copper parallel (the Gold is #'d/125)

Viewed this way, it is clear that the market views Price's 2007 Bowman Chrome Draft card – his first Bowman Chrome card – as his key non-auto, as its Gold Refractor parallel is significantly more highly valued than any of his 2009 RC-year gold refractors. Meanwhile, his 2008 Bowman Chrome Prospects auto stands out more in Gold Refractor #'d/50 form, though it's worth noting that there is no 2007 Bowman Sterling gold refractor parallel – only Refractors #'d/199 and Black Refractors #'d/25, in addition to 1/1s.

Among his 2009 RC non-auto refractors, the Bowman Chrome Gold Refractor #'d/50 stands out, though the Upper Deck Gold #'d/99 is technically more highly valued in the book.

The 2009 Finest David Price autos are patch autos split into five different groups – one for each letter of Price's last name. As such, he actually has five sets of Gold Refractors, each #'d/10 in reality, but valued like a card #'d/50. Meanwhile, the 2009 SP Authentic David Price RC Autos have a Gold parallel #'d/125, but a Copper parallel #'d/50; the Copper pricing is used in the table.

Price does have a variety of 2005-06 and 2006-07 Upper Deck USA Baseball cards, though the autos are of lesser value compared to the 2007 Bowman Sterling Prospects and 2008 Bowman Chrome Prospects autos, while the 2005-06 and 2006-07 USA non-autos carry ungraded values of $3 (no graded value given) and have no rarer parallels.

Stephen Strasburg

Washington Nationals RHP Stephen Strasburg was the No. 1 overall pick of the 2009 MLB First-Year Player Draft. Considered a generational talent, Strasburg was the first of a series of uber prospects that would ignite the resurgence of the hobby (though Trout came out of the same draft, his hype engine would develop much later, emerging over 2010 but not shifting into overdrive until his 2012 official rookie campaign). In contrast to David Price, Strasburg did not have a Bowman card issued in his draft year, with Topps – aided by its newly exclusive MLB license – instead choosing to use Strasburg to market its 2010-year product lines. The spring 2010 Bowman release included Strasburg's first Bowman Prospects and Bowman Chrome Prospects cards, as well as a Bowman Prospects (paper) auto.

His 2010 Bowman Chrome Prospects Superfractor 1/1 would make waves when it sold on eBay at auction for $16,043 on May 12, 2010, setting a new record for a 1/1 superfractor,[52] while sparking interest that would drive heightened demand and production as early as the fall 2010 Bowman Chrome release.

Topps' plan was likely to save Strasburg's Bowman Chrome Prospects auto for the 2010 Bowman Chrome release, but Strasburg changed that plan. After only 11 games in the minors between Class AA Harrisburg and Class AAA Syracuse in which he gave up all of eight earned runs while striking out 65 batters in 55.1 innings for a 1.30 ERA, Strasburg made his major league debut on June 8, 2010, striking out 14 batters and yielding two earned runs in seven innings, recording the win.

As a consequence of the quick path to the majors, Strasburg also has 2010-year RCs, and his first Bowman Chrome auto is not a prospect auto, but rather his 2010 Bowman Chrome RC-logo auto. Strasburg also has a 2010 Bowman Chrome Draft RC auto that carries a higher base card value due to a significantly smaller print run (the Bowman Chrome Draft autos are #'d/99, there are no parallels, and only three are graded BGS 9.5).

Stephen Strasburg: Prospect Cards and RCs

Card	#	Ungraded BV	BGS 9.5	Adj. Multiple
2010 Bowman Prospects Stephen Strasburg Auto	BP1	$150	$400	2.5x
2010 Bowman Prospects Stephen Strasburg	BP1	$4	$30	2.1x

---

[52] www.cardboardconnection.com/stephen-strasburg-2010-bowman-superfractor-raffle

Card	#	Ungraded BV	BGS 9.5	Adj. Multiple
2010 Bowman Chrome Prospects Stephen Strasburg	BCP1	$5	$60	4.0x
2010 Bowman Platinum Stephen Strasburg RC Relic Auto Refractor #/240	SS	$200	–	–
RC Non-Autos				
2010 Bowman Chrome Stephen Strasburg RC	205	$12	$50	2.3x
2010 Bowman Chrome Draft Stephen Strasburg RC	BDP1	$6	$25	1.6x
2010 Bowman Draft Stephen Strasburg RC	BDP1	$4	$20	1.4x
2010 Topps Chrome Stephen Strasburg RC	212	$8	$30	1.7x
2010 Finest Rookie Redemption #6 Stephen Strasburg	6	$10	–	–
2010 Bowman Sterling Stephen Strasburg RC	1	$12	–	–
2010 Topps Sterling Stephen Strasburg RC #/250	37	$30	–	–
2010 Bowman Platinum Stephen Strasburg RC	1	$8	$30	1.7x
2010 Topps Stephen Strasburg RC	661	$12	–	–
2010 Topps 206 Stephen Strasburg RC	55	$6	$30	1.9x
RC Autos				
2010 Bowman Chrome Stephen Strasburg RC Auto	205	$150	$350	2.2x
2010 Bowman Chrome Draft Stephen Strasburg RC Auto	BDP1	$250	$400	1.5x
2010 Topps Chrome Stephen Strasburg RC Auto	212	$100	–	–
2010 Bowman Sterling Stephen Strasburg RC Auto	1	$100	$200	1.8x
2010 Topps Triple Threads Stephen Strasburg RC Jsy Auto #/99	171	$120	–	–

Source: Beckett.com, December 2013

And the gold refractor view:

Stephen Strasburg: Gold Refractors

Card	#	Base	Gold #/50	Gold-Base Multiple
2010 Bowman Chrome Prospects Stephen Strasburg	BCP1	$5	$700	140.0x
2010 Bowman Platinum Stephen Strasburg RC Relic Auto Refractor #/240*	SS	$200	$400	2.0x
RC Non-Autos				
2010 Bowman Chrome Stephen Strasburg RC	205	$12	$150	12.5x

Card	#	Base	Gold #/50	Gold-Base Multiple
2010 Bowman Chrome Draft Stephen Strasburg RC	BDP1	$6	$100	16.7x
2010 Topps Chrome Stephen Strasburg RC	212	$8	$60	7.5x
2010 Finest Rookie Redemption #6 Stephen Strasburg	6	$10	$80	8.0x
2010 Bowman Sterling Stephen Strasburg RC	1	$12	$60	5.0x
2010 Topps Sterling Stephen Strasburg RC #/250**	37	$30	$40	1.3x
RC Autos				
2010 Bowman Chrome Stephen Strasburg RC Auto	205	$150	$600	4.0x
2010 Topps Chrome Stephen Strasburg RC Auto	212	$100	$300	3.0x
2010 Bowman Sterling Stephen Strasburg RC Auto	1	$100	$350	3.5x
2010 Topps Triple Threads Stephen Strasburg RC Jsy Auto #/99***	171	$120	$120	1.0x

Source: Beckett.com, December 2013

*Blue Refractor #/50

**Framed White #/50

***Emerald #/50

The base 2010 Bowman Chrome Prospects card was downgraded to $5 from $20 towards the end of 2013, while the other base card values were unchanged. It's conceivable that this is attributable to price guide variance – where one value has changed but the value of comparable cards and parallels have not changed, whether because they haven't traded (as is often the case with rare parallels and graded card values) – or price guide error, as this is the first time the Bowman Chrome Prospects card has carried a lower base card value than the comparable RCs.

That said, there's little question from the gold refractor view that Strasburg's key non-auto is his 2010 Bowman Chrome Prospects card, and that his key RC-logo non-auto is his 2010 Bowman Chrome card, as evidenced by both graded BGS 9.5 book values and Gold Refractor #/50 values. I also think it's pretty clear that the 2010 Bowman Chrome RC auto is the clear key RC-logo auto, given its parallel value.

The better question is whether or not the 2010 Bowman Chrome RC auto – Strasburg's first Bowman Chrome auto – is preferable to the paper 2010 Bowman Prospects auto, despite being an RC-logo card and thus being explicitly in a different class.

The answer is that it's hard to say. The 2010 Bowman Prospects auto and 2010 Bowman Chrome RC auto appear to be close in value, though the base paper

Prospects auto does seem to trade at a slight premium to the base Bowman Chrome RC auto. That said, there are a couple of variables that make this comparison difficult.

One is that real prices across the board fell considerably over 2013 as Strasburg put up solid – but not necessarily elite – numbers, two seasons removed from Tommy John surgery; according to data from Terapeak.com, prices of the Bowman Prospects auto graded BGS 9.5 with a 10 auto fell from the $300-$350 range over the first half of 2013 down to under $200 by the end of the season, with two sales at auction at around $180 – one on Oct. 9th, and the other on Nov. 27th. Meanwhile, there are only 16 2010 Bowman Chrome Stephen Strasburg RC base autos graded BGS 9.5 Gem Mint in the Beckett.com population report (compared to 218 Bowman Prospects autos graded BGS 9.5 Gem Mint), and *only one* such example sold on eBay all year – a March 8 sale for $275 at auction.

So while the Bowman Prospects card does carry a slightly higher graded book value and the Bowman Chrome auto graded BGS 9.5/10 sold for $275 at a time when graded BGS 9.5 Bowman Prospects paper autos were trading at $300-$350, it was only one sale for comparison.

But as we've done with Trout and Price, we can try to look to the high-end parallels for guidance. However, there is unfortunately little guidance from Beckett on this front regarding higher-end parallels – while the Bowman Chrome auto has Refractors #'d/500, Blue Refractors #'d/150 and Gold Refractors #'d/50 (along with an Orange Refractor #'d/25, Red Refractor #'d/5, and 1/1 Superfractor) with prices listed on Beckett.com, the Bowman Prospects paper auto only has Blue #/250 and Orange #/25 parallels, but only the Blue #/250 values are listed on Beckett. com. The Bowman Chrome RC Blue Refractor #'d/150 is listed at $300, while Bowman Prospects Blue parallel #'d/250 is listed at $200, but that comparison is of little help as the chrome blue refractor is rarer.

The next step is to look at actual eBay sales. And in January 2013, a Bowman Chrome Orange Refractor #'d/25 graded BGS 9.5/10 sold for $1,750, while a Gold Refractor #'d/50 graded BGS 9.5/10 sold for $1,100. And for a more direct comparison, a PSA 9 Mint Bowman Chrome Orange Refractor auto #'d/25 sold for $931 at auction on 3/5/13, while a pair of BGS 9 Mint Bowman Prospect Orange parallel paper autos #'d/25 sold for $610.37 on 4/30/13 and $535.88 on 4/29/13.[53]

---

[53] Terapeak does show an April 14th sale of an Bowman Prospect Orange #/25 auto at $902, but it's unclear from Terapeak whether the card was graded, and if so what its grade was; regardless, its sale price was lower than that of the PSA 9 Mint Bowman Chrome Orange Refractor #'d/25.

Now all that said, while the base Bowman Chrome and Bowman Prospects autos appear to be close in value – and with perhaps a small edge to the paper Bowman Prospects auto – if I had to bet on the high end, I would lean towards the Gold Refractors #'d/50-and-better Bowman Chrome RC autos as Strasburg's key autos most unlikely to be trumped.

Strasburg also has a wide array of USA Baseball cards issued by Upper Deck in various sets between 2008 and 2009. The 2008-09 USA Baseball Stephen Strasburg non-auto carries an ungraded value of $15 and a graded BGS 9.5 book value of $100 – higher than the base value of the 2010 Bowman Chrome Prospects card – but has no rarer parallel. Other USA cards range from a 2008-09 USA Baseball National Team Jersey Patch #'d/149 with an ungraded book value of $60 to a 2008-09 USA Baseball Autographs Gold card #'d/175 with an ungraded book value of $250, to a 2008-09 USA Baseball National Team Patriot Patches auto #'d/50 (BV: $500) and a 2008 Sweet Spot USA Signatures Red-Blue Stitch Black Ink auto #'d/37 with an ungraded book value of $600, not to mention rarer parallels too rare to price.

Bryce Harper

Washington Nationals OF Bryce Harper was arguably the most-hyped prospect in the history of the game, and – for better or for worse – has a prospect card pipeline to match.

Harper was the No. 1 overall pick of the June 2010 MLB First-Year Player Draft. As it did with Strasburg, Topps chose to save Harper's first cards in a Washington Nationals uniform to highlight the 2011-year Bowman releases. However, Harper had already had several cards issued before that.

Like Strasburg, Harper had several high value cards issued in Upper Deck's USA Baseball sets between 2008 and 2009. Among the more notable ones are a 2008-09 USA Baseball 16U National Team Jersey Patch auto #'d/50 with an ungraded book value of $1,500 (a BGS 9 Mint copy sold in December 2013 for $2,000), as well as the 2008-09 USA Baseball non-auto with an ungraded book value of $120 and a graded BGS 9.5 book value of $200. However, none of these cards were issued in major league sets.

Harper's first Bowman Chrome card – and first card released as part of a major league set – was the 2010 Bowman Chrome 18U USA card issued in the spring 2010 Bowman release. Despite carrying a slightly lower graded book value compared to the 2008-09 USA Baseball card, the 2010 Bowman Chrome 18U USA card is undoubtedly Harper's key non-auto card, which becomes evident when we look at the parallels (the 2008-09 USA Baseball card has none) – the Gold Refractor #'d/50 carries an ungraded value at $600 that is higher than any of Harper's non-autos.

Notably, the 2010 Bowman Chrome 18U USA Superfractor 1/1 sold for $12,500 in September 2010, despite having a raised edge and being essentially ungradable.[54]

100 copies of the 2010 Bowman Chrome 18U USA card were bought back, signed, numbered, and issued in packs as part of a wrapper redemption program associated with the 2010 Bowman release. Harper also had a limited print paper Bowman Draft AFLAC auto issued in the 2010 Bowman Draft release.

---

[54] www.beckett.com/news/2010/09/bryce-harper-superfractor-sale-confirmed-at-12500

Bryce Harper: Prospect Cards

Card	#	Ungraded BV	BGS 9.5	Adj. Multiple
2008-09 USA Baseball 16U National Team Jersey Patch Autographs Bryce Harper #/50	BH	$1,500	–	–
2008-09 USA Baseball Bryce Harper	47	$120	$200	1.5x
2009-10 USA Baseball Bryce Harper Auto #/502	USA83	$300	–	–
2009-10 USA Baseball Bryce Harper	USA30	$40	$60	1.2x
2009 Upper Deck Signature Stars USA National Team Future Watch Jersey Autographs Bryce Harper #/899	30	$150	$300	1.9x
2010 Bowman Chrome 18U USA Bryce Harper	18BC8	$60	$150	2.1x
2010 Bowman Chrome 18U USA Bryce Harper Buyback Autographs #/100	18BC8	$1,000	–	–
2010 Bowman Draft AFLAC Bryce Harper Auto #/230	9	$600	$1,200	2.0x
2011 Bowman Prospects Bryce Harper	BP1	$15	$40	1.6x
2011 Bowman Prospects Bryce Harper Auto	BP1	$200	$400	1.9x
2011 Bowman Chrome Prospects Bryce Harper	BCP1	$20	$40	1.3x
2011 Bowman Chrome Prospects Bryce Harper	BCP111	$20	$40	1.3x
2011 Bowman Chrome Prospects Bryce Harper Auto	BCP111	$350	$500	1.4x
2011 Bowman Platinum Prospects Bryce Harper	BPP1	$20	–	–
2011 Bowman Platinum Prospects Bryce Harper Auto Refractor	BH	$200	$300	1.4x
2011 Bowman Sterling Prospects Bryce Harper	1	$30	–	–
2011 Bowman Sterling Prospects Bryce Harper Auto Refractor #/109	BH	$300	–	–
2011 Bowman Draft Bryce Harper Green Border Auto #/350	BH	$400	–	–
2011 Bowman Draft Relic Autographs Bryce Harper #/69	BHAR1A	$250	–	–
2012 Bowman Prospects Bryce Harper	BP10	$4	$25	1.8x
2012 Bowman Prospect Autographs Bryce Harper	BH	$200	–	–

Card	#	Ungraded BV	BGS 9.5	Adj. Multiple
2012 Bowman Chrome Prospects Bryce Harper	BCP10	$6	$30	1.9x
2012 Bowman Platinum Bryce Harper Jumbo Relic Auto Refractor	BH	$200	–	–

Source: Beckett.com, December 2013

The spring 2011 Bowman release included Harper's first Bowman Prospects and Bowman Chrome Prospects cards (BP1 and BCP1, respectively), as well as his first Bowman Prospects paper auto. Meanwhile, the fall 2011 Bowman Chrome release included an additional Bowman Chrome Prospects card of equal value (both are 2011-year Bowman Chrome Prospects cards, but neither is Harper's first Bowman Chrome card – that was his 2010 Bowman Chrome 18U USA card), as well as Harper's first Bowman Chrome Prospects auto.

In addition to 2011-year prospect autos issued in Bowman Platinum and Bowman Sterling, Harper also had a green-bordered paper auto #'d/350 and a relic auto #'d/69 issued in the 2011 Bowman Draft set.

Milking the kid for all he's worth, Topps also included Harper Bowman Prospects/ Bowman Chrome Prospects cards, as well as another Bowman Prospect paper auto in the spring 2012 Bowman release.

Among the non-autos, the hierarchy is clear, as the 2011 Bowman Chrome Prospects cards are worth less than the 2010 Bowman Chrome 18U USA card, and the 2012 Bowman Chrome Prospect card is worth less than the 2011 Bowman Chrome Prospects cards. Meanwhile, the 2011 Bowman Chrome Prospects auto is Harper's clear key card – period – as evidenced by the gold refractor ungraded value at $3,000.

It's interesting to note that there is no confusion as to whether the 2011 Bowman Chrome Prospects auto issued in Bowman Chrome is more desirable than the 2011 Bowman Prospects paper auto, perhaps because both are prospect-level cards. This is in contrast to Strasburg, where at least there is reasonable doubt as to whether the base 2010 Bowman Chrome RC auto is worth a premium to the 2010 Bowman Prospects paper auto (which seems to be the case at least with the high-end parallels).

It's also interesting to note that the 2011 Bowman Chrome Prospects auto Gold Refractors #'d/50 and better trump the 2010 Bowman Chrome USA Baseball Buyback auto. The 2011 Bowman Chrome Prospects auto Blue Refractor #'d/150 has the same $1,000 ungraded value as the 2010 Bowman Chrome USA Baseball Buyback auto, though I suspect that a graded BGS 9.5/10 copy of the 2010 Bowman Chrome USA Baseball Buyback auto is worth materially more than a BGS 9.5/10 copy of the 2011 Bowman Chrome Prospects Blue Refractors #'d/150; only one such 2010 Bowman Chrome USA Baseball Buyback auto sold in 2013, for $3,500 – higher than any BGS 9.5 2011 Bowman Chrome Prospects Blue Refractor #'d/150, though a BGS 10 Blue Refractor auto did sell for $5,000.

Meanwhile, a graded BGS 9.5/10 Orange Refractor #/25 variation of the 2011 Bowman Chrome Prospects auto reached a 2013 high of $6,000 in a sale dated 8/8/13, while a BGS 9.5/10 Gold Refractor sold for $4,000 in April 2013.

Bryce Harper: Prospect Gold Refractors

Card	#	Base	Gold #/50	Gold-Base Multiple
2008-09 USA Baseball 16U National Team Jersey Patch Autographs Bryce Harper #/50*	BH	–	$1,500	–
2009 Upper Deck Signature Stars USA National Team Future Watch Jersey Autographs Bryce Harper #/899	30	$150	$700	4.7x
2010 Bowman Chrome 18U USA Bryce Harper	18BC8	$60	$600	10.0x
2011 Bowman Prospects Bryce Harper Auto**	BP1	$200	$600	3.0x
2011 Bowman Chrome Prospects Bryce Harper	BCP1	$20	$500	25.0x
2011 Bowman Chrome Prospects Bryce Harper	BCP111	$20	$500	25.0x
2011 Bowman Chrome Prospects Bryce Harper Auto	BCP111	$350	$3,000	8.6x
2011 Bowman Platinum Prospects Bryce Harper	BPP1	$20	$300	15.0x
2011 Bowman Platinum Prospects Bryce Harper Auto Refractor	BH	$200	$600	3.0x
2011 Bowman Sterling Prospects Bryce Harper	1	$30	$400	13.3x
2011 Bowman Sterling Prospects Bryce Harper Auto Refractor #/109	BH	$300	$600	2.0x
2011 Bowman Draft Relic Autographs Bryce Harper #/69***	BHAR1A	$250	$250	1.0x
2012 Bowman Prospects Autographs Bryce Harper****	BH	$200	$300	1.5x
2012 Bowman Chrome Prospects Bryce Harper	BCP10	$6	$125	20.1x
2012 Bowman Platinum Bryce Harper Jumbo Relic Auto Refractor	BH	$200	$300	1.5x

Source: Beckett.com, December 2013
*Not gold parallel; base is #'d/50
**Purple parallel #'d/55
***Blue parallel #'d/50
****Blue parallel #'d/35

Harper made his major league debut on April 27, 2012 at age 19. That year, he became the youngest position player to ever make an All-Star roster (aided by a third-place finish in the All-Star Final Vote and a pair of injuries to other All Stars), and went on to win the NL Rookie of the Year award after finishing with one of the best age-19 seasons on record, hitting .270/.340/.477 with 22 HRs, 98 runs scored, and 18 SBs, and recording 4.5 FanGraphs WAR (wins above replacement).

Harper's early season debut allowed Topps to capitalize with RCs across much of its product lines in 2012. This included short-printed (SP) or super-short printed (SSP) RCs in 2012 Topps and 2012 Topps Archives, as well as short-printed RC autos in Topps, Topps Mini, Topps Archives, Topps Allen & Ginter, and Topps Heritage.

The 2012 Topps Heritage RC non-auto was included in the 2012 Topps Heritage High Number set with a stated print run of 1,000 sets. Consequently, this RC carries a relatively high ungraded book value of $120, and a graded BGS 9.5 book value of $350.

In 2012, Topps also introduced Topps Five Star, a super high-end release on super-thick stock including five cards per box at a price of $500 per box. Harper's base RC non-auto is #'d/80 with a Rainbow parallel #'d/10, while his base auto is #'d/150 with a Rainbow parallel #'d/25. Harper has a number of other patch cards, patch autos, jumbo relic auto books, and combination cards with other players issued in the release as well.

Bryce Harper: RCs

Card	#	Ungraded BV	BGS 9.5	Adj. Multiple
RC Non-Autos				
2012 Bowman Chrome Bryce Harper RC	214	$8	$40	2.2x
2012 Bowman Chrome Draft Bryce Harper RC	10	$8	$30	1.7x
2012 Bowman Draft Bryce Harper RC	10	$5	$25	1.6x
2012 Topps Chrome Bryce Harper RC	196	$10	$50	2.5x
2012 Finest Bryce Harper RC	73	$10	$40	2.0x
2012 Bowman Sterling Bryce Harper RC	1	$50	–	–
2012 Bowman Platinum Bryce Harper RC	56	$8	$40	2.2x
2012 Topps Allen and Ginter Bryce Harper RC	12	$10	$30	1.5x
2012 Topps Mini Bryce Harper RC	661	$30	$60	1.5x
2012 Topps Bryce Harper RC SP	661	$250	–	–

Card	#	Ungraded BV	BGS 9.5	Adj. Multiple
2012 Topps Update Bryce Harper RC	US183, US299	$6	$50	3.3x
2012 Topps Archive Bryce Harper RC SP	241	$500	–	–
2012 Topps Five Star Bryce Harper RC #/80	1	$250	–	–
2012 Topps Heritage Bryce Harper RC (print run: 1,000)	H650	$120	$350	2.7x
2012 Panini Prizm Bryce Harper RC	152	$10	$50	2.5x
2012 Panini National Treasures Bryce Harper RC Jsy	160	$120	–	–
2012 Panini Signature Series Bryce Harper RC	18	$10	–	–
2012 Prime Cuts Bryce Harper RC Jsy #/99	10	$40	–	–
RC Autos				
2012 Bowman Chrome Bryce Harper RC Auto	BH	$250*	–	–
2012 Bowman Chrome Draft Bryce Harper RC Auto	BH	$400*	–	–
2012 Topps Chrome Bryce Harper RC Auto	BH	$200	–	–
2012 Finest Bryce Harper RC Auto Refractor #/198	BH	$200	–	–
2012 Finest Bryce Harper RC Jumbo Relic Auto Refractor	BH	$200	–	–
2012 Bowman Sterling Bryce Harper RC Auto	BH	$250	–	–
2012 Topps Bryce Harper RC Auto	661	$400		
2012 Topps Allen and Ginter Bryce Harper RC Auto	BY	$250	–	–
2012 Topps Mini Bryce Harper RC Auto	MA1	$400	–	–
2012 Topps Archive Bryce Harper RC Auto	BHA	$550	–	–
2012 Topps Five Star Active Autographs Bryce Harper RC Auto #/150	BH	$250	–	–
2012 Topps Heritage Bryce Harper RC Auto	BH	$800	–	–
2012 Topps Tier One On the Rise Autographs Bryce Harper	BH	$500	–	–
2012 Topps Triple Threads Bryce Harper RC Jsy Auto #/99	129	$250	–	–

Source: Beckett.com, December 2013

*Same card

Still, once we examine the gold refractor values, what we come back to is that the 2012 Bowman Chrome RC – or rather, its #'d refractor parallels – is Harper's key RC-logo non-auto. Meanwhile, the values of the base 2012 Bowman Chrome and Bowman Chrome Draft RCs are higher than that of the 2012 Bowman Chrome Prospects card, while the Bowman Chrome RC Gold Refractor #'d/50 also carries a higher book value than the 2012 Bowman Chrome Prospects Gold Refractor #'d/50, suggesting that RC-logo cards carry more value than third-year chrome or second-year chrome prospects cards.

The 2012 Bowman Sterling issue is interesting for a number of reasons. The Bowman Sterling RC Gold Refractor #'d/50 carries the same valuation as the 2012 Bowman Chrome RC Gold Refractor #'d/50, but the value of the base Bowman Sterling RC is significantly higher. This is because in the 2012 Bowman Sterling release, there were three autos per pack, but only one base RC or prospect card per pack, making base cards relatively rare, and enhancing the value of the base cards of a high-demand player like Bryce Harper even more so than the other players in the set.

The 2012 Bowman Sterling release is also notable because for the first time, the autos in the set were predominantly on-card autos rather than sticker autos. The Harper autos from this set were inserted as redemptions, and went live in the fall of 2013.

The 2012 Bowman Chrome RC autos were included as redemptions in 2012 Bowman Chrome; the base auto was relatively short-printed, while the Blue Refractor autos were #'d/99. On the other hand, the 2012 Bowman Chrome Draft RC autos were inserted directly into Bowman Draft packs, and only Orange Refractors #'d/25, Purple Refractors #'d/10, Red Refractors #'d/5, and 1/1 Superfractor parallels were included in Bowman Draft (i.e. there was no regular refractor, Blue Refractor #'d/150 or otherwise, or Gold Refractor #'d/50). Meanwhile, the Bowman Chrome Draft base auto was thought to be super-short printed, with a print run possibly as low as roughly 50 copies.

The Bowman Chrome base, Blue Refractor #'d/99, and Gold Refractor #'d/50 auto redemptions went live (came back) in April 2013. And as it turned out, the base Bowman Chrome RC auto was *identical* to the Bowman Chrome Draft RC auto. In other words, the Bowman Chrome Draft auto is not nearly as rare as previously thought – the Bowman Chrome Draft auto can't be worth $400 while the Bowman Chrome base auto has a $250 valuation, as they are literally the same card. Meanwhile, the Blue Refractors #'d/99 and Gold Refractors #'d/50 from

Bowman Chrome, as well as the Orange Refractors #'d/25, Purple Refractors #'d/10, Red Refractors #'d/5, and 1/1 Superfractor from Bowman Chrome Draft are all parallels of the same cards.

Interestingly, the Orange Refractor, Purple Refractor, and Red Refractor RC auto redemptions from the 2012 Bowman Chrome release have yet to come live as of the end of 2013.

Bryce Harper: RC Gold Refractors

Card	#	Base	Gold #/50	Gold-Base Multiple
RC Non-Autos				
2012 Bowman Chrome Bryce Harper RC	214	$8	$150	18.8x
2012 Bowman Chrome Draft Bryce Harper RC	10	$8	$120	15.0x
2012 Topps Chrome Bryce Harper RC	196A	$10	$100	10.0x
2012 Finest Bryce Harper RC	73	$10	$100	10.0x
2012 Bowman Sterling Bryce Harper RC	1	$50	$150	3.0x
2012 Topps Mini Bryce Harper RC*	661	$30	$150	5.0x
2012 Topps Update Bryce Harper RC**	US183, US299	$6	$100	16.7x
RC Autos				
2012 Bowman Chrome Bryce Harper RC Auto	BH	$250	$600	2.4x
2012 Topps Chrome Bryce Harper RC Auto	BH	$200	$500	2.5x
2012 Finest Bryce Harper RC Auto Refractor #/198	BH	$200	$300	1.5x
2012 Bowman Sterling Bryce Harper RC Auto	BH	$250	$700	2.8x
2012 Topps Triple Threads Bryce Harper RC Jsy Auto #/99***	129	$250	$250	1.0x

Source: Beckett.com, December 2013

*Gold parallel #'d/61

**Black parallel #'d/61

***Emerald parallel #'d/50

Despite the fact that the Bowman Sterling Gold Refractor auto technically carries a higher ungraded book value at $700, the 2012 Bowman Chrome autos are still the key RC autos. For one thing, though the $600 book value of the 2012 Bowman Chrome RC Gold Refractor autos #'d/50 seems reasonable based on late 2013 sales (and in fact is up from what had been a $500 book valuation until a price change recorded on December 18, 2013), the card had traded significantly higher through much of 2013, while the 2012 Bowman Sterling RC Gold Refractor autos #'d/50 are likely overstated.

In 2013, prices of the 2012 Bowman Chrome RC Gold Refractor autos generally ranged from $700 to $1,000, with one recorded outlier sale at $1,250. In contrast, the value of the Bowman Sterling Gold Refractor auto redemptions peaked near $550 in December 2012 shortly after release; the now-live Gold Refractors #'d/50 were selling ungraded in the $200-$250 range by late 2013, along with a general decline in the value of Harper's cards following a relatively disappointing, injury-shortened 2013 season in which he hit .274/.368/.486 with 20 HRs in 118 games and generally struggled mightily against left-handed pitching.

We'll discuss the 2012 Bowman Chrome Bryce Harper RC autos again in Part VI: The Supply Chain and the Value Cycle.

Yu Darvish

Texas Rangers RHP Yu Darvish presents a different scenario, where Darvish has 2009-year Bowman Chrome World Baseball Classic prospect cards, but does not have his first Bowman Chrome autos until his 2012 RC-year Bowman Chrome RC autos, of which he has *three*.

Born in Japan to an Iranian father and Japanese mother, Darvish began his professional baseball career as a star pitcher for the Hokkaido Nippon-Ham Fighters of the Pacific League of Nippon Professional Baseball from 2005 to 2011. Darvish has many Japanese baseball cards between 2005 and 2008, though the only two which show up with valuations on Beckett.com are the 2005 BBM Japan Rookie Edition cards #116 with an ungraded book value of $30 (no BGS value listed) and card #12 with an ungraded book value of $25 and a graded BGS 9.5 Gem Mint book value of $60.

Darvish represented Japan in the 2008 Beijing Olympics and the 2009 World Baseball Classic. From the latter experience, Topps managed to slip a Bowman Sterling WBC Patch card #'d/65 into the *2008* Bowman Sterling boxes as a redemption; that card was Darvish's first card issued as part of an MLB-licensed set, and carries an ungraded book value of $250, though Terapeak shows four sales of the card in 2013 in BGS 9.5 Gem Mint condition with prices ranging from $86 to $133. Darvish has 2009-year Bowman Chrome, Bowman Chrome Draft, Topps Chrome, and Bowman Sterling WBC cards (among several others, including paper Bowman and Bowman Draft WBC Prospects cards).

The short-printed 2008 Bowman Sterling patch aside, the 2009 Bowman Chrome WBC Prospects card is identifiable as Darvish's key non-auto, though a case can be made for his 2009 Topps Chrome WBC card based on gold refractor valuations.

Darvish was posted to Major League Baseball by the Hokkaido Nippon-Ham Fighters prior to the 2012 season. And after paying a $51.7 million posting fee, the Texas Rangers signed Darvish to a six-year, $60 million contract. Darvish made his major league debut in April 2012, and has a complete slate of 2012-year RCs.

The highlights are listed in the table below. Not listed are various Topps, Topps Mini, Topps Archives, and two Topps Update RCs, all of which are paper RCs with ungraded values of $5 and graded values between $25 and $30 (aside from the two Topps Update RCs, for which no graded value is listed).

Yu Darvish: Prospect Cards and RC Non-Autos

Card	#	Ungraded BV	BGS 9.5	Adj. Multiple
2005 BBM Japan Rookie Edition Yu Darvish	116	$30	–	–
2005 BBM Japan Rookie Edition Yu Darvish	12	$25	$60	1.7x
2008 Bowman Sterling WBC Yu Darvish Patch #/65	1	$250	–	–
2009 Bowman Chrome WBC Prospects Yu Darvish	BCW1	$8	$40	2.2x
2009 Bowman Chrome Draft WBC Prospects Yu Darvish	BDPW2	$6	$30	1.8x
2009 Topps Chrome WBC Yu Darvish	W1	$8	–	–
2009 Bowman Sterling WBC Relics Yu Darvish	YD	$30	–	–
RC Non-Autos				
2012 Bowman Yu Darvish RC	209	$8	$30	1.7x
2012 Bowman Chrome Yu Darvish RC	84	$6	$25	1.6x
2012 Bowman Chrome Draft Yu Darvish RC	50	$6	$25	1.6x
2012 Bowman Draft Yu Darvish RC	50	$4	$25	1.8x
2012 Bowman Platinum Yu Darvish RC	9	$6	$25	1.6x
2012 Topps Chrome Yu Darvish RC	151	$8	$50	2.8x
2012 Finest Yu Darvish RC	35	$8	$40	2.2x
2012 Topps Mini Yu Davish RC	660	$5	$25	1.7x
2012 Topps Allen and Ginter Yu Darvish RC	4	$8	$25	1.4x
2012 Bowman Sterling Yu Darvish RC	10	$12	–	–
2012 Topps Heritage	H600	$12	–	–
2012 Topps Gypsy Queen Yu Darvish RC SP	288	$200	–	–
2012 Topps Five Star Yu Darvish RC #/80	61	$80	–	–
2012 Panini Prizm Yu Darvish RC	151	$8	$40	2.2x
2012 Panini National Treasures Yu Darvish Jsy RC #/99	224	$40	–	–
2012 Panini Signature Series Yu Darvish RC	100	$8	–	–
2012 Prime Cuts Yu Darvish Jsy RC #/99	50	$25	–	–

Source: Beckett.com, December 2013

The 2012 Topps Gypsy Queen Yu Darvish RC is super short-printed, hence the $200 ungraded valuation. And along with Bryce Harper, Yu Darvish was the only other player with an RC in 2012 Topps Five Star, with a base card #'d/80.

The gold refractor view suggests that the Bowman Chrome RCs parallels are still the key RCs. That the Bowman Chrome Draft RC Gold Refractor carries a higher ungraded book value than the Bowman Chrome Gold Refractor can likely be attributable to price guide variance, as there is nothing special about the Bowman Chrome Draft set that would make it more valuable; as it is, the 2012 Bowman Chrome Bryce Harper RC Gold Refractor carries a higher valuation than his 2012 Bowman Chrome Draft Gold Refractor.

The better bet is likely that the two Bowman Chrome RC Gold Refractors are equal in value to the Bowman Sterling Gold Refractor #'d/50, and all three are worth a slight premium to the Topps Chrome and Finest RC Gold Refractors #'d/50.

Yu Darvish: Prospect and RC Gold Refractor Non-Autos

Card	#	Base	Gold #/50	Gold-Base Multiple
2008 Bowman Sterling WBC Yu Darvish Patch #/65*	1	–	$250	–
2009 Bowman Chrome WBC Prospects Yu Darvish	BCW1	$8	$120	15.0x
2009 Bowman Chrome Draft WBC Prospects Yu Darvish	BDPW2	$6	$60	10.0x
2009 Topps Chrome WBC Yu Darvish	W1	$8	$150	18.8x
2009 Bowman Sterling WBC Relics Yu Darvish	YD	$30	$60	2.0x
RC Non-Autos				
2012 Bowman Chrome Yu Darvish RC	84	$6	$60	10.0x
2012 Bowman Chrome Draft Yu Darvish RC	50	$6	$80	13.3x
2012 Topps Chrome Yu Darvish RC	151	$8	$60	7.5x
2012 Topps Mini Yu Darvish RC**	660	$5	$50	10.0x
2012 Finest Yu Darvish RC	35	$10	$60	6.0x
2012 Bowman Sterling Yu Darvish RC	10	$12	$80	6.7x

Source: Beckett.com, December 2013
*2008 Bowman Sterling Patch is #'d/65
**2012 Topps Mini Gold parallel is #'d/61

The auto story is more interesting. Darvish does not have an auto of any kind before his 2012-year RCs. His only prospect auto is the 2012 Bowman Platinum Prospects auto, which doesn't really trump anything because it is a prospect card only in the sense that it is part of a prospect autograph set (through 2013, the Bowman Platinum has yet to include RC autos); as was the case with Stephen

Strasburg in 2010 Bowman Platinum and Bryce Harper also in 2012 Bowman Platinum, the 2012 Bowman Platinum set includes a Darvish RC non-auto along with a prospect auto. Moreover, by the July 25, 2012 release date, Darvish had already had his key RC autos come out.

The spring 2012 Bowman release included Darvish's first Bowman Chrome auto, which is a Bowman Chrome RC parallel of his regular Bowman paper RC, number 209 in the Bowman set. The black-bordered base auto was short-printed, and there is no regular refractor – only Blue Refractors #'d/250, Gold Refractors #'d/50, Orange Refractors #'d/25, Red Refractors #'d/5, and the 1/1 Superfractor. As of December 2013, only 28 BGS 9.5 Gem Mint base autos appear in the Beckett.com population report – compared to 45 BGS 9.5 Blue Refractor autos and 14 Gold Refractor autos – suggesting a base card print run in the 100-150 range, which would make it even rarer than the Blue Refractor.

The spring 2012 Bowman release also included a Bowman paper auto with a different picture but also #209 in the set, and was included in retail packs. This auto appears to be even rarer, with only four copies appearing in the Beckett.com population report, and all four of them are graded BGS 9 Mint.

Darvish also has distinct Bowman Chrome RC autos issued in the 2012 Bowman Chrome and Bowman Chrome Draft sets, essentially giving Darvish three distinct sets of Bowman Chrome RC-logo autos. Both the 2012 Bowman Chrome and 2012 Bowman Chrome Draft base autos are similarly short-printed, and both have the numbering RA-YD on the back, though both are quite distinct (unlike the identical Bryce Harper 2012 Bowman Chrome and Bowman Chrome Draft RC base autos). The 2012 Bowman Chrome RA-YD autos also have no regular refractor parallel, while the Blue Refractor is #'d/99, to go with a Gold Refractor #'d/50, Orange Refractor #'d/25, Purple Refractor #'d/10, Red Refractor #'d/5, and 1/1 Superfractor. Meanwhile, the Bowman Chrome Draft RC autos have no refractor, blue refractor, or gold refractor parallels – only the Orange Refractors #'d/25, Purple Refractors #'d/10, Red Refractors #'d/5, and Superfractor 1/1.

Like Harper, Darvish has a wide array of RC autos across Topps' product lines in 2012. Some of them – including the Topps Gypsy Queen, Allen and Ginter, and Tier One autos – technically aren't RCs, and do not carry the RC logo. Others – including the Finest and Topps Chrome autos – carry the RC logo, but technically aren't RCs by official definition because they are not part of the base set. Still, these cards are still RCs for any practical purpose (this is the case for many of cards discussed in this chapter).

Yu Darvish: Prospect and RC Autos

Card	#	Ungraded BV	BGS 9.5	Adj. Multiple
2012 Bowman Platinum Prospects Yu Darvish Auto	YD	$100	–	–
RC Autos				
2012 Bowman Yu Darvish RC Auto	209	$200	–	–
2012 Bowman Chrome Yu Darvish RC Auto	209	$200	$350e	1.7x
2012 Bowman Chrome Yu Darvish RC Auto	YD	$200	$250	1.2x
2012 Bowman Chrome Draft Yu Darvish RC Auto	YD	$200	–	–
2012 Topps Chrome Yu Darvish RC Auto	151	$150	–	–
2012 Finest Yu Darvish RC Auto Refractor #/198	YD	$200	–	–
2012 Finest Yu Darvish RC Jumbo Relic Auto Refractor	YD	$150	–	–
2012 Bowman Sterling Yu Darvish RC Auto	YD	$150	–	–
2012 Topps Mini Yu Darvish RC Auto	MA10	$200	–	–
2012 Topps Archives Yu Darvish RC Auto	YD	$200	–	–
2012 Topps Allen and Ginter Yu Darvish RC Auto	YD	$200	–	–
2012 Topps Gypsy Queen Yu Darvish RC Auto	YD	$400	–	–
2012 Topps Five Star Yu Darvish RC Auto #/150	YD	$200	–	–
2012 Topps Tier One Yu Darvish RC Auto #/225	YD	$175	–	–
2012 Topps Triple Threads Yu Darvish RC Jsy Auto #/99	139	$200	–	–

Source: Beckett.com, December 2013
*2012 Bowman Chrome Yu Darvish RC Auto #209 BGS 9.5 value is estimated based on actual sales

From the gold refractor view, it is clear that the Bowman Chrome RC autos are the clear key autos. That said, Beckett lists the three Bowman Chrome autos as having equal valuations, though sales in late 2013 suggest that the original Bowman Chrome #209 (issued in the spring Bowman release) – Darvish's first Bowman Chrome auto – still carries a premium somewhere in the 50%-100% range, with graded #209s running in the $250-$350 range, and the Bowman Chrome RA-YD and Bowman Chrome Draft RA-YD autos trading in the $130-$200 range. Meanwhile, a Bowman Chrome #RA-YD Gold Refractor #'d/50 graded PSA 10 sold for $315 at auction on 10/27/13, and a graded BGS 9.5/10 Orange Refractor #'d/25 sold for $572 at auction on 11/10/13, while an *ungraded* Bowman Chrome #209 Gold Refractor #'d/50 sold for a Buy It Now price of $609 on 11/11/13.

In other words, though Beckett for the moment views all three Bowman Chrome RC autos as being equivalent cards, the market through 2013 appears to favor the first Bowman Chrome RC auto #209 as the premium Bowman Chrome RC auto, and thus the boss Darvish card.

Yu Darvish: Prospect and RC Auto Gold Refractors

Card	#	Base	Gold #/50	Gold-Base Multiple
2012 Bowman Platinum Prospects Yu Darvish Auto	YD	$100	$400	4.0x
RC Autos				
2012 Bowman Chrome Yu Darvish RC Auto	209	$200	$800	4.0x
2012 Bowman Chrome Yu Darvish RC Auto	YD	$200	$800	4.0x
2012 Topps Chrome Yu Darvish RC Auto	151	$150	$500	3.3x
2012 Finest Yu Darvish RC Auto Refractor #/198	YD	$200	$250	1.3x
2012 Finest Yu Darvish RC Jumbo Relic Auto Refractor	YD	$150	$200	1.3x
2012 Bowman Sterling Yu Darvish RC Auto	YD	$150	$300	2.0x
2012 Topps Triple Threads Yu Darvish RC Jsy Auto*	139	$200	$250	1.3x

Source: Beckett.com, December 2013
*Emerald #'d/50

It's hard to fault Beckett for taking a point of view, as there is no precedent for a player having three sets of effectively equivalent Bowman Chrome RC autos in the same year. The closest comp is the 2011 Bowman Chrome Prospects Bryce Harper cards BCP1 and BCP111 issued in the spring Bowman release and fall Bowman Chrome release, respectively; both are equivalent Bowman Chrome Prospects cards with equal valuations, as Harper already had his first Bowman Chrome card in the 2010 Bowman Chrome 18U USA card. This essentially makes the 2011 Bowman Chrome Prospects cards equivalent second-year Bowman Chrome cards in the same way that Harper has equivalent 2012 Bowman Chrome and Bowman Chrome Draft non-auto RCs.

On the other hand, the 2011 Bowman Chrome Prospects cards are equivalent second-year cards, while the 2012 Bowman Chrome #209 Yu Darvish auto is his first Bowman Chrome auto.

I think legitimate arguments could be made either way, and it's possible that in the long run that the market will view the three Bowman Chrome autos and their parallels as being equivalent. But personally, I tend to think of the original Bowman Chrome #209 Yu Darvish as being the first Bowman Chrome auto and thus the key card, and as of late 2013 the market appears to view it the same way.

Key Observations

Having examined a variety of prospect-RC structures, we can begin to make generalizations regarding key cards, starting with:

1. A player's truest key card is generally his first Bowman Chrome auto, while his key non-auto is generally his first Bowman Chrome non-auto, or some parallel of it.

2. While a player may have several high-end, short-printed RCs of value, his key RC autos and non-autos are often the premium refractor parallels of his Bowman Chrome RC autos and non-autos.

The first point – that the truest key card is generally a player's first Bowman Chrome auto – is the main point of the exercise, but the second point about the RCs is also extremely important. Because Bowman Chrome base cards aren't particularly rare, we find that the base RCs in higher-end sets like Bowman Sterling or Topps Five Star carry shorter print numbers (sometimes serialized, as is the case with Topps Five Star) and consequently often significantly higher valuations than the base Bowman Chrome RCs. However, the market still generally keys on the rarest Bowman Chrome parallels as a player's most desirable RCs.

Premium Color vs. Secondary Color

Though we only used the gold refractor #/50 parallels (and gold refractor comparables) in the tables in this chapter, we've previously discussed the relationship between the relative scarcity of parallels and relative value – that is, the rarer the parallel, generally the more valuable the card. That said, as we also previously discussed, it's important to note that not all refractor or other parallels are functionally equal – the rarest parallels are the most likely to be the best available on the market, and thus are most likely to have pricing power, and thus benefit from multiple expansion and generate outsized returns over the long run.[55]

On the other hand, more common parallels – even serialized ones – are more likely to face like or superior competition in the marketplace, and thus generally have less pricing power, and functionally have more in common with base cards than the highest-end parallels.

In 2001, Topps first introduced the Gold Refractor to the Bowman Chrome line as a #/99 (the Gold Refractor had previously been introduced to the Finest product lines); in 2002, the Gold Refractor became #'d/50 and was also introduced to

---

[55] See Relative and Absolute Scarcity in Part I: The Value of Scarcity

Bowman Chrome Draft. Aside from the odd 2003 Bowman Chrome issue in which Gold Refractors were included at a rate of one per hobby box as a box loader and were #'d/170, the Gold Refractor has been a standard #/50 in Bowman Chrome issues ever since, and has become a staple #/50 in the Finest and Topps Chrome lines (though with some numbering exceptions, particularly in football and basketball variations of these product lines).

When the Gold Refractor was first introduced to Bowman Chrome in 2001, the Gold Refractor was the rarest parallel and thus easily identifiable as the boss parallel. Over the years, Topps has added other, rarer parallels, including the Superfractor 1/1s, Red Refractors #'d/5 (first introduced as a 1/1 in 2004 and 2005 Bowman Chrome Draft, becoming the standard #/5 in 2005 Bowman Chrome), Purple Refractor autos #'d/10 (autos only, first introduced in 2011 Bowman Chrome Draft and becoming standard in the 2012 and 2013 Bowman Chrome lines), and Orange Refractors #'d/25 (2006-present).

In 2013, with growing supply to meet growing demand (at least at the case breaker level – we'll discuss these guys in Part VI), Topps added Black Refractors #'d/99 to the Bowman Chrome Prospects set issued in the spring 2013 Bowman release; Yellow Refractors #'d/10, Black Refractors #'d/15, and Magenta Refractors #'d/35 in 2013 Bowman Chrome; and Silver Wave Refractors #'d/25, Red Wave Refractors #'d/25 (previously issued as a redemption), Black Refractors #'d/35, and Green Refractors #'d/75 in 2013 Bowman Chrome Draft. And for the first time, Beckett.com included pricing for the Orange Refractors #'d/25 in both 2013 Bowman Chrome and Bowman Chrome Draft, as well as the Red Wave and Silver Wave Refractors #'d/25 in Bowman Chrome Draft.

Nevertheless, the Gold Refractor #'d/50 remains a useful cutoff point between the premium colored refractors and everything else. Despite the rarer color additions to the refractor lineup, the gold refractors are generally rare enough to command pricing power over the long run. Meanwhile, for Bowman Chrome issues prior to 2013, Beckett considered anything rarer than the Bowman Chrome Gold Refractor #'d/50 to be too rare to price (though in rare cases Beckett.com does include pricing for rarer parallels in some other product lines, though typically in sports other than baseball).

That said, at least for the time being, we will consider Gold Refractors #'d/50 (and equivalents) and rarer parallels to be **premium color**, and everything else to be of **secondary color**.

On-Card Autos vs. Sticker Autos vs. Cut Autos

There is a distinct difference in value between on-card autos – when the player signs the card directly – and sticker autos, where a player signs a sticker which is later placed on the card. Pretty much without exception – all else being equal – an on-card auto is worth more than a sticker auto.

One of the main attractions to the Bowman Chrome autos is that they are typically signed on-card. This is one of the main reasons why a player's Bowman Chrome prospect auto tends to carry a premium over his Bowman Sterling counterpart, which prior to 2012 Bowman Sterling were typically sticker autos (in 2012 Bowman Sterling, most of the autos were on-card autos; in 2013 Bowman Sterling, the prospect autos were typically on-card, while the RC autos were typically sticker autos). Meanwhile, some players will have both a Finest RC on-card auto and a Finest RC jersey/patch card with a sticker auto issued in the same set; in this case, the edge generally goes to the on-card auto.

Key point: An on-card auto is generally more valuable than a sticker auto, all else being equal.

Another type of auto is the **cut signature**, where the manufacturer literally cuts a signature from another source (typically a photograph or some other document) and attaches it to a card. This is a non-standard – but not terribly uncommon – practice generally used when the manufacturer can't get a player to sign a card directly, either because the player (or other subject) is deceased or for some other licensing-related issue. A notable example of the latter case was the 2013 Leaf Metal Draft and Leaf Valiant football sets, which included Texas A&M QB Johnny Manziel cards with cut signatures as redemptions; Leaf stated that it had acquired the signatures through a third party, as NCAA rules prohibit players from receiving compensation.[56]

A cut signature is clearly inferior to an on-card signature – all else being equal – but also an inescapable necessity for players (or other subjects) no longer around to sign cards.

Brand vs. Brand

It's also important to note the general relationship in value amongst the different brands. We can see that among prospect autos, the Bowman Chrome prospect autos are generally worth a premium to the equivalent Bowman Sterling prospect

---

[56] www.beckett.com/news/2013/03/leaf-announces-johnny-manziel-as-mystery-redemption

autos, and the discrepancy is especially apparent in gold refractor #/50 valuations. Among non-auto prospect cards – as in the case with the 2011-year Bryce Harpers – the Bowman Sterling base prospect cards are generally worth a premium to the equivalent Bowman Chrome Prospects and Bowman Platinum Prospects cards, but the Bowman Chrome Prospects Gold Refractors #'d/50 are worth a premium to the Bowman Sterling Gold Refractors #'d/50, which are worth a premium to the Bowman Platinum Gold Refractors #'d/50.

Among RCs, there is a tendency for the Topps Chrome RCs to carry higher base card valuations than Bowman Chrome or Finest RCs, but the dominance of the Bowman Chrome brand tends to show up in the premium color valuations.

Patches/Relics

Memorabilia cards might include anything from bat knobs to dirt or even somebody's hair, but the most commonly used memorabilia are jerseys. Among jersey or "patch" cards, multi-colored patches (which might include part of a jersey number, the player's name, or a sleeve, among other possibilities) are generally more desirable than plain, single-color jersey swatches.

The most valuable patch cards include autos, which unfortunately are often sticker autos. But again, the most desirable among these tend to be the patch cards with the on-card autos. Be aware that some sets which may include patch cards with on-card autos (like Topps Tribute or Topps Triple Threads, or high-end Panini products like Panini Black Football or even Panini National Treasures) may not be exclusively on-card auto sets, and may include sticker autos as well. Also be aware that while Beckett.com does list whether a card is an on-card or sticker auto in a card's profile, the distinction may not show up in the pricing.

But I'll put it his way: Would *you* rather have a card that is actually signed, or a card in which somebody placed a sticker with a player's signature on it?

Relative Valuation: Rarer Parallels and Printing Plates

Except in some relatively rare circumstances, Beckett has generally considered anything rarer than the gold refractors #'d/50 (and equivalents) to be too rare to price. Still, while the prices of rarer parallels may vary wildly, it is worth the effort to at least formulate some general guidelines for rarer refractors and 1/1 Printing Plates.

Our best approach is to start by relating to gold refractor #/50 values rather than base card values, as base card values can be distorted by differences in base card print runs, while some base cards – typically autos – may be short printed. After that, our next step is to adjust for other factors which may affect relative valuations.

#/25 vs. #/50

Since 2006 Bowman Chrome, the staple Orange Refractor in Bowman Chrome has been #'d/25, while the standard #'d/25 in Topps Chrome in recent issues has been the Red Refractor, and the #'d/25 refractor in Bowman Sterling Baseball has been a Black Refractor until 2012 (the 2013 Bowman Sterling #/25 is a Blue Refractor).

As a starting point, a decent rule of thumb is that a #/25 is generally worth a 25%-50% premium to the gold refractor #'d/50. But even in Beckett.com's pricing, refractors #'d/25 show a premium range from as low as 17% (for some 2013 Bowman Chrome and Bowman Chrome Draft RCs such as Jose Fernandez) to at least as high as 122% for the 2012 Finest Andrew Luck RC Red Refractor #'d/25.

There are at least a couple of main factors to consider when making adjustments. The first is how many refractors in a given set there are which are either equal to or rarer than the #/25s. For example, for 2013 Bowman Chrome non autos, there are Yellow Refractors #'d/10 and Black Refractors #'d/15 above the Orange Refractors #'d/25, in addition to the staple Red Refractors #'d/5 and the 1/1 Superfractor. Meanwhile, in 2013 Bowman Chrome Draft, Red Wave Refractors #'d/25 and Silver Wave Refractors #'d/25 were also inserted into packs.

These extra refractors equal to or superior than the Orange Refractors #'d/25 place the Orange Refractors #'d/25 further down the refractor hierarchy, while creating relative pricing pressure on the Orange Refractors #'d/25. This should theoretically result in multiple compression, helping explain the lower premiums for the #/25s in the 2013 Bowman Chrome and Bowman Chrome Draft sets.

On the other end of the spectrum, two factors which enable multiple expansion (increased premiums) are:

1. A lack of refractors superior to the #/25s, and

2. Star power.

In the case of the 2012 Finest Andrew Luck RCs, only the Pulsar Refractors #'d/10 and 1/1 Superfractor are superior to the Red Refractors #'d/25, placing only 11 cards ahead of the #/25s rather than 31 cards as in the case of the 2013 Bowman Chrome set (or six superior refractors and 50 roughly equivalents in 2013 Bowman Chrome Draft). Meanwhile, entering the 2012 NFL Draft, Andrew Luck was widely considered to be one of the best quarterback prospects in the history of the game, and has led the Indianapolis Colts to the playoffs in each of his first two seasons in the league.

And as we know, the greater the star power, the greater the propensity for multiple expansion.

#/10

The Purple Refractor autos #'d/10 were introduced in 2011 Bowman Chrome Draft, and in 2012 and 2013 were staple refractors in the Bowman Chrome and Bowman Chrome Draft prospect auto lineups. Though Yellow Refractors #'d/10 were included in 2013 Bowman Chrome, #/10s have not been a standard non-auto included in Bowman Chrome sets. However, #/10 non-autos have appeared in other product lines.

That said, a decent rule of thumb might peg the value of a #/10 at somewhere between a 50% and 100% premium to the Gold Refractors #'d/50, though it may be considerably less for more common players for whom there is little-to-no market, and it may be considerably higher for superstar players.

#/5

The Red Refractor #'d/5 has been a staple #/5 since 2005 Bowman Chrome. A good rule of thumb might peg the value of a #/5 at about 2x to 3x the value of a Gold Refractor #'d/50, though there have been examples where a superstar-valued player like Bryce Harper has traded at roughly 4x to 5x.

Between November 11 and December 15, 2012, all five 2012 Bowman Chrome Bryce Harper RC Red Refractor auto redemptions #'d/5 sold with prices ranging from $1,699 to $3,000, with the $3,000 sale an extreme outlier as the middle three sold with prices ranging from $2,000 to $2,337. In contrast, the Gold Refractor #/50 redemptions had sold generally in a range of $450-$550.

1/1 Superfractor

Prices of 1/1 Superfractors are all over the map, though I think it's a safe bet to peg the value of the 1/1 Superfractor at about 5x to 10x the value of a Gold Refractor, with significant upside for superstar players.

1/1 Printing Plates

The **Printing Plates** used to manufacture the cards are typically inserted to packs and issued as 1/1s, but are better thought of as a set of four 1/1s (Black, Cyan, Magenta, and Yellow) rather than being individual 1/1s. Printing plates appear to range from being generally equivalent to ungraded Gold Refractors #'d/50 in value, to being significantly higher. The challenge in valuing anything this rare is that they can sell for significantly higher if someone wants them bad enough.

Bookends (e.g. #1/50 and #50/50) and Jersey Numbers

The bookends – the first and last cards in a serialized parallel set (e.g. Gold Refractors #1/50 and #50/50) – are generally worth a premium. As a rule of thumb, a Gold Refractor #1/50 may be worth a roughly 25% to 50% premium over the other Gold Refractors (in other words, if an ungraded Gold Refractor has a street value of about 67% or two-thirds of ungraded book value, then the #1/50 might be worth as much as full book). On the other hand, the last card – say the #50/50 – is also generally worth a premium, but generally less than that of the #1/50.

Another popular serial number is the jersey number of the player. For example, everybody knows that #23 is Michael Jordan's most notable jersey number from virtually his entire career with the Chicago Bulls, and as such, any Michael Jordan card with a serial number of 23 is generally worth a premium to the rest. My guess is that somebody somewhere started the jersey number thing as a gimmick to sell a card at a premium; but regardless of the origin, jersey numbered cards sometimes trade at absurd premiums.

Personally, I don't value the jersey number more than the #1/XX, but enough collectors seem to value the jersey number enough that it is often worth more than the #1/XX on the open market.

The bookend cards and jersey numbers are loosely considered to be 1/1s.

Part III: Key Concepts

Knowing what we know, we can boil down our list of potentially desirable cards with potential investment value in terms of three key concepts:

1. **Focus on key cards, and generally in Gem Mint or better condition.**
   We know that a given player's key cards graded in BGS 9.5 Gem Mint or BGS 10 Pristine condition have an overwhelming tendency to benefit most from multiple expansion over time. We also know that a player's key card overwhelmingly tends to be a player's first Bowman Chrome auto.

2. **Focus on premium color.** Particularly when dealing with non-autos, secondary key cards (like RC-logo cards when a player has preceding prospect cards), and/or secondary stars, it is generally best to focus on the premium color parallels (generally – but not necessarily limited to – Gold Refractors #'d/50 and better). Premium color parallels are the most likely to have pricing power and thus generate multiple expansion, while more common parallels may lack such pricing power, and may tend to be functionally little different from base cards, particularly for lesser stars or more common players.

3. **Prefer on-card autos.** On-card autos are fundamentally superior to sticker autos. There are few absolutes in this game, but if there is one, it is that an on-card auto is always superior to a sticker auto, all else being equal. Tend to avoid sticker autos.

Part IV: The Baseball Prospecting Game

Playing baseball's next big stars, and introducing the EV Comp approach to prospect valuation.

In June 2009, the Los Angeles Angels selected a high school outfielder from Millville, N.J. named Mike Trout with the 25th overall pick in the MLB First-Year Player Draft. Built like an NFL safety and possessing the speed of a track star, a line drive swing, and off-the-charts baseball sense, Trout dominated the Rookie-level Arizona League that summer, posting a .360/.418/.506 AVG/OBP/SLG line with 13 stolen bases, 7 doubles, 7 triples and a home run over 187 plate appearances in 39 games, earning Baseball America's honor as the top prospect in the Arizona League.

Trout entered the 2010 season rated by Baseball America as the No. 85 prospect in all of baseball, and the No. 3 prospect in the Angels organization, behind only C Hank Conger and OF Peter Bourjos. The April/May 2010 issue of Beckett Baseball magazine listed the value of Trout's 2009 Bowman Chrome Draft Prospects Autograph card at $30 – tied for the highest value among players in the 2009 Bowman Chrome Draft Prospects set, and behind only Atlanta Braves RHP Tommy Hanson and Chicago White Sox OF Dayan Viciedo among all players with 2009-year Bowman Chrome prospect autos.

Still just 18 years old, Trout hit .348/.429/.490 with 10 HRs and 56 SBs over 131 games between low single-A ball and high single-A ball in 2010, and ranked as Baseball America's No. 1 prospect in both the low Class A Midwest League and high Class A California League.

Trout entered the 2011 season as Baseball America's No. 2 overall prospect, behind Washington Nationals OF Bryce Harper, the #1 overall pick in the 2010 MLB First-Year Player Draft. Accordingly, by the spring of 2011, the ungraded book value of Trout's 2009 Bowman Chrome Draft auto had quadrupled to $120. Trout did not disappoint that summer, hitting .326/.414/.544 with 11 HRs and 33 SBs in 91 games of Class AA ball, before getting the call up to the majors.

In 40 games at the major league level, Trout struggled at the plate, hitting only .220/.281/.390 with 5 HRs and 4 SBs over 135 plate appearances. Still, Trout managed to generate 0.7 FanGraphs WAR (Wins Above Replacement as calculated by fangraphs.com), attributable to his base running and defense.

Trout entered the 2012 season as Baseball America's No. 3 prospect – behind Harper and now Tampa Bay Rays LHP Matt Moore. His cardboard stock remained unchanged, with the ungraded value of his 2009 Bowman Chrome Draft auto still at $120. However, though he still retained his rookie eligibility for the Rookie of the Year voting in real baseball, his official RCs had come out in 2011, clocking in at a modest $6 for both his 2011 Bowman Chrome and 2011 Finest RCs; $5 for his 2011 Bowman Chrome Draft RC; and $10 for his 2011 Bowman Sterling RC.

Inexplicably, Trout was left off the Angels' major league roster at the start of the 2012 season. Despite high hopes after signing the great 1B Albert Pujols away from the St. Louis Cardinals, the Angels got off to a dismal start, with a 6-14 record as of April 27. Meanwhile, Trout was hitting .403/.467/.623 with a HR and 6 SBs in 20 games at the AAA level.

Trout made his season debut on April 28, and went on to have arguably the greatest rookie season – and one of the greatest seasons, period – on record. For the year, Trout hit .326/.399/.564 with 30 HRs and 49 SBs, while scoring 120 runs and registering 83 RBI. Adding in Gold Glove-caliber defense while leading the league with 23 defensive runs saved (DRS) when playing centerfield, Trout recorded 10.0 FanGraphs WAR – easily the best in baseball.

Meanwhile, with Trout setting the table from the leadoff spot and patrolling centerfield, the Angels went 83-59 the rest of the way, narrowly missing the playoffs.

By the end of the summer of 2012, Trout's cards had multiplied in value. Prices of his 2009 Bowman Chrome Draft autos graded BGS 9.5/10 were trading in the $500-$600 range, while his 2009 Bowman Sterling Prospects auto in BGS 9.5/10 condition had hit the $300-$350 range. Graded BGS 9.5 Gem Mint copies of his 2011 Bowman Chrome, Bowman Chrome Draft, and Finest RCs were in the $40-$50 range, with raw (ungraded) copies going in the $15-$20 range.

By the end of 2012, Trout had taken home the AL Rookie of the Year (ROY) award, and came close to claiming the AL MVP award – in what would be a hotly contested debate primarily in the Internet media, Trout lost the MVP vote to Detroit Tigers 3B Miguel Cabrera, who was the first Triple Crown winner (winning the AL batting average, home run, and RBI titles) since 1967, hitting .330/.393/.606 with 44 HRs and 139 RBI.

Many statistically-oriented observers felt that Trout deserved the MVP trophy primarily by virtue of the WAR statistic, which accounts for the value of base running and makes an attempt to account for the value of defense – two areas where Trout held a clear advantage over Cabrera. By FanGraphs WAR, Trout held a considerable 10.0 to 6.8 advantage.

These same statistically-oriented observers also felt Trout deserved to win the Rawlings Gold Glove award as well. Though Trout led AL centerfielders with 23 defensive runs saved, the player who ultimately won the Gold Glove – Baltimore Orioles OF Adam Jones – posted a DRS of -16, meaning that Jones' defense *cost* his team runs.

Coming off his age-20 season, Trout was already considered by many to be the best player in the game, and a generational talent only rivaled by long-time uber-prospect Bryce Harper, who himself had just completed a historic age-19 season in which he claimed the NL ROY award. Meanwhile, Trout's cardboard stocks had set a new standard as the most valuable player in the modern hobby.

Collector-investors who had bought Mike Trout the earliest would have generated the biggest gains.

Mike Trout: Key Cards

Card	April/ May 2010	April 2011	April 2012	April 2013	December 2013	BGS 9.5
2009 Bowman Chrome Draft Draft Picks Auto	$30	$120	$120	$400	$500	$800
2009 Bowman Sterling Prospects Auto	$15	$80	$80	$350	$350	$450
2010 Bowman Platinum Prospects	–	$8	$8	$15	$20	$50
2010 Bowman Platinum Prospects Auto Refractor	–	$50	$50	$200	$200	$300
2011 Bowman Chrome RC	–	–	$6	$25	$30	$60
2011 Bowman Chrome Draft RC	–	–	$5	$20	$25	$80
2011 Finest RC	–	–	$6	$25	$30	$50
2011 Bowman Sterling RC	–	–	$10	$50	$80	$120
2011 Finest RC Auto Refractor #/499	–	–	$40	$250	$250	–

Sources: Beckett Baseball magazines dated April/May 2010, April 2011, March and May 2012, April 2013; Beckett.com, Dec. 2013

Unfortunately, the game is not that simple.

The Prospecting Game

In the baseball card equivalent of a stock IPO (initial public offering), every year collectors await the release of the Bowman, Bowman Chrome, and Bowman Draft sets in anticipation of the first Bowman Chrome cards – and especially the 1st Bowman Chrome autos – of the next round of baseball's top prospects and rookies. The goal of the game is to acquire the key cards of baseball's future stars before they become stars, much the same way that some investors and speculators in the stock market look to buy the stocks of the next big thing in hopes that it pays off with outsized returns when the company hits it big.

In other words, the game is to buy Google before it becomes Google, and to buy Mike Trout before he becomes Mike Trout.

As we saw in the case of Mike Trout, the potential rewards can be huge. However, there are several challenges with regard to attempting this strategy, chiefly:

1. The prospect washout rate, and

2. Top prospect bubbles.

Let's examine these issues, and then we'll discuss the Expected Value Comparison Approach to prospect valuation.

The Prospect Washout Rate

"He's still going to get better. He looks like the next Cal Ripken to me."

– San Jose Manager Lenn Sakata, on former Angels prospect Brandon Wood[57]

One of the challenges with trying to find the next Mike Trout every year is that generational talents, by definition, do not come along every year. But that's not even really the biggest problem: The bigger problem is that – in stark contrast to football, basketball, and hockey, where a player has to play at the major league level in order to have a rookie card – the key Bowman Chrome auto for the vast majority of baseball players is not their official RC, but rather a prospect card of minor league players who are often several years away from making the big leagues; and that's assuming they even make it at all.

This in itself makes the concept of prospecting quite speculative by default. But it gets worse.

In 2001, the 2001 Bowman Chrome set included a total of 20 RC autos (recall that the Bowman Chrome and Bowman Chrome Draft RC autos from 2001-2005 are the equivalent of the prospect autos from 2006-present). In 2007, there were a combined 66 Bowman Chrome Prospects/Draft Picks autos. By 2013, the Bowman Chrome Prospect/Draft Pick autograph lineup had widened considerably: Between 2013 Bowman and 2013 Bowman Chrome, there were a total of 99 Bowman Chrome Prospects autographs; add in 47 draft pick autos from Bowman Chrome Draft, and there were a total of 146 Bowman Chrome prospect autos in 2013.

What this means is that the pool of Bowman Chrome prospect autos has grown considerably even more speculative. In 2013, instead of having a cherry-picked lineup of 20 top prospects with 1st Bowman Chrome autos, we had a vastly diluted pool of nearly 150 players with 1st Bowman Chrome autos, many of whom will never play a game in the major leagues, and only a handful of which project to become stars.

There are three keywords in the last sentence: "many," "never," and "project."

The washout rate for prospects is extremely high, even among the best prospects in the game. Sometimes it's due to injury; in other cases, the prospect either just doesn't have it, or otherwise never makes the adjustments to the opposition at the big league level. Or perhaps the player was simply overrated. Whatever the

---

[57] www.baseballamerica.com/today/prospects/rankings/top-100-prospects/2006/26660.html

reason, the odds of true stardom – and thus the prospect for spectacular returns – are stacked against even the top prospects in the game.

Let's take a look at some of the most highly valued RC and prospect autos from the 2006 Bowman Chrome and Bowman Chrome Draft prospect auto class.

2006 Bowman Chrome and Bowman Chrome Draft: Top RC and Prospect Autos

Card	#	April 2007	April/ May 2010	Dec 2013	BGS 9.5 2013	Adj. Multiple
Kenji Johjima RC	219a	$120	$25	$15	–	–
Prince Fielder (RC)	221	$40	$50	$50	$120	2.0x
James Loney (RC)	224	$25	$15	$15	–	–
Alex Gordon	BC221	$250	$50	$25	$50	1.4x
Justin Upton	BC223	$200	$120	$80	$200	2.2x
Jon Lester	BC239	$40	$50	$30	$60	1.5x
Chris Iannetta	BC229	$30	$30	$15	–	–
Brandon Wood	BC231	$25	$20	$15	–	–
Matt Garza	BC234	$25	$25	$15	–	–
Kendry Morales	BC240	$25	$20	$15	$40	1.6x
Jose Bautista	BC242	$15	$15	$40	–	–
Evan Longoria	66	$120	$250	$120	$250	1.9x
Clayton Kershaw	84	$60	$100	$250	$300	1.2x
Cody Johnson	67	$40	$30	$10	–	–
Adrian Cardenas	71	$40	$40	$10	–	–
Matt Antonelli	72	$25	$50	$10	–	–

Sources: Beckett Baseball Magazine April 2007 and April/May 2010; Beckett.com Dec. 2013

Note first of all that this is a cherry picked list – there are many other prospects from this year who had inconsequential value back then in the spring of 2007, and still have inconsequential value now. There are also other guys like Chad Huffman, Cory Rasmus, Kyler Burke, and Stephen Englund who had $20 valuations back then, but are commons now.

The first three players – Johjima, Fielder, and Loney – are Rookie Card-logo autos from the regular Bowman Chrome set. Technically, both Fielder and Loney had rookie cards under the pre-2006 definition, but these are the first Bowman Chrome autos for all three players. The players from Alex Gordon down to Jose Bautista are Bowman Chrome Prospects autos, while Evan Longoria down to Matt Antonelli are draft pick autos from Bowman Chrome Draft.

What should be striking about this list is that, with the exception of Prince Fielder, Jon Lester, Jose Bautista, Evan Longoria, and Clayton Kershaw, the rest of this cherry picked group of prospects from the 2006-year Bowman Chrome prospect auto class have seen their values essentially *evaporate*. Meanwhile, factoring graded values, only Fielder, Lester, Bautista, Longoria, and Kershaw have seen a material appreciation in value since April 2007.

After hitting .291/.332/.451 as a 30-year-old for the Seattle Mariners in 2006 and then .287/.322/.433 in 2007, the Japanese catcher Kenji Johjima struggled in 2008 and 2009, and subsequently left the league to return to Japan. Consequently, the player once tied for the third-most valuable player in the 2006 Bowman Chrome RC/prospect auto class has since been relegated to a more common status.

Entering the 2007 season, Kansas City Royals 3B Alex Gordon was Baseball America's No. 2 prospect. Though he hasn't quite lived up to that lofty status and struggled to make an impact at the major league level until 2011, Gordon has actually had a pretty good career so far, winning three Gold Gloves (2011, 2012, and 2013) and making the 2013 All-Star Game. Still, $50 in graded BGS 9.5/10 value is a long way from $250 ungraded.

Then-Arizona Diamondbacks OF Justin Upton was Baseball America's No. 9 prospect entering the 2007 season. He hasn't quite lived up to the hype, either. He has, however, had a couple of really good seasons so far in his career, including the 2011 season in which he hit .289/.369/.529 with 31 HRs and 105 RBIs, plus 21 SBs. His stock is generally down, but factoring graded values has actually held up relatively speaking.

Only one player, then-Pittsburgh Pirates prospect and current Toronto Blue Jays OF Jose Bautista, has risen from common status to semi-star value, after smashing 54 HRs in 2010 and 43 HRs in 2011. Bautista, incidentally, has several official 2002-year RCs – including a Bowman Chrome one – and is one of the rare players to have a Bowman Chrome Prospects auto after having an officially designated rookie card.

So the prospect picture is generally negative overall. Of course, it's also possible that 2006 was just a bad year. What about 2007?

2007 Bowman Chrome and Bowman Chrome Draft: Top Prospect Autos

Card	#	April/ May 2008	April/ May 2010	Dec 2013	BGS 9.5 2013	Adj. Multiple
Joba Chamberlain	BC236	$200	$80	$12	$30	1.4x
Fernando Martinez	BC221	$100	$40	$15	–	–
Tim Lincecum	BC238	$80	$175	$120	$200	1.5x
Dellin Betances	BC249	$50	$30	$15	–	–
Hunter Pence	BC248	$40	$20	$25	–	–
Cedric Hunter	BC255	$40	$15	$8	–	–
J.R. Towles	BC225	$30	$12	$8		
Jeff Samardzija	BC227	$30	$25	$25	–	–
Luke Hochevar	BC230	$30	$12	$12	–	–
Trevor Cahill	BC234	$30	$30	$10	$25	1.3x
Chris Coghlan	BC233	$20	$25	$10	–	–
Beau Mills	BDPP114	$40	$30	$8	–	–
Nick Noonan	BDPP131	$40	$20	$8	–	–
Nick Hagadone	BDPP134	$30	$15	$8	–	–
Devin Mesoraco	BDPP115	$20	$15	$15	–	–
Peter Kozma	BDPP118	$20	$12	$8	–	–
Todd Frazier	BDPP128	$25	$12	$12	–	–
Tim Alderson	BDPP113	$25	$30	$8	–	–
Travis d'Arnaud	BDPP140	$15	$15	$25	$60	1.7x

Sources: Beckett Baseball Magazine April/May 2008 and April/May 2010; Beckett.com Dec. 2013

2007 was even uglier. Only one true star player has emerged from the 2007 Bowman Chrome prospects auto class in San Francisco Giants RHP Tim Lincecum, who has won two NL Cy Young Awards, made four All Star Games, won two World Series, and led the NL in strikeouts on three occasions.

But the top two players from that class entering the 2008 season – New York Yankees RHP Joba Chamberlain and then-New York Mets OF Fernando Martinez – have fallen from future star to little better than common status. Chamberlain at least had initial success, posting a 0.38 ERA in 24 innings of relief for the Yankees in 2007, a stat line and uniform which provoked the $200 valuation. Chamberlain followed with a 2.60 ERA over 100 innings in 42 games including 12 starts in 2008. However, he has for the most part struggled since – failing in an attempt to become a starting pitcher – and subsequently fell out of favor in New York. Chamberlain signed a 1-year, $2.5 million deal with the Detroit Tigers prior to the 2014 season.

Martinez, on the other hand, has yet to find any success at the major league level. And to make matters worse, in August 2013, Martinez was suspended 50 games in connection to the Biogenesis clinic PED scandal.

Chamberlain and Martinez were ranked Baseball America's No. 3 and No. 20 prospects heading into the 2008 season.

A couple of plausible semi-stars have emerged in OF Hunter Pence (another player who previously had an official RC) and Chicago Cubs RHP Jeff Samardzija, while two other plausible every day players have developed in Cincinnati Reds 3B Todd Frazier and C Devin Mesoraco. Chris Coghlan of the Florida Marlins won the NL Rookie of the Year award in 2009, but has struggled to maintain an everyday job at the major league level since. St. Louis Cardinals SS Pete Kozma was the starting shortstop when the Cardinals won the World Series in 2012 and when they lost to the Boston Red Sox in the 2013 World Series, but for the most part has struggled to hit at every level. As a result, most onlookers do not view Kozma as anything more than a defensive backup long term, hence the common player value.

One player – former Toronto Blue Jays prospect C Travis d'Arnaud – has emerged from a common to a top prospect, and was the key piece in the trade that brought 2012 NL Cy Young award winner R.A. Dickey from the New York Mets to the Blue Jays prior to the 2013 season. His story has yet to be written.

But you get the picture:

1. Most prospects wind up in the dumpster.
2. There is little value in merely being an everyday player.
3. It is very unlikely for a common player to rise to star status, much less superstar status, and
4. Even the odds on high-profile prospects are not very good.

And it gets worse.

Top Prospect Bubble Behavior

You've done your homework. You've parsed the Baseball America top prospects lists and read all of the scouting reports, analyzed the FanGraphs data, and have consulted the Baseball Prospectus for additional opinion. You've narrowed down your list of high-potential prospects to a few key desirables for potential investment.

But then you go to eBay, and find you've got another problem: Some of the very best prospects on your list are wildly overpriced.

Baltimore Orioles RHP Dylan Bundy was the fourth overall pick in the 2011 MLB First-Year Player Draft. In a draft class stacked with high-end power arms – including Pittsburgh Pirates RHP Gerrit Cole (No. 1 overall) and 2013 NL ROY winner Miami Marlins RHP Jose Fernandez (No. 14), not to mention Seattle Mariners LHP Danny Hultzen (No. 2), since-traded Arizona Diamondbacks RHP Trevor Bauer (No. 3), and Arizona Diamondbacks RHP Archie Bradley (No. 7) – Bundy was the highest-rated high school pitcher in the draft, and thought to be the "most advanced prep pitcher in years."[58] Having yet to throw a pitch at the professional level, Bundy entered the 2012 season as the Orioles' top prospect, and Baseball America's No. 10 prospect overall.

In 2012, Bundy blew away all expectations. In 30 innings over eight starts at low-A ball, Bundy struck out 40 batters while issuing only two walks, and did not yield a single earned run. High-A ball was little problem, either, as Bundy struck out 66 batters in 57 innings over 12 starts, with a 2.84 ERA. Bundy then pitched 16.2 innings at the Double-A level to finish the season, registering 13 Ks and a 3.24 ERA.

After the minor league season was over, Bundy went to the instructional league. But in a surprise move, the Orioles – in the midst of a playoff run and in need of relief pitching – called up Bundy for support. Bundy threw 1.2 scoreless innings in his brief stint; the Orioles made the playoffs, but left Bundy off the playoff roster.

Nevertheless, Bundy's status as a top prospect was cemented. Bundy entered the 2013 season as Baseball America's No. 2 prospect, behind only Texas Rangers SS Jurickson Profar. Meanwhile, the ungraded value of Bundy's 2011 Bowman Chrome Draft prospect auto had climbed from $60 in April 2012 to $100, with BGS 9.5/10 copies trading in the $120-$150 range.

---

[58] www.baseballamerica.com/online/prospects/rankings/organization-top-10-prospects/2013/2614249. html

At the same time, the trading ranges for BGS 9.5/10 copies of the comparable Bowman Chrome Prospect/RC autos of established major league stars looked something like this:

BGS 9.5/10 Trading Ranges, Pre-Season 2013

Player	#	BGS 9.5/10
2005 Bowman Chrome Justin Verlander RC Auto	331	$200-$300
2004 Bowman Chrome Felix Hernandez RC Auto	345	$125-$190
2010 Bowman Chrome Stephen Strasburg RC Auto	205	$275
2007 Bowman Chrome Prospects Tim Lincecum Auto	BC238	$90-$225
2006 Bowman Chrome Draft Draft Picks Clayton Kershaw Auto	84	$130-$150

Source: Terapeak.com

The problem with the $120-$150 price tag for Dylan Bundy is that at that price, the market was essentially assuming that Bundy is either going to have a better career than Clayton Kershaw, or that he is going to be the equivalent of Kershaw but with no margin for error. At this point, Kershaw was just entering his age-25 season, had already been to the All Star game twice, won the Cy Young and NL Triple Crown (leading the league in wins, strikeouts, and ERA) in 2011, was runner up in the Cy Young voting in 2012, and was already widely considered to be one of the top two or three pitchers in the game. Bundy, on the other hand, had pitched all of 1.2 innings of relief at the major league level.

And so at this price, the probability was that either Kershaw was undervalued or that Bundy was overvalued (though it's possible that both were undervalued or overvalued).

Looking past Kershaw, Detroit Tigers RHP Justin Verlander entered the 2013 season as a five-time All Star who had won both the AL Cy Young and MVP awards in 2011, and narrowly finished second in the 2012 Cy Young vote. Seattle Mariners RHP Felix Hernandez was already a three-time All Star entering his age-27 season, and had won the AL Cy Young award in 2010 after finishing second in the 2009 Cy Young vote. And San Francisco Giants RHP Tim Lincecum had already won the NL Cy Young award twice, to go with two World Series rings.

Even if you thought there was a 100 percent chance that Bundy was going to accomplish any of that and be worth $180-$200 by 2018 (before accounting for inflation), you're looking at a very modest real return at best with little-to-no margin for error. And so, in order for Bundy to be worth $120-$150 before accomplishing anything at the major league level, you'd have to project Bundy as a multiple Cy Young award winner.

As it turned out, Bundy never threw a pitch at any level in 2013, and underwent Tommy John surgery that June. By fall 2013, his 2011 Bowman Chrome Draft auto in BGS 9.5/10 condition was trading in the $50-$70 range.

Other Cases: Jurickson Profar and Oscar Taveras

Bundy is far from an isolated case. Texas Rangers SS Jurickson Profar entered the 2013 season as Baseball America's No. 1 prospect. Following a strong .286/.368/.452 showing as a 19-year-old in Class AA ball, Profar earned a late-season call up, and promptly hit a home run in his first major league at bat.

Leading up to the 2013 season, Profar's 2011 Bowman Chrome Prospects auto in BGS 9.5/10 condition were trading in the $160-$180 range – or nearly in the same range as the 1st Bowman Chrome autos of San Francisco Giants C Buster Posey, the 2012 NL MVP and two-time World Series champion; Miami Marlins OF Giancarlo Stanton; Los Angeles Dodgers OF Matt Kemp, the two-time All Star and runner up in the 2011 NL MVP vote; and Milwaukee Brewers OF Ryan Braun, the 2011 NL MVP and 2012 runner up for MVP (or at least Braun was in this range prior to his devaluation related to the Biogenesis PED scandal).

Profar began the 2013 season at the AAA level, and hit .278/.370/.438 with 4 HRs and 6 SBs in 37 games before getting the call up to replace the injured 2B Ian Kinsler. Blocked at his natural shortstop position by two-time All Star SS Elvis Andrus and at second base by three-time All Star 2B Ian Kinsler upon Kinsler's return from the disabled list, Profar spent the rest of the year in a super utility role, splitting time primarily at shortstop and second base and as the designated hitter (DH), while getting additional time on the field by playing third base and even left field. Perhaps distracted in part by having to learn and play new positions, Profar struggled mightily at the plate, hitting only .234/.308/.336 with 6 HRs and 2 SBs in 85 games.

Profar's cardboard stock suffered mightily as well, as BGS 9.5/10 copies of his 2011 Bowman Chrome Prospects auto had fallen into the $60-$70 range by the end of the season.

Baseball America's No. 3 prospect heading into the 2013 season was St. Louis Cardinals OF Oscar Taveras. The biggest name in the 2012 Bowman Chrome prospects auto class, Taveras' 2012 Bowman Chrome Prospects auto in BGS

9.5/10 condition were trading in the $200-$250 range by the spring of 2013. Part of the value is due to condition scarcity – many of Taveras' autos have been graded a 9 rather than a perfect 10, making a BGS 9.5 Gem Mint grade with a 10 Auto grade relatively rare. Still, the only players in the Bowman Chrome auto era with higher comparable values at the time were Mike Trout and Bryce Harper.

After hitting .321/.380/.572 with 23 HRs and 94 RBIs in 124 games as a 20-year old at the Class AA level in 2012, Taveras hit .306/.341/.462 with 5 HRs in 46 games at the Class AAA level before suffering a season-ending ankle injury. By the end of the season, BGS 9.5/10 copies of his 202 Bowman Chrome Prospects auto had fallen back into the $120-$140 range.

Systematic Bubble Behavior

What we've just observed are representative examples of the systematic bubbling in the prices of top prospects. Speculators routinely bid up the prices of the most desirable prospects in the game with little regard to valuation – all you have to do is look at established players with similar cards (Bowman Chrome autos) to see that the going rate for a top prospect often does not make sense.

What this means is that the time when a prospect is most desirable – when his story is perfect and he has never failed – is often the worst time to buy.

Biggest Bubbles to Burst: 2001-2008 RC/Prospect Autos

Player/Card	#	Peak Ungraded BV	Peak Date*	Dec 2013 Ungraded BV	Dec. 2013 Graded BV
2001 Bowman Chrome Greg Nash RC Auto #/500	331	$120	2002	$15	–
2001 Bowman Chrome Tony Blanco RC Auto #/500	348	$150	2002	$15	–
2001 Bowman Chrome Ron Davenport RC Auto #/500	347	$200	2005	$15	–
2002 Bowman Chrome David Wright RC Auto	385	$600	2007	$120	$250
2002 Bowman Chrome Kazuhisa Ishii RC Auto	403	$120	2003	$50	–
2003 Bowman Chrome Draft Delmon Young RC Auto	176	$175	2007	$20	$30
2003 Bowman Chrome Draft Brandon Wood RC Auto	170	$100	2006	$12	$25

Player/Card	#	Peak Ungraded BV	Peak Date*	Dec 2013 Ungraded BV	Dec. 2013 Graded BV
2003 Bowman Chrome Jose Contreras RC Auto	332	$200	2004	$30	–
2004 Bowman Chrome Draft Philip Hughes RC Auto	174	$175	2007	$12	$100
2004 Bowman Chrome Draft Homer Bailey	170	$120	2007	$20	$40
2004 Bowman Chrome Draft AFLAC Cameron Maybin Auto Refractors #/125	CM	$700	2008	$150	–
2005 Bowman Chrome Draft Stephen Drew RC Auto	166	$120	2007	$15	–
2005 Bowman Chrome Draft Colby Rasmus RC Auto	175	$120	2008	$15	$30
2006 Bowman Chrome Kenji Johjima RC Auto	219	$120	2007	$15	–
2006 Bowman Chrome Prospects Alex Gordon Auto	BC221	$250	2007	$25	$50
2007 SPx Daisuke Matsuzaka RC Auto	128	$300	2008	$50	$120
2007 Bowman Chrome Prospects Joba Chamberlain Auto	BC236	$200	2008	$12	$30
2007 Bowman Chrome Prospects Fernando Martinez Auto	BC221	$100	2008	$15	–
2008 Bowman Chrome Prospects Lars Anderson Auto	BC249	$100	2009	$10	–
2008 Bowman Chrome Prospects Jason Heyward Auto	BC121	$200	2010	$60	$100
2008 Bowman Chrome Draft Prospects Jesus Montero Auto	BDPP127	$100	2010	$15	$30

Sources: Beckett Baseball magazines dated April 2002-2010; Beckett.com
*Peak date as of April issue for each given year

The flip side is that prospect bubbles routinely burst, and often dramatically so. Whether this is due to injury (Bundy, Taveras), unusual circumstances (Profar), or unrealistic expectations (rookies are *supposed* to struggle), bursting bubbles may create potential buying opportunities.

And sometimes, the market focuses on certain prospects so much that other top prospects go overlooked.

Hidden Gems

In an Internet age where everybody has access to a wealth of information regarding prospects in general, the market is very good at identifying who the top prospects are. Still, some prospects may simply go overlooked – if only briefly.

In June 2011, the Florida Marlins selected a Cuban-born, high school pitcher out of Florida named Jose Fernandez with the 14th overall pick in the First-Year Player Draft. The seventh pitcher taken in the draft, Fernandez was solidly built at 6-3, 215 lbs., and flashed an explosive mid-90s fastball with a plus slider, a killer curveball later nicknamed "The Defector," and a changeup that was already developing into a plus pitch. Fernandez pitched two scoreless innings in rookie ball that summer, followed by 2.1 innings at short-season Jamestown in which he hit a batter, issued three walks, allowed four hits, and gave up five earned runs for a 19.29 ERA.

Fernandez entered the 2012 season rated by Baseball America as the No. 3 prospect in the Marlins organization, behind OF Christian Yelich and OF Marcell Ozuna. The name Jose Fernandez was nowhere to be found Baseball America's Top 100 prospects list. Meanwhile, as a common prospect, the 2011 Bowman Chrome Draft Prospects Jose Fernandez auto is not listed in the April 2012 Beckett Baseball magazine; the value of a common prospect auto in that set is listed at $10.

During the summer of 2012, Fernandez was nearly unhittable. In 14 starts at low Class A Greensboro, Fernandez struck out 99 batters while walking only 18 in 79 innings, and allowed only a .177 batting average against, resulting in a 1.59 ERA. Fernandez was nearly as effective in 11 starts at high Class A Jupiter, striking out 59 batters in 55 innings with a .187 batting average against and a 1.96 ERA. Overall, Fernandez led the minor leagues with an 0.93 WHIP (walks plus hits per innings pitched), and was rated Baseball America's No. 1 prospect in both the low Class A South Atlantic League and high Class A Florida State League.

Though by this point Fernandez was well known to the prospecting media, the general populous was slower to catch on: In milb.com's (the official site for Minor League Baseball) annual MiLBY end-of-season awards, the milb.com staff chose Fernandez as the best starting pitcher in the minors in 2012; but in the fan voting, Fernandez only took fourth place behind Dylan Bundy, Philadelphia Phillies prospect Tyler Cloyd, and then-Arizona Diamondbacks prospect Trevor Bauer.

Fernandez entered the spring of 2013 as Baseball America's No. 5 overall prospect, behind Profar, Bundy, Taveras, and Tampa Bay Rays OF Wil Myers. His cardboard stock was on the rise – the April 2013 issue of Beckett Baseball magazine lists the ungraded value of his 2011 Bowman Chrome Draft prospect auto at $40, while BGS 9.5/10 copies were trading in the $60-$70 range.

Though highly touted, all expectations were that Fernandez would begin the year at Class AA Jacksonville.

The Marlins invited Fernandez to spring training, but sent him to minor league camp in mid-March – several weeks before the major league season began. But after injuries to starting pitchers Nathan Eovaldi and Henderson Alvarez created a temporary spot in the major league rotation, the Marlins decided to fill it permanently, placing Fernandez on the 25-man Opening Day roster despite the fact that Fernandez had yet to throw a pitch above the single-A level.

The Marlins' plan was to keep Fernandez for the whole season, but on a 150-170 inning limit.

On April 7, 2013, Fernandez made his major league debut against the New York Mets, striking out eight batters and allowing only one run in five innings, earning a no decision in the 4-3 loss. Though he struggled somewhat initially, posting a 4.50 ERA over 24 innings in the month of April, Fernandez improved considerably by the month. After making a July 1 start against the San Diego Padres in which he struck out 10 batters while walking one and giving up only two hits in 8.0 scoreless innings, Fernandez had compiled a sparkling 2.72 ERA with 96 Ks over 92.2 innings.

On July 6th, Fernandez was named the Marlins' representative in the 2013 Major League Baseball All Star Game at Citi Field in New York. In the July 16th game, Fernandez pitched one inning and faced three batters, striking out Boston Red Sox 2B Dustin Pedroia; getting reigning AL MVP Miguel Cabrera out on a pop up; and then striking out Baltimore Orioles 1B Chris Davis, a player who would lead the major leagues with 53 HRs and 139 RBIs in 2013.

Fernandez was unhittable the rest of the season. In six August starts, Fernandez struck out 49 batters while yielding only 22 hits and five earned runs in 39.0 innings for a 1.15 ERA. In two September starts, he was even better, allowing only a single earned run on six hits in 14.0 innings for a 0.64 ERA. Fernandez was shut down the rest of the way after crossing the 170-inning limit.

Month	IP	H	BB	SO	ERA
April	24.0	20	11	23	4.50
May	28.1	24	10	29	3.18
June	32.1	19	11	32	1.67
July	35.0	20	10	40	2.06
August	39.0	22	11	49	1.15
September	14.0	6	5	14	0.64
Total	172.2	111	58	187	2.19

All told, Fernandez compiled a 12-6 record on a Marlins team that was a National League-worst 62-100, striking out 187 batters with a 2.19 ERA over 172.2 innings in one of the greatest age-20 seasons on record. His 2.19 ERA was good for second-best in the major leagues, behind only Los Angeles Dodgers ace Clayton Kershaw's 1.83 ERA. Fernandez ran away in the NL Rookie of the Year voting, besting Dodgers phenom Yasiel Puig by taking 26 of 30 1st place votes. He also placed third in the NL Cy Young vote, behind Clayton Kershaw and St. Louis Cardinals RHP Adam Wainwright.

By the end of 2013, BGS 9.5/10 copies of the 2011 Bowman Chrome Draft Prospects Jose Fernandez auto were trading in the $100-$120 range, with the ungraded book value reaching $100.

The EV Comp Approach to Prospect Valuation

In real estate appraisal, the most widely used valuation method is the sales comparison approach. Anybody who has ever bought a home has used comparable sales – comps – using recent sales of other homes in the same neighborhood or like homes with similar features in different neighborhoods in order to determine the value of a home before making an offer. This typically involves the use of the price per square foot metric, while making adjustments for things like the number of bedrooms or the presence of a pool, or other amenities.

For baseball cards, we can also use the comp approach to compare the values of the cards of current prospects to the values of similar cards of comparable – but more established – major league players. And then, by estimating the probability of certain outcomes (i.e. the probability of reaching certain levels of potential), we can develop estimates of expected value for a given prospect card.

This is the **Expected Value Comp Approach**, or EV Comp for short.

Let's say, for example, that we estimate that the graded BGS 9.5/10 value for the Bowman Chrome prospect auto of player we'll call Prospect A has three potential outcomes in a simplified scenario:

1. A 10% chance of being a generational talent – equivalent of Los Angeles Angels OF Mike Trout – with a potential value of $800,

2. A 40% chance of being a superstar – or the equivalent of Los Angeles Dodgers OF Matt Kemp – with a potential value of $250, and

3. A 50% chance of being a bust or other common player, with an assumed value of $20.

Now to determine the expected value of Prospect A, all we need to do is multiply the potential value of each of the three potential outcomes by the probability of each potential outcome in order to get the expected value of each outcome, and then add up the expected values in order to get a total expected value.

And in this scenario, a 10% probability of being the equivalent of Mike Trout is worth $800 x 10% = $80, while a 40% probability of reaching the equivalent value of Matt Kemp is worth $250 x 40% = $100, and a 50% chance of winding up a bust or other common player is worth $20 x 50% = $10. Add it all up, and the total expected value of the player in this simplified scenario is $80 + $100 + $10 = $190.

Prospect A

Comp Player	Potential Value	Probability	Expected Value
Generational Talent	$800	10%	$80
Superstar	$250	40%	$100
Bust or Other Common	$20	50%	$10
Total Expected Value			**$190**

Now let's try this exercise on Byron Buxton's 2013 Bowman Chrome prospects auto. We'll start by projecting graded value, and then reconcile to both ungraded book value and initial ungraded street values.

Byron Buxton, OF, Minnesota Twins

Key Card: 2013 Bowman Chrome Prospects Autographs

Minnesota Twins OF prospect Byron Buxton was the second overall pick in the 2012 MLB First-Year Player Draft, but was widely considered to be the best prospect in the 2012 draft class both before and after the draft, and certainly after the summer of 2013. Read any baseball prospect guide, and you'll find that Buxton projects as a potential five-tool talent (he can potentially hit for average, hit for power, run the bases, play defense, and has a gun for an arm).

As such, for the purposes of this exercise, I selected four comp players representing four potential value outcomes – Mike Trout, Matt Kemp, Atlanta Braves OF Jason Heyward, and Kansas City Royals OF Alex Gordon – plus a fifth outcome representing a bust or other common.

On the top tier, Mike Trout is nearly the epitome of a five tool player, with a .326/.399/.564 line with 129 runs scored, 30 home runs, and 49 stolen bases to go with Gold Glove-caliber defense in his 2012 rookie year good enough for 10.0 FanGraphs WAR, followed by a 2013 season in which he generated 10.4 FanGraphs WAR while hitting .323/.432/.557 with 27 HRs, 33 SBs, 109 runs scored and 97 RBIs. The only tool that most observers don't grade as a plus is his arm. Trout is widely considered to be a generational talent, with some using the words "second coming of Mickey Mantle." Trout's 2009 Bowman Chrome Draft auto carries an ungraded book value of $500 and a graded BGS 9.5 book value of $800.

Entering the 2013 season, most prospect guides didn't have Buxton quite pegged as a generational talent; rather, the comp most cited as Buxton's ceiling was Pittsburgh Pirates OF Andrew McCutchen, the 2013 NL MVP. But after a season in which

Buxton destroyed both low-A ball (.341/.431/.559 with 15 doubles, 10 triples, 8 HRs and 32 SBs in 68 games) and high-A ball (.326/.415/.472 including 8 triples, 4 HRs and 23 SBs in 57 games) with Trout-like numbers, the Trout comparisons have become more frequent.

For the purpose of this exercise, we'll give Buxton a 5% chance of reaching Mike Trout's level.

On the next level in the "Superstar" category, we'll give Buxton a 30% of reaching Matt Kemp's level as a five-tool, MVP-level talent (again, Andrew McCutchen is probably the better comp and would probably slot in or near this area, except he doesn't have a directly comparable Bowman Chrome prospect auto), with an ungraded book value of $120 and a graded BGS 9.5 book value of $250.

In the "Star" category, we'll assign a 30% probability of reaching Jason Heyward's level, with an ungraded book value of $60 and a graded BGS 9.5/10 book value of $100. The caveat to the Jason Heyward comp is that Heyward himself is only 24 years old and may still have considerable upside left.

In the "Semistar" category, we'll give Buxton a 10% probability of being the equivalent of Alex Gordon, who has three Gold Gloves and an All Star Game appearance on his resume.

And then finally, we'll give Buxton a 25% chance of being a bust, with an assumed ungraded value of $10 and graded BGS 9.5/10 value of $20 (essentially ungraded book value plus $10, or the assumed cost of getting a card graded).

Byron Buxton: 2013 Bowman Chrome Prospect Auto Expected Graded Book Value

Player/Card	BGS 9.5 BV	Probability	BGS 9.5 Expected BV
2009 Bowman Chrome Draft Mike Trout Auto	$800	5%	$40
2005 Bowman Chrome Matt Kemp Auto	$250	30%	$75
2008 Bowman Chrome Jason Heyward Auto	$100	30%	$30
2006 Bowman Chrome Alex Gordon Auto	$50	10%	$5
Bust or Other Common	$20	25%	$5
Total Expected Value			**$155**

*Source: Beckett.com, December 2013

Using these probabilities and potential outcome values, the 5% chance of being Mike Trout is worth $40 in graded BGS 9.5 book value, while the 30% of being

Matt Kemp is worth $75 in graded BGS 9.5 book value. The 30% chance of being Jason Heyward is worth $30 in graded BGS 9.5 book value, while the 10% chance of being Alex Gordon is worth $5 in graded value, and the 25% bust scenario is also worth $5 in graded value.

Adding it all up, and the 2013 Bowman Chrome Byron Buxton auto has an expected BGS 9.5/10 graded book value of $155 in this scenario, which we can round to $150 for simplicity.

Reconciling to Initial Ungraded Book Value and Initial Street Value

The next step is to reconcile our estimate of graded BGS 9.5/10 book value to an initial estimate of ungraded book value, which in turn will allow us to project what actual street values should be. This will help us determine whether or not – and at what price – we should buy ungraded cards of key prospects upon the initial release of a new set.

We know from studying the multiples of Bowman Chrome prospect autos that graded BGS 9.5/10 book values of more recent years (generally within three years of release) generally run at about a 25% premium to ungraded book value (or put differently, ungraded book value generally runs at about a 20% discount to graded book value). Working backwards, a graded BGS 9.5/10 value of $150 implies an ungraded book value of about $120.

We also know that street values generally run at a discount to book values, generally somewhere around 60% to 80% of book value, give or take. Roughly speaking, this would peg the initial ungraded street value at around $80 to $100 (Note: We'll see later that ungraded value deteriorates after initial release due to card removal, which we'll discuss in greater depth in Part VII).

Mitigating Factors

There are a lot of mitigating factors to consider.

For starters, this is just one estimate: Playing around with the numbers can have a dramatic impact on results. For example, let's say instead we think Buxton has zero chance of reaching Mike Trout's level as a projected generational talent. Taking Trout's five percent and giving it to Matt Kemp would cause a drop in graded BGS 9.5/10 value from $155 to $127.50, pegging ungraded book value at about $100, and ungraded initial street value at about $60-$80.

The numbers can be played with a lot of different ways, and the art of projecting values can be quite subjective. But anyone who has any experience doing appraisals or financial forecasting can tell you that the actual practice of projecting values can be a lot more subjective than you'd think it is or would like it to be.

Another factor is the potential difference in print run sizes. Some hobbyist estimates peg the print run of the 2013 Bowman chrome prospect autos at an average of up to 2,200 copies for the base autos for each given player, or approaching 3,000 including the refractors. By way of comparison, the stated print run on 2003 Bowman Chrome autos was 2,500 (1,700 base autos), while the stated print run on 2004 Bowman Chrome autos was 2,800 (2,000 base autos).

In contrast, I estimate from the stated odds that the print run for the 2012 Bowman Chrome Draft prospect (Draft Pick) autos was about 1,000 for the base autos – or potentially less than half that for the 2013 Bowman Chrome prospect base autos – and around 1,700 to 1,800 total autos on average for each player.

Though it's probably true that the 2012 Bowman Chrome Draft set may be an outlier itself on the low end of print runs (the production runs on the 2013 Bowman Draft and thus Bowman Chrome Draft set appear to be roughly 50% higher), if the high estimates are true regarding the 2013 Bowman Chrome prospect autos, then it's possible that the base autos (the print runs of the serialized, numbered refractors are consistent with previous years) may be somewhat devalued relative to comparable cards from previous years.

Sidebar: A Note on Multiple Expansion, Ungraded Values, and the EV Comp Approach

You might have noticed that we did not use the EV Comp approach directly on ungraded book values, and instead simply used it on graded book values and then worked backwards. The reason we did not use the approach directly on ungraded values is because the relationship between ungraded and graded values becomes skewed over time due to multiple expansion.

You may recall from the Introduction to the book that the multiples for the Bowman Chrome autos from 2007-2011 were generally in 1.2x to 1.6x range, while the multiples for the cards from 2001-2006 were generally in the 1.7x to 2.5x range.

As previously discussed, multiple expansion may be a natural product of time (i.e. given growing demand, older cards naturally carry larger premiums over time), or more likely a combination of time and the card removal effect. That is, over time, the best examples of a given card get graded and are thus removed from the pool of ungraded cards; and, as a consequence, the value of ungraded cards declines in relation to the value of graded cards, also resulting in multiple expansion.

Regardless of the cause, what this means is that the ungraded value of the 2005 Bowman Chrome Matt Kemp auto is less reliable as a comp for ungraded values of more recent issues. As such, our best bet is to rely more on graded BGS 9.5 values and then work backwards to ungraded values, using the multiples of more recent issues.

To illustrate the difference, using the EV Comp approach directly using ungraded values would have resulted in an ungraded expected book value of $84, compared to our $120 estimate.

Byron Buxton: 2013 Bowman Chrome Prospect Auto EV (Including Ungraded BV)

Player/Card	Ungraded BV	BGS 9.5 BV	Probability	Ungraded Expected BV	BGS 9.5 Expected BV
2009 Bowman Chrome Draft Mike Trout Auto	$500	$800	5%	$25	$40
2005 Bowman Chrome Matt Kemp Auto	$120	$250	30%	$36	$75
2008 Bowman Chrome Jason Heyward Auto	$60	$100	30%	$18	$30
2006 Bowman Chrome Alex Gordon Auto	$25	$50	10%	$2.50	$5
Bust or Other Common	$10	$20	25%	$2.50	$5
Total Expected Value				**$84**	**$155**

Source: Ungraded and graded BVs where available from Beckett.com

Meanwhile, based on an expected graded book value of $155, the adjusted multiple would have been 1.6x, or a bit higher than our 1.25x assumed multiple. For reference, as of December 2013, Beckett.com lists the ungraded book value for the 2013 Bowman Chrome Buxton auto at $200 and graded BGS 9.5 book value at $250 – a 1.2x adjusted multiple.

The Plus Side

The EV Comp approach provides a useful framework for thinking about valuation in a marketplace where valuation often seems to be disregarded. But if the top prospects are, in effect, "taken" due to absurd prices, and the vast majority of other prospects are destined to wipeout, is there a good way to play the prospect game?

There are several bits of good news on this front:

1. The current, highest profile prospects aren't the only prospects in the game.
2. Sometimes prospects simply go overlooked.
3. Prospects take time to develop.
4. Many of the prospects autos are of teenage players who are either international players, or just drafted out of high school.
5. Bubbles are meant to burst.

As we saw with Jose Fernandez, sometimes prospects simply go overlooked. With all of four innings of professional work to go on – including two really bad ones in short season ball – Baseball America had Fernandez pegged with the upside of a potential No. 2 starter going into the 2012 season. Moreover, it was easy to look past Fernandez in a draft class stacked with high end power arms, including Gerrit Cole, Dylan Bundy, Archie Bradley, Trevor Bauer, and Danny Hultzen.

Mike Trout, a 2009 draftee out of high school with a 2009 Bowman Chrome Draft auto, was similarly overlooked.

St. Louis Cardinals pitcher Michael Wacha was also similarly overlooked. Wacha was the eighth pitcher taken and the 19th overall pick in the 2012 MLB First-Year Player Draft. A college arm out of Texas A&M, Wacha breezed through the minors in 2012, striking out 40 batters and giving up only two runs in 21 innings between rookie ball, high Class A ball, and Double-A.

Wacha went into 2013 ranked by Baseball America as the Cardinals' No. 6 prospect, and the No. 76 prospect in baseball. His 2012 Bowman Chrome Draft auto was listed at $25 in the April 2013 issue of Beckett Baseball magazine. Wacha then breezed through Triple-A before posting a 2.78 ERA in 64.2 innings pitched over 15 appearances, including 9 starts at the major league level during the regular season.

And then in three starts during the NLDS against the Pirates and the NLCS against the Dodgers, Wacha went 3-0, while striking out 22 batters and allowing only eight hits and a run in 21 innings, earning the NLCS MVP award in the process. He did get scored on in two games against the Red Sox in the World Series, but he managed to win a game as well.

By the end of 2013, Wacha's 2012 Bowman Chrome Draft auto had an ungraded book value of $100 and a graded BGS 9.5 book value of $120.

Teenagers Have Room to Grow

Points #3 and #4 are related. Many of the prospects with Bowman Chrome prospects autos are teenagers. Teenagers are often difficult to project with any precision, and generally have room to grow both physically and mentally. Consequently, prospective investors may have more time to pick up on such prospects.

The 2013 AL ROY award winner, Tampa Bay Rays OF Wil Myers, was a 2009 3rd-round draft pick of the Kansas City Royals out of high school. Myers has a 2010 Bowman Chrome Prospects auto, which the March 2011 issue of Beckett Baseball magazine listed at $40. Myers was Baseball America's No. 4 prospect entering the 2013 season; by the end of 2013, Beckett.com pegged the ungraded value at $120, and the graded BGS 9.5 book value at $200.

Jurickson Profar was an international prospect who had just turned 18 years old when his 2011 Bowman Chrome Prospects auto was released in the spring of 2011. The November 2011 issue of Beckett Baseball magazine listed the value of the auto at $40, with the value in the April 2012 issue listed at $60, before the price took off.

Minnesota Twins prospects Miguel Sano and Max Kepler are both international prospects who were 17-year-olds when their 2010 Bowman Chrome Prospects autos were issued. The March 2011 issue of Beckett Baseball magazine listed their values at $50 and $20, respectively. Sano has since developed into one of the top power hitting prospects in the game, and as of Dec. 2013, his auto has an ungraded book value of $100 and a graded BGS 9.5 value of $150. Kepler, on the other hand, remains a speculative prospect having struggled in his first crack at full-season, low Class A ball in 2013.

Bubbles Are Meant to Burst

A big part of the reason bubbles persist is because speculators and collectors alike fear missing out on the upswing, albeit for different reasons. Speculators (gamblers) fear that prices are going to go up without them; as such, they chase gains with no regard to valuation (often largely because they don't understand the concept), driving up prices to the point where sufficient gains are no longer available – or worse. Collectors who "just want one," on the other hand, see prices going up and buy now to avoid having to pay a higher price later (and also because they fear prices are going to go up without them).

But at some point, most all bubbles tend to burst, whether due to injury or unreasonable expectations or for some other reason.

It's remarkable that while Dylan Bundy's 2011 Bowman Chrome Draft auto in BGS 9.5/10 condition was trading for $120-$150 in early 2013, that BGS 9.5/10 copies of Clayton Kershaw's 2006 Bowman Chrome Draft auto were readily available for $130-$150 a pop. That bubbles burst is bad news if you paid $150 for Dylan Bundy, but it is great news if you were in the market for Clayton Kershaw.

By late 2013, BGS 9.5/10 copies of the 2003 Bowman Chrome Hanley Ramirez Refractor auto were going in the $120-$150 range. Ramirez had compiled a total of 37.1 FanGraphs WAR before the age of 30, and just came off a season in which he had come back from injury to hit .345/.402/.638 in 86 games (5.1 WAR) to help lead the Dodgers to the playoffs.

Meanwhile, BGS 9.5/10 copies of the 2013 Bowman Chrome Prospects Carlos Correa Refractor #/500 were going in the $150-$200 range. The Houston Astros selected Correa – a shortstop like Ramirez – first overall in the 2012 MLB First-Year Player Draft, ahead of Byron Buxton. While Correa is generally thought highly of as a prospect, nobody has him on par with Buxton, and I don't think anybody is of the opinion that he is a favorite to outperform Hanley Ramirez.

And if Hanley Ramirez's Refractor auto can be had for $120-$150, how can Correa's be worth $150-$200?

The Grand Scheme

Prospecting can be a very high risk game presenting a number of challenges. One is that the prospect washout rate is exceptionally high, even for the best prospects in the game. Another is that as the Bowman Chrome prospect auto lineup has grown from a cherry picked list of 20 players in the initial 2001 season to 146 players (everybody gets one) in 2013, the overall prospect pool has become increasingly speculative. But the biggest challenge is that even as we narrow down our list of prospects to the highest-percentage and highest-potential prospects, the going market prices for top prospects are often such that there may not be sufficient reward to justify paying up for them.

Markets in general have a tendency to be short-sighted at times, and this seems to be especially true in the baseball prospect market where the tendency to bubble is very strong. Year in and year out, the market seems to make the same mistake of only comparing the prices of current prospects to the prices of other current prospects, when all you have to do is look back a few years at the prices of more established players to see that doing so is missing the big picture.

To that end, as noted, the EV Comp approach provides a useful framework for thinking about prospect valuation in a marketplace where valuation seems to be often disregarded.

The gist of it is that you're probably not going to make a killing by betting the crap out of wildly overpriced prospects, almost no matter how good they are. This isn't to say that you can't go ahead and overpay for one for collection's sake – if you really want one, that's certainly your choice. But for investment purposes – acquiring more than one copy – your best strategy when dealing with overpriced prospects is often to sit back and wait for a better opportunity, or otherwise look elsewhere for better potential values.

Prospecting: Key Concepts

Three key takeaways:

1. **Be wary of piling on "hot" prospects.** Top prospects are prone to bubble behavior. In addition to comparing prospects to one another, be sure to examine valuation in the context of established players using the EV Comp approach.

2. **Established players often yield relative values.** Established players can often be had relatively cheaply compared to prospects, and are simultaneously far less risky. Consequently, the best strategy with some of the top prospects may often be to sit back and wait.

3. **Look for top prospects who are being underappreciated.** Markets tend to fixate on the "hot" players, leaving potential values to be found elsewhere. Look for less obvious guys like Mike Trout or Jose Fernandez who haven't been hyped out of the gate.

Part V: Value Investing and the Gem Mint Game

A value investor's approach to the game.

"A simple rule dictates my buying: Be fearful when others are greedy, and be greedy when others are fearful."

– Warren Buffett

Value investing is a general approach to investing most often associated with investing in common stocks. Though the authors don't use the term "value investing" in the book, the origins of the approach are universally attributable to the 1934 book *Security Analysis* by Benjamin Graham and David Dodd, based largely on classes Graham taught at Columbia Business School beginning in 1928. And though *Security Analysis* is generally considered to be the bible of value investing, it is Graham's later 1949 classic *The Intelligent Investor* that is more widely read today, and regarded by Warren Buffett – Graham's most famous student – as "by far the best book on investing ever written."

Value investing is not necessarily any one specific strategy; nor is it an idea restricted only to stocks. Rather, value investing is perhaps best thought of as a general philosophy: If you focus on high quality assets and consistently pay less than the assets are fundamentally worth and while factoring in a margin of safety, you will tend to come out ahead in the long run.

There are many interpretations of what value investing means and many different value-oriented investing strategies to go with them. Some people – mostly detractors – think value investing only means investing in low P/E ratio stocks, or only looking at stocks that nobody else would ever want, or that "growth" stocks are fundamentally different and exclusive from "value" stocks. But these are far too narrow views on what is a fundamentally broad concept with essentially universal application.

At its core, there are at least three main elements to value investing:

1. Focus on quality
2. Focus on value
3. Margin of safety

Focus on Quality

Quality is an important factor in the value of stocks, but it is especially important when it comes to baseball cards where certain types of shares – that is, premium color limited print, serialized parallels, particularly when graded in BGS 9.5 Gem Mint or BGS 10 Pristine condition – are significantly rarer and often exponentially more desirable than either more common variations, or like variations in lesser condition. Meanwhile, graded BGS 9.5 Gem Mint or BGS 10 Pristine copies of the key cards of the game's biggest stars stand to benefit the most from multiple expansion over time, and have a significant advantage over the same cards in lesser condition, over a player's lesser prospect or RC cards, and over the key cards of lesser players.

Quality is so fundamental that we spent the first three chapters of this book defining it and demonstrating its relative power in this game of collectibles real estate.

Focus on Value

Though quality is paramount in this game, getting value is at least equally important. As we know from our discussion of prospect value in Part IV: The Baseball Prospecting Game, identifying the game's next big stars is only half the battle, as we cannot acquire these players' key cards and expect to generate a return regardless of cost – nor can we simply acquire the key cards of more established stars and expect to generate a return within a reasonable time frame regardless of cost. Rather, for anything other than the purpose of collecting for the sake of collecting, we need to be able to acquire these key cards at a reasonable price such that the potential return can justify the risk.

The simple fact is this: The lower the price we pay relative to fair value, the lower the risk and the higher the potential return.

Recall this table from our presentation of the EV Comp Approach to prospect valuation in Part IV, using the 2013 Bowman Chrome Prospects Byron Buxton auto as an example.

Byron Buxton: 2013 Bowman Chrome Prospect Auto Expected Graded Book Value

Player/Card	BGS 9.5 BV*	Probability	BGS 9.5 Expected BV
2009 Bowman Chrome Draft Mike Trout Auto	$800	5%	$40
2005 Bowman Chrome Matt Kemp Auto	$250	30%	$75
2008 Bowman Chrome Jason Heyward Auto	$100	30%	$30
2006 Bowman Chrome Alex Gordon Auto	$50	10%	$5
Bust or Other Common	$20	25%	$5
Total Expected Value			**$155**

*Source: Beckett.com, December 2013

In relative terms, we know fundamentally that Buxton cannot be worth $800 in graded BGS 9.5 book value, as that would imply that there is a 100% probability that Buxton turns into Mike Trout and does things in his age-20 and age-21 seasons that have never been done before. And aside from Bryce Harper – another player considered to be a generational talent – the next tier of star position players with comparable Bowman Chrome autos includes Los Angeles Dodgers OF Matt Kemp, New York Mets 3B David Wright, San Francisco Giants C Buster Posey, and Miami Marlins OF Giancarlo Stanton, all whose comparable Bowman Chrome autos have graded book values of $250, which imply street values in about the $175-$225 range, give or take.

Well, we also know that unless Buxton – who finished 2013 in high-Class A ball – has a legitimate (non-zero) chance of being Mike Trout, that he also cannot be worth $250 in graded book value or $175-$225 in street value, either, unless you give him a 100% chance of being an MVP contender (or winner in the case of Buster Posey). And yet, for much of 2013, graded BGS 9.5/10 copies of the Buxton traded at or around that $175-$225 range, and in fact traded at a range of roughly $150-$215 in December 2013, after registering a few trades in the $130 range in November.

This is not to say that Buxton will or will not turn into Mike Trout, or that he won't compete for MVP titles; it only means that – at least in comparative terms – the probability that he will do so is not likely to justify a graded BGS 9.5 book value of $250, and thus a street value in the $175-$225 range. Instead, at least in this projection using somewhat admittedly arbitrary outcome probabilities (but no more or less arbitrary than methods "professionals" use to forecast things such as company earnings), the 2013 Bowman Chrome Prospects Byron Buxton auto has a graded BGS 9.5 book value of $155, implying a street value of about $120, give or take.

The reality is that Byron Buxton is going to do what Byron Buxton is going to do, and we have no control over his outcome. The only thing we can control is the price we choose to pay, should we choose to pay it. Ideally – assuming we are comfortable with our $155 graded BGS 9.5 BV projection – we'd like to pay some discount to $120 in order to bet on Byron Buxton. And the lower the price we pay, both the lower the risk and the higher the potential return.

The table below illustrates the relationship between price paid and potential return or potential loss.

Potential Return (or Loss) vs. Price Paid

Price Paid	Outcome Value					
	$20 (Common)	$50 (Gordon)	$100 (Heyward)	$200 (Kemp)	$500 (Harper)	$800 (Trout)
$200	-90%	-75%	-50%	0%	150%	300%
$150	-87%	-67%	-33%	33%	233%	433%
$100	-80%	-50%	0%	100%	400%	700%
$50	-60%	0%	100%	300%	900%	1,500%
$20	0%	150%	400%	900%	2,400%	3,900%

Margin of Safety

The projection we used to arrive at the $155 estimated BGS 9.5 book value represents only one estimate of potential outcome probabilities and values, and is unfortunately quite subject to error. For one thing, it is quite possible that Mike Trout is overvalued; assigning Trout a value of $600 instead of $800 alone would knock $10 off our estimate value (our value attributable to the Trout outcome would drop from 5% of $800 to 5% of $600, or from $40 to $30), dropping our overall estimated value for Buxton from $155 to $145.

Or what if instead we thought the chance of Buxton becoming Mike Trout was zero, and instead thought it was slightly more likely that Buxton would turn into former elite prospect and San Diego Padres OF Cameron Maybin, who is still a decent Major League player, but effectively not much different than a common in value?[59]

In that case, taking Trout's 5% and adding it to the "Bust or Other Common" outcome, Buxton's projection would look more like this:

[59] Unfortunately, Maybin does not have a comparable Bowman Chrome prospect auto – only a 2004 Bowman Chrome Draft AAFLAC auto refractor #'d/125, currently with a book value of $150.

Byron Buxton: 2013 Bowman Chrome Prospect Auto Expected Graded Book Value

Player/Card	BGS 9.5 BV*	Probability	BGS 9.5 Expected BV
2005 Bowman Chrome Matt Kemp Auto	$250	30%	$75
2008 Bowman Chrome Jason Heyward Auto	$100	30%	$30
2006 Bowman Chrome Alex Gordon Auto	$50	10%	$5
Bust or Other Common	$20	30%	$6
Total Expected Value			$116

*Source: Beckett.com

This brings us to Graham's **margin of safety** principle, which essentially dictates that we should look to buy at a sufficient enough discount to our estimation of fair value in order to account for errors in projection or other adverse outcome. Moreover, the greater the risk of default, the bigger the margin of safety we require.

There's less player-specific risk in buying somebody like Miami Heat F LeBron James, for example, who could retire today (end of 2013, or the middle of the 2013-14 NBA season) at age-29 with four MVP awards, two championship rings, and two NBA Finals MVP awards and wind up in the Hall of Fame. This – in addition to star power – is one of the reasons his cards carry huge premiums. There's also less risk in players like former St. Louis Cardinals and current Los Angeles Angels 1B/DH Albert Pujols, or New York Yankees SS Derek Jeter.

There is still risk in Mike Trout – who after 2013 is only two full seasons into his Major League career – but there is little doubt that he has already established himself as one of the best players (if not *the* best player) in the game. And as of the end of the 2013 season, there is also still risk in Bryce Harper – who may be an injury risk throughout his career, or who may never learn to hit lefties – though there is little doubt they he will be at the very least a productive major leaguer, and at age-21 in 2014 is still on track to be a perennial All Star, if not more.

While there is still risk in overpaying for these players, there is relatively little risk that these players will bust completely and turn into commons.

But with a prospect like Byron Buxton – who has yet to see Double-A pitching entering 2014 at age-20, and still has a wide range of potential outcomes – we should prefer to err on the side of caution. If we believe in the slim possibility of a Trout outcome and that Buxton is worth $155 in graded BGS 9.5 book value and thus roughly $120 in street value, then it is probably generally OK to pay $120 –

estimated fair value – and add Buxton to the collection. However, we would need a significant discount to $120 before we start betting the crap out of him.

Viewed from the bottom up, at $20 or common pricing, we would be **freerolling** – we basically can't lose, but have much to gain – but we would never get that price while Buxton still has prospect value. At $50 or some discount to it – Alex Gordon pricing – we would be freerolling if we thought Buxton's floor was three-time Gold Glove winner and one-time All Star by age-29. We would be *not quite* freerolling at $50 if we think Cameron Maybin is a potential outcome, but it would still be an excellent bet given Buxton's upside, and are most probably still in "bet the crap out of him" territory.

But at around a $100 or some discount to it – Jason Heyward range, with a Gold Glove and an All Star selection by age-23 – we've reached the point where Buxton is probably still a very a good bet completely discounting the possibility of a Trout outcome, though no longer necessarily in "bet the crap out of it" territory.

Value Investing and the Gem Mint Game

Value investors typically try to do at least one of two things:

1. Acquire great assets at good prices, or
2. Acquire good assets at great prices.

Our focus is on #1, but we will also do #2. Our primary goal is to acquire premium assets without paying a premium for them, though we may also be willing to acquire secondary assets if we can get them at steal prices.

Premium assets generally refer to key autos and their parallels of star players, graded in BGS 9.5/10 or better condition (includes PSA 10 if the auto would warrant a 10 Autograph grade under the BGS grading system); premium color parallels (~gold refractors #'d/50 or better) of the key non-autos of star players, graded in BGS 9.5 Gem Mint or better condition; or premium color key autos of secondary stars (semi-stars) in BGS 9.5/10 or better condition.

These are the cards that tend to benefit most from pricing power, and for which we are willing to pay a fair price for.

Secondary assets generally refer to premium color parallels (#/50 or better) of the key autos of star players in BGS 9 Mint condition with a 10 Autograph grade, or in BGS 9.5 or BGS 10 condition with 9 Autograph grades (or their PSA-equivalents, which are cards graded PSA 10 with poor autographs likely to grade a 9 under the BGS grading system, or cards graded PSA 9 Mint with autos likely to grade a 10 under the BGS grading system); secondary color or (to a lesser extent) base versions of key non-autos of star players graded in BGS 9.5 Gem Mint or better condition; or the key autos (secondary or base) and premium color key non-autos of secondary stars (semi-stars) in graded BGS 9.5 Gem Mint or better condition. Also included are premium color key autos of lesser players.

Secondary assets are the cards we may be willing to take if we can get them at steal prices.

Premium Assets vs. Secondary Assets

Premium Assets	Secondary Assets
• Key autos and parallels of star players graded BGS 9.5/10 or BGS 10/10 condition (or PSA 10, if the autograph would grade a 10 under BGS system)	• Premium color (#/50 or better) parallels of key autos of star players in BGS 9 Mint with 10 Autos, or BGS 9.5 or BGS 10 with 9 Autos
• Premium color (#/50 or better) parallels of key non-autos of star players in BGS 9.5 or BGS 10 condition, or PSA 10 Gem Mint condition	• Secondary color or (to a lesser extent) base versions of key non-autos of star players in BGS 9.5 Gem Mint or better condition
• Premium color (#/50 or better) key autos of secondary stars (semi-stars) in BGS 9.5/10 or better condition	• Key autos (secondary and base) and premium color key non-autos of secondary stars (semi-stars) in BGS 9.5 Gem Mint or better condition
	• Premium color key autos of lesser players in graded BGS 9.5/10 or better condition

Essentially, we are looking to avoid paying prices that can't be right, while looking to acquire at prices that can't be wrong. We are looking for freerolls and layups.

And though we can often generate short-term profits by virtue of pricing power when dealing with high-grade, scarce cards, our basic aim is to profit in the long run through rising values as a result of some combination of pricing power, growing player demand (star power), scarcity-induced leverage, and multiple expansion.

That said, there are two basic ways we can acquire such gems. We can:

1. **Build it.** We can look to acquire ungraded cards and have them graded ourselves, which we will discuss more in depth in Part VIII: Building Gems.

2. **Buy it.** We can purchase graded cards directly, whether on eBay, through online discussion forums and trading sites, in card stores, or at card shows.

We'll discuss specific types of value plays at the end of this chapter. But before we can talk about buying cards for less than they are fundamentally worth, we first need to conceptualize the way we think about the terms *price* and *value*.

Price vs. Value

"Long ago, Ben Graham taught me that 'Price is what you pay; value is what you get.'"

– Warren Buffett

The basic premise of value investing in common stocks is that the stock of a given company has an underlying or **intrinsic value** based on some combination of asset value and the ability to generate income. This value is different from the going price of a given stock – sometimes the going prices overvalue the prospects of a given company; sometimes the going prices undervalue the prospects of a given company; and other times the going prices are within fair value range.

In principle, value investors look to buy undervalued stocks, betting that prices in the long run will ultimately approach fair value and produce outsized gains relatively to risk. *In the long run*, the terms *price* and potentially realizable *value* are fundamentally different.

However, on a day-to-day basis, price and *immediately realizable* value are actually the same with regard to stocks. Because stocks are relatively liquid – some more than others – ordinary investors cannot trade at prices substantially above or below going market prices. As such, if you are looking to buy or sell *today*, the going market price *is* essentially what a stock is worth.

That said, the basic implication is that investors with a long-term focus can take advantage when others have a short-term focus, or otherwise fundamentally undervalue the prospects of a given company.

Baseball cards are similar in this respect, but different in another.

Auction Variance and Liquidity

Because individual high-grade modern baseball cards are scarcer and don't trade in large volumes, they are often materially less liquid than most stocks. As a consequence, auction prices sometimes vary wildly, such that identical cards trading even within minutes or hours may have materially different prices.

This may happen for any number of reasons. It could be that there were two bidders for a given copy of a card; but once a buyer won that auction, he may not be in the market for a second copy, thus leaving only one bidder for the second copy, resulting in a lower price. Often the reverse happens, and the first card goes at a lower price because the presence of the second card creates pricing pressure on the first card – potential buyers may be less willing to commit if they know a second copy is available.

The time an auction ends may also impact the result. Auctions that end during work hours may limit potential buyers, as might auctions that end late at night on the west coast (removing some potential east coast bidders) or early morning on the east coast (removing some potential west coast bidders). Sometimes auctions that end during prime hours may be hurt when a flood of other auctions run at the same time, which may limit potential buyers simply by diverting attention.

Moreover, some cards or players are more liquid than others, and the same factors that drive demand are the ones that impact liquidity:

1. **Star power.** The bigger the star, the more liquid his cards will be.

2. **Grade.** High-grade graded cards will generally be more liquid than lesser-graded cards.

3. **Brand.** Key brands such as Bowman Chrome are generally more liquid than secondary brands.

4. **Key cards.** A player's key cards will generally be more liquid than his secondary cards.

5. **Hot lists.** Cards and players that appear on current hot lists will generally be more liquid than those that aren't.

There are two key points to be made here. One is that the concept of price is not necessarily a simple one with regard to baseball cards. Where stocks investors can simply point to the price of the last trade as a proxy for the going prices of a given stock, he cannot do the same for baseball cards, as baseball card prices may be much more fluid.

And the second key point is that the cards that aren't in current high demand may be materially less liquid than what's currently trending. This is important, because when auctions run for cards where nobody is looking, often times these auctions run at steep discounts to what somebody would pay for the same card in a fixed price Buy It Now listing – had they happened to be looking for it – even under the prevailing current market equilibrium values.

We can use this to our advantage when bargain hunting.

Appraisal: Replacement Cost and Relative Valuation

Now that we've conceptualized *price*, we can begin to conceptualize the term *value*. Let's start by talking about valuation in the context of appraisal.

In real estate appraisal, there are three basic approaches to valuation:

1. **The cost approach.** The cost approach essentially uses replacement cost as a value ceiling. If you can build an asset for $100, then the value of a like asset on the market cannot be worth more than $100 under this approach.

2. **The sales comparison approach.** The sales comparison approach uses recent sales of comparable assets – comps – as a proxy for valuation. The EV Comp approach to prospect valuation presented in Part IV is a variation of this approach. The sales comparison approach is the most widely used – if not always the most heavily weighted – approach.

3. **The income approach.** The income approach uses the discounted value of anticipated future income as an estimation of value. This is generally the most heavily weighted approach when applicable.

These approaches are not mutually exclusive, and are often used in conjunction with one another. Unfortunately, as baseball cards are fundamentally *not* income-generating assets, the income approach does not apply to baseball cards. But the other two approaches *do* have useful application.

The Cost Approach

The gist of the cost approach is that if you can build a BGS 9.5 card for $100 – say, by spending $90 on an ungraded card and $10 to have it graded – then the value of a graded BGS 9.5 copy of the same card cannot be worth more than $100 under this approach. This is fundamentally why, in the short run (generally within the first few months after initial release of a new issue for rarer parallels, but longer for more common base cards), graded cards often warrant a relatively small premium over ungraded cards – because at this early stage after initial release, gems can often still be readily built.

But the limitation of the cost approach is immediately apparent where rarer cards such as a 1/1 superfractor – for example – literally cannot be replaced.

One of the key attributes of rare, serialized key cards of star players is that the highest-quality examples ultimately get graded. In the long run, as the supply of gradable cards approaches exhaustion, high-grade copies of these cards can no longer be built. As a result, the spread in value between the "irreplaceable" high-grade copies and the ungradable ones tends to widen.

We can also use replacement cost a different way.

Replacement Cost as a Value Floor

Not only can we use replacement cost as a value ceiling, but we can also use replacement cost as a proxy for a valuation floor. Let's say a common prospect auto carries an ungraded book value of $8, but trades for $5. Assuming that the cost of grading is $10, then the value of a graded BGS 9.5/10 copy is *fundamentally* worth at least ($5 + $10) = $15.[60]

Note that at replacement cost, we are acquiring the graded BGS 9.5/10 card without paying a premium – that is, we are doing this without the risk that an ungraded card will not grade out.

In this manner, we can also use **book value replacement** cost as a proxy, and then discount from there.

Book Value Replacement Cost = Ungraded BV + $10

A BGS 9.5/10 copy of a common prospect auto with an ungraded BV of $8 and an assumed cost of grading of $10 carries a book value replacement cost of $8 + $10 = $18. Thus, if you can acquire a BGS 9.5/10 copy at a discount to the book value replacement cost of $18, you should generally make out OK strictly in terms of value.

Alternatively, let's say a top prospect from a newly released set is trading at $70 to $80, implying a book value of about $100. *Assuming the card is not being overvalued*, a graded BGS 9.5/10 copy cannot be worth less than $80 to $90 (the $10 cost of grading plus the $70-$80 acquisition cost), while you are probably doing OK if you can acquire a BGS 9.5/10 copy at a discount to implied book value replacement cost of $110 (implied book value of $100 + $10).

The Sales Comparison Approach and Relative Valuation

The sales comparison approach uses recent sales of comparable assets as a proxy for valuation. With regard to baseball cards, we can use sales comps in a variety

---

[60] It's conceivable that demand never materializes for such a common, in which case the common may not justify the cost of grading.

of ways:

1. Same card, same condition
2. Same card, different condition
3. Same player, different sets
4. Parallels of the same card
5. Different players, same set
6. Comparable cards of comparable players, different years

Same Card, Same Condition

If the last dozen 2011 Bowman Chrome Mike Trout RCs graded BGS 9.5 traded for $50 each over the last month, then there's a strong probability that the current going rate for the card is $50.

Same Card, Different Condition

A BGS 9.5 Gem Mint copy of a card is worth more than a BGS 9 Mint copy, while a BGS 10 Pristine copy is worth a premium to a BGS 9.5 copy.

Same Player, Different Sets

We can compare a player's RCs among the different brands (i.e. Finest vs. Topps Chrome vs. Bowman Chrome vs. Bowman Chrome Draft vs. Bowman Sterling, etc.), and we can do this among base cards, among gold refractors, or among autos.

For example, we know generally speaking that Topps Chrome base RCs generally carry a slight but negligible premium to Bowman Chrome, and that Bowman Chrome RCs historically carried a premium to their Bowman Chrome Draft counterparts until 2012 (when Bowman Draft became a Hobby-only product benefitting from a smaller production run).

On a gold refractor level, we know that a player's Bowman Chrome RC Gold Refractor #'d/50 generally trumps gold refractors from other brands, and is generally equal to or more highly valued than its Bowman Chrome Draft counterpart (and when the Bowman Chrome Draft RC gold refractor carries a higher book value than the Bowman Chrome RC Gold Refractor of the same player, it is generally attributable to price guide variance).

This is helpful knowledge when comparing available cards in the marketplace, and when evaluating new issues. For example, when 2013 Topps Chrome was released in late September 2013, the 2013 Topps Chrome Jose Fernandez RC

Gold Refractor auto redemptions were trading for roughly $100 each. Two weeks later, 2013 Finest was released, and included redemptions for the 2013 Finest Jose Fernandez Gold Refractor autos. We know historically that Finest RC Gold Refractor autos generally trade at a discount to Topps Chrome RC Gold Refractor autos; as such, when a seller argues that the Finest Gold Refractor auto is worth $100 because the Topps Chrome Gold Refractor auto sold for $100, we know that this is incorrect.

We also know that on-card autos are more valuable than sticker autos. Whereas 2012 Bowman Sterling Baseball was primarily on-card autos where previous issues were sticker autos, the 2013 Bowman Sterling set was mixed – while prospect autos were generally on-card, the RC autos appeared to be either primarily or exclusively sticker autos. And again, the 2013 Bowman Sterling Jose Fernandez RC autos were issued as redemptions; as such, based on the probability that these cards will turn out to be sticker autos, we could safely assume that the Bowman Sterling Jose Fernandez RC Gold Refractor autos should trade at a discount to the Topps Chrome Gold Refractors autos, and probably the Finest ones as well.[61]

Parallels of the Same Card

The general rule is that the rarer the parallel, the more valuable the card. This isn't quite 100% – some parallels are hideous and strain desirability – but it's close enough. But we know that a Blue Refractor #'d/150 graded BGS 9.5 is probably not worth more than a Gold Refractor #'d/50 also graded BGS 9.5.

Different Players, Same Set

Assuming comparable print runs (i.e. one player is not short-printed), you can decide if you think Michael Wacha's 2013 Finest RCs are worth more than those of Jose Fernandez, for example.

Comparable Cards of Comparable Players, Different Years

Using the EV Comp approach, we showed how we can compare Bowman Chrome/ Bowman Chrome Draft prospect autos of different players from different years. This can be done for any type of card from any type of set. For example, is a 2012 Finest Bryce Harper RC Gold Refractor #'d/50 worth more than a 2013 Finest Manny Machado RC Gold Refractor #'d/50?

---

[61] As it turned out, the Jose Fernandez RC autos from 2013 Bowman Sterling turned out to be on-card autos.

That said, we do need to account for differences in each player's prospect-RC structure. The best comparison for Bryce Harper's 2012-year RCs is the 2011-year Mike Trout RCs. However, Trout's Bowman Chrome RC is his first Bowman Chrome non-auto, while Bryce Harper had already had a 2010 Bowman Chrome non-auto; *two* 2011 Bowman Chrome Prospects non-autos; *and* a 2012 Bowman Chrome Prospects non-auto before his 2012 Bowman Chrome RC arrived. As such, it's not surprising that Trout's 2011 Bowman Chrome RC carries an ungraded BV of $30, while Harper's books for $8.

The more interesting question is how the value of the Bowman Chrome RC Gold Refractors #'d/50 compare. Is the 2012 Bowman Chrome Bryce Harper RC Gold Refractor #'d/50 directly comparable to the 2011 Bowman Chrome Mike Trout RC Gold Refractor #'d/50? Or is it an inferior class of card?

This can be argued both ways. Personally, I'd lean towards the Bowman Chrome RC Gold Refractors being comparable or near comparable, with Harper's 2012 Bowman Chrome Prospects card (his 4th set of prospect cards) being a bastardization. On the other hand, I wouldn't necessarily pay comparable value for it; in other words, I might look to buy the 2012 Bowman Chrome Bryce Harper RC Gold Refractors #'d/50 as if it was an inferior class of card, but would look to sell it as if it were comparable in class to the 2011 Bowman Chrome Mike Trout RC Gold Refractors #'d/50.

The Greater Fool Theory and Equilibrium Collectible Value

The biggest challenge with baseball cards is – and always will be – that we can never argue with any certainty what the underlying value of a given baseball card is; because baseball cards are not cash-generating assets, all we have to go on are a series of relative valuations.

The limitation of relative valuation is that we can logically argue with great conviction, for example, that a 2009 Bowman Chrome Draft Mike Trout prospect auto graded BGS 9.5/10 would be a steal at $50 when compared to the universe of players with Bowman Chrome prospect autos; however, the underlying assumption is that all other players with Bowman Chrome prospect autos are not being overvalued.

And if baseball cards are just pieces of cardboard with no underlying value, then it's also conceivable that Mike Trout would be overvalued even at $50.

As such, baseball cards will always on some level be subject to the oft-cited **greater fool theory**.

The Greater Fool Theory

There isn't a standard definition of the greater fool theory, but the gist of it is that you can justify buying anything at any price if you think somebody else will pay more for it. Typically, when referenced with regard to stocks, the greater fool theory refers to buying overpriced stocks on the rise in the hope that prices will continue to rise and people dumber than you will pay more (not a good strategy). However, when evoked with regards to baseball cards, the term "greater fool theory" is sometimes effectively meant to imply that *any* investment in baseball cards depends on finding buyers dumber than you, with the underlying assumption being that baseball cards have no underlying value.

The greater fool theory is often quite valid with regard to baseball cards at the high end of the hobby (meaning high-end scarce – which is often but not necessarily high dollar amount), where it only takes one buyer with the scrap and the desire for a given card to overpay for it. This is very much often the justification for the sometimes absurd prices of 1/1s, and is in fact the justification Bruce McNall used when he and Wayne Gretzky purchased the Gretzky T206 Wagner, if you recall this quote from the beginning of Part I:

> "My philosophy was, if you buy something that is absolutely the best in the world, you'd be okay because there is always another buyer for something at the top end."

On the other hand, the sometimes implied assumption that baseball cards have no underlying value is easily disprovable as being the default case – after all, Gurksy's *Rhein II* is just a photograph anyone can download to their phone, and Leonardo da Vinci's *Mona Lisa* (1503-1506) is merely oil on canvas. Each of these things has some underlying value beyond economic utility, if quantifiable only in relative terms.

Would you, for example, pay $5 for the original *Mona Lisa*? Of course you would, if only because somebody else would pay more than $5 for it.

It might seem we've invoked the greater fool theory – we can justify paying $5 for a piece of oil on canvas simply because we think somebody else would pay more. However, invoking the greater fool theory would imply that the *Mona Lisa* is not worth $5 – an insane assumption, considering that most of us have paid more than $5 for posters we put up on our bedroom walls as kids, while many have paid significantly more than $5 for a decent copy of the *Mona Lisa* (in fact, you can find them on eBay).

But what about $100,000? $1 million? $10 million? $100 million? $1 billion? $2 billion?

For reference, *Guinness World Records* lists the *Mona Lisa* with the highest insurance value ever assessed for a painting at $100 million on December 14, 1962, for a move from the Louvre in Paris, France to Washington, D.C. and then New York City for a series of exhibitions through March 1963;[62] factoring inflation, that $100 million valuation translates to $771 million in 2013 dollars. Incidentally, the most expensive painting ever *sold* was *The Card Players* (1892-93) by Paul Cézanne, which sold in April 2011 to the Royal Family of Qatar for a price variously reported to be between $250 million and $300 million.[63]

Equilibrium Collectible Value

The point is, all things have some underlying, theoretical **equilibrium collectible value** based on supply and demand. Some things (like late 1980s common baseball cards) have negligible collectible value, while other things like the *Mona Lisa, Rhein II*, and the Gretzky Wagner have considerable collectible value.

Much like stocks, all collectibles can be overvalued, undervalued, or fairly valued as compared to their underlying equilibrium collectible values. Consequently, the

---

[62] www.guinnessworldrecords.com/records-10000/highest-insurance-valuation-for-a-painting
[63] en.wikipedia.org/wiki/The_Card_Players

greater fool theory cannot be used as a blanket default explanation for baseball card values, as that would imply that *all* baseball cards have no underlying value; instead, much like stocks, the concept of the greater fool theory only applies to cards overvalued compared to their underlying equilibrium collectible value.

Again, the challenge with baseball cards (and other collectibles) is that all we have to go on are a series of relative valuations, which break down when the market as a whole is overvalued or undervalued; as such, this equilibrium collectible value can't be calculated with any precision, and can only be conceptualized. That said, though we can't argue with any precision what the underlying value of a given baseball card is, what we *can* do is argue that the potential collector base is largely untapped, in which case the market at large could be primed for a mass re-valuation.

Multiple Expansion and Relative Multiples

Much like there is a supply and demand for baseball cards, there is a supply and demand for stocks. If you follow the stock market at all, you'll often hear an analyst or other market commentator attribute a rise in prices for a given stock or the stock market in general to multiple expansion. When somebody attributes a rise in prices to **multiple expansion**, what they are saying is that prices have risen relative to earnings – that is, the price-to-earnings ratio (P/E ratio) has risen – for no real reason other than that the demand for investments in a given stock or the stock market in general have risen.

In other words, there is no real catalyst or change in fundamental business value, and prices are rising simply because people want in. And so, when multiple expansion occurs, it means not only that the demand for investments has risen, but also that stocks have become relatively more expensive as compared to their underlying values.

The occurrence of multiple expansion in itself is neither fundamentally a good or bad thing. A stock that is undervalued may see its multiple expand towards its underlying value, which we generally expect, and is good for value-oriented investors (unless you were looking to buy more!). Alternatively, a stock that is fairly valued might see its multiple expand and become overvalued, while overvalued stocks might bubble further and become even more overvalued (as they did in the tech stock bubble of the 1990s).

The latter is a less healthy outcome, and one that speculators/gamblers often illogically depend on occurring for short-term gain (hence the greater fool theory).

That said, there are logical reasons why some companies fundamentally carry higher multiples than other comparable companies, chiefly:

1. **Projected earnings growth rate.** Companies that project to grow faster than its competitors will carry higher P/E multiples in anticipation of earnings growth.

2. **Earnings risk.** The more dependable a company's earnings are, the more that company's earnings are worth – after all, a 100% chance at earning $1 is worth a $1, while a 50% chance at earning $1 is worth only 50 cents. Consequently, companies with strong, durable competitive advantages often carry premium valuations over their competitors.

Baseball Cards

With regard to baseball cards, we've used multiple expansion to describe the relationship among cards between graded values and ungraded book values, and between gold refractor #/50 parallels and base cards. What fundamentally causes some cards to warrant higher multiples than comparable cards of comparable players, or different cards of the same player?

As we have seen, there are many potential causes:

1. **Star power.** The bigger the star and the higher the demand, the bigger the premium collectors/investors/speculators will pay for the highest-quality assets.

2. **Key cards.** As demand is often greatest for key cards, high-grade key cards often command a premium over a player's secondary cards.

3. **Star power and star "earnings" risk.** As a player builds Hall of Fame credentials by racking up such things as MVP awards, Cy Young awards, championships, or All-Star Game appearances, the player is both fundamentally building star power and reducing player-specific risk.

4. **Scarcity-induced leverage.** As a player builds star power, high-leverage cards – the rarest, most desirable parallels – benefit the most, increasing the spread between the high-end parallels and the base cards.

5. **Grade scarcity.** When high-grade cards are difficult to build, the spread between the values of the high-grade cards and lesser graded cards grows. This and the card removal effect will both be discussed in greater detail in Part VII.

6. **Card removal.** As the highest quality examples of a given card get graded, eventually the supply of potential gems becomes exhausted and gems can no longer be built. As this happens, the spread between graded gems and ungraded cards widens.

7. **Time.** Time alone is not enough to cause multiple expansion; rather, it is the things that happen over time that do so, chiefly card removal and the development of star power.

Multiple Contraction

In the same way that multiples expand when demand rises, multiples can also contract when demand falls and/or people start selling. This could happen when rookie or prospect bubbles burst; it could also happen when a player goes on a luck-driven hot streak, his cards bubble, and then the bubble bursts once the market figures out how much of the hot streak was attributable to luck. It might happen when injury occurs; or it might be more subtle, where a star player matures and becomes forgotten as the market fixates on the next hot player.

Sometimes multiple contraction is not so subtle – and the bigger the premiums being paid, the farther the player has to fall.

You only have to go back to 2012, when the 1994 SP Alex Rodriguez RC carried an ungraded book value of $80 and a graded BGS 9.5 book value of $2,500, for an adjusted multiple of 27.8x. By January 2013, the Biogenesis PED scandal had broken; and on August 5, 2013, Rodriguez was among 13 players suspended by Major League Baseball for use of banned substances provided by the South Florida-based anti-aging clinic Biogenesis of America, namely human growth hormone (HGH) in Rodriguez's case.[64] On January 11, 2014, Rodriguez saw his suspension reduced from 211 games to 162 games, still keeping Rodriguez off the field in 2014.[65]

By this point, the damage to A-Rod's card values had long been done. Graded BGS 9.5 copies of the 1994 SP Alex Rodriguez RC had fallen to the $600-$700 range by the spring of 2013, down to the $300 range by the summer 2013, and traded as low as $250 by December 2013. And by December 2013, the 1994 SP Alex Rodriguez RC carried an ungraded BV of $40, and a graded BGS 9.5 book value of $400, for an adjusted multiple of only 8.0x.

The Tech Stock/Graded Card Bubble

As we've established from the start of this book, investment-grade (BGS 9.5+ and PSA10) graded cards of Hall of Fame-level players have long achieved prices never attained by their ungraded counterparts – and this is true even for players with rookie cards from the 1980s and 1990s. However, graded cards are far from immune to bubbles. And along with the absurd prices in the stock market of the late 1990s came absurd prices in graded cards with extreme multiples relative to ungraded cards.

---

[64] espn.go.com/mlb/story/_/id/9540755/mlb-bans-13-including-alex-rodriguez-new-york-yankees-2014
[65] espn.go.com/new-york/mlb/story/_/id/10278277/alex-rodriguez-suspension-reduced-162-games

The table below shows the April 2001 pricing of notable key RCs from the 1980s and early 1990s. Ungraded and BGS 9.5 Gem Mint book values are from the April 2001 issue of Beckett Baseball Card Monthly.

Notable RCs from 1982-1994: April 2001 Pricing

Card	#	Ungraded BV	BGS 9.5 Gem Mint	Adj. Multiple
1982 Topps Traded Cal Ripken Jr. RC	98T	$200	$2,500	11.9x
1983 Topps Tony Gwynn RC	482	$40	$3,500	70.0x
1983 Topps Wade Boggs RC	498	$25	$1,000	28.6x
1983 Topps Ryne Sandberg RC	83	$20	$600	20.0x
1984 Donruss Don Mattingly RC	248	$30	$600	15.0x
1984 Donruss Joe Carter RC	41	$10	$250	12.5x
1984 Donruss Darryl Strawberry RC	68	$5	$80	5.3x
1984 Fleer Update Roger Clemens XRC	27	$150	$1,500	9.4x
1984 Fleer Update Kirby Puckett XRC	92	$100	$600	5.5x
1985 Topps Mark McGwire RC	401	$150	$5,000	31.3x
1986 Donruss Jose Canseco RC	38	$25	$400	11.4x
1986 Donruss Fred McGriff RC	28	$8	$150	8.3x
1987 Fleer Barry Bonds RC	604	$30	$1,500	37.5x
1987 Fleer Barry Larkin RC	204	$5	$150	10.0x
1987 Donruss Greg Maddux RC	36	$15	$400	16.0x
1989 Upper Deck Ken Griffey Jr. RC	1	$150	$2,500	15.6x
1990 Leaf Frank Thomas RC	300	$40	$350	7.0x
1990 Leaf Sammy Sosa RC	220	$50	$600	10.0x
1992 Bowman Mariano Rivera RC	302	$10	$120	6.0x
1992 Bowman Mike Piazza RC	461	$70	$500	6.3x
1993 SP Derek Jeter RC	279	$120	$24,000*	184.6x*
1994 SP Alex Rodriguez RC	15	$100	$12,000*	109.1x*

Source: Beckett Baseball Card Monthly April 2001
*Reflects PSA 10 values; PSA's April 2001 Sports Market Report lists 1993 SP Derek Jeter RC PSA 10 at $14,500 and 1994 SP Alex Rodriguez RC PSA 10 at $12,500

Aside from the high graded card prices, the most notable thing about this table is that the ungraded values of these cards weren't exactly flying off the charts; the absurd prices of graded cards appear to be attributable almost entirely to multiple expansion (and steroids). This becomes even more absurd when you consider that unopened boxes of many of these sets were printed in such numbers that – even 13 years later – unopened boxes are still in seemingly endless supply.

Regarding the 1993 SP Derek Jeter RC and 1994 SP Alex Rodriguez RC, we noted earlier in this book the discrepancy between the BGS 9.5 Gem Mint and PSA 10 Gem Mint populations of these cards, contributing to the outsized valuation of the PSA 10 graded copies of these cards. The April 2001 Beckett Baseball Card Monthly magazine explicitly accounts for PSA (and SGC or Sportscard Guaranty, another grading company) values in its pricing, while the current Beckett.com online price guide clearly does not, or at least not with regard to these two cards.

Compare the prices from April 2001 to those from Beckett.com as of December 2013.

Notable RCs from 1982-1994: December 2013 Pricing

Card	#	Ungraded BV	BGS 9.5 Gem Mint	Adj. Multiple
1982 Topps Traded Cal Ripken Jr. RC	98T	$120	$1,200	9.2x
1983 Topps Tony Gwynn RC	482	$25	$500	14.3x
1983 Topps Wade Boggs RC	498	$15	$400	16.0x
1983 Topps Ryne Sandberg RC	83	$20	$300	10.0x
1984 Donruss Don Mattingly RC	248	$40	$500	10.0x
1984 Donruss Joe Carter RC	41	$8	$120	6.7x
1984 Donruss Darryl Strawberry RC	68	$8	$60	3.3x
1984 Fleer Update Roger Clemens XRC	27	$120	$600	4.6x
1984 Fleer Update Kirby Puckett XRC	92	$100	$500	4.6x
1985 Topps Mark McGwire RC	401	$20	$400	13.3x
1986 Donruss Jose Canseco RC	38	$12	$100	4.6x
1986 Donruss Fred McGriff RC	28	$8	$60	3.3x
1987 Fleer Barry Bonds RC	604	$12	$120	5.5x
1987 Fleer Barry Larkin RC	204	$8	$60	3.3x
1987 Donruss Greg Maddux RC	36	$10	$100	5.0x
1989 Upper Deck Ken Griffey Jr. RC	1	$40	$300	6.0x
1990 Leaf Frank Thomas RC	300	$20	$100	3.3x
1990 Leaf Sammy Sosa RC	220	$12	$40	1.8x
1992 Bowman Mariano Rivera RC	302	$60	$250	3.6x
1992 Bowman Mike Piazza RC	461	$20	$80	2.7x
1993 SP Derek Jeter RC	279	$150	$2,000*	12.5x*
1994 SP Alex Rodriguez RC	15	$40	$400*	8.0x*

Source: Beckett.com, December 2013
*Reflects BGS 9.5 pricing; PSA 10 1993 SP Derek Jeter is listed at $28,000 on PSAcard.com as of 1/1/14, while PSA 10 1994 SP Alex Rodriguez is listed at $900

Both ungraded and graded prices have come down considerably from those April 2001 bubble levels, but multiple contraction has meant that graded prices have burst the hardest.

A big part of the bubble was pure bubble behavior. For example, at least in retrospect, it's really difficult to see the 1983 Topps Tony Gwynn at 70.0x adjusted ungraded value, or the 1987 Fleer Barry Bonds RC at 37.5x, particularly given the availability of unopened boxes.

Another cause of the bursting of the bubble was likely the rapid growth in graded card supply, thanks to a combination of the fact that card grading was still relatively new back in 2001, as well as the aforementioned unending availability of unopened boxes from this time period. For one thing, BGS did not begin grading cards until 1999. And for another, from the inception of PSA in 1991 through its fiscal year ended June 30, 2001, PSA had graded over 4 million cards; but by the fiscal year ended June 30, 2013, that number had reached over 21 million cards total.[66] Moreover, those extra 17 million cards weren't all modern Chrome Era cards, an area where BGS is dominant – through the beginning of 2014, PSA had graded less than 500,000 baseball cards issued from 2001-2013 *total*, and fewer than 1.1 million combined baseball, football, basketball, and hockey cards issued from 2001-2013.

In other words, it's a virtual certainty that the unending supply of unopened boxes from this time period helped to drive new graded card supply for cards from this time period, and thus drive down multiples.

Beyond mere bubble bursting, many of the players on this list also lost considerable value due to the discovery of steroid use, including Roger Clemens, Mark McGwire, Jose Canseco, Barry Bonds, Sammy Sosa, and Alex Rodriguez. Meanwhile, the only two cards to show any real appreciation from these bubble levels are the 1992 Bowman Mariano Rivera RC and the 1993 SP Derek Jeter RC, the latter which again recorded a pair of PSA 10 Gem Mint sales at $32,500 in December 2013.

---

[66] Source: Collector's Universe 2001 and 2013 10-Ks

Value Hunting

By now, we know what kinds of cards we are looking for, and we have at least a framework for thinking about valuation. We know we want to buy cards on the cheap, getting premium cards of premium players without paying a premium, or picking up secondary key cards at steal prices. We are looking to pay prices that can't be wrong, and avoid paying prices that can't be right.

The next question is, how do we go about finding such values?

Before we get into specific types of situations, there are at least four key principles:

1. **Be patient.** Unfortunately, not every player will be playable when you want them to be playable – in fact, most won't be at the very moment you first think of them. Wait for opportunities to develop.

2. **You don't need to win every player – only the ones you bet the crap out of.** While it's natural to want to try to profit off a top prospect like Byron Buxton, it's conceivable that the opportunity to "bet the crap out of" Byron Buxton may never present itself. It's OK to try to get decent prices and pick at a Byron Buxton here and there for your collection, but for investment purposes, you are better off picking your spots and looking for layups.

3. **Avoid the hot lists.** When players are in the playoffs or are on hot streaks, they are getting free advertising and often approach bubble prices; they also often wind up on hot lists. Over the summer of 2013, as it appeared that Detroit Tigers 3B Miguel Cabrera had a good shot at becoming the first repeat Triple Crown winner (leading the league in batting average, HRs, and RBIs), prices of BGS 9.5 copies of his 2000 Topps Chrome Traded RC had zoomed up to around $400 a pop; by the end of 2013 – after he didn't do it – they were back down as low as $170.

4. **Look where and when nobody else is looking.** The best values are found when the market's attention is focused elsewhere – during the offseason; when other teams are in the playoffs; when other players are on hot streaks; when other prospects or RCs are hot; or at hours when much of the country is sleeping or working. When sellers run auctions where nobody is looking, excellent – and sometimes extreme – values can be found.

Let's talk about some specific types of value plays.

Overlooked/Undervalued Stars

As players mature, they shed the hot young player label and often go forgotten. As we noted in Part IV, BGS 9.5/10 copies of the Bowman Chrome Hanley Ramirez RC Auto *Refractors* were going in the $120-$150 range as of the end of 2013 – this, after Ramirez had compiled a total of 37.1 FanGraphs WAR before the age of 30, and after Ramirez had just came off a season in which he had come back from injury to hit .345/.402/.638 in 86 games (5.1 WAR) to help lead the Dodgers to the playoffs. Meanwhile, a 2002 Bowman Chrome Joe Mauer Auto X-Fractor #'d/250 and graded BGS 9.5/10 could be had for $350 – not bad for a former #1 overall pick who had compiled 44.0 FanGraphs WAR by age 30 with six All Star Game appearances, five Silver Slugger awards, three Gold Glove awards, and an MVP award as a catcher.

It's also remarkable that BGS 9.5/10 copies of the 2006 Bowman Chrome Draft Clayton Kershaw prospect auto were trading and readily available in the $130-$150 range as recently as the spring of 2013, while a PSA 10 Gold Refractor auto #'d/50 sold for $1,050 in a fixed price listing on 4/15/13. At the time, Kershaw was entering his age-25 season, and was already widely considered to be one of the top two or three pitchers in the league, if not *the* best pitcher in the league. Kershaw won the NL Cy Young Award in 2011, and was runner up to R.A. Dickey in 2012. And yet, Kershaw was trading at roughly a 25% discount to the comparable 2005 Bowman Chrome Justin Verlander RC auto and 2004 Bowman Chrome Felix Hernandez RC auto, and in about the same range as the 2011 Bowman Chrome Draft Dylan Bundy prospect auto.

In the midst of a 2013 age-25 season in which Kershaw won his second NL Cy Young Award – going 16-9 with a 1.83 ERA and 232 Ks in 236 innings – three BGS 9.5/10 Orange Refractor autos #'d/25 sold between $3,450 and $4,100 in August-September. At the same time, a BGS 9.5/10 Gold Refractor auto #'d/50 sold for $2,550 on 9/2/13, while a PSA 10 copy sold for $2,050 on 9/5/13. Base autos graded BGS 9.5/10 were up in the $300-$330 range.

It's also notable that by the end of 2013 – long after the season was over – the base 2006 Bowman Chrome Draft autos graded BGS 9.5/10 were trading down in the $220-$250 range, and that a BGS 9.5/10 Orange Refractor #'d/25 sold for $2,227 at auction on 11/20/13. And then in January 2014, a BGS 9.5/10 Gold Refractor #'d/50 sold for $2,900, while a base auto graded BGS 9.5/10 and another graded PSA 10 both sold for $350.

Overlooked Prospects

Sometimes top prospects get overlooked by the market, particularly if they are in the minor league systems of small market teams, or if they don't debut with the hype of a Bryce Harper or Byron Buxton. Mike Trout entered the 2010 season as Baseball America's No. 85-ranked prospect after dominating the Rookie-level Arizona League; his 2009 Bowman Chrome Draft prospect auto is listed in the April/May 2010 issue of Beckett Baseball magazine with an ungraded value at $30.

Miami Marlins RHP Jose Fernandez was even more overlooked, entering the 2012 season valued as a common. Entering the spring of 2013, the 2011 Bowman Chrome Draft Jose Fernandez prospect auto graded BGS 9.5/10 could still be had in the $60-$70 range, even after he went a combined 14-1 with a 1.75 ERA and 158 Ks in 134 innings between low Class A Greensboro and high Class A Jupiter in 2012, and entered the 2013 season as Baseball America's No. 5-ranked prospect.

After the Prospect-RC Bubble Bursts

Rookies are supposed to fail – even Mike Trout struggled in his first crack at the majors, hitting .220/.281/.390 in 40 games in his 2011 RC year, before dominating in his 2012 official rookie year. And yet, though top prospects and hot rookies are often (wildly) overpriced and consequently unbuyable as prospects, potential buying opportunities often present themselves as the first sign of weakness causes their prospect or rookie bubbles to burst.

As we discussed in Part IV, Texas Rangers SS Jurickson Profar entered the 2013 season as Baseball America's No. 1 prospect, with graded BGS 9.5/10 copies of his 2011 Bowman Chrome Prospects auto trading in the $160-$180 range by early spring 2013; also recorded were a BGS 9.5/10 Orange Refractor auto #/25 sale at $1,600 on 4/16/13, and a BGS 9.5/10 Gold Refractor auto #/50 sale at $1,250 on 3/2/13. Profar began the season at Triple-A Round Rock, but was called up in May to replace the injured 2B Ian Kinsler.

Blocked at his natural shortstop position by Elvis Andrus and at second base by Ian Kinsler upon Kinsler's return from the disabled list – but apparently too advanced for Triple-A ball – the Rangers kept Profar at the major league level in a super utility role. Profar struggled, hitting only .234/.308/.336 with 6 HRs and 2 SBs in 85 games while playing four different positions as a 20-year-old.

By the end of 2013, Profar's top prospect shine had faded, and BGS 9.5/10 copies of his 2011 Bowman Chrome Prospects auto had fallen into the $60-$70 range.

Meanwhile, a Gold Refractor auto #'d/50 and graded BGS 9.5/10 sold at auction on 1/8/14 for $455.

As with any young player, Profar may or may not pan out. And while Profar is now officially neither a prospect nor even a rookie, he will play the 2014 season at age 21. And depending on your opinion of Profar from this point, he may or may not be an excellent buy at $60-$70.

Turnaround Plays

Atlanta Braves RF Jason Heyward entered the 2010 season as Baseball America's No. 1-ranked prospect in all of baseball after dominating three minor league levels to the tune of .323/.408/.555 in 2009 – including a .352/.446/.611 showing in 47 games at the Double-A level – flashing five tools and incredible plate discipline. As a rookie in 2010, Heyward hit .277/.393/.456 with 18 HRs and 11 SBs, making the All Star Game and finishing second in the NL Rookie of the Year voting to San Francisco Giants C Buster Posey. Heyward was on fire, with his 2008 Bowman Chrome Prospects auto carrying a $200 ungraded book value entering the spring of 2011.

Heyward then proceeded to hit a dismal .227/.319/.389 in 2011, before rebounding in 2012 to hit .269/.335/.479 with 27 HRs and 21 SBs and winning a Gold Glove in the process. And prior to the 2013 season, Heyward was ranked No. 3 on Keith Law's list of the top 25 players under the age of 25 on ESPN.com.[67]

Regardless, Heyward's stock had already been hit, such that graded BGS 9.5/10 copies of his 2008 Bowman Chrome Prospects auto could be had for $80-$100 entering the 2013 season. In an injury-shortened 2013 season, Heyward hit only .254/.349/.427 with 14 HRs and only 2 SBs in 104 games. And by the end of 2013, BGS 9.5/10 copies of the 2008 Bowman Chrome Prospects auto were trading in the $50-$60 range.

It's entirely possible that the 2013 Jason Heyward is what Jason Heyward is and will be. On the other hand, Heyward is still only 24 years old entering the 2014 season, and may yet present upside at $50-$60.

Injury Turnaround Plays

When a star player sustains a major injury, the market often panics such that prices may fall farther than the nature of the injury might suggest.

---

[67] insider.espn.go.com/mlb/story/_/id/8821510/mike-trout-bryce-harper-top-25-players-age-25-mlb

After posting a 2.73 ERA with 70 Ks in 59.1 innings pitched over 10 starts as a rookie in 2012, New York Mets RHP Matt Harvey entered the 2013 season in demand. In April 2013, his 2010 Bowman Chrome Draft 1/1 Superfractor auto sold for $8,200; a half a dozen Orange Refractor autos #'d/25 and graded BGS 9.5/10 sold between $700 and $850, while the Orange Refractor auto #1/25 and also graded BGS 9.5/10 sold for $1,100. Meanwhile, BGS 9.5/10 copies of his Gold Refractor autos #'d/50 were trading in the $500-$650 range.

Over the season, Harvey got hotter, establishing himself as arguably one of the top two or three pitchers in the game while going 9-5 on a bad Mets team, and posting a 2.27 ERA with 191 Ks in 178.1 innings pitched before being shut down on August 26 with a partial tear of the ulnar collateral ligament (UCL) that would ultimately require Tommy John surgery. But prior to the initial injury announcement, the BGS 9.5/10 Orange Refractor autos #'d/25 had reached $1,200 by June, with a $1,750 sale in July, and another outlier sale at $3,500 in an auction dated August 27 (a perhaps questionable sale following the injury announcement); meanwhile, BGS 9.5/10 copies of the Gold Refractor auto #'d/50 had reached $975.

In the days following the injury announcement, a BGS 9.5/10 Orange Refractor auto #'d/25 sold for $1,048 at auction on 9/1/14, and for $850 in a fixed-price listing on 9/2/14. And between 8/29/13 and 9/17/13, three BGS 9.5/10 Gold Refractor autos #'d/50 sold between $400 and $433.

So in a span of days, Matt Harvey went from being valued like a budding superstar playing for a big market team to being valued more like David Price (who is probably undervalued, playing for a small-market team in Tampa Bay).

But how serious is the injury? While Tommy John surgery is nothing to sneeze at, it is not uncommon; in an article dated July 17, 2013, Will Carroll of the Bleacher Report reported that a whopping 124 of the 360 pitchers who began the 2013 at the major league level – that is, one-third of major league pitchers – have had Tommy John surgery at some point in their careers.[68]

Moreover, it is something players often come back from quite strongly. After missing virtually all of the 2011 season to Tommy John surgery, Washington Nationals RHP Stephen Strasburg came back in 2012 to pitch 159.2 innings, going 15-6 with a 3.12 ERA while striking out 11 batters per nine innings. When then-Florida Marlins RHP Josh Johnson went down in 2007, he looked like a solid

---

[68] bleacherreport.com/articles/1699659-the-alarming-increase-in-mlb-pitchers-whove-had-tommy-john-surgery

No. 2 kind of pitcher with a fastball in the low-90s; when he came back in 2008 following Tommy John surgery, he looked like an ace who suddenly had mid-90s fastball and touched 97 mph. In 2009, Johnson went 15-5 with a 3.23 ERA and 191 Ks in 209 innings pitched, while going 11-6 with a 2.30 ERA and 186 Ks over 183.2 innings in 2010.

Matt Harvey may or may not come back in 2015 as strong as he was before; but if you believe that's the case, then you might think he looks pretty good with BGS 9.5/10 Gold Refractor autos at under $500.

Newly Issued Ungraded Cards

The ability to acquire newly issued ungraded cards and build gems opens up a world of additional opportunities to gain value. We'll discuss these opportunities and the ins and outs of acquiring ungraded cards – including buying strategies and evaluating case breaks – in Part VIII: Building Gems. But before we can do that, we have much else to discuss.

Part VI: The Supply Chain and the Value Cycle

The supply chain, the Value Cycle, and the logistics and impact of supply growth.

One of our primary strategies for getting value involves acquiring ungraded cards and building long-term investment assets in the form of Gem Mint-or-better graded cards. But if this is such a great strategy, why isn't everybody else doing it? And where does this value come from?

The answers lie in the supply chain.

The first thing you realize is that not everybody is playing the same game. In the modern baseball card industry, there are many different players up and down the supply chain, from the manufacturers to the distributors; to the retailers, hobby shops, and case breakers (more on these guys in a minute); down to the hobbyist investors, speculators, and collectors. Some deal in unopened boxes or cases, while others deal in sets, ungraded singles and/or bulk lots; and still others deal in graded cards. Some employ mixed strategies, while others specialize in only one function.

But regardless of strategy, most players in the supply chain have a very short-term focus. And, as we know, players with a short-term focus are the most likely to yield long-term values.

Understanding the supply chain is the key to identifying which sellers are most likely to be selling ungraded cards which are potential gems, and which sellers are completely unlikely to sell potential gems.

Understanding the supply chain is also important for another reason. As we have seen time and time again, the baseball card industry as a whole is extremely prone to bubble behaviors. We've seen it at the industry level with the bubble of the late 1980s and early '90s, and we see it at the collector level on an annual basis with every hot new rookie and prospect.

That said, there is a sensitive relationship between secondary market values for singles and box demand; between box demand and future supply; and between future supply and future secondary market values.

This set of relationships form the basis of the Value Cycle.

As secondary market values for singles in a given set rise, demand for unopened boxes from that set also rise. This leads to increased demand for future boxes, which in turn leads to greater supply. When supply rises faster than collector demand – as was the case in the late 1980s and early '90s – secondary market values for these issues fall, leading to declines in box values for those issues and box demand for future issues.

The demand for Topps' three Bowman Chrome product lines (Bowman, Bowman Chrome, and Bowman Draft) has grown considerably over the past several years, but the supply has grown along with it. Moreover, the rapid emergence of the case breaker segment of the supply chain – combined with Topps' policy of printing to pre-order demand – has a number of potential consequences. Chief among them is an acceleration of the Value Cycle, which could lead to mini boom-bust cycles with wild swings in supply – far wilder than actual changes in collector demand – with evidence of this already present in 2013 (and in fact, as we will see later here in Part VI, there is evidence that this has already occurred even in just the past five years, most notably in 2010 between the smash hit spring 2010 Bowman release and the apparently wildly overproduced 2010 Bowman Chrome set released later that year).

Meanwhile, growing demand and the accompanying growth in supply in the Bowman Chrome product lines present a number of challenges for Topps with regard to both product configuration and product value.

We'll discuss these challenges and Topps' past, present, and future responses to them in a minute. We will also discuss the impact that Topps' responses have on card and box values. But first, let's break down the supply chain.

The Supply Chain

The modern baseball card supply chain is relatively simple. Unopened cases go from the **manufacturers** (Topps, Panini, Upper Deck, Leaf, etc.) to **distributors**. Distributors then distribute unopened cases to **retailers** such as Target and Walmart; to **hobby dealers** including local brick-and-mortar card stores or online wholesalers; and to case breakers, which we'll discuss in depth in a minute.

The Supply Chain: Cases, Boxes, and Ungraded Singles

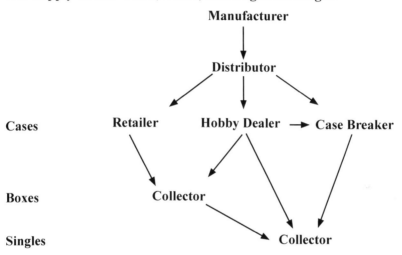

Unopened boxes come in two basic, distinct varieties: Retail (distributed to retailers) and Hobby (distributed to hobby dealers and case breakers). That said, for a product like Bowman Chrome or Topps Chrome, the distinction is extremely important, because the bulk of the high value cards – the on-card autographs, and rarest parallels (chiefly the 1/1 superfractors) – are typically found in the Hobby product, while lesser value items such as sticker autos and memorabilia cards are more likely to be found in Retail product.

Moreover, it is exceptionally rare that Retail product is worth its retail price, meaning that it is very unlikely that you can go to Target or Walmart and make a killing by buying the crap out of unopened boxes. One notable exception was 2012 Topps Chrome Football, which was a perfect storm of a high-value rookie class including QBs Andrew Luck, Robert Griffin III, Russell Wilson, and Ryan Tannehill, as well as Tampa Bay Buccaneers RB Doug Martin (5th in the NFL in rushing yards) and Carolina Panthers LB Luke Kuechly (1st in NFL in tackles); as well as general box value including a healthy dose of refractors, and appealing insert RCs in the form of cards based on the 1957, 1965 and 1984 Topps Football designs. By the spring of 2013, blaster boxes which sold for $20 at retail at Target and Walmart were going for $30-$35 a pop on eBay.

Though some of the larger hobby dealers (typically online wholesalers) also carry retail product, some product lines – such as Bowman Sterling and Finest – are hobby-only products, meaning you won't find them at Target or Walmart in any form. Meanwhile, in 2012, Bowman Draft became a hobby-only product.

Collectors typically purchase unopened cases and boxes from retailers and hobby dealers. When these boxes are opened, singles are either sold or traded to other collectors, typically via eBay or other online forums where collectors meet. Hobby shops also typically open boxes and sell ungraded singles upon release as well.

But in recent years, one of the biggest sources of ungraded singles for any new issue has been the case breaker.

Case Breakers

Case breakers – also called group breakers – are a relatively new breed of service provider, and essentially perform commercialized **group breaks**. In a group break, multiple collectors pool together resources to purchase unopened boxes or cases that an individual might not otherwise be able to acquire. The cards that come out of a break might be divided any number of ways, but the general goal for the participant is to improve his or her chances of getting the high-end hits that don't appear every box, and/or to build investment lots of certain key players.

Commercial case breakers come in many different varieties, but the basic principle is the same: A case breaker will bust open a case or multiple cases, and sell portions of the cards, generally prior to the actual break.

Some case breakers sell complete sets, team sets, or insert sets, while others sell team lots (all cards for players on a given team) or player lots (all cards of that player), or for specific types of cards that might appear (autos, superfractors, or other parallels). Some case breakers pre-sell lots for a fixed price directly on their website or in their brick-and-mortar card shop, while some pre-sell lots at auction on eBay; some case breakers do both.

A case breaker could be a local card shop, or it could be a guy or group of guys in a home office or basement. Regardless, when lots are pre-sold, the actual case break is generally filmed and broadcast live over the Internet.

Case breakers as a class have grown to the point that they have become an officially recognized part of the supply chain. And in August 2013, Upper Deck announced that it was working on an "Authorized Group Breaker" program.[69] Meanwhile, in October 2013, Panini announced the creation of the "Authorized Case Breaker" designation, creating a separate category class in its distribution model.[70]

The biggest, most recognized case breakers generally acquire cases directly from distributors. But technically speaking, anybody can perform the case breaker function, and there are many, many smaller players who bust boxes acquired from online wholesalers or even their local card store.

The largest case breakers perform primarily a "rip and flip" function, meaning that they generally sell everything that comes out of the break. Some case breakers – or "collectors who bust cases" – might keep certain hits and have cards graded, while selling off unwanted cards either as ungraded singles or in bulk lots.

Graded Cards

A collector/investor typically obtains graded cards from one of three sources:

1. **Build it.** The end collector/investor opens boxes or acquires ungraded singles from hobby dealers, case breakers, or other collectors, and then has them graded himself.

2. **Hobby dealers.** The end collector/investor can acquire graded cards from hobby dealers, who either build them from cases they open, or otherwise acquire them from collectors.

3. **Other collectors.** The end collector/investor can acquire graded cards from other collector/investors.

---

[69] www.cardboardconnection.com/news/upper-deck-working-on-program-to-support-dealers-and-group-breaks

[70] paniniamerica.wordpress.com/2013/10/18/panini-america-announces-authorized-case-breaker-designation-other-enhancements

The Supply Chain: Graded Cards

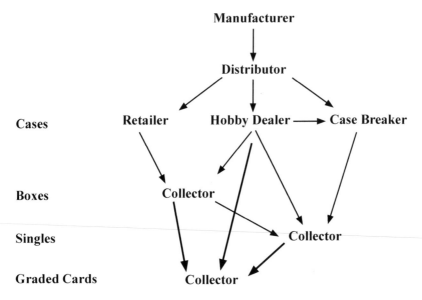

Investment Time Frame

Another key attribute for each player in the supply chain is their typical holding period or investment time frame, which for most players is exceptionally short.

Manufacturers take orders, then print and ship when the time comes, and consequently don't have a holding period. The investment time frame for the distributor is similarly short. Case breakers also have a short holding period, in some cases selling out lots even in advance of delivery.

Retailers such as Target and Walmart also have a short-term holding period. With fixed maximum prices and comparably little box value compared to hobby products, the ideal holding period for retailers is as close to zero as possible. When a product is strong, it generally sells quickly; when a product is weak, it ultimately either gets marked down or returned. Regardless, retailers do not sit on product indefinitely.

Hobby dealers are a mixed breed and often use mixed strategies which may differ amongst dealers. Like the retailers, hobby dealers generally have short holding periods on new, unopened boxes. However, in contrast to the retailers, hobby dealers have the freedom and sometimes – depending on the product – the box value to raise prices as the market dictates, and consequently may have potentially much longer holding periods.

Some hobby dealers perform case break functions, while some simply break cases and sell off the parts.

While hobby dealers might grade cards that come out of a break, they generally don't do so with the purpose of stuffing the cards in a vault as long-term investments. Rather, most every card in a hobby dealer's inventory is generally available for sale. Hobby dealers are generally in the transaction business, and will tend to take short-term profits when available. Consequently, though holding periods may be indefinite, the investment time frame for graded cards at the hobby dealer level is generally short rather than long.

Collectors are also a mixed breed. Some have only one strategy, while others use mixed strategies. When a collector buys unopened boxes, it is typically a short-term affair, as the presence of expiring redemption cards for autos hurts the long-term value of unopened boxes.

When a collector opens boxes, some of the cards are often sold or traded (short-term holding period), while other cards either get graded and kept (long-term investment time frame) or flipped (short-term investment time frame), and some ungraded cards are kept as part of the collection. When a collector acquires ungraded singles, some of those cards are graded and either kept (long) or flipped (short), while ungradable cards are often thrown back into the market (short) or otherwise added to the collection (long).

It is the collector who deals in graded cards that generally has the longest investment time frame. We know that ungraded cards typically don't fare as well as investments over the long run, except perhaps the rarest parallels and other 1/1s. Graded cards, on the other hand, make *by far* the best buy-and-hold investments. Consequently, though even collectors who deal in graded cards often flip them, these collectors generally have a long-term investment time frame.

Supply Chain by Investment Time Frame: Long vs. Short

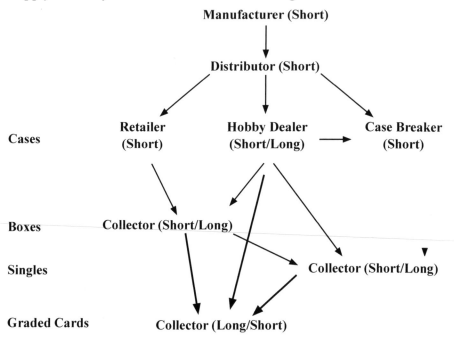

The Value Cycle

One thing that should be clear is that secondary market values drive the entire value/supply chain. When supply is favorable and demand is relatively high, then secondary market values are high, and thus box demand is high; collector-investor confidence is also high, helping drive future box demand. But when supply is too high and secondary market values are correspondingly weak – as was the case with the late 1980s and early 1990s issues – people stop buying unopened boxes; collector-investor confidence weakens, future box demand drops, and the entire supply chain fails.

Subsequently, new supply falls to potentially more attractive levels such that secondary market values may return, enabling box demand to rise once again.

That secondary market value drives box value is easy enough to demonstrate. Let's say you have a card with an average street value of $50, and it appears at a rate of one per box. In this case, an unopened box is generally worth at least $50. But if the value of the card rises to $100, the value of an unopened box generally also rises to at least $100.

That said, the challenge for the collector – and everybody else in the supply chain – is that when conditions are favorable and supply is relatively low, such conditions cannot be expected to persist indefinitely. This is because when excess value exists on the secondary market, other players in the supply chain – from the manufacturers down to the case breakers – will attempt to capture it.

These attempts to capture value inevitably result in increased supply.

Manufacturer Forces

Manufacturers typically have two basic methods of capturing excess value:

1. Raise prices
2. Expand supply

A manufacturer might raise prices by raising wholesale prices of the staple product lines like Topps or Bowman Chrome, with rising costs working their way down the supply chain.

Alternatively, a manufacturer might simply include less per pack or fewer packs per box. Retail blasters, for example, generally have a fixed price of $20; a manufacturer may adjust the contents of those blasters from year to year or set to set. Another example is Bowman Sterling: 2011 Bowman Sterling Baseball included five cards per pack, including two autos, a relic, an RC and a prospect card; 2012 Bowman Sterling Baseball included only four cards per pack, including three autos and one base RC or prospect card.

In addition, manufacturers might introduce increasingly "high end" products, such as Upper Deck Exquisite Collection, Topps Five Star or Panini National Treasures, which might run $500+ a box with one pack per box; another example is 2012-13 Panini Flawless Basketball, which was released on October 2013 with a suggested retail price of $1,250 per pack/box and came in a briefcase (by the end of November, prices of Panini Flawless had passed $2,000 per briefcase).[71]

But the "easy" approach to capturing value is simply to expand supply.

Now it should first be pointed out that a manufacturer can't print a product and – if it's successful in the secondary market – simply go back to the well and print more of it (don't worry – Topps has other ways of doing this). For one thing, Topps prints to pre-order demand; and for another, Topps can't print more 1/1 superfractors, or another set of #/5 red refractors for the same set, etc. But more to the point, the day that Topps goes back to the well would be the end of the game, because the whole market depends on the assurance of a fixed print size, and that the manufacturer is not going to screw the supply chain.

Consequently, when a product performs well, the manufacturer must capture value in later issues, whether in the same product year or the next one. That said, card manufacturers can increase supply in two basic ways:

1. **Add new product lines.** In addition to its staple Bowman, Bowman Chrome, and Bowman Draft products, Topps has added new products to its Bowman prospecting lineup in Bowman Sterling (2004), Bowman Platinum (2010), and Bowman Inception (2013).

2. **Expand existing lines.** Increase the production sizes of the existing product lines (a.k.a. attempting to print money).

Neither option benefits secondary market values, but the expansion of existing lines is potentially of greater negative impact. However, to the extent that Topps prints to pre-order demand, the company is essentially trying to let the market dictate growth, rather than simply expand supply on its own accord.

---

[71] msn.foxsports.com/nba/story/panini-flawless-basketball-cards-costs-1800-dollars-per-pack-and-are-very-popular-110413

But as we are about see, Topps' policy of printing to pre-order demand comes with hazards.

Case Breaker Forces

Any time there is an easy profit to be made and little barrier to entry, you are going to attract competition. Or put differently, if it is possible to turn meaningful profits simply by opening a box of baseball cards and selling the contents, then a lot of other people are going to want to do it as well.

As we know, competition creates pricing pressure and squeezes profits. But in the baseball card business, this winds up being a double whammy.

Why? Because in this case, the competition is also pumping up supply and devaluing the product in the process.

The emergence of the profitable case breaker has led to the emergence of many other case breakers chasing case breaker profit. As a result – whether it is large case breakers ordering through distributors or smaller case-breaking collectors ordering cases through online wholesalers – pre-order demand rises accordingly. And because Topps prints to pre-order demand, supply also rises along with it.

Growing supply in itself is not necessarily problematic, so long as collector demand is growing along with it. But when the case breaker segment of the supply chain is growing significantly faster than actual collector demand, secondary market values will suffer and case breaker profits will be squeezed even further.

There are signs that this has happened in 2013. In his mid-year review on The Cardboard Connection website, noted case breaker Brent Williams (a.k.a. brentandbecca) reported that he had been generating his lowest ROI (return on investment) on case breaks since 2009.[72] And in the fall of 2013, Topps provided a triple whammy when it released its 2013 Topps Chrome, 2013 Bowman Chrome, and 2013 Finest – three of its biggest releases for mid- to high-end collectors – all within a span of two weeks (In 2012, Finest and Topps Chrome were August releases separated by two weeks, while Bowman Chrome was an October release).

As we'll discuss in Part VIII, the first two-to-four weeks following the initial release of a new card issue are key for collector-investors looking to acquire the rarest parallels because the bulk of the new supply is broken within the first two weeks, thus creating both availability and pricing pressure for rare cards. But with

---

[72] www.cardboardconnection.com/2013-topps-baseball-card-mid-year-review

three big releases within two weeks, an incredible amount of supply was dumped on the market by case breakers in an incredibly short period of time, with the ultimate result being that some incredible values on anything other than Yasiel Puig (bubble) were easily found, despite being an unusually strong RC-logo (but not prospect) class including Yasiel Puig, Manny Machado, Jose Fernandez, Wil Myers, Gerrit Cole, Michael Wacha, Hyun-Jin Ryu, Shelby Miller, Jedd Gyorko, and Christian Yelich (plus several other notables), not to mention some other high-end RC-year players who may yet pan out in Dylan Bundy, Jurickson Profar, and Mike Zunino.

If nothing else, the probability is that by the time the 2013 Finest release rolled around, collectors had simply run out of money.

Moreover, the other thing that was noticeably clear about the 2013 Topps Chrome and 2013 Bowman Chrome releases in particular was that print runs were up significantly from 2012. Judging from the pack odds on the 1/1 Superfractors, roughly 3,865 hobby cases of 2013 Topps Chrome were produced, up 32% from roughly 2,927 hobby cases of 2012 Topps Chrome.[73] Other clues were the inclusion of new, limited print, serialized refractors in both Bowman Chrome and Topps Chrome *in addition* to the standard color refractors (more on this in a minute).

Unless we see a large bump in collector demand, then at some point – if it hasn't happened already – we are going to see some case breakers squeezed out of the market, while others peel back on orders, until some point where box value returns.

And so, though Topps policy of printing to pre-order demand was probably intended to let actual collector demand dictate the growth of supply, what's actually happening is that Topps' policy is letting the supply chain determine supply, and at the peril of the market. And as a result, the market may be prone to accelerated value cycles with wild swings in supply – swings much greater than changes in actual collector demand. These swings might occur *not* in the long run, but rather from year-to-year or even set-to-set.

Meanwhile, growing supply – whether sustained or temporary – creates logistical issues of importance to the collector and manufacturer alike.

---

[73] Found by taking the Superfractor odds (1:3,832 Hobby packs in 2012, and 1:5,060 Hobby packs in 2013), multiplying by 220 (the number of cards in each set) to get the total number of packs produced, then dividing by 24 packs per box, and 12 boxes per case. Note that this case figure is not precise, as it does not account for cards that Topps may hold back for use as replacements.

The #'d Refractor, the Auto, and the Logistics of Supply Growth

When conditions are favorable, demand grows and supply grows along with it. And as we just discussed, manufacturers typically use two basic methods of expanding supply: They can either add new product lines, or expand the production runs on existing lines.

That said, the expansion of existing lines creates logistical issues for the manufacturer. Any time production rises, the manufacturer must make decisions regarding at least four basic areas of set configuration, all of which impact box value:

1. Base set production
2. Inserts
3. #'d refractors
4. Autos

Base set production is an easy subject, as the manufacturer can either expand the checklist, or simply increase the production size. Usually, expanding the checklist is not a realistic option; with a set like Finest, which has an annual base set checklist of 100-150 players (100 players in 2011, 2012, and 2013) composed primarily of RCs and stars, you can't typically expand the checklist, as doing so will necessarily add less desirable players and thus weaken the checklist, ultimately hurting box value.

When people buy boxes and wind up with boxes full of commons, people stop buying boxes.

Inserts are also relatively easy, though not always value added. When the need arises, the manufacturer can either print more inserts along with the base set, or it can add more insert sets.

The 2012 Topps Chrome Football set did this to great effect. Among the insert sets were three rookie insert sets utilizing the designs of the 1957 Topps, 1965 Topps, and 1984 Topps sets, to go with a Red Zone Rookies insert set. The 1957 insert set consisted of 30 cards, while the others included 35, and the throwback cards in particular have added value as cards that don't necessarily look like inserts, and yet function as effective RCs (though without the RC logo, as the original 1957, 1965, and 1984 designs did not have such logos) while allowing Topps to constrain base set production. It doesn't hurt to have Andrew Luck, Robert Griffin III, Russell Wilson, and Ryan Tannehill (not to mention Doug Martin and Nick Foles) to add punch.

But going back to baseball, insert sets are not always helpful, particularly if they have absurd checklist sizes themselves filled with common (or future common) prospects.

When you get really desperate and growth explodes, you see things like in the 2010 Bowman Chrome set, which included the Bowman Chrome Topps 100 Prospects – a 100-card *insert* set (a chrome version of the paper Bowman Topps 100 Prospects set included in 2010 Bowman) with a print run of 999 sets, plus 499 Refractor parallels, 50 Gold Refractor parallels, and a Superfractor parallel. Meanwhile, the 2013 Bowman paper release included not only a chrome Bowman Top 100 Prospects insert set, but also a 150-card Bowman Chrome Cream of the Crop Mini Refractors set, composed of the top five prospects from each of the 30 teams in Major League Baseball.

When checklists get long, box value erodes.

Meanwhile, the limited print, serialized refractors and the autos present even greater challenges.

#'d Refractors

The challenge with refractors is that when you keep a fixed checklist size, the high-end refractors necessarily become harder to hit as production rises.

This is easy to figure: In a set like Finest with a base set checklist of 100 players with 50 Gold Refractors #'d/50 each, there will be 5,000 base set Gold Refractor parallels every year. But when demand grows and base set production grows, more cases will be produced, while the number of Gold Refractors #'d/50 remains fixed at 5,000. Consequently, the more production increases, the less likely you will be to open a box and find a Gold Refractor #'d/50.

One common solution is to add rare insert parallels to fill the need for box hits. But this only goes so far, and at some point the manufacturer will respond by adding more refractors to the lineup.

The table on the next page shows the pack odds of hitting a Gold Refractor from Bowman Chrome Hobby and Bowman Draft Hobby issues from 2001-2005. In 2001, the Gold Refractor was introduced to the Bowman Chrome lineup and was #'d/99. In 2002, the Gold Refractor changed to its now-standard #/50, and was also introduced to Bowman Draft. The Gold Refractor has been #'d/50 ever since, except in the 2003 Bowman Chrome set in which they were #'d/170 and inserted as a box loader at a rate of one per box (2003 Bowman Chrome Draft Gold Refractors were #'d/50).

Note the general trend of rising odds against drawing a Gold Refractor, as well as Topps' responses to this trend under "Notes" on the right.

Bowman Chrome Gold Refractor Odds : 2001-2005

Year	Bowman Chrome Hobby	Bowman Draft Hobby	Notes
2001	1:47*		Gold Refractor #/99 introduced
2002	1:56	1:67	Gold Refractor becomes #/50; X-Fractor #/250 introduced to Bowman Chrome, and is #/150 in Bowman Chrome Draft
2003	1:18**	1:98	Gold Refractor non-autos are #/170 in Bowman Chrome and inserted one per box loader; X-Fractor not numbered; X-Fractor in Bowman Chrome Draft is #/130
2004	1:60	1:119	X-Fractor is #/172 in Bowman Chrome and #/125 in Bowman Chrome Draft; 1/1 Red Refractor included in Bowman Chrome Draft
2005	1:61	1:155	1/1 Superfractor and #/5 Red Refractor introduced; Red Refractor remains 1/1 in Bowman Chrome Draft; Blue Refractor #/150 introduced; X-Fractor #/250 in Bowman Chrome and #/225 in Bowman Chrome Draft

*In 2001, Gold Refractors were #'d/99
**In 2003 Bowman Chrome, Gold Refractors were not inserted into packs, but rather were inserted in box loader packs at a rate of one per box loader and #'d/170

The first thing that happened was that there was an apparently large drop in production between 2001 Bowman Chrome and 2002 Bowman Chrome, perhaps not distantly related to the fallout from the bursting of the tech stock (dot-com) bubble of the late 1990s. Whatever the cause, Topps' apparent response was to drop the print run of Gold Refractors effectively in half from #/99 in 2001 Bowman Chrome to #/50 in 2002 Bowman Chrome, with total Hobby case production falling less than that. This resulted in worse Gold Refractor pack odds – about 19% worse in 2002 – and Topps compensated by including a #/250 X-Fractor in Bowman Chrome, and a #/150 X-Fractor in Bowman Chrome Draft.

From here, the trend is pretty clear: As demand and thus supply increase and the Gold Refractor odds get worse, Topps responds by adding more and more variations of refractors to its lineup in order to support box value.

As noted, in 2003, Gold Refractors were #'d/170 and inserted as box loaders at a rate of one per box, or one for every 18 packs. From a production standpoint, this is the equivalent of producing Gold Refractors #'d/50 at a rate of one every 61 packs, meaning that the production size of Hobby boxes appear to be roughly the same for

Bowman Chrome in 2003, 2004, and 2005 (Note: This method is a rough proxy, as it does not factor retail production). Meanwhile, Bowman Draft grew rapidly.

By 2004, the Gold Refractor odds in Bowman Draft were nearly twice as bad as they were in 2002. That year, Topps responded to the need for high-end value by introducing a 1/1 Red Refractor.

In 2005, Topps introduced its now ubiquitous 1/1 Superfractor across its chrome-based product lines. Topps also introduced the #/5 Red Refractor to 2005 Bowman Chrome, though the Red Refractor would remain a 1/1 in Bowman Chrome Draft for 2005 before becoming a #/5 across Bowman Chrome lines from 2006 to present. That year, Topps also introduced the Blue Refractor, #'d/150.

Bowman Chrome Gold Refractor Odds: 2006-2010

Year	Bowman Hobby	Bowman Jumbo	Bowman Chrome Hobby	Bowman Draft Hobby	Notes
2006	1:355	1:116	1:74	1:197	Orange Refractor #/25 introduced; #/5 Red Refractor standard in both Bowman Chrome and Bowman Chrome Draft; in Bowman Chrome Draft, Blue Refractors are #/199 and X-Fractors #/299; Bowman Jumbo boxes introduced
2007	1:481	1:80	1:88	1:232	
2008	1:380	1:63	1:131*	1:150	In Bowman Chrome Draft, Blue Refractors are #/99 and X-Fractors are #/199
2009	1:271	1:57	1:50	1:96	
2010	1:228	1:64	1:142	1:160	#'d X-Fractor removed; Green X-Fractor is prospects-only, and included in Bowman Chrome Retail. Bowman Chrome Draft Blue Refractor is #/199. 2010 Bowman Chrome Prospects from 2010 Bowman (BCP1-BCP110) is another discussion in itself.

*Stated odds are 1:393 for Bowman Chrome Prospects, but 1:197 for Bowman Chrome (RCs and veterans); 2008 is the only year where this is broken down; 1:131 represents blended figure, factoring three combined Gold Refractors per 393 packs

In 2006 with the new MLBPA RC rules, Topps began including Bowman Prospects and Bowman Chrome Prospects cards as "inserts" in its regular Bowman paper line, with the Bowman Chrome Prospects set numbering continued into the Bowman

Chrome Prospects cards later included as "inserts" in the Bowman Chrome product. That year, Topps also introduced Jumbo packs to the regular Bowman release – with more cards per pack and more hits per box – giving collectors two Hobby-only options. But with the addition of the Bowman Chrome Prospects, Bowman packs from 2006-present include Bowman Chrome Prospects Gold Refractors #'d/50.

You can see supply growing, as Hobby pack odds on Gold Refractors were 21% worse in Bowman Chrome and 27% worse in Bowman Draft than in 2005. And in 2006, Topps compensated by inserting another high-end refractor above the Gold, with the introduction of the now-staple Orange Refractor #'d/25.

Supply continued to grow in 2007, with Gold Refractor odds worsening by 19% in Bowman Chrome and 18% in Bowman Draft.

In 2008, the Gold Refractor odds were nearly 50% worse in Bowman Chrome than in 2007 – and nearly twice as bad as in 2006. However, the Gold Refractor odds were significantly better in Bowman and in Bowman Draft.

Whether it was due to lack of demand due to a weak prospect/RC class, fallout from the bursting real estate bubble, or a negative reaction to the worsening pack odds and wild overproduction of the preceding years, 2009 saw major declines to very attractive levels. Compared to 2008, Gold Refractor odds improved a healthy 29% in Bowman Hobby and 21% in Bowman Jumbo, and 36% in Bowman Draft. But even more dramatically, Gold Refractor odds improved a whopping 62% in Bowman Chrome, going from the worst odds to date in the history of Bowman Chrome in 2008 to the best year based solely on Gold Refractor odds in 2009 – and even better, once you factor the addition of the Orange Refractors #'d/25, Red Refractors #'d/5, and 1/1 Superfractor.

2010 Bowman turned out to be a landmark set. For starters, in Topps' first Bowman issue as an exclusive licensee of Major League Baseball, the 2010 release combined the first Bowman Chrome cards of two generational talents – Washington Nationals pitcher Stephen Strasburg and future Washington Nationals OF Bryce Harper, whose 18U Team USA card is featured in the set – to go with Strasburg's Bowman Prospects auto (a paper auto). It also included the first Bowman Chrome card of Baltimore Orioles 3B Manny Machado (an 18U USA card), as well as the Bowman Chrome Prospects autos of Wil Myers, Starlin Castro, Dustin Ackley, and Anthony Rizzo. As a bonus, it also included a Bowman Chrome Jason Heyward RC auto. Meanwhile, coming off the low print runs of the 2009 sets, the 2010 Bowman set also featured the best high-end refractor odds of any Bowman release to date.

Notably, Strasburg's 2010 Bowman Chrome Prospects Superfractor 1/1 would set a record for a sale of a 1/1 Superfractor – twice. According to The Cardboard Connection, the card was pulled on May 12, 2010 by a collector named Leo Kim. Later that month – in an auction watched by over 10,000 people[74] – the card sold at auction on eBay for a record $16,043 to a collector named Robert Power. That June, Power put the card up for auction, and sent the card to BGS to be graded during the auction; though the card was noticeably off-center, the card came back graded BGS 9.5 Gem Mint prior to the end of the auction. That auction ended at a price of $25,000, but the sale fell through. Power later sold the card for $21,403 to Brian Gray, owner of Razor Entertainment, who used it as part of a re-package product called 2010 Razor Rookie Retro.[75]

Later in September 2010, the 2010 Bowman Chrome 18U USA Bryce Harper Superfractor 1/1 sold for $12,500 on eBay at auction, despite having a bad edge and being essentially ungradable.[76]

Though the Harper sale came later, the success of the 2010 Bowman set undoubtedly drove pre-orders of the 2010 Bowman Chrome and 2010 Bowman Draft issues, as the 2010 Bowman Chrome set in particular was wildly overproduced. Because not a year after having the best high-end refractor odds in the history of Bowman Chrome, the 2010 Bowman Chrome Hobby packs had the worst high-end refractor odds in the history of Bowman Chrome, with Gold Refractors coming in at a rate of one every 142 packs – nearly three times worse than in 2009.

Instead, we find 2010 Bowman Chrome boxes stuffed with inserts – namely the Bowman Chrome Topps 100 Prospects. Weak box value is apparent given the long odds on the high-end refractors, but will become even more apparent when we talk about the autos.

Meanwhile, Gold Refractor odds on Bowman Draft Hobby were 67% worse than in 2009, but basically in line with the average odds from the previous six years (2004-2009).

Note: Note again that these odds are not precise measures of production, as they do not include Retail box production. That said, the odds should provide a reasonable proxy for tracking changes in production for the purposes of discussion.

---

[74] www.cardboardconnection.com/news/over-10000-watch-strasburg-superfractor-auction-come-to-a-close

[75] www.cardboardconnection.com/stephen-strasburg-2010-bowman-superfractor-raffle

[76] www.beckett.com/news/2010/09/bryce-harper-superfractor-sale-confirmed-at-12500

Bowman Chrome Gold Refractor Odds: 2011-2013

Year	Bowman Hobby	Bowman Jumbo	Bowman Chrome Hobby	Bowman Draft Hobby	Notes
2011	1:542	1:88	1:94	1:162	Bowman Draft Jumbo boxes introduced
2012	1:544	1:83	1:96	1:128	Bowman Chrome Blue Refractor is #'d/250, while Purple Refractor #'d/199 is added to Bowman and Bowman Chrome. Bowman Chrome includes X-Fractor and Green Refractor, neither of which are #'d. Bowman Draft becomes Hobby-only product
2013	1:670	1:209	1:105*	1:185	Black Refractor #'d/99 introduced to Bowman Chrome Prospects in Bowman release. Yellow #/10, Black #/15, Magenta #/35 introduced to Bowman Chrome; Bowman Chrome Jumbo boxes introduced. Black #/35, Green #/75 introduced, and Blue is #/99 in Bowman Chrome Draft; Silver Wave Refractors #/25 (new), Red Wave Refractors #/25, Blue Wave Refractors and Black Wave Refractors (new) are inserted to Bowman Draft packs.

*Bowman Chrome Hobby odds only; in 2013, Bowman Chrome Jumbo boxes were introduced

By 2011, we are facing a new reality, and from here the three main Bowman lines should be discussed separately.

Production and thus Gold Refractor odds were up in 2011 Bowman compared to the exceptionally favorable 2010 Bowman release, and then remained roughly the same in 2012. But production of 2013 was up considerably from that of 2012. Gold Refractor odds were 23% worse in Bowman Hobby, but 152% worse in Bowman Jumbo (the discrepancy due to a refractor bias towards the Hobby issue which featured one auto per box, while Jumbo boxes included three autos per box). But as a result, for the first time, the Bowman Chrome Prospects included in 2013 Bowman had a Black Refractor parallel #'d/99.

Following the 2010 Bowman Chrome debacle, Bowman Chrome production returned to more reasonable levels, though Gold Refractor odds at 1:94 in 2011 were still higher than pre-2008 levels, and stayed roughly the same in 2012. The 2011 Bowman Chrome set was particularly strong, including the Mike Trout RC and Bryce Harper's Bowman Chrome Prospects auto; and as of late 2013, box prices continue to rise on the secondary market.

But 2013 Bowman Chrome will make an excellent case study. Since the beginning of Bowman Chrome in 1997, Bowman Chrome Hobby packs came with 4 cards per pack and 18 packs per box, with chrome autos included at a rate of one per box going back to 2003. For the first time – thanks to considerable demand – Bowman Chrome would see Bowman Chrome Jumbo packs with 13 cards per pack, 8 packs per box, and 3 autos per box.

Production growth in 2013 Bowman Chrome is extremely apparent in a couple ways. One is that Gold Refractor odds on Bowman Chrome Hobby rose considerably to 1:105 – nearly double the 2002 odds – despite benefitting from an apparent refractor bias towards Hobby boxes (to illustrate, Gold Refractor odds in Jumbo packs were 1:52 – or only twice as frequent as Hobby packs, despite including 3.25 times as many cards per pack). But the biggest clues were that, for the first time, Bowman Chrome included Black Refractors #'d/15 (Jumbo-only), Magenta Refractors #'d/35 (Hobby-only), and Yellow Refractors #'d/10 (Retail-only).

In other words, Topps is compensating for growth in supply with the inclusion of more, rarer, high-end refractors slotting above the Gold Refractor #'d/50.

In 2011, Topps introduced the Jumbo box to Bowman Draft. In 2012, Bowman Draft became a hobby-only product, meaning that boxes were only released in Hobby and Jumbo varieties, and no longer at retail outlets. The result was a significant overall decline in production to favorable levels, which came with the second-best Gold Refractor odds since 2004 Bowman Draft.

But in 2013, Gold Refractor odds rose a whopping 45%, reflecting a similar increase in overall production. And to compensate, Topps included even more new additions to the refractor lineup:

- Red Wave Refractors #'d/25, previously a wrapper redemption feature in 2012
- Silver Wave Refractors #'d/25 (new)
- Blue Wave Refractors, previously a wrapper redemption feature
- Black Wave Refractors (new)
- Black Refractors #'d/35 (new)
- Green Refractors #'d/75 (new)
- Blue Refractors #'d/99, previously #'d/250 in 2012

Autograph Production

Autograph RC/Prospect cards present another interesting challenge. Chrome autos have been inserted at a rate of one per Hobby box since 2003 Bowman Chrome, and three chrome autos per Bowman Jumbo box since 2010. And as the production of the Bowman lines continued to grow – and more and more boxes are printed with one auto per Hobby box and three autos per Jumbo box – this means that Topps must print more autographed cards along with increases in the base set print runs.

There are two ways Topps can do this:

1. Print more autographs per player, or
2. Widen the autograph checklist.

We know from stated print runs that the auto print run for 2003 Bowman Chrome totaled 2,500 autographs per player, including 1,700 base autos, 500 Refractor autos, 250 X-Fractor autos, and 50 Gold Refractor autos. And we also know from stated print runs that that number grew to 2,800 in 2004 Bowman Chrome, with base auto production rising to 2,000 per player.[77]

Though Topps no longer states print runs on base autos, the good news for the investment-minded collector is that auto print runs don't appear to have changed much: Based on the pack odds, the Bowman Chrome prospect auto print runs in 2012 Bowman Draft appear to be about 1,741 (give or take) per player including 1,000 base autos, though this number grew to more normalized levels in 2013. On the other hand, the bad news for anyone who enjoys opening boxes is that option #2 – widening the autograph checklist – is decidedly the dominant option.

The table below shows the growth of the Bowman Chrome prospect/draft pick auto checklist by set and by year. Note that from 2001-2007, Bowman Chrome autos only appeared in Bowman Chrome and Bowman Draft boxes. In 2008, Bowman Chrome Prospects autos appeared in the regular Bowman paper product, joining the regular, non-auto Bowman Chrome Prospects set that was introduced to Bowman in 2006. Consequently, Bowman Chrome prospect autos appeared in three different Bowman products from 2008-present.

Meanwhile, from 2006 to present, Bowman Chrome Draft prospect autos have been variously labeled "Draft Pick" or "Prospects" autographs depending on the year, but are effectively in the same product line regardless of the label.

---

[77] Source: Beckett.com

The auto checklist growth has been spectacular, nearly tripling between 2005 and 2013 when factoring the Bowman Chrome and Bowman Draft releases alone.

Bowman Chrome Prospect Autos by Set and Year

Year	Bowman	Bowman Chrome*	Bowman Draft*	Total
2001	–	20	–	20
2002	–	22	10	32
2003	–	22	11	33
2004	–	20	10	30
2005	–	23	15	38
2006	–	25	25	50
2007	–	36	30	66
2008	20	45	19	84
2009	17	24	22	63
2010	31	40	32	103
2011	33	37	34	104
2012	38	41	40	119
2013	42	57	47	146

Source: Beckett.com, cardboardconnection.com, sportscardradio.com
*Bowman Chrome and Bowman Chrome Draft autos from 2001-2005 are RCs by official designation, but comparable to Bowman Chrome prospect autos from 2006-present

Note that the wildly overproduced 2008 Bowman Chrome set came with a prospect auto checklist including a whopping 45 players – a number that wouldn't be surpassed until 2013. A similarly overproduced 2010 Bowman Chrome set had 40 prospects. And in 2012 – likely in recognition of weakening box value due to the widened checklist – Topps began inserting an extra auto for every three boxes in 2012 Bowman Chrome Hobby boxes. In fact, in March 2014, Topps announced that 2014 Bowman Chrome would be released with *five* autos per Jumbo box, to go with *two* autos per Hobby box.[78]

---

[78] www.beckett.com/news/2014/02/first-look-2014-bowman-chrome-baseball-cards

In addition to the growth in chrome prospect autos, Topps has shown an increasing reliance on Bowman Chrome RC autos in order to satisfy chrome autograph demands. Some of these RC autos are the first Bowman Chrome autos for some players, including Prince Fielder and Kenji Johjima (2006), Stephen Strasburg (2010), Eric Hosmer (2011), and Yu Darvish (2013), while many of these are players who had already had Bowman Chrome Prospects autos, including Clayton Kershaw and Evan Longoria (2008), Jason Heyward (2010), Bryce Harper (2012), and Manny Machado, Dylan Bundy, Jurickson Profar, Wil Myers, and Yasiel Puig (2013).

Some players have multiple Bowman Chrome RC autos spread across the Bowman product lines (obviously in the same year, per the RC rules), including Strasburg (2010 Bowman Chrome and Bowman Chrome Draft), Bryce Harper (2012 Bowman Chrome and Bowman Chrome Draft, though these are actually the same card released in two different sets, but short-printed overall), Yu Darvish (2012 Bowman, Bowman Chrome, and Bowman Chrome Draft, all short-printed), and Jurickson Profar (2013 Bowman and Bowman Chrome).

Factor in the Bowman Chrome RC autos, and the chrome auto lineups in recent years become even larger.

Bowman Chrome RC Autos: 2006-2013

Year	Bowman	Bowman Chrome	Bowman Draft	Total RC Autos	Total Prospect Autos	Total RC + Prospect Autos
2006	–	5	0	5	50	55
2007	–	0	0	0	66	66
2008	–	0	5	5	84	89
2009	–	0	0	0	63	63
2010	14	1	1	16	103	119
2011	–	2	0	2	104	106
2012	12	4	2	18	119	137
2013	14	7	1	22	144	166

Source: Beckett.com, cardboardconnection.com, sportscardradio.com

And this doesn't include the various chrome USA Baseball sticker autos included in the 2010 and 2011 Bowman Chrome and Bowman Draft sets.

Multiple Chromes Risk: How Topps Goes Back to the Well

In December 2011, the Texas Rangers paid the Nippon Ham Fighters of Japan's Nippon Professional Baseball league $51.7 million for the right to negotiate a major league contract with their star pitcher, a 25-year-old right-hander named Yu Darvish. Darvish signed in January 2012 for $60 million over six years.

That April, Darvish made his first five major league starts, going 4-0 with a 2.18 ERA and 33 strikeouts in 33.0 innings – and that's even after giving up five earned runs over 5.2 innings in the first of those five starts.

In May 2012, the new 2012 Bowman set hit the streets. Naturally, the most highly anticipated card in the release was the 2012 Bowman Chrome Yu Darvish Rookie Autographs card, card #209 in the set. The base auto had a black border and is thought to be short-printed – likely rarer than the Blue Refractor auto parallel #'d/250. And given that there is no regular (non-color) refractor parallel, the Bowman Chrome Yu Darvish RC Autos with the #209 on the back is quite rare, and with an entire print run likely under 500 including the Blue Refractors #'d/250, Gold Refractors #'d/50, Orange Refractors #'d/25, Red Refractors #'d/5, and Superfractor 1/1.

In the first week after release, two Orange Refractors #'d/25 sold on eBay for $2,250 and $2,325. Six Gold Refractors #'d/50 went between $1,250 and $1,599, while a base black-bordered auto sold for $950. All of those cards were raw (ungraded). The book had the base auto listed that summer at $600, the Blue Refractors #'d/250 at $900, and the Gold Refractors #'d/50 at $1,500.[79]

However, after the hot start, Darvish struggled through much of the summer, and by August 6, his ERA sat at a much less impressive 4.57. But in his last six starts of the regular season, Darvish was nearly unhittable, going 4-0 with a 1.85 ERA over 43.2 innings, before losing in the one-game Wild Card playoff game against the Baltimore Orioles. Darvish finished his rookie year with a 16-9 record, a 3.90 ERA and 221 strikeouts in 191.1 innings.

But by then, the bubble had burst: In September-October 2012, the base autos graded BGS 9.5 Gem Mint with a 10 Auto were going for $350 a pop, while the Blue Refractors #'d/250 graded BGS 9.5/10 were going in the $450-$550 range, a Gold Refractor #'d/50 graded BGS 9.5/10 sold for $1,000, and an ungraded Orange Refractor #'d/25 sold for $900.

---

[79] www.cardboardconnection.com/hottest-cards-in-2012-bowman-baseball

At this point, these cards look like a decent value:

1. Darvish looks every bit like he's going to be an ace in this league.

2. This is Darvish's first Bowman Chrome auto, and cannot be trumped by another Bowman Chrome auto.

3. There are likely fewer than 500 total of the 2012 Bowman Chrome Yu Darvish RC autos with the card number 209 on the back.

4. Graded base autos are trading for about half of ungraded book value.

5. At $350 for the base auto in BGS 9.5/10 condition, it is roughly double the price of a 2007 Bowman Chrome Prospects Tim Lincecum auto similarly graded BGS 9.5/10; which sounds reasonable when you consider that there are about ten times as many such Lincecum base autos (for reference, as of December 2013 there were 418 Lincecum base autos in the Beckett population report, including 263 BGS 9.5s and 14 BGS 10 Pristines; in contrast, there were only 35 such Darvish autos in the population report, including 28 BGS 9.5s and 1 BGS 10 Pristine).

Right?

But there are a couple of other crucial elements not yet accounted for. One is that Beckett pricings are reactive to market conditions, and are not predictive by nature. And the other is that *Topps does not care what you, me, or anyone else paid for its cards on the secondary market.*

On October 17, 2012, the 2012 Bowman Chrome issue was released. In addition to the Bowman Chrome Prospects autos, the set included four Rookie Autographs not previously announced on the pre-release sell sheet or checklist: Yu Darvish, Bryce Harper, Will Middlebrooks, and Trevor Bauer. These cards were included as redemptions, and were similarly short-printed, with no regular refractors, but Blue Refractors, Gold Refractors #'d/50, Orange Refractors #'d/25, Purple Refractors #'d/10, Red Refractors #'d/5, and a 1/1 Superfractor.

The new 2012 Bowman Chrome Yu Darvish RC autos have the number RA-YD on the back, but have the same RC logo as the one issued in the 2012 Bowman release. When the Blue Refractor redemptions came back the following spring, they turned out to be #'d/99, meaning that once you factor all of the refractor parallels, the RA-YD Bowman Chrome Yu Darvish RC autos may be even rarer than the original one.

Upon release, the base auto redemptions were trading in roughly the $100-$120 range.

It gets worse. On November 28, 2012, the 2012 Bowman Draft set hit the market, including Bowman Chrome Draft RC autos of Darvish and Harper. This was not a surprise, as the sell sheet for the Bowman Draft set included an image of a Yu Darvish Blue Refractor auto, as well as a Bryce Harper Gold Refractor auto. However, neither of those cards exist; not only were the images used for the actual cards different from the images in the sell sheet, but there were no refractor, blue refractor, or gold refractor variations of the Bowman Chrome Draft base autos. Instead, only the base autos, Orange Refractors #'d/25, Purple Refractors #'d/10, Red Refractors #'d/5, and Superfractor 1/1 were issued.

Moreover, pack odds from the 2012 Bowman Draft Hobby and Jumbo boxes (no Retail boxes were issued) suggest that from the 2012 Bowman Chrome Draft Rookie Autographs set – including only Darvish and Harper – only 254 base autos (give or take) were inserted into packs. Meanwhile, early eBay sales suggest that the Darvish autos (inserted as redemptions) outnumbered the Harper autos (actual card inserted in packs) by perhaps a 3:1 or 4:1 ratio, pegging the print run of base Darvish autos at around 150-200. But including the #'d refractors, this puts the entire run of 2012 Bowman Chrome Draft Yu Darvish RC autos at only about 200-250, making *these* Darvish autos the rarest of the bunch.

And upon release of 2012 Bowman Draft, these base auto redemptions traded in the $75-$125 range.

And so, while Topps could not go back and print more of the #209 Bowman Chrome Yu Darvish autos released in 2012 Bowman boxes, Topps does in fact have a method of capturing excess secondary market value by virtue of its ability to print more Bowman Chrome RC autos by using its Bowman Chrome and Bowman Draft releases.

And while the original #209 Bowman Chrome RC auto has not been trumped, it apparently has been equaled: By the end of 2013, Beckett.com has all three 2012 Bowman Chrome Yu Darvish RC autos – the 2012 Bowman Chrome #209, 2012 Bowman Chrome #RA-YD, and 2012 Bowman Chrome Draft #RA-YD – listed with equal $200 ungraded valuations. And while market trades as of late 2013 suggest that the original #209 autos still carry a premium over the others in the minds of collectors, there is evidence to suggest that, in the long run, nobody will remember which Bowman Chrome Darvish auto came first.

2011 Bowman Chrome Prospects Bryce Harper BCP1

There are many examples of players who have had their 1st Bowman Chrome card released in Bowman, and then either had an RC released in Bowman Chrome or Bowman Chrome Draft later in the same year, or had a lesser recognized – and lesser valued – chrome prospect card released in Bowman Chrome Draft. What makes the Yu Darvish 2012 Bowman Chrome/Draft autos unique is that he has three Bowman Chrome autos released in three different sets, and all are in the books as being equivalent RCs with equivalent value (actually, technically none are official RCs in the Beckett book, as the original is technically a parallel of the base Bowman RC, and the other two are technically insert autos by Beckett's definition).

But Darvish was not the first player to have a key card released in Bowman in the spring, only to have its value gutted by an equivalent card produced in the Bowman Chrome release in the fall.

The 2011 Bowman release included Bryce Harper's first Bowman Chrome card in a Washington Nationals uniform. The card – #'d BCP1 in the Bowman Chrome Prospects set – was in the books that summer (as of the November 2011 issue of Beckett Baseball magazine) at $25, with the Gold Refractor #'d/50 at $900.

Later that fall, Harper had another Bowman Chrome Prospects card – #'d BCP111 in the Bowman Chrome Prospects set – included in the 2011 Bowman Chrome release.

By the end of the winter, it was clear that the market viewed these two cards as having equivalent value: The April 2012 issue of Beckett Baseball magazine pegged the ungraded value of both versions at only $10 a pop. Meanwhile, by the end of the summer of 2012, graded BGS 9.5 copies of both cards could be had for about $20 a pop, even as Harper put together a historic age-19 season and NL ROY campaign.

Both cards, incidentally, rank among the most graded cards in the Bowman Chrome Era, with over 1,800 BCP1s and over 1,000 BCP111s in Beckett's population report as of December 2013.

Is this an example of a prospect bubble bursting? Likely. But it is also an example of Topps trying to print money in 2011 Bowman Chrome, to the detriment of anybody who had purchased 2011 Bowman.

There is also another important point to be made, and it is that these were not Harper's 1st Bowman Chrome Cards – that card was his 2010 Bowman Chrome 18U USA Baseball card. So in effect, the market simply views these cards as equivalent Bowman Chrome Prospects cards appearing in the same year, much the same way as Bryce Harper has equivalent 2012 Bowman Chrome and 2012 Bowman Chrome Draft RCs – both of which are more highly valued than his 2012 Bowman Chrome Prospects card (yet another!) released in 2012 Bowman.

The Reverse Screw: The 2012 Bowman Chrome Draft Bryce Harper RC Auto

In addition to the Darvish autos, the 2012 Bowman Chrome set released in mid-October 2012 included the short-printed 2012 Bowman Chrome Bryce Harper RC autos. These autos – #'d RA-BH on the back – were inserted into packs as redemptions. And over the next couple of months, the short-printed base auto redemptions traded in roughly the $130-$160 range, with the Blue Refractor redemptions thought to be #'d/250 trading in about the $225-$275 range, the Gold Refractor redemptions #'d/50 in about the $450-$550 range, the Orange Refractors #'d/25 in about the $600-$700 range, and the Purple Refractors #'d/10 roughly in the $800-$1,000 range. All five Red Refractor #'d/5 redemptions sold between November 11 and December 15, with prices ranging from $1,699 to $3,000.

In late November, the 2012 Bowman Draft set was released, including the Rookie Autographs of only two players: Bryce Harper and Yu Darvish. Though the Darvish autos were inserted into packs as redemptions, the Harper autos were live and inserted directly into packs.

As noted earlier, that the Harper and Darvish autos were included in Bowman Draft was not a surprise, as the pre-release sell sheet shows images of a Bryce Harper gold refractor auto and a Yu Darvish blue refractor auto. What was a surprise, however, was just how rare these autos were – especially the Bryce Harper autos.

Despite the images on the sell sheet, there were no blue refractors or gold refractors autos of either player inserted into packs. The only refractor variations were Orange Refractors #'d/25, Purple Refractors #'d/10, Red Refractors #'d/5, and Superfractors 1/1, for a total of 41 refractor autos per player.

The base autos were also rare as a group. The table below shows the stated insertion rates of the Rookie Autographs in Bowman Draft Jumbo and Hobby packs, as well as the distribution between Jumbo and Hobby for the base autos and each parallel. Note that there are only two players in the Rookie Autographs set for Bowman Chrome Draft; as such, the two players have a combined print run of two Superfractors, 10 Red Refractors #'d/5, etc. Aside from the Superfractor odds – which look fairly precise – the other stated odds appear to be rounded approximations. Consequently, the distributions may also be approximations, and in some cases do not quite add up to total actual print run (another possibility is that some cards were held back by Topps as replacements for damaged cards).

2012 Bowman Chrome Draft Rookie Autographs: Odds and Distribution

	Combined Print Run	Jumbo Pack Odds	Hobby Pack Odds	Jumbo Distribution	Hobby Distribution	Total Pack Distribution
Superfractor	2	1:75,816	1:1,251,840	1	1	2
Red Refractor	10	1:25,000	1:178,000	3	7	10
Purple Refractor	20	1:15,000	1:90,000	5	14	19
Orange Refractor	50	1:6,000	1:36,000	13	35	48
Base Auto	?	1:1,125	1:6,700	67	187	254
Total				89	244	333

*Pack odds are as stated on Jumbo and Hobby pack wrappers; distributions are approximate

The key figure is that between Harper and Darvish, there were only 254 base autos combined, give or take a dozen or so. But as it turned out, it appeared that the Harper base auto was significantly rarer than the Darvish one.

In the first week after release, only one Harper base auto went up for auction on eBay, but that auction quickly ended without a recognized sale, likely indicating that the card was sold off site. But over the next three months, 2012 Bowman Chrome Draft Darvish base auto sales outnumbered those of the Harper autos by 33-8 on eBay, suggesting that the Darvish base autos might outnumber the Harper base autos by a 4:1 ratio.

What this means is that there might only be 50-60 2012 Bowman Chrome Draft Bryce Harper RC base autos, and possibly *fewer than 100* **total** including the refractors. This would make the 2012 Bowman Chrome Draft Bryce Harper RC auto the rarest of all of Harper's chrome autos.

The market reflected this. According to data from Terapeak.com, of those eight sales on eBay through the end of February 2013, one went for $285, while the other seven sold between $299.99 and $300.50 (actually six of them sold between $299.99 and $300.00 a piece, making the $300.50 sale an outlier, relatively speaking) – or double the price of the equivalent Bowman Chrome base auto redemptions. This is despite the fact that Harper's autos from this set were notoriously streaky – the vast majority of the autos from this set would receive a BGS Auto grade of 9 or less.

Meanwhile, the 2012 Bowman Chrome Draft Bryce Harper RC auto went into the books at $400 on Beckett.com.

The Return of the 2012 Bowman Chrome Redemptions

Harper got off to a hot start in 2013, hitting .400/.442/.800 with 5 HRs and 10 RBIs over the first 10 games from April 1 through April 12. If he cooled off the rest of the month, it wasn't by much, as he finished the month of April hitting .340/.430/.720 with 9 HRs and 18 RBIs in 26 games.

By this point, the prices on the 2012 Bowman Chrome Draft refractor autos had multiplied. Between the late November 2012 release date and the end of December, two Orange Refractors #'d/25 sold for $600 and $650, while two Purple Refractors #'d/10 sold for $767 and $1,000. But in April 2013, an ungraded Orange Refractor #'d/25 sold for $1,200, while one graded BGS 9 Mint with a 9 Auto sold for $1,400, and another graded BGS 9.5 Gem Mint with a 9 Auto sold for $1,800. Meanwhile, a Purple Refractor #'d/10 graded BGS 9 Mint with an 8 Auto – in fact the one that had previously sold ungraded for $767 in December – sold for $2,000 on eBay.

Around the same time, an ungraded base auto sold for $329.99, while a copy graded BGS 9.5 Gem Mint with a 10 Auto sold for $499.99. As an aside, to give you an idea how rare the 10 Auto grade is for these Harper autos, of all of the Bowman Chrome Draft auto refractors that have been graded through December 2013 and the seven base autos graded through April 2013, only two had received a 10 Auto grade.

2012 Bowman Chrome Draft Bryce Harper RC Auto eBay Sales: April 2013

Card	Grade	Sale Price	Date
Purple Auto Refractor #/10	BGS 9/8	$2,000	4/22/13
Orange Auto Refractor #/25	BGS 9.5/9	$1,800	4/22/13
Orange Auto Refractor #/25	BGS 9/9	$1,400	4/20/13
Orange Auto Refractor #/25	Ungraded	$1,200	4/1/13
Base Auto	BGS 9.5/10	$499.99	4/1/13
Base Auto	Ungraded	$329.99	4/7/13

Source: Data from Terapeak.com

The April cutoff date for the Bowman Chrome Draft autos in the Beckett population report is relevant for a reason: Because on or just before April 15, 2013, the redemptions from the 2012 Bowman Chrome Bryce Harper RC autos began coming back from Topps, and immediately started hitting the market. Or more specifically, the base autos, the Blue Refractor autos which turned out to be #'d/99, and the Gold Refractors #'d/50 came back, while the Orange Refractors #'d/25, Purple Refractors #'d/10, and Red Refractors #'d/5 remained unaccounted for.

And here's the bomb: The cards that came back were *identical* to the Bowman Chrome Draft Bryce Harper RC autos.

That is, the base auto redemptions that had sold for $150 a pop in October were the exact same card as the base autos released in Bowman Draft that were going for $300 in January, with the same card number (RA-BH) and same photo. Meanwhile, the Blue Refractors #'d/99 and Gold Refractors #'d/50 were parallels of the same cards.

In other words, the base autos from both Bowman Chrome and Bowman Chrome Draft, the Blue and Gold Refractor autos from Bowman Chrome, and the Orange, Purple, Red, and Superfractor autos from Bowman Chrome Draft all made up one set.

This has a couple of major implications. For one, the base Bowman Chrome Draft RC autos are not nearly as rare as previously thought, and are identical in value to the Bowman Chrome RC autos that just came back from Topps – they are, after all, the same card, regardless of origin. For reference, by March, the Bowman Chrome base redemption cards were going in the $200-$230 range; by mid-late April, the now-live cards that came back from Topps were up in the $300 range, before retreating back towards $200 by early May. And after this point, whatever base autos that surfaced from Bowman Draft boxes were indistinguishable.

But this also means that – unless the Bowman Chrome Orange Refractors #'d/25, Purple Refractors #'d/10, and Red Refractors #'d/5 are an identical set also #'d/25, #'d/10, and #'d/5 (which would be a complete disaster for Topps and the entire industry) – then the Bowman Chrome Red #/5, Purple #/10, and Orange #/25 refractors are Harper's rarest Chrome autos, with a total combined print run of 41 including the 1/1 Superfractor.

As of December 2013, the Bowman Chrome Orange, Purple, and Red Refractor redemptions had yet to come back from Topps.

Sidebar: 2012 Bowman Chrome Draft Bryce Harper RC Auto Grades

We noted earlier than the 10 Auto grade on the 2012 Bowman Chrome Draft Bryce Harper autos was extremely rare. In fact, including all of the Bowman Chrome Draft refractor autos and the seven Bowman Chrome Draft base autos graded through April 2013, only two had come back with a 10 auto.

The table below shows the distribution of Auto grades among graded cards in the Beckett.com population report as of December 2013 for the refractors, and the six base autos graded through April 2013. Note that the colored, #'d refractors in the population report on Beckett.com are mistakenly split: Some are listed as being Bowman Chrome Draft Rookie Autographs, while some are listed as Bowman Chrome Rookie Autographs EXCH (for exchange, indicating acquired via redemption card). That said, we know that as of December 2013, the Red, Purple, and Orange redemptions hadn't come back yet, so all of the refractors in the population report through December 2013 are from Bowman Chrome Draft.

Meanwhile, the Bowman Chrome Draft base autos that appear in the population report after April 2013 are naturally suspect, as many of them are likely to have come from Bowman Chrome redemptions and mistakenly identified as being from Bowman Chrome Draft (though technically it makes little difference as they are the same card).

2012 Bowman Chrome Draft Bryce Harper RC Autos: Auto Grades

Card	8	9	10	Authentic	Total
Red #/5	–	2	–	1	3
Purple #/10	2	4	–	–	6
Orange Refractor #/25	4	8	–	1	13
Base	1	4	2	–	7
Total	7	18	2	2	29

Source: Beckett.com, Dec. 2013, adjusted

Conclusions: The Impact on Card Value and Box Value

This is a constantly changing game. And going forward, it is important to be able to understand how and why the game changes, as well as how these changes affect card values and box values.

Through 2013, the industry – and particularly the Bowman Chrome family of lines – appeared to be growing, and quite rapidly so. While growing supply is never a good thing for card values, it is not necessarily bad, so long as collector demand is rising along with it. That said, regardless of any arguments regarding the state or potential state of collector demand, we've seen that growth in supply creates a number of logistics-related challenges for the card manufacturers regarding base set production, inserts, #'d refractors, and autos.

But what does this mean?

The Auto and the Decline of Box Value

We know that there are two basic ways a company can grow supply: It can add new product lines, or expand existing ones. The advantage of adding new product lines is that it allows the manufacturer to keep print runs down for each given product, preserving secondary market value on some level; the disadvantage is that as a manufacturer continues to add more and more new product lines, each product starts to lose brand identity.

The identity issue is not a problem for the Bowman Chrome family of products – namely Bowman, Bowman Chrome, and Bowman Draft, which deliver the most desired chrome prospect autos year in, and year out. Instead, what we've seen is a growing fixation of the market on the three Bowman Chrome lines, resulting in incredible growth.

That said, we also know that when a company expands production of an existing product line but maintains a fixed auto insertion rate, this means that more autos need to be produced as well. Meanwhile, there are two ways a company can expand the supply of autos: It can print and include more autos per player, or it can add more players and expand the auto checklist.

And herein lies the quandary: If Topps were to expand the auto print run per player, it would run the risk of damaging secondary market values, which could collapse the whole system.

Instead, what we've seen is that Topps has wisely chosen to maintain auto print run sizes in its Bowman Chrome product lines in order to maintain secondary market values for its new prospect pool every year. However, in doing so, Topps has chosen to sacrifice box value by virtue of expanding the auto checklist.

As we noted earlier, the auto checklist between Bowman Chrome and Bowman Draft alone nearly tripled between 2005 and 2013; meanwhile, the 2013 Bowman release included 42 more prospects, for a total of 146 Bowman Chrome prospect autos in 2013, compared to just 38 cherry-picked prospects in 2005. Unfortunately, these new additions are not proportional in quality. And as a result, the auto checklists have become increasingly more common in nature, while making key players harder to hit.

This necessarily weakens box value, as for many collectors, it is devastating to spend $60 or $70 on a box to consistently wind up with a $5 auto. Meanwhile, it is even more devastating for an enterprising individual to spend $1,000 on an 8-box case of 2013 Bowman Jumbo with 24 autos hoping to hit at least one of four or five key players, and instead hit none of them and wind up with the autos of a few decent prospects and 21 present or future commons.

This makes it much more attractive for collectors to buy singles on the secondary market rather than bother opening boxes. And ultimately, unless Topps provides more value by other means (as noted earlier, Topps has announced its intention to now include *two* autos per Bowman Chrome Hobby box and *five* autos per Bowman Chrome Jumbo box in 2014), there is a very strong possibility that we will either see a pullback in box demand and thus supply (a good thing) – and thus a smaller auto checklist in turn – or that we are otherwise facing a permanent loss of box value.

The #'d Refractor and Multiple Compression

The other trend that we noted was that as production and thus supply of the Bowman Chrome lines have grown, Topps has continually responded by adding more and more high-end refractors to the lineup. In 2012, the top of the color lineup across all Bowman Chrome lines for non-autos was Superfractor 1/1, Red Refractor #/5, Orange Refractor #/25, Gold Refractor #/50. In 2013 Bowman Chrome, the non-auto color lineup was Superfractor 1/1, Red Refractor #/5, Yellow Refractor #/10, Black Refractor #/15, Orange Refractor #/25, Magenta Refractor #/35, Gold Refractor #/50. And in 2013 Bowman Chrome Draft, the non-auto color lineup was Superfractor 1/1, Red Refractor #/5, Orange Refractor #/25, Red Wave Refractor #/25, Silver Wave Refractor #/25, Black Refractor #/35, Gold Refractor #/50, Green Refractor #/75, and Blue Refractor #/99.

Well we know that Topps can't print money. What I mean is, it is not reasonable to expect that Topps can simply keep adding more and more high-end refractors without affecting valuations.

That said, there are two basic arguments we can make about valuation:

1. **The Gold Refractor Standard.** That is, a 2013 Gold Refractor #'d/50 = a 2012 Gold Refractor #'d/50, or

2. **Distance from the Top.** In 2012, there were 31 refractors higher than a Gold Refractor #'d/50, while in 2013 Bowman Chrome, there were 91 refractors higher up in the hierarchy than the Gold Refractors #'d/50, and in 2013 Bowman Chrome Draft there were 116 rarer refractors.

The Gold Refractor Standard argument is essentially that: (1) a 2013 Bowman Chrome Bryce Harper RC Gold Refractor #'d/50 would be equal in value to the 2012 Bowman Chrome Bryce Harper RC Gold Refractor #'d/50 he actually has, and (2) all other refractors should be evaluated relative to the value of the Gold Refractor #'d/50. In contrast, the "Distance from the Top" argument is that we start with the value of the 1/1 Superfractor, and the further away from the top the card is, the less it is worth; consequently, the Gold Refractors #'d/50 in 2013 Bowman Chrome and Bowman Chrome Draft are worth less than a Gold Refractor #'d/50 in 2012.

Both arguments are quite valid, though one (the Gold Refractor Standard argument) is easier to poke holes in than the other. That said, it turns out that these arguments are not mutually exclusive, and in fact are quite compatible with each other.

Recall from our discussion on the value of #/25s vs. #/50s in Part III: RC-Prospect Structures (2006-Present) that any time you add a rarer refractor such as a #/10 or a #/15, you are creating extra pricing pressure on the #/25s. What this means is that the value of an Orange Refractor #'d/25 compared to a Gold Refractor #'d/50 is potentially greater when there is no #/10 or #/15 than it is once you insert the #/10 or #/15 refractors.

Consequently, whenever you add more higher-end refractors, the result is multiple compression.

First, let's talk about the Gold Refractor Standard argument. The table below lists some of the top RC-logo players from 2011, 2012, and 2013 Bowman Chrome releases (i.e. excluding Bowman, and excluding Bowman Chrome Draft), including their base RC and Gold Refractor #/50 ungraded book values. Just sampling these players, Beckett's view of the market seems to support the idea of a Gold Standard.

Notable Bowman Chrome RC Base-Gold Multiples: 2011-2013

Player/Card	Base	Gold #/50	Multiple
2011 Bowman Chrome Mike Trout RC	$30	$250	8.3x
2011 Bowman Chrome Freddie Freeman RC	$4	$30	7.5x
2011 Bowman Chrome Dustin Ackley RC	$4	$30	7.5x
2012 Bowman Chrome Bryce Harper RC	$8	$150	18.9x
2012 Bowman Chrome Yu Darvish RC	$6	$60	10.0x
2012 Bowman Chrome Yoenis Cespedes RC	$3	$50	16.7x
2013 Bowman Chrome Yasiel Puig RC	$8	$200	25.0x
2013 Bowman Chrome Manny Machado RC	$6	$80	13.3x
2013 Bowman Chrome Jose Fernandez RC	$5	$50	10.0x
2013 Bowman Chrome Wil Myers RC	$4	$50	12.5x
2013 Bowman Chrome Michael Wacha RC	$5	$40	8.0x

Source: Beckett.com, Dec. 2013

There are plenty of mitigating factors to consider – chiefly, that Trout's 2011 Bowman Chrome RC is his first Bowman Chrome non-auto, protecting base card value (perhaps explaining the relatively small multiple; either that, or the Gold Refractor is undervalued); that Harper's Bowman Chrome RC is his 5th Bowman Chrome non-auto; that Yasiel Puig's Bowman Chrome RC is his first Bowman Chrome card, not counting the mini-refractors released in 2013 Bowman boxes; that Puig's base card value was downgraded in December 2013, and that the Gold Refractor value had yet to follow in the books (meaning that the multiple is potentially overstated as of December 2013); and that the print run in 2013 was significantly higher than in previous years, which could result in a higher spread between Gold #/50 and base card values.

But at the very least, there is not yet enough to disprove the Gold Refractor Standard.

Now let's take a look at the spreads between the Gold Refractors #'d/50 and the Magenta Refractors #'d/35 and Orange Refractors #'d/25 in 2013 Bowman Chrome. Prior to 2013 Bowman Chrome, Beckett previously considered anything rarer than the Gold Refractors #'d/50 to be too rare to price, but apparently with the influx of new rare refractors comes more data points.

2013 Bowman Chrome Notable RCs: Gold #/50, Magenta #/35, Orange #/25

Player/Card	Gold #/50	Magenta #/35	Orange #/25	Orange-Gold Multiple
2013 Bowman Chrome Yasiel Puig RC	$200	$120	$300	1.5x
2013 Bowman Chrome Manny Machado RC	$80	$80	$100	1.3x
2013 Bowman Chrome Jose Fernandez RC	$50	$50	$60	1.2x
2013 Bowman Chrome Wil Myers RC	$50	$50	$60	1.2x
2013 Bowman Chrome Michael Wacha RC	$40	$50	$50	1.3x
2013 Bowman Chrome Mike Zunino RC	$40	$40	$50	1.3x
2013 Bowman Chrome Jurickson Profar RC	$20	$25	$25	1.3x
2013 Bowman Chrome Gerrit Cole RC	$20	$50	$60	3.0x

Source: Beckett.com, December 2013

Aside from the one price guide anomaly (Cole), what we're seeing in Beckett's view of the market is a remarkably small spread between the values of the Gold #/50, Magenta #/35, and Orange #/25 refractors. For most of the players on the list, the Orange Refractors #'d/25 are basically worth a relatively small 17%-25% premium over the Gold Refractors #'d/50, while the Magenta Refractors #'d/35 are variously listed as being equivalent to either the Gold or the Orange.

The Puig cards are in general due for a downgrade (the base RC is down to $8 as of December 2013, compared to its initial $12 valuation), so either: (a) the Magenta #/35 value is the most accurate; (b) the market just doesn't like the Magenta Puig card in particular; or (c) it is a pricing error. That said, we know that higher value players tend to warrant higher multiples, which explains the comparatively high 1.5x multiple or 50% premium in the value of Puig's Orange Refractor #'d/25 vs. the Gold Refractor #'d/50.

The Impact of Multiple Chrome Risk

As we saw with the examples of the 2012 Bowman Chrome Yu Darvish RC auto #209 and 2011 Bowman Chrome Prospects Bryce Harper BCP1, Topps' practice of producing multiple equivalent Bowman Chrome cards in the same year creates risk on the secondary markets, which ultimately will impact initial box value. If there is a card issued in the spring Bowman release that you want, but you are concerned that Topps can produce an identically-valued – and thus value-destructing – card later in Bowman Chrome and/or Bowman Draft, then you are less likely to pay up in the spring time. This risk ultimately will drive down secondary values of certain cards issued in the spring Bowman release, which will hurt case breakers, and then drive down pre-order demand, and eventually bring supply down.

In fact, Topps did it again in 2013, releasing Bowman Chrome Jurickson Profar RC autos in both Bowman and Bowman Chrome, with different photos but identically numbered RA-JP.

The 2012 Bowman Chrome Draft Bryce Harper RC auto is another story. Collectors take risks based on certain implicit assumptions, one key one being that you can't put the same card in two different sets without informing the collector that you're doing so. And when a manufacturer includes the same card in different sets when the implication is that they are a different card – or, worse, includes an actual picture of a different card in a pre-release sell sheet, as Topps did – it creates a lot of risk on the secondary market, as well as a general lack of trust that the manufacturer will not screw the collector.

This is the kind of practice that could destroy the industry.

The fact is, this a completely unregulated industry. There are no rules – only the competing interests of all of the players in the game, up and down the supply chain from the manufacturer down to the collector. That said, it's probably too much to assume that manufacturers are on the side of the collector; however, for the sake of the industry as a going concern, the one thing for certain is that the manufacturer should not be playing against the collector, either.

Part VII: Grade Scarcity, Card Removal, and the BGS Grading System

Grading systems, the card removal effect, and related topics further examined.

A casual collector can go quite far in this game without being an expert grader, and without really needing to understand all of the nuances of the BGS or PSA grading systems. Unless you are planning on having cards graded yourself, all you really need to know about the grading systems from a collector/investor standpoint is that a card graded BGS 9.5 or PSA 10 is in Gem Mint condition, and a card graded BGS 10 Pristine card is in BGS 10 Pristine condition.

That said, the ability to acquire ungraded cards and build gems yourself opens up additional opportunities to gain value. And in order to do that, you should have a good understanding of how the grading systems work.

Here in Part VII, we'll begin by discussing how the BGS grading system works, and compare the BGS grade definitions to those of PSA. Understanding the grading systems will allow us to tackle a few other key topics in greater depth – namely grade scarcity and the card removal effect – before we are ready to discuss building gems next in Part VIII.

The BGS Grading System

As we've discussed, the BGS grade scale is a 10-pt. grading scale in half-point increments. The final score – BGS 10 Pristine, BGS 9.5 Gem Mint, BGS 9 Mint, BGS 8.5 NM-MT+, etc. – is a composite of four subgrades, which are also on a 10-pt. scale in half-point increments:

1. Centering

2. Corners

3. Edges

4. Surface

When centering or corners are the lowest subgrade, a card's final score cannot be more than 0.5 points above the lowest subgrade (i.e. a card with 8.5 centering or 8.5 corners cannot grade above BGS 9 Mint). When edges or surface are the lowest subgrade, a card may grade up to a full point above the lowest subgrade (i.e. a card with an 8.5 edges or 8.5 surface grade may grade BGS 9.5 Gem Mint if the other three subgrades are all 10s, but a card with 7 edges or 7 surface cannot grade above BGS 8 NM-MT).

Autographed cards have a fifth, separate grade for the quality of the auto, which is a whole-point scale that only runs from 5 to 10, and is not factored into the final score of the main card.

Minimum Subgrade Requirements: BGS 10 Pristine and BGS 9.5 Gem Mint

In order for a card to be graded BGS 10 Pristine, it must have either three 10 subgrades and one 9.5 subgrade, or all 10 subgrades (which is quite rare).

In order for a card to be graded BGS 9.5 Gem Mint, a card needs to have minimum subgrades consisting of either:

1. Three 9.5 subgrades and one 9 subgrade, or

2. Three 10 subgrades and one 8.5 subgrade (if the 8.5 subgrade is edges or surface).

Essentially, a minimum requirement of three 9.5 subgrades and one 9 subgrade means that a card needs to be generally perfect in at least three dimensions with an allowance of one minor blemish, whether the card is slightly off-center; *or* shows light corner wear in one corner (or maybe negligible wear in two); *or* may have a light surface scratch or other light surface blemish; *or* a slightly rough edge.

Cards with three 10 subgrades and one 8.5 subgrade are relatively rare, though if you grade enough cards you will see more than a handful. Probably the most likely scenario for a card to have three 10s and an 8.5 is for the surface grade to be the 8.5, if only because the surface is the easiest for the novice grader to overlook, and also because surface issues are more common in modern chromes.

Centering

Generally speaking, the main focus of the centering grade is on the front of the card rather than the back. According to Beckett.com, Beckett defines 10 centering as perfect 50/50 centering on the front, with 60/40 or better centering on the back. A 9.5 centering score is 50/50 centering one way (i.e. vertical or horizontal orientation) and 55/45 the other way on the front, and with 60/40 or better centering on the back. Meanwhile, 9 centering is defined as 55/45 centering both ways on the front, and 70/30 centering or better on the back.

To the naked eye, the difference between 9.5 and 10 centering is pretty slight. On the other hand, a card with 9 centering is generally noticeably off-center such that you know that the card is off-center, but not hideously so. Some cards that get 8.5 centering might be 9s on another day, but there should be little dispute about cards that grade worse than that.

Corners

Beckett defines 10 corners as "perfect to the naked eye and Mint under magnification," while 9.5 corners are perfect to the naked eye, but may have slight imperfections under magnification. 9 corners are "Mint under close inspection," but with a "speck of wear" allowed under close scrutiny.

BGS is fairly consistent with corner grades, and you should be able to spot a 9 pretty easily, at least on paper cards with dark borders, or chromes with dark borders on the back. Chrome cards generally are going to look pretty sharp on the front, but if you have a graded card with 9 corners, you should be able to flip the card over and identify the 9 corner, as you are likely to see a little bit of white on a dark border. In some cases, you might see a card with extremely light wear on two corners get graded a 9, but generally any more than that and you are probably looking at something less than 9 corners.

Edges

As with corners, Beckett defines 10 edges as "perfect to the naked eye and Mint under magnification," with 9.5 edges defined as being "virtually Mint" to the naked eye, but with a "speck of wear" allowed under intense scrutiny. A 9 edge is also essentially Mint to the naked eye, but with minor chipping allowed.

For the most part, 9 edges are going to be fairly subtle, while anything noticeably wrong is likely to be something less than a 9 edge.

Surface

The surface grade is the trickiest subject, though it becomes easier to figure out once you know what to look for. Let's start with Beckett's grade definitions:

- **10:** No print spots. Flawless color, devoid of registration or focus imperfections. Perfect gloss, devoid of scratches and metallic print lines.

- **9.5:** A few extremely minor print spots, detectable only under intense scrutiny. Deep color, devoid of registration or focus imperfections. Perfect gloss, devoid of scratches and metallic print lines.

- **9:** A handful of printing specks or one minor spot. Very minor focus or color imperfections. Clean gloss with one or two tiny scratches barely noticeable to the naked eye. One faint, unobtrusive metallic print line is allowed.

Much like cards from as recent as the 1980s were prone to wax or gum stains, modern chrome cards are prone to surface scratches. Chrome cards may pick up scratches or stains from being handled, but it is unfortunately quite common for cards to come with scratches or print lines straight out of the pack. In any case, surface scratches can be devastating to a card's overall grade.

One of the challenges of buying ungraded cards over the Internet is that surface scratches generally do not show up in pictures – even high-quality scans. In fact, surface scratches can be hard to detect even when holding a graded card in its slabbing.

Moreover, a person with an untrained eye can look at a scratch and not know that it's a scratch.

The key is to know what to look for. And generally, what you are looking for are lines that look like somebody slashed the card with a box cutter, or a rash of scratches, or sometimes stains that cannot simply be wiped away. While it is generally recommended that you look at a card with a magnifying glass, you should be able to see these things simply by looking at the card at an angle under a light.

One or two short, light lines might grade a 9, but you are generally out of luck with deeper or longer lines, or with multiple lines. With an 8.5 surface grade, you need each of the other three subgrades to be 10s in order to get a BGS 9.5 Gem Mint grade. While not impossible, that is no small order.

Fingerprints are also a concern with modern chrome cards, though these can generally be wiped away with a microfiber cloth.

Autos

Autographs are graded on a 10-pt. scale in whole-pt. increments from 5 to 10. The vast majority of autographs are generally 10s and 9s. 8s are less common though not rare, while worse grades are not terribly common and are generally horrible examples.

Beckett defines its Auto grades as follows:

- **10:** A beautiful, boldly signed autograph that appears nearly perfect to the naked eye. Under normal viewing, it looks like an aesthetically-pleasing autograph.

- **9:** This is a signature that is also very pleasing, but has slight imperfections that barely detract from the autograph. Very light bubbling or micro scratching is allowable, but no yellowing, fading, or smearing. Positioning should be nearly perfect - with just the very tips of a letter or two cut off or hidden.

- **8:** At this level, some flaws begin to stand out slightly. Signature is still solid and pleasing, but might be somewhat bubbled throughout, or have areas of minor scuffing/scratching that detracts from the aesthetic beauty of the signature. Only lightly visible yellowing or fading or smearing is allowed. A cut signature may only have 10% of the signature hidden (or missing, when referring to a sticker autograph). Only a very small tip of the signature may run off or bleed onto the edge.

A 10 is essentially a perfectly bold, clear auto, with the score having nothing to do with style. A 9 auto grade simply means that there is something wrong with it – the auto might be streaky, or the player's signature might run off the card. An 8 is unusually bad.

The difference in value between a 10 and a 9 auto is substantial, with a BGS 9.5 Gem Mint card with a 9 Autograph grade often similarly valued as a BGS 9 Mint card with a 10 Autograph grade; in fact, depending on who you ask, some collectors value a BGS 9 Mint with a 10 Auto *more* than a BGS 9.5 Gem Mint with a 9 Auto. For that reason, it is not uncommon for collectors to send cards with poor autographs to PSA instead of BGS, as PSA neither has a separate Auto grade, nor factors the quality of the auto into its final score.

As an example, the 2012 Bowman Chrome and Bowman Chrome Draft Bryce Harper RC autos are notorious for having poor autographs, the vast majority of which have graded 9 or worse; meanwhile, there are several PSA 10 copies of the card with autographs that would obviously grade 9 or worse had they been submitted to BGS.

And so, in the same way that PSA 10 Gem Mint copies of cards from the 1980s sometimes trade at a meaningful premium to BGS 9.5 Gem Mint copies of the same cards, BGS 9.5 Gem Mint cards with 10 Autos sometimes trade at a meaningful premium to PSA 10 copies of the same cards.

Comparing BGS and PSA Grading Definitions

Let's compare the BGS definitions for BGS 9.5 Gem Mint and BGS 9 Mint to PSA's definitions for their PSA 10 Gem Mint and PSA 9 Mint grades (termed GEM-MT 10 and MINT 9 by PSA):

– **PSA 10 Gem Mint:** A PSA Gem Mint 10 card is a virtually perfect card. Attributes include four perfectly sharp corners, sharp focus and full original gloss. A PSA Gem Mint 10 card must be free of staining of any kind, but an allowance may be made for a slight printing imperfection, if it doesn't impair the overall appeal of the card. The image must be centered on the card within a tolerance not to exceed approximately 55/45 to 60/40 percent on the front, and 75/25 percent on the reverse.

The two keys here are the "four perfectly sharp corners" and the tolerance for centering. While the BGS definition of BGS 9.5 Gem Mint allows for one slight blemish – whether the card is slightly off-center; *or* shows light corner wear; *or* has a light surface scratch or other light surface blemish; *or* a slightly rough edge – PSA is explicit that what would effectively be a 9 corner is not allowed.

On the other hand, the PSA 10 Gem Mint grade shows a higher tolerance for centering, with a tolerance of "approximately 55/45 to 60/40 percent on the front, and 75/25 percent on the reverse." In contrast, BGS' definition of 9 centering is "55/45 centering both ways on the front, and 70/30 centering or better on the back," while BGS' definition of 8 centering is "60/40 both ways or better on the front, 80/20 or better on the back."

It's not necessarily a matter of "right" or "wrong," but these differences in grading definitions do represent differences in grading philosophy. The PSA 10 Gem Mint grade seems to place a slightly greater emphasis on the physical card in not allowing the equivalent of 9 corners, but seemingly allowing the equivalent of 8.5 centering. In contrast, the BGS 9.5 Gem Mint grade places a slightly greater emphasis on the totality of the card, including centering.

– **PSA 9 Mint:** A PSA Mint 9 is a superb condition card that exhibits only one of the following minor flaws: a very slight wax stain on reverse, a minor printing imperfection or slightly off-white borders. Centering must be approximately 60/40 to 65/35 or better on the front and 90/10 or better on the reverse.

The PSA 9 Mint definition appears to allow for the equivalent of 9 corners, *or* 9 edges, *or* a 9 surface, while allowing for a tolerance for centering equivalent to

BGS 7 or 7.5 centering. The definition for BGS 7 Near Mint centering: "65/35 both ways or better on the front," and "90/10 or better" on the back.

Again, the PSA 9 Mint grade places a significantly greater emphasis on the physical card, while the BGS 9 Mint grade places a greater emphasis on the totality of the card including centering.

Here the line between PSA and BGS is quite blurred. By definition, some PSA 9s would grade BGS 9.5 – a card with three 9.5s but 9 corners would be BGS 9.5 Gem Mint but PSA 9 Mint due to the corner grade. On the other hand, due to the tolerance for centering, some PSA 9s might not grade BGS 8.5 NM-MT+ (a card with 7.5 centering and three 9.5 subgrades would be a BGS 8 NM-MT; when centering is the lowest subgrade, a card generally will not grade more than a half-point above the centering grade).

As we noted in Part I in our discussion of the 1993 SP Derek Jeter RC – a card notorious for chipping and weak corners, but apparently no centering issues – these discrepancies in definition are likely what has allowed only 12 out of nearly 11,000 PSA slabs to grade PSA 10 Gem Mint, while 139 out of nearly 11,000 BGS slabs have graded BGS 9.5 Gem Mint. On the other hand, the allowance for centering is likely what has allowed the PSA 10 Gem Mint grade to appear to be slightly easier than the BGS 9.5 Gem Mint grade on the 1993 Topps Derek Jeter RC.

Sidebar: A Note on Comparing BGS and PSA Gem Mint Frequencies

So far, we've used Gem Mint frequency – that is, the number of graded Gem Mint copies of a given card as a percentage of all copies of a given card that have been graded – to compare how tough the PSA 10 Gem Mint grade is on the 1993 SP Derek Jeter RC as compared to a BGS 9.5 Gem Mint grade on the same card, as well as for the 1993 Topps Derek Jeter RC.

Gem Mint Frequency = Graded Gem Mint Copies / Total Cards Slabbed

It should be noted that the comparison between BGS and PSA Gem Mint frequencies may not be valid on lower-value cards where a BGS 9 Mint grade or a BGS 8.5 NM-MT+ grade have little-to-negative value, particularly in more recent Bowman Chrome Era issues. This is because BGS has a "min-grade" or "no-grade" option (which PSA does not offer as of this writing) that is not advertised but is available to bulk graders, where for a small fee per card (typically $1 or $2, depending on the size of the order and desired turnaround time), BGS will review every card you submit, but only grade and slab – and thus charge a full grading fee (though typically higher than the normal grading fee) – the cards that meet the desired minimum grade (e.g. BGS 9.5 Gem Mint).[77]

Let's say, for example, you have 100 copies of a base card with an ungraded BV of $4, for which grading BGS 9 Mint would likely be value destructive. You submit your 100-card order with a desired min-grade of BGS 9.5; 50 of the cards come back graded BGS 9.5 Gem Mint, while the other 50 come back ungraded, having not met the minimum requirements for a BGS 9.5 Gem Mint grade.

What's happened is that instead of having 50% of this card grade BGS 9.5 Gem Mint, 100% of the cards that BGS *has slabbed* from your order have graded BGS 9.5 Gem Mint, thus skewing the BGS Gem Mint frequency as compared to PSA's.

---

[80] Technically, both BGS and PSA offer a "min-grade/no-grade" option on normal orders, but charge the full grading fee regardless. So if you're grading at $10 per card and declare that you don't want the card graded and slabbed unless the card meets the minimum requirements for BGS 9.5 or PSA 10, you will pay the full $10 regardless of whether the card meets the minimum requirements or not.

241

Grade Scarcity and Multiple Expansion

Grade scarcity deals with the scarcity of cards in a certain grade. For example, out of the more than 20,000 1993 SP Derek Jeter RCs graded and slabbed by BGS and PSA combined through early 2014, there are only 139 BGS 9.5 Gem Mint copies and 12 PSA 10 copies carrying book values of $2,000 and $28,000, respectively, compared to an ungraded book value of $150. There are zero BGS 10 Pristine copies of the card.

On the other hand, there are only five 1986-87 Fleer Michael Jordan RCs graded BGS 10 Pristine, the last which sold for $100,000 in a June 2011 Memory Lane Inc. auction.[81] In contrast, there are 332 BGS 9.5 copies of the card out of over 7,000 slabbed by BGS, which by the end of 2013 and early 2014 were generally running around $3,500-$4,500, but up to $7,000 with higher subgrades (a 10 and three 9.5 subgrades) and would run significantly higher with two 10s and two 9.5 subgrades. Meanwhile, only 180 of nearly 14,000 such cards graded by PSA have graded PSA 10 Gem Mint, and traded at prices hovering around $10,000.

Indeed, one of the main advantages that professional grading services provide is, in effect, certification that a given card in a given condition is in fact both authentic and in a certain condition, in a class above either lesser-graded or ungraded copies of the same card. And when high-grade copies of a given card are both rare and difficult to build, multiple expansion – the spread in value between high-graded and lesser-graded or ungraded cards – occurs.

In the modern BGS 9.5 Gem Mint+ game, there are two basic causes of grade scarcity:

1. Low print numbers
2. Condition sensitivity

Low Print Numbers

Low print numbers contribute to grade scarcity by limiting the number of potential high-grade cards. If there are only five Bowman Chrome Red Refractors #'d/5, then there physically cannot be more than five Bowman Chrome Red Refractors #'d/5 graded BGS 9.5 Gem Mint or BGS 10 Pristine.

This has extreme implications. Consider that when the last BGS 10 Pristine 1986-87 Fleer Michael Jordan sold for $100,000 at auction in June 2011, the population

---

[81] www.beckett.com/news/2011/06/perfect-michael-jordan-rookie-card-sells-for-100000

of BGS 10 Pristine cards was only three; nearly three years later, that number has risen to five. Whether the source of new BGS 10s came (and may continue to come) from PSA 10s; from BGS 9.5s receiving grade bumps through BGS' Graded Card Review;[82] or from the supply of unopened 1986-87 Fleer boxes which seem to have dried up, it may be a while before we can determine what the final number of BGS 10 Pristine 1986-87 Fleer Michael Jordan RCs is (though it's a safe bet that most centered PSA 10s and most BGS 9.5s with high sub-grades have been reviewed by BGS by 2014).

Condition Sensitivity

A card issue is generally considered to be **condition sensitive** when relatively few high-quality examples exist in comparison to the total print run, thus placing an extra premium in value on the highest quality examples. The 1993 SP Derek Jeter RC, for example, is not particularly rare, but is exceptionally condition sensitive.

While the term "condition sensitive" is generally reserved for issues which are exceptionally so, the concept of condition sensitivity applies to all issues to varying degrees.

Vintage (pre-1981) issues, for example, are held to a different standard than modern issues. In the Beckett price guides, the prices of vintage issues are listed in Near Mint (NM) condition, while cards in PSA 9 Mint condition carry large premiums even for issues through 1980; cards graded PSA 10 Gem Mint are so exceedingly rare and exceptionally valued that PSA does not include PSA 10 Gem Mint pricing for cards issued prior to 1973. PSAcard.com lists the value of a PSA 9 Mint 1952 Topps Mickey Mantle card (Population: 6) at $420,000, compared to a Beckett ungraded book value of $30,000. Meanwhile, Beckett lists the 1980 Topps Rickey Henderson RC with an ungraded value of $80, while PSAcard.com lists the value of a PSA 9 Mint copy (Pop: 1,385) at $325, and a PSA 10 Gem Mint copy (Pop: 11) at a whopping $9,000.

On the other hand, for cards issued from 1981 to present, ungraded prices are listed in NM-MT+ condition; PSA 9 and BGS 9 Mint grades are generally not worth a meaningful premium except for rare or higher-value cards over the long run, and PSA 10 and BGS 9.5 Gem Mint grades are standard investment grade. And so, in general terms, vintage issues can be said to be more condition sensitive than modern card issues.

---

[82] a service in which BGS will review already-graded cards for a fee to determine whether a card may justify a bump in grade, typically no more than a half-point bump in one of the four subgrades if at all

Why the different standards between vintage and modern issues? There are really two parts to the answer. The first part is that fewer Mint- or Gem Mint-quality examples have survived from vintage times when there were no widespread standards for storing and protecting cards, and many of the kids who collected them were still flipping cards and putting them in bicycle spokes. And the second part is that print numbers got so high by the 1980s that unopened boxes from the late-1980s in particular still remain in large quantities; and so, even if kids from the late 1980s and early 90s were to have destroyed cards by flipping them and putting them in bicycle spokes, there is still a supply of essentially brand new cards to replace them.

That said, in the modern BGS 9.5 Gem Mint+ game, there are many reasons why a particular issue may be exceptionally condition sensitive.

The 1985-1991 Donruss issues, for example, were printed on exceptionally thin stock; these cards are prone to bad corners out of the box, and cannot be expected to survive any amount of handling and still be gradable, as you run the risk of blunting a corner even just trying to stick the card in a sleeve. Topps issues from the 1980s through 1991 came with gum, and cards were prone to gum and wax stains when pulled from wax packs (Hint: Go for the rack packs).

If these sets were printed in smaller numbers and the biggest stars with RCs from this time period weren't predominantly steroid users, the probability is that Gem Mint+ graded cards from this time period would be exponentially more valuable than they are.

Centering is a universally major problem, even for cards issued in 2013. The vaunted 2012 Topps Chrome Football set unfortunately has major centering issues, while the Bowman Chrome and Topps Chrome brands in general have been anything but slam dunks when it comes to centering.

Though modern chrome cards generally benefit from sharp corners, they are subject to surface scratching, fingerprints, and surface stains. And some issues like 2012 Topps Five Star are printed on extra thick paper stock which can be prone to chipping, yielding exceptionally few BGS 9.5 Gem Mint grades.

It is because of these constant defects that graded, Gem Mint condition cards carry premiums even in modern issues.

Another source of condition sensitivity among modern chromes are autos, which are player dependent and sometimes issue dependent. While the 2011 Bowman

Chrome Prospects Bryce Harper autos are largely 10s, the 2012 Bowman Chrome and Bowman Chrome Draft Bryce Harper RC autos are notoriously streaky, with the vast majority of autos grading 9 or less. Thus, a 2012 Bowman Chrome or Bowman Chrome Draft Bryce Harper auto graded BGS 9.5 Gem Mint with a 10 auto is bound to trade at a significant premium – more than usual – over a BGS 9.5/9 or a PSA 10 copy for which there is no auto grade.

Other notable cards where 10 auto grades are unusually rare are the 2012 Bowman Chrome Prospects Oscar Taveras autos, and the 2012 Bowman Chrome Prospects Jonathan Singleton autos.

These are some of the more obvious examples of grade scarcity. Now let's take a look at a couple of more subtle examples.

The 1982 Fleer Cal Ripken, Jr. RC

The table below shows the ungraded and graded BGS 9.5 and PSA 10 Gem Mint book values for the 1982-year RCs of Baltimore Orioles Hall of Fame shortstop Cal Ripken, Jr. The 1982 Topps Traded Cal Ripken, Jr. is notable as Ripken's first solo Topps card – his 1982 Topps RC is shared with two other players of no real consequence (Bob Bonner and Jeff Schneider). While technically neither an RC nor XRC by the RC definitions of the day (the Topps Traded card came after 1982 Topps RC was issued), the 1982 Topps Traded card is Ripken's clear key card.

The ungraded and BGS 9.5 values are from Beckett.com, while the PSA 10 Gem Mint values are from PSAcard.com. Note again that PSA's prices are meant to reflect average dealer selling prices, rather than Beckett's "Hi" values.

See if you notice anything unusual.

1982 Cal Ripken RCs

Card	#	Ungraded BV	PSA 10 Gem Mint	Adj. Multiple	BGS 9.5 Gem Mint	Adj. Multiple
1982 Topps Traded Cal Ripken	98T	$120	$1,250	9.6x	$1,400	10.8x
1982 Topps Cal Ripken RC	21	$30	$515	12.9x	$500	12.5x
1982 Fleer Cal Ripken RC	176	$25	$500	14.3x	$700	20.0x
1982 Donruss Cal Ripken RC	405	$30	$240	6.0x	$300	7.5x

Sources: Beckett.com, PSAcard.com, January 2014

The discrepancies between the PSA and BGS values are neither here nor there, as they can be chalked up to differences in price guide methodology. What's most notable is that despite the fact that the 1982 Fleer Cal Ripken, Jr. RC has the lowest ungraded book value among the three official RCs, it carries easily the highest multiple using both PSA and BGS graded values, while its graded Gem Mint values are *more than double* that of the 1982 Donruss RC in both the PSA and BGS pricing.

Why? The most likely explanation is relative grade scarcity, as it turns out that PSA 10 and BGS 9.5 Gem Mint+ examples of the 1982 Fleer RC are actually quite rare compared to the other RCs. Checking the population reports from Beckett.com and PSAcard.com, there are only 185 combined PSA 10 Gem Mint and BGS 9.5 Gem Mint examples of the 1982 Fleer RC in existence as of January 2014, which is well less than half that of both the 1982 Topps RC and 1982 Donruss RC, and still considerably less than that of even the key 1982 Topps Traded card.

Cal Ripken, Jr. RC Gem Mint+ Population Report

Card	PSA 10 Gem Mint	BGS 9.5 Gem Mint	BGS 10 Pristine	Total
1982 Topps Traded	180	97	2	279
1982 Topps RC	301	173	1	475
1982 Fleer RC	160	25	0	185
1982 Donruss RC	338	119	6	463
Total	979	414	9	1,402

Sources: Beckett.com, PSAcard.com, January 2014

The next test is Gem Mint+ frequency. The table below compares the combined PSA 10, BGS 9.5, and BGS 10 populations for each card with the total PSA and BGS populations for each card. And though the 1982 Fleer RC is not particularly rare with combined PSA and BGS graded population just under 10,000 – not much lower than, and in the same general vicinity as the 1982 Donruss RC and 1982 Topps Traded card – it has a Gem Mint+ frequency less than half that of the 1982 Donruss card.

1982 Cal Ripken, Jr. RCs: Gem Mint+ Frequency

Card	Total PSA + BGS Gem Mint+	Total PSA + BGS Population	Gem Mint+ Percentage
1982 Topps Traded	279	12,245	2.3%
1982 Topps RC	475	31,319	1.5%
1982 Fleer RC	185	9,938	1.9%
1982 Donruss RC	463	11,640	4.0%
Total	1,402	65,142	2.2%

Source: Beckett.com, PSAcard.com, January 2014

Incidentally, the 1982 Topps RC has the lowest Gem Mint+ frequency, though this may be a function of simply having about three times as many cards submitted for grading as the other issues, and many lower quality copies among them.

The 1990 Bowman Sammy Sosa RC

The 1990 Sammy Sosa RCs present another interesting scenario, this one from a period of vast oversupply. Sosa's key card is generally his once-iconic 1990 Leaf RC, but his most valuable RCs are limited print parallels in the 1990 Bowman Tiffany RC with a print run of 3,000, and the 1990 Topps Tiffany RC with a print run of 15,000.

And yet, the card with the highest graded BGS 9.5 book value and *by far* the highest adjusted multiple is the regular 1990 Bowman RC, which in ungraded form is one of the more populous and lower value cards.

1990 Sammy Sosa RCs

Card	#	Ungraded BV	PSA 10	Adj. Multiple	BGS 9.5	Adj. Multiple
1990 Bowman Sammy Sosa RC	312	$3	–	–	$100	7.7x
1990 Bowman Tiffany Sammy Sosa RC	312	$20	$35	1.2x	$80	2.7x
1990 Leaf Sammy Sosa RC	220	$12	$30	1.4x	$40	1.8x
1990 Upper Deck Sammy Sosa RC	17	$3	–	–	$25	1.9x
1990 Topps Sammy Sosa RC	692	$2.50	–	–	$25	2.0x
1990 Topps Tiffany Sammy Sosa RC	692	$15	$40	1.6x	$50	2.0x
1990 Fleer Sammy Sosa RC	548	$2.50	–	–	$20	1.6x
1990 Donruss Sammy Sosa RC	489	$2.50	–	–	$25	2.0x
1990 Score Sammy Sosa RC	558	$2.50	–	–	$25	2.0x

Source: Beckett.com, January 2014

One possible explanation is grade scarcity. Among Sosa's 1990 RCs, the 1990 Bowman RC has by far the lowest population of PSA 10, BGS 9.5, and BGS 10 graded cards. With a combined Gem Mint+ population of 104, it is rarer than even the 1990 Bowman Tiffany, despite the fact that the Bowman Tiffany has a lower print run of only 3,000 copies.

1990 Sammy Sosa RCs: Gem Mint+ Populations

Card	PSA 10 Gem Mint	BGS 9.5 Gem Mint	BGS 10 Pristine	Total
1990 Bowman	84	20	0	104
1990 Bowman Tiffany	68	101	1	170
1990 Leaf	1,350	767	19	2,136
1990 Upper Deck	1,878	768	7	2,653
1990 Topps	764	115	2	881
1990 Topps Tiffany	116	91	6	213
1990 Fleer	1,515	246	4	1,765
1990 Donruss	975	636	6	1,617
1990 Score	177	38	0	215
Total	6,927	2,782	45	9,754

Source: Beckett.com, PSAcard.com, January 2014

That there are more Gem Mint+ 1990 Bowman Tiffany RCs than 1990 Bowman RCs is not in itself unusual, as your first thought should be that relatively few 1990 Bowman RCs were submitted for grading; by way of comparison, there are nearly twice as many 2011 Bowman Chrome Draft Mike Trout RCs (450) in the BGS population report as there are 2011 Bowman Draft Mike Trout RCs (249), which makes sense in that there is more value in the chrome variation and less value risk in having it graded and turn up BGS 9 Mint (or worse) rather than BGS 9.5.[83] However, this is not the case with the 1990 Bowman Sammy Sosa RC, as the total population of PSA and BGS graded cards is 4,956, or nearly triple that of the 1990 Bowman Tiffany, and is in fact higher than the total print run of the 1990 Bowman Tiffany, period.

Where the 1990 Bowman RC really stands out is Gem Mint+ Frequency, which at 2.1% is easily the lowest among all 1990 Sammy Sosa RCs. The only one even close is the less desirable 1990 Score RC.

---

[83] It also makes sense for another reason: Paper cards are more condition sensitive and thus far less likely to grade BGS 9.5 Gem Mint than chrome cards are. Moreover, the fact that Trout did not skyrocket in value until the summer of 2012 meant that many of Trout's Bowman Draft paper RCs were likely to be poorly handled upon the late 2011 release of 2011 Bowman Draft.

1990 Sammy Sosa RCs: Gem Mint+ Frequency

Card	Total PSA + BGS Gem Mint+	Total PSA + BGS Population	Gem Mint+ Percentage
1990 Bowman	104	4,956	2.1%
1990 Bowman Tiffany	170	1,684	10.1%
1990 Leaf	2,136	34,530	6.2%
1990 Upper Deck	2,653	27,848	9.5%
1990 Topps	881	15,864	5.6%
1990 Topps Tiffany	213	945	22.5%
1990 Fleer	1,765	12,208	14.5%
1990 Donruss	1,617	11,440	14.1%
1990 Score	215	7,308	2.9%
Total	9,754	116,783	8.4%

Source: Beckett.com, PSAcard.com, January 2014

But there is one other possible explanation for the outsized BGS 9.5 value of the 1990 Bowman RC, which is price guide variance. That is, there may evidence to suggest that the graded PSA 10/BGS 9.5 Gem Mint 1990 Bowman RC and 1990 Bowman Tiffany RCs are close in value, but perhaps not enough to suggest that the 1990 Bowman RC is worth a premium.

In 2013, Terapeak.com recorded a half a dozen sales of PSA 10 Gem Mint 1990 Bowman Tiffany Sammy Sosa RCs in roughly the $45-$55 range including shipping, with a few sales in the $30-$35 range, and one outlier sale around $20 ($18.37 before shipping, with shipping cost not indicated in Terapeak.com data). Another BGS 9.5 Gem Mint copy of the 1990 Bowman Tiffany RC sold for $75 (shipping not indicated) in April 2013.

At the same time, there were three sales of the PSA 10 Gem Mint 1990 Bowman RCs in the $45-$55 range including shipping, one at $41 including shipping, another at $26 before shipping (not indicated in Terapeak), and one extreme outlier sale at $10.49 shipped on November 19, 2013. One BGS 9.5 Gem Mint copy sold for $30 shipped.

So what do we make of this? Well I think for one thing, it is notable that several of the PSA 10 1990 Bowman RCs sold in the same $45-$55 range as many of the PSA 10 1990 Bowman Tiffany RCs. At the same time, there were over a dozen recorded sales of BGS 9.5 and PSA 10 1990 Leaf Sammy Sosa RCs in the $25-$40 range in the fourth quarter of 2013 alone.

If nothing else, this is evidence that at least one buyer appreciates the relative grade scarcity of the regular 1990 Bowman issue, and that the general hierarchy of BGS 9.5/PSA 10 1990 Bowman over the 1990 Leaf RC is quite plausibly correct.

It is also notable that there are more 1990 Bowman Sammy Sosa PSA 10s than 1990 Bowman Tiffany Sammy Sosa PSA 10s, while BGS 9.5 1990 Bowman Sammy Sosas are significantly rarer than BGS 9.5 1990 Bowman Tiffany ones; incidentally, PSA does not include pricing for the regular 1990 Bowman Sosa (while seemingly undervaluing the PSA 10 1990 Bowman Tiffany Sosa at $35). That said, it's also possible that Beckett's pricing simply reflects the scarcity of specifically the BGS 9.5 Gem Mint grade on the 1990 Bowman Sammy Sosa.

Meanwhile, the single Buy It Now sale of a BGS 9.5 1990 Bowman Sammy Sosa at $30 isn't enough data in itself to disprove the $100 valuation, as that one sale can plausibly be attributed to seller error. However, it is also entirely conceivable that Beckett's pricing either overvalues the card, or that its BGS 9.5 value for the 1990 Bowman Sammy Sosa – and perhaps the 1990 Bowman Tiffany as well – may be due for a markdown.

Grade Scarcity and Box Value

As of January 2014, unopened wax boxes of 1987 Donruss could be had for $20 to $30 per box, with multi-box lots and 20-box cases running for as little as under $20 per box. Each box contains 36 packs with 15 cards per pack, for a total of 540 cards per box. There are 660 total cards in the 1987 Donruss set; as such – assuming equal print numbers – if you open a random box, you will pull a given card 540/660 or 81.8% of the time on average.

Put differently, if you purchase a box and open every pack, you will pull 0.818 Greg Maddux RCs per box, with an ungraded book value of $10 and a graded BGS 9.5 Gem Mint book value of $100.

For reference, in the three months from August to October 2013, there were 30 actual sales of such BGS 9.5 Gem Mint copies and 27 sales of PSA 10 Gem Mint copies on eBay, ranging from $45 to $107 each including shipping (BGS 9.5 copies marked both the bottom and top end of the range, with BGS 9.5 and PSA 10 copies otherwise generally selling in roughly the same range). By December 2013 – ahead of the January 8 Hall of Fame vote – PSA 10 copies were consistently in the $100+ range, with one sale at $129 shipped. And upon Maddux' easy vote into the Baseball Hall of Fame on January 8, 2014, another PSA 10 copy sold at auction for $130.50 shipped.

Think about that for a minute. Let's assume for a moment that every Greg Maddux you pull will grade Gem Mint, and that the cost of grading is $10. Let's also be conservative and assume that the actual street value of a BGS 9.5 or PSA 10 Gem Mint 1987 Donruss Greg Maddux RC is $70 on average.

In this scenario, you will on average pull 0.818 Gem Mint Greg Maddux RCs worth $70 each, for an average value of ($70 x 0.818) or $57.26 per box. The average cost of grading per box will be ($10 x 0.818) or $8.18 per box, yielding a net value of ($57.26 - $8.18) or $49.08 in Greg Maddux RCs per box.

Considering that the cost of a box is $20 to $30 (or potentially less if you buy in bulk), if every Greg Maddux you pulled was Gem Mint, you would turn a profit of about $20 to $30 per box on Greg Maddux alone for a gross return on investment (ROI) of 66.7% to 150% (before backing out shipping costs and eBay and PayPal fees on the sale). Moreover, the Greg Maddux RC is not the only card of value in the set, which includes the rookie cards of Barry Bonds, Barry Larkin, Bo Jackson, Rafael Palmeiro, and Will Clark, as well as Mark McGwire's first card in an Oakland A's uniform (officially, the 1985 Topps Team USA Olympic card is McGwire's only RC) – all yielding additional potential value.

1987 Donruss: Notable Cards

Player	#	Ungraded BV	BGS 9 Mint	BGS 9.5 Gem Mint	BGS 9.5 Adj. Multiple
Greg Maddux RC	36	$10	$25	$100	5.0x
Barry Bonds RC	361	$12	$20	$40	1.8x
Barry Larkin RC	492	$4	$20	$40	2.9x
Bo Jackson RC	35	$5	$20	$50	3.3x
Mark McGwire	46	$8	$20	$30	1.7x
Rafael Palmeiro RC	43	$5	$10	$25	1.7x
Will Clark RC	66	$1.50	$8	$20	1.7x

Source: Beckett.com, Dec. 2013

So if a BGS 9.5 or PSA 10 Gem Mint 1987 Donruss Greg Maddux RC is pushing $100+ a pop, and Greg Maddux RCs fall at a rate of about four Greg Maddux RCs every five boxes, how can it be that unopened boxes of 1987 Donruss can be routinely had for $20 to $30 per box?

The answer is simple: Though Greg Maddux RCs in general are easy to pull, *Gem Mint condition copies of the 1987 Donruss Greg Maddux RC are quite difficult to pull.*

Anybody who's handled Donruss cards from 1985 to 1991 knows that the cards from these issues are thin, flimsy, and fragile. Cards pulled from wax packs from this time period are liable to have bent corners or rough edges, while the front and back cards in a pack might have wax stuck to it, destroying any chance at a passable (9 or better) surface grade. And then even if you can pull a card in perfect condition, it must also be centered properly in order to attain a BGS 9.5 or PSA 10 Gem Mint grade, which itself is no small hurdle.

The more likely scenario is that you might open 10 boxes of 1987 Donruss, pull eight Greg Maddux RCs, and have five that look clean enough but only one that will actually grade Gem Mint. Moreover, the penalty for grading below Gem Mint is steep in this case – even in late 2013, PSA 9 copies were running in the $15-$20 range with a few outlier sales as high as $25-$30, while BGS 9 copies (which nobody really looks for) were running as low as $10-$15 each.

That said, when gems are difficult to build even out of the box, box value deteriorates.

The Card Removal Effect

We've discussed card removal and the card removal effect numerous times throughout this book. The concept of card removal is exceptionally important to understand, as it is fundamental to multiple expansion in graded cards, which itself is in part a function of the relative devaluation of ungraded cards over time.

Card removal is a term that will be quite familiar to advantage gamblers. Card counting blackjack players know that presence of tens and aces in the deck are favorable to the player, while 2s through 7s are favorable to the dealer. Essentially, when tens and aces are dealt, they are no longer available in the remaining deck, and the composition of the remaining deck becomes more favorable to the dealer on the next hand; conversely, when 2s through 7s are dealt, the composition of the remaining deck becomes more favorable to the player on the next hand. And if enough smaller cards are dealt relative to tens and aces, the remaining deck composition will become favorable enough to the player that he can have positive expectation on the next hand.

Card removal also has a variety of applications in poker games as well. If you are holding AK before the flop in hold'em, then it becomes mathematically less likely that another player has AA or KK. Alternatively, if you have three to a spade flush on third street in seven card stud and you see a bunch of spades out on the table in other players' hands, then the odds of drawing to a flush become progressively worse the more spades you see in your opponents' hands.

In baseball cards, the **card removal effect** is when the highest-quality copies of a given card become graded and thus removed from the pool of ungraded cards, resulting in a lower average quality and thus lower average value of the remaining pool of ungraded cards. In the process, the spread in value between graded Gem Mint or better cards and the value of ungraded cards thus tends to widen by default, which by definition results in multiple expansion.

Maximum Leverage and Premium Class

Though some multiple expansion is a natural function of the devaluation of ungraded cards due to card removal, the card removal effect also promotes further multiple expansion by providing value enhancement in graded cards in a couple of ways.

For starters, when print numbers are relatively low and a given card is widely deemed valuable enough to grade, more and more high quality examples will become graded to the point that eventually Gem Mint+ cards can no longer be built. When Gem Mint+ quality cards no longer exist in the pool of ungraded cards, the supply of Gem Mint+ cards stops growing. At this point, Gem Mint+ copies of a given card have reached **maximum leverage**,[84] allowing further multiple expansion to occur with any positive change in demand.

This effect is stunted in issues burdened by oversupply – chiefly, issues from the late 1980s and early 1990s, for which an endless supply of unopened boxes remain. This effect is also stunted for cards of players for which there is little demand, as for these players there may not be enough demand to justify grading cards to the point that Gem Mint+ cards can no longer be built.

On the other hand, this effect is enhanced in issues with small print runs – particularly in limited print, serialized cards – and for key cards of players in high demand. When print runs are small or a player is in high demand, the probability is enhanced that the entire (or at least the bulk of) pool of Gem Mint+ quality copies of a given card become graded, thus helping the card achieve maximum leverage.

At the same time, graded cards create a new hierarchy – a premium class – among copies of a given card. If there are 50 gold refractors and only 15 ultimately grade BGS 9.5 Gem Mint and two others grade BGS 10 Pristine, the 15 BGS 9.5 Gem Mint copies are no longer one gold refractor out of 50, but are rather one of 15 BGS 9.5 Gem Mint copies, while the BGS 10 Pristine copies are now one of two atop the gold refractor hierarchy.

The presence of maximum leverage, combined with the creation of a premium class of high-grade cards, is fundamentally what has enabled high-grade vintage baseball cards to reach their current heights. It is also why the outlook for Gem Mint+, premium-color, serialized cards of modern ilk is far superior to that of the overproduced cards issued in the late 1980s and early 1990s.

---

[84] See Part I: The Value of Scarcity

Card Removal: A Demonstration

Let's demonstrate how card removal works in practice. Let's say you have a newly released card with a reasonably favorable print run of 2,000 to 3,000 copies (or roughly the same as the Bowman Chrome Prospects autos), and the card is a key RC or prospect card of a generational talent (think Mike Trout, Bryce Harper, LeBron James, Andrew Luck, Sidney Crosby, etc.). We'll make the following assumptions:

1. Upon initial release, all cards are ungraded.

2. Upon initial release, reasonably well-centered (potential gems) copies generally run in the $70-$80 range online.

3. The cost of getting a card graded is $10.

4. The projected initial street value of a BGS 9.5 Gem Mint copy is $100-$120.

5. Ungradable cards have a terminal value of $50.

6. The card is fairly valued at these prices.

At this stage, the card will likely go into the book with an ungraded value of $100, and at some point after graded cards hit the market will perhaps go into the books with a graded BGS 9.5 value between $120 and $150 for an adjusted multiple of 1.1x to 1.4x.

There are a number of key observations to be made at this point.

Initial Ungraded Book Value

Even if the card never sells for $100 in ungraded form *online*, the $100 ungraded book value is quite reasonable. This is because if you were an expert grader and could see a card in person and could ascertain that the card has a 100% chance of grading at least a BGS 9.5 Gem Mint with an initial street value of $100-$120 – and with a slight possibility of grading BGS 10 Pristine with a value likely in the $150- $200 range – you would gladly pay $100 for this card, as your cost of building a Gem Mint or better copy will be $100 + $10 = $110.

In terms of expectation, you would essentially be paying fair value with a freeroll at even greater returns should the card grade BGS 10 Pristine. Thus, in effect, a $70-$80 online trading range represents a 20%-30% discount to book value, attributable to the risk of buying a card online without being able to see it in person.

Initial BGS 9.5 Gem Mint Value and Pricing Pressure from Ungraded Cards

Based on initial ungraded sales of $70 to $80, it is reasonable to expect that the initial street value of BGS 9.5 Gem Mint copies would run in the $100 to $120 range, representing roughly a 50% premium. That said, it should be noted that in the short run – say, within the first three to six months after initial release or so – the potential for a prospective buyer to be able to acquire ungraded cards at $70 to $80 and build Gem Mint+ cards himself places pricing pressure on graded BGS 9.5 Gem Mint cards.

If you can buy ungraded cards at $70 to $80 and potentially build BGS 9.5 Gem Mint or BGS 10 Pristine cards for $80 to $90, how likely are you to pay $120 for a BGS 9.5 Gem Mint copy? $150? $200?

Oddly, the reality is sometimes a bit different than logic would dictate, as it is not uncommon for the first graded BGS 9.5 Gem Mint cards to hit the market often to carry outsized premiums. Why? Because when no or few end collectors yet have a BGS 9.5 Gem Mint copy, the supply-demand relationship is skewed such that when the first few graded copies hit the market, the maximum number of potential buyers (based on current demand) is often bidding on one copy or relatively few copies.

As we know, it only takes two bidders to drive up prices in an auction, and only one buyer to make a Buy It Now mistake. Consequently, when the first graded BGS 9.5 Gem Mint cards hit the market, bubble pricing often occurs, particularly in high-demand prospects and RCs.

Initial BGS 9 Mint Value

In the short run, the prospect for building gems also negatively impacts BGS 9 Mint copies such that a BGS 9 Mint card is often worth less than a reasonably well-centered, ungraded card. If you can buy a BGS 9.5 Gem Mint copy for $120 to $130 or still have a reasonable chance to potentially build one (or better) for $80 to $90, then how willing are you to pay $70 to $80 for a BGS 9 Mint copy that is essentially guaranteed to be BGS 9 Mint?[85]

That said, BGS 9 Mint cards are generally value destructive in the short run, and may not be worth a meaningful premium to ungraded value in the long run except in some exceptionally condition sensitive issues, in high-value cards, or cards in

---

[85] It's not quite 100% for reasons probably beyond the scope of this book.

either high enough demand or sufficiently limited supply such that gems can no longer be built.

Devaluation of Ungraded Cards

The bulk of supply for a new issue is often released to the market – much of it by case breakers – within the first two to four weeks of a new release. During this stage, the potential gems are generally sent off for grading. Some likely BGS 9s – generally well-centered cards with surface issues, or otherwise clean cards that are too off-center, or slightly off-center cards that may have other slight blemishes – are often sold or re-sold rather than graded.

The grading process might be done in a day at a card show at a relatively high cost, and some people do this for high-demand cards in order to take advantage of favorable short-term economics of having the first and only BGS 9.5s on the market. But at the most cost-effective bulk grading rates, the process often takes one to two months. As noted earlier, BGS has a "no-grade" or "min-grade" option available to bulk graders (see the end of Part VIII, next) which is not advertised, but where for a small fee (generally a fraction of grading costs, usually $1-$2 depending on order size and turnaround time, but subject to change), BGS will look at a card and only grade it if the card meets a minimum grade standard; in other words, if you request a min-grade of BGS 9.5, BGS will only grade and slab the card if the card will grade BGS 9.5 Gem Mint or better, while charging the $1-$2 fee in either case.

What all of this means is that the odds that an ungraded card on the market will grade BGS 9.5 or better starts to fall dramatically after about a month after release, and get progressively worse as time wears on. After about two to four months after release, many of the cards submitted for grading that fail to meet a min-grade of BGS 9.5 are now back in play, further weakening the composition of available ungraded cards.

By this point, the demand for ungraded cards has already weakened.

Theoretically speaking, in the long run – assuming a given card is sufficiently desirable and in short enough supply – all potential Gem Mint+ cards will get graded. When the supply of potential Gem Mint+ cards is exhausted or is approaching exhaustion, the relative demand for ungraded copies will fall, and the remaining pool of ungraded cards will ultimately approach our assumed terminal value for ungradable copies of $50 (again assuming no change in player demand).

As prices of ungraded cards fall, ungraded book value will eventually fall along with it. Let's assume that initial BGS 9.5 book value is $120-$150, and also that ungraded book value will settle at $60 in the long run; in this case, the adjusted multiple will expand from our initial estimate of 1.1x-1.4x to between 1.7x and 2.1x based on deterioration in ungraded book value alone.

Maximum Leverage and Upside Multiple Expansion

When the supply of potential gems is exhausted and gems can no longer be built, the card has reached maximum leverage. At this stage, any positive change in demand for the player's key cards will tend to cause graded BGS 9.5 prices to rise, and result in upside multiple expansion.

Impact of Card Removal on Ungraded Buying Strategy

As we noted, as time wears on following the release of a new issue, the odds of being able to build gems simply by buying ungraded singles and having them graded drops significantly. That said, you should be less likely to buy ungraded cards after the first month or two after release even though prices may be declining, simply because the average quality of ungraded cards is also materially worse.

Part VIII: Building Gems

Busting boxes, buying ungraded cards, and getting cards graded.

The first two to four weeks following the initial release of a new set on the market are prime time for collector-investors looking to acquire ungraded cards in order to build BGS 9.5 Gem Mint or BGS 10 Pristine graded cards. During this time, a flood of new supply often hits the market in an exceptionally short period of time as case breakers bust much of the supply of a given issue. Rare, premium color parallels are readily available such that pricing pressure is present on the high end during this window.

Moreover, these first few weeks present a window in which you are most likely to find case breakers whose strategy is to rip and flip (rather than grade) high end cards; and thus, you are also more likely to be able to find gradable, ungraded cards which haven't already been examined and subsequently released.

That said, this is a period of many, many competing forces. Namely:

1. Top prospect/RC bubbles

2. Overlooked values

3. Card removal, buyer exhaustion, and falling demand

4. Temporary high-end pricing pressure

Top Prospect/RC Bubbles and Overlooked Values

In a seemingly annual (or set-by-set) occurrence, the market tends to converge on hot new prospects and RC-year players such that they tend to bubble. Helping to drive these bubbles are the initial sales – when the first cards of a given player hits the market with every new release, you have the maximum number of potential collectors/investors/speculators who don't have a card bidding on the fewest number of cards. In addition, these collectors/investors/speculators often lack a frame of reference to compare the values of new prospects; this helps contribute to inordinately high initial prices before the remainder of the supply hits the market, and prices move (generally downward) toward a more true equilibrium level.

On the flip side, the attention paid to the hottest prospects/RCs often means that other top prospects/RCs may go overlooked, resulting in sometimes extreme values at auction upon initial release, before moving (generally upward) toward a more true equilibrium level.

Card Removal, Buyer Exhaustion, and Falling Demand

Case breakers often observe a general decline in prices in the time following initial release. While this is often attributed to a simple decline in demand following initial release, we know that can't be the whole story – if that were the case, then buyers would simply wait for prices to fall after initial release before buying.

Instead, we can surmise with a little logic that a big part of any decline in prices can be attributable to a number of factors:

1. **Initial bubble correction.** As noted, prices for top prospects and RCs often start at unreasonably high levels before correcting downward towards equilibrium prices (which are often still too high).

2. **Card removal.** As the flood of new supply hits the market and settles into the hands of collectors/investors/speculators, high-grade examples get graded while lower-quality examples stay ungraded, ultimately resulting in a lower average quality of the remaining pool of ungraded cards. This in turn leads to lower demand, and thus lower prices.

3. **Buyer exhaustion.** Collectors have budgets. At some point after initial release – particularly in periods of oversupply and/or weak RC classes – collectors/investors/speculators either run out of money or simply lose interest.

High-End Pricing Pressure

The flood of new supply in the first two to four weeks after initial release creates a unique window in which there is persistent pricing pressure on high-end, premium color parallels. While this may or may not be enough to go after top prospects or RCs who are in bubble mode and thus are being wildly overvalued, this pricing pressure may enable us to snap up high-end color of undervalued prospects or RCs at reasonable – or better – prices.

Building Gems

If you've read this far, then you should know what cards you want to acquire – key cards of top players or prospects in Gem Mint or better condition. You should also have a framework for thinking about valuation, as well as an understanding of our general approach to value investing.

Here in Part VIII, we will discuss building graded BGS 9.5 Gem Mint or better cards from the ground up. With regard to buying ungraded singles in order to build gems, we will discuss:

- What card types to avoid
- Seller tells, and what types of sellers or listing types to avoid
- Higher probability options
- Redemptions
- Buying strategies
- Buying and evaluating player case break auction lots

We will also cover submitting your cards for grading, and discuss BGS' "no-grade/min-grade" option, group or bulk submissions, and prepping your cards for grading.

But first, let's talk about the four basic types of strategies for ungraded cards.

The Four Basic Types of Ungraded Strategies

When it comes to ungraded cards, players in the game generally employ at least one of four basic types of strategies:

1. Case breaker

2. Case breaker/grader

3. Boxes

4. Singles

It should go without saying that in a game where autos often come at a rate of one or two per box, you should not be buying packs out of unopened boxes. For starters, it's not very cost effective to buy packs, because they are generally wildly overpriced, particularly compared to boxes. But more to the point – and I'm not saying that people do this (but people *do* do this) – it's quite possible (or probable) that if someone is selling packs, that the key box hit (the auto) has already been found.

This may or may not be the case at your local card store, but it's simply not worth the money or the risk to buy packs, at least for the purposes of our game.

Case Breaker

A pure case breaker strategy is a purely rip and flip strategy – everything that comes out of a break gets sold, often before the break actually takes place. This can be done any number of ways – some case breakers pre-sell team lots (sometimes random teams); others pre-sell player lots (say, for all base cards and parallels, or in some cases only for autos, etc.); still others pre-sell sets and sell off the hits individually.

On the plus side, this is a *potentially* low-risk strategy given favorable conditions, particularly for established case breakers who can acquire cases directly from a distributor, and who have built regular clientele. The downside is that literally anybody can break a case and dump supply on the market, and consequently there are little-to-no barriers to entry. Worse, when it is profitable to simply break cases and sell the contents, new case breakers will be attracted to the market.

This results in the double whammy of not only further flooding the market with new supply and thus depressing prices for other case breakers upon initial release, but also pumping up pre-order demand and thus supply, depressing secondary market values even further.

As a general rule, a pure case breaker's strategy often depends on turning around and selling what comes out of a break, rather than taking the time and risk of sending off cards to get graded. As such, these are generally the guys we are looking to buy premium color, ungraded singles from in those first two to four weeks after initial release.

Pros: A *potentially* low-risk strategy under favorable conditions

Cons: Time intensive; likely cyclical; conditions subject to competition, supply, and product; little-to-no barrier to entry; probably not as easy as it sounds

Case Breaker/Grader

Some case breakers will grade the gradable hits, while preselling sets or base card lots. Other collectors will break cases in search of gradable hits, and sell off much of the scraps *after* the break. Still other collector/investor types will grade anything gradable that comes out of a break, while selling off the scraps.

Assuming reasonable supply conditions, this concept of breaking cases in search of hits, grading the gradable hits (and other cards of value) while selling off everything else is essentially a perfect strategy. By breaking cases yourself, you vastly improve your chances of obtaining key hits without the risk of having someone else examine such cards and only selling the undesirables.

The downside to this strategy is that it can be very capital intensive if you aren't pre-selling lots, and it can be very time intensive regardless. It can also be value destructive unless you have the time and will to sell off the unwanted parts, or under unfavorable market conditions.

Pros: Improve chances at obtaining hits without someone else searching it first

Cons: Capital/time intensive; can be value destructive unless you have time and will to sell discards, or under unfavorable market conditions

Boxes

Boxes are a bit like slot machines in that some are designed to have many lower value payouts, while others are designed to have fewer payouts with larger potential jackpots. Topps Chrome Baseball, for example, generally comes with two RC autos per Hobby box; however, these RC autos generally aren't as valuable as the Bowman Chrome Prospects or RC autos which come at a lower rate (generally one per Bowman Hobby or three per Jumbo box) and have significantly more speculative checklists, but also have significantly higher upside.

And so on the plus side, if you're into gambling, buying boxes can allow you to obtain potentially super high-end hits at a relatively low cost. The downside to opening boxes is that it can be an extremely high-variance exercise where boxes are often expensive and most of the "hits" wind up being duds. And even more troublesome is that, as we discussed in Part VI: The Supply Chain and the Value Cycle, high-end hits become increasingly harder to hit with the widening auto checklists that come with increasing supply.

Pros: Can potentially obtain high-end hits at relatively low cost, much like a slot machine or a lottery

Cons: Can be high variance, particularly in sets where most "hits" are duds

Ungraded Singles

In this game of hits, our default strategy revolves around ungraded singles and lots. Buying ungraded singles directly is generally significantly more capital-friendly than buying boxes or cases in search of hits. If done correctly, you can often obtain singles or bulk values. And once you've gotten a handle on the BGS grading standards and submission process, you will know which cards are gradable, while the ungradables you acquire can be held or resold, or in some cases returned to the seller.

The biggest risk with ungraded cards is that when you purchase singles or lots, you run the risk that the cards you acquire have already been searched through. Meanwhile, you also run the risk that the cards you purchase even from established case breakers may not have been handled properly.

Pros: Capital-friendly, bypassing box risk; can obtain singles or bulk values; gradables can be graded, while ungradables can often be returned, or held and/or resold

Cons: Cards are often examined, and player lots are often searched through prior to sale unless presold through case break; cards can be subject to over-handling

The remainder of Part VIII will deal with ungraded singles and lots. And the first trick is to figure out what types of cards, what types of sellers, and what types of listings we should avoid.

Card Types to Avoid

Certain types of cards are significantly less likely to yield gems than others, either because they cannot stand more than a minimal amount of handling, or because they might have other issues out of the pack.

These types include:

1. Paper cards

2. Memorabilia cards

3. Other super thick stock (75 pt. or greater) cards

Thin stock paper cards like Bowman paper or Topps paper cannot stand up to more than a minimal amount of handling, as these cards are vulnerable to any number of defects due to over handling, with bent corners being a chief one.

The problem with memorabilia and other super thick stock cards is that there is an unfortunate tendency for people to try to stuff cards in sleeves that are too small, frequently resulting in corner or edge wear, thus making your "brand new" card ungradable. Meanwhile, some high-end issues printed on super thick stock like 2012 Topps Five Star Baseball or 2012 Panini Black Football (for example) are similarly sensitive to over handling, but may also be prone to chipping issues straight out of the pack.

This is not to say that you can't buy such cards for the sake of collection – only that the odds of being able to build gems by acquiring these cards second-hand is not very good.

It's an unfortunate reality of life that many of the people you will potentially buy from may not handle the cards they are selling the same way they would if they planned to keep them or have them graded themselves. If you're opening up packs yourself, you'd probably want to make sure your hands are clean, while any cards of note that you pull will go straight into a sleeve and then into either a top loader or a graded card submission holder, or otherwise straight into a one-touch magnetic holder. You'd probably want to handle the card by its sides so as to avoid putting fingerprints on the face of the card.

However, there are no official regulations as to how cards are handled in this game, and case breakers or other collectors may not engage in the same practices as you would with your own cards. Some guys opening boxes or cases may do so while eating pizza or other foods that may stain the cards. And while some guys will put key hits straight into sleeves, other guys might put these cards (or lesser cards that they think don't have value, but which you might want) into a stack before sorting, meaning that the card will be handled once more.

Seller Tells: Types of Sellers and Sales Types to Avoid

Poker players are familiar with the concept of tells – clues a player may provide as to the strength of his hand, whether as a function of body language, or other physical or verbal action. Similarly, sellers on eBay yield all kinds of information by virtue of their handles and/or what they are selling. And since our game is to acquire gradable cards, we want to avoid sellers who are not likely to sell gradable cards, and we want to avoid buying cards or lots that have been searched through.

Beware:

1. People with handles that include the letters "BGS" or "PSA"
2   Catch-and-release types
3. High-volume graders, and other people who have graded cards for sale
4. People who have a lot of cards of the same player for sale
5. Sellers who try to sell ungraded cards as "must grade"
6. Singles of high profile players after the first few months after initial release
7. Large player lots after the first few weeks of release
8. Cards confirmed sold and later relisted

People With Handles That Include the Letters "BGS" or "PSA"

If a guy on eBay has a handle that includes the letters "BGS" or "PSA" in it, it is a pretty strong clue that the guy grades cards. And if a guy is grading cards and has an ungraded card that you *really* want, chances are that you don't really want it because it's not going to be gradable.

Catch-and-Release Types

A common strategy – in fact, the very ungraded singles strategy proposed here – is to acquire high-end (rare, but not necessarily high dollar amount) ungraded cards, send the gradable ones off to BGS with a "min-grade BGS 9.5," and resell (or return) the ungradables. Even an expert grader is likely to send some borderline cards to BGS given a min-grade option on the off chance that it will grade BGS 9.5. But as an end result, some of these cards are going to come back ungraded having not met the requirements for a BGS 9.5 Gem Mint grade, and ultimately wind up back on the market for sale.

We want to avoid these sellers. And the strongest clue is a guy who has an inordinate amount of ungraded, high-end scarce cards for sale, and usually very little (if any) crap. Either this guy is the luckiest guy in the world and only pulls hits, or he is very likely employing the strategy indicated above.

High-Volume Graders, and Others with Graded Cards for Sale

Sellers with an unusually large amount of graded cards for sale are not messing around, and can generally be expected to be grading anything worth grading. These are sellers that should probably be avoided.

The presence of graded cards is fundamentally what separates a purely commercial case breaker from somebody who is simply breaking cases. A guy who is breaking cases is likely going after hits, and likely grading many of the cards worth grading (value-wise), whether he intends to keep them for his personal collection or otherwise intends to sell them once the graded slabs are returned from BGS or PSA.

People with graded cards for sale in general are also red flags. It's not to say that these guys never sell cards worth grading – the fact is, different people value different things differently, and some cards you might want are cards that others may not think are worth the time and investment to grade. But generally speaking, I would be wary of a seller who is also selling graded cards.

People Who Have a Lot of Cards of the Same Player for Sale

Somebody who has an unusually large number of cards of the same player for sale is a dead giveaway, particularly if these include a number of autos and/ or premium color parallels, and *especially* if some of them are graded. This is indicative of someone who has made a concerted effort to invest in a given player and is dumping off the ungradables. As such, you are *extremely* unlikely to acquire ungraded gems from this seller.

This tell is about 99% accurate when the seller has only ungraded cards, and about 100% accurate when he has graded cards for sale.

Sellers Who Try to Sell a Card as "Must Grade"

On occasion, you will come across a listing in which the seller says a card "Must be graded!" or "Must grade!" while qualifying that statement by noting that he is "not a professional grader." Much of the time, the seller is full of shit. If a card is in reasonable demand (a star player) and the seller thinks the card is gradable, the seller is more likely to have the card graded himself.

This is exponentially more true if somebody is trying to sell a multi-card lot this way. "I'm not a grader, but if I was, I would grade these eight 2010 Bowman Chrome Draft Buster Posey RCs for sure."

Bullshit. There's no reason for anybody to have eight of anything, unless he either intended to have them graded and determined they weren't gradable, or unless he just broke a case (which you would be able to tell from the seller's other listings).

Other times, a seller will use the words "well centered" to describe a card. Usually, this is a good sign that there is something else wrong with the card, with surface scratches being the most likely culprit (as usual).

And every once in a while, when 10 autograph grades are rare for a given card (like 2012 Bowman Chrome and Bowman Chrome Draft Bryce Harper autos, or 2012 Bowman Chrome Prospects Oscar Taveras autos, for example), somebody will say the card for sale has a "rare BOLD autograph." If the seller knows enough to know that graded 10 autos are rare, then he knows enough to know that the card he is selling is not gradable (or is being overvalued).

Singles of High Profile Players after the First Few Months after Initial Release

As we've discussed, the odds of being able to acquire ungraded potential gems goes down dramatically following the first two to four months after the initial release of a new issue, as the bulk of new supply is broken in the first two to four weeks, and subsequently searched through and graded, or otherwise not graded and resold. Moreover, the higher profile the player, the more likely it is that that player's cards have been searched through, and thus the less likely it is that ungraded cards will yield gems.

This is not 100%, as not all supply is broken in the first two to four weeks – for some issues, cases continue to be broken months after release, while boxes might take several years to reach exhaustion or near exhaustion, depending on the brand, year, and print run of the issue. Meanwhile, not all lower value cards (generally < $10 in ungraded value) get graded or searched through.

But as a generality, the older the issue and the higher profile the player, the lower the odds of being able to acquire ungraded potential gems.

Large Player Lots after the First Few Weeks of Release

During the first few weeks after release, you will see many player lots go up for auction. Many will be pre-sell lots sold by case breakers; others will be lots sold by people who break cases. The pre-sell lots sold by case breakers are generally higher-percentage, though still subject to centering issues and other surface issues out of the box. The lots sold by people breaking cases will be hit or miss; some of these lots are from people who have searched through the lots, picked the best ones for grading, and are selling the rest.

But after the first few weeks after a new release, your odds of finding gems in these lots starts to fall dramatically, as the probability goes up that the people selling these lots are people who have acquired bulk lots and have already searched through them for gradable potential gems, and are selling off the ungradables in bulk lots.

This isn't 100%, but is a general truth.

On the other hand, you might still find guys breaking new cases up to several months after release, particularly for high profile issues like Bowman or Bowman Chrome. When these guys are selling player lots before the break, it is generally OK, though you still need to be mindful of the price you are paying (more on this later here in Part VIII).

Cards Confirmed Sold and Later Relisted

Let's say you are looking at a particular ungraded card serial #2/5, and it sells at auction for $240. Two weeks later, the seller relists the same card with the same #2/5 serial number. What happened?

The two most likely explanations are:

1. The buyer never paid, or
2. The buyer paid, the seller shipped, and then the buyer returned the card.

The buyer not paying is a distinct possibility, and probably occurs more than you might think. Sometimes the buyer does not have the funds, or is having other issues with PayPal or whatever. But this does not really concern us at this juncture.

The second possibility is more concerning to us as prospective buyers. Because when the buyer pays and the seller ships the card – completing the transaction – and the buyer subsequently returns it, it means there is something wrong with the card. And in the case of chromes, the overwhelming probability is that there are surface issues, typically scratches.

Upon relisting, some sellers will note the surface issues; some won't.

There is also a third possibility, which is **shill bidding** – that is, the seller (via a second account) or a cohort bids up the prices of the auction. This is expressly forbidden on eBay, though it does occur. And in the odd case that the shill bidder ends up winning the auction, obviously the shill bidder is not going to pay (otherwise the seller would pay eBay and PayPal fees).

Shill bidding is sometimes easy to spot by going through the bid history. The bid history will have a list of bidders and bid amounts. Clicking on the bidder will show the bidder's 30-day bid history, including the categories of items bid on, the seller of those items, and the "bid activity" with the seller of the item in question. The bid activity is the percentage of bidder's bids over the last 30 days that were on items listed by the seller in question. An abnormally high bid activity percentage with this seller on a number of different items is a strong possible indicator of shill bidding.

Other potential clues are bidders with new accounts, or those with little-to-no feedback.

Higher Probability Cards: What to Look For

Unfortunately, there is no 100% foolproof method for acquiring ungraded cards, particularly since cards aren't even reliable to come out Gem Mint straight out of the pack. But now that we have a good idea of what to avoid, we can discuss some higher probability options and perhaps shade the odds a bit in our favor.

We should focus on:

1. Probable 9.5 centering
2. Corners and auto quality
3. Chromes
4. Premium color chrome refractors
5. High volume sellers with tons of feedback

Probable 9.5 Centering

Centering for any card is the first thing you should be looking at, in part because it is the only subgrade that can – for the most part – be reliably judged by looking at a picture on your computer or cell phone.

In order for a card to grade BGS 9.5 Gem Mint, a card must have at least three 9.5 subgrades and a 9 subgrade, or three 10 subgrades with an 8.5 subgrade. And the problem with cards that are likely to turn up with 9 centering is that *each* of the other three subgrades need to grade 9.5 or better. Meanwhile, a card with 8.5 centering *cannot* be BGS 9.5 Gem Mint – when centering or corners are the lowest grade, a card's final grade cannot be more than 0.5-pt. higher than the lowest grade.

As such, a card with 8.5 centering cannot grade higher than BGS 9 Mint.

But if you start with a card likely to grade 9.5 centering or better, then you only need two out of the other three subgrades to grade 9.5 or better, with the third subgrade only needing to be a 9, which is a significantly easier hurdle to overcome.

Corners and Auto Quality

While edge and surface issues are often difficult to judge from pictures, corners and autos are often easier to judge. On cards with dark borders – most often on the back of the card – generally if you can see a speck of white on one corner, you are probably looking at a 9 corner; if you see white on multiple corners, you're probably looking at less.

As with centering, a card with 8.5 corners cannot grade higher than BGS 9 Mint, either.

Autos might take some experience to judge, but this is easy to get – start by running searches on eBay for "auto BGS" or "chrome auto BGS" for any given player, and examine the differences between 10 autos and 9 autos (also be sure to check the pictures in the center of this book). On the 2012 Bowman Chrome and Bowman Chrome Draft Bryce Harper RC autos, you can see a lot of white in Harper's signature, as if he was running out of ink; these autos are generally 9s at best. Also look for autos that are cut off – a player's signature might run off the card on an on-card auto (not good), or off the sticker on a sticker auto (also not good, and shame on the manufacturer). These are also 9s at best.

Chromes

Chrome (chromium) cards are generally more desirable than paper cards. But beyond that, chrome cards are significantly better constructed than thin paper cards, and are significantly more likely to survive handling intact with sharp corners and healthy edges.

Consequently, chromes are significantly higher-percentage cards than paper cards.

Premium Color Chrome Refractors

We should tend to focus on premium color – generally gold refractors #'d/50 or better – for a number of reasons related to both quality and relative quality.

For starters, these cards have a significantly better chance of being handled properly out of the pack. While case breakers (or box breakers) might not pay much attention to base cards or other cards of little value, they are more likely to be more careful with premium color refractors simply because they are worth more.

Secondly, should the card turn out to be ungradable or a BGS 9-quality (which you may or may not want to grade), the card has a better chance of having resale value, either in the near-term or in the long run. While ungraded base cards in particular may lose value or otherwise have little chance for appreciation in the long run, premium color refractors will more often still be in demand, and may have reasonable pricing power.

But even in the short run (generally within six months of release, but certainly less than a year, especially for high profile cards) premium color refractors may have pricing power, even over confirmed (slabbed) BGS 9s. Once the smoke clears from the case breaker rush upon initial release – after much of the other premium color refractors have sold – premium color refractors may benefit by being the only ones on the market.

High Volume Sellers with Tons of Feedback

High volume sellers with tons of feedback are often our bread-and-butter, as these generally indicate case breaking types of sellers. These are the guys we are looking for, as their strategy is often *dependent* on ripping and flipping, as opposed to ripping and grading.

That said, this again is not 100%, as some of these guys are guys breaking cases and dumping parts while looking for hits. Many of the guys breaking cases are grading the gradables, whether to keep or to flip at a greater profit.

These are the guys you need to sort out. One way to do so is to run a search for "Finest BGS" or "Bowman Chrome BGS" or "Topps Chrome BGS" and make a note of who is selling graded cards, and what their threshold for grading is. Are they grading only the big hits, or seemingly anything worth grading?

If you see a guy who seemingly grades *everything* later busting cases and selling a lot of singles out of them, you know to avoid them completely. But if a guy only grades super high-end stuff, then some of the lower-end cards might still be ripe for picking.

Redemptions

With the explosion in autograph subjects (players) and widening of product lines over the past decade or so, the use of redemption cards for autographs have, for better or for worse, become increasingly and necessarily more common. That said, this is very much a plus-minus game.

The biggest complaint that collectors have about redemptions is that redemptions can take an indefinite period to be fulfilled. A redemption might take anywhere from a few weeks to several months – and in some cases well over a year – to be fulfilled. Sometimes a player never signs and returns the cards, in which case those redemptions might automatically be replaced by other cards (in other cases, a collector can request a replacement from Topps for redemptions before fulfillment).

Another major issue with redemptions is that even though the cards come straight from the manufacturer, there are no guarantees that the cards will come gem. Rather, these cards are subject to the same centering and surface scratch issues as a card pulled from a pack – only in this case, we don't get to cherry pick the well-centered examples.

Moreover, Topps' storage and shipping standards leave something to be desired. Jersey autos and other super thick stock cards are often stuffed in sleeves that are too tight, and thus are subject to corner and edge issues. And where chrome cards should be placed in 55-pt. top loaders, Topps' standard seems to be to stuff them into 35-pt. top loaders; worse, for customers with a lot of redemptions, Topps also appears to fulfill some orders by bypassing sleeves and top loaders and simply stuffing cards – even high value ones up to $500+ value in my experience – in snap cases (the same kind of 25-ct. or so clear boxes you might use to hold commons).[86]

Still, these very concerns are what make redemptions sometimes very attractive options.

The Pros

Many collectors hate waiting for redemptions to be fulfilled, and loathe the risk that a redemption may take a year or longer to be fulfilled. Meanwhile, most case breakers' very rip-and-flip strategy often *depends* on selling the redemptions rather than waiting for fulfillment. And as a consequence, there seems to be a general short-term oriented sell bias in the market regarding redemptions.

---

[86] There is a very unfortunate addendum to this part of the discussion in the Closing Thoughts.

This is a large potential plus for value hunters, as redemptions sometimes trade at healthy discounts to anticipated fair value.

A second – and crucial – benefit is that, while redemptions are far from guaranteed to come back gem mint, they also have not been searched through, either. What this means is that redemptions have a longer shelf life than ungraded cards pulled from packs. One key implication is that where case breakers often observe a decline in ungraded prices over time following the initial release of a new set due to falling demand (in part due to card removal, particularly on the high end of a set), if the prices of redemptions fall along with the rest of the set, redemptions may provide even more attractive values. This is because the underlying value of a redemption card cannot be impacted by card removal.

A third benefit of redemptions is a shot at hitting key serial numbers without paying a premium for it. As discussed in Part III, these key serial numbers include the first and last serial numbers of a series (i.e. #1/50 and #50/50) or a player's jersey number (e.g. #23 for Michael Jordan, #27 for Mike Trout, #34 for Bryce Harper, #11 for Yu Darvish).

Card Selection: Value Plays

When it comes to buying newly released ungraded cards, all of the same concepts we've discussed thus far regarding value investing, and both player and card selection apply here as well. But one key difference is that when dealing with ungraded new issues, we are often dealing primarily with current-year rookies and prospects, many of whom are in bubble mode.

"Second-Best" Plays That Aren't Second Best

As we've discussed, there is an overwhelming tendency for the market to focus on a few key prospects or rookies. For 2013 Topps Chrome, Bowman Chrome, and Finest – all released within a span of two weeks from late September into early October – the bubbly RCs were Los Angeles Dodgers OF Yasiel Puig and St. Louis Cardinals RHP Michael Wacha, who benefited greatly from playing (and starring, particularly in the case of Wacha) in the playoffs.

Meanwhile, other high-end RC-year players on teams either not in the playoffs or otherwise eliminated from the playoffs early on went comparatively overlooked, including Baltimore Orioles 3B Manny Machado (also hurt by a late-season injury), Miami Marlins RHP Jose Fernandez, and Pittsburgh Pirates RHP Gerrit Cole.

Post-Bubble RC Turnaround Plays

Rookies are supposed to fail. As such, it is a common occurrence that bubbly top prospects see their cardboard stocks hammered when they make it to the big leagues and don't start off as hot as Yasiel Puig – even Mike Trout struggled in his first crack at the majors, hitting .220/.281/.390 in 40 games in his 2011 RC year, before dominating in his 2012 official rookie year. That said, top prospects with 2013-year RCs who saw their stocks fall after making the majors and not performing up to veteran expectations include Texas Rangers SS/2B Jurickson Profar, Seattle Mariners C Mike Zunino, and Miami Marlins OF Christian Yelich.

Yelich, for example, entered the 2013 season as Baseball America's 15th-ranked prospect in all of baseball. In May 2013, Terapeak.com recorded sales of three BGS 9.5/10 copies of the 2010 Bowman Chrome Draft Christian Yelich Refractor autos #'d/500 at prices between $145 and $165; in October 2013 – after Yelich had hit a respectable .288/.370/.396 in 62 games after being rushed to the majors – two copies sold for $75 each. Yelich's only chrome on-card RC autos are his 2013 Topps Chrome RC autos; upon release in September 2013, the Gold Refractor autos #'d/50 sold generally in the modest $40-$50 range.

Zunino, the No. 3 overall pick in the 2012 First Year Player Draft, entered the 2013 season as Baseball America's 17th-ranked prospect. In April 2013 alone, Zunino's base 2012 Bowman Chrome Draft auto graded BGS 9.5/10 saw *eight* sales at prices ranging roughly from $120 to $160, with another outlier sale at $260. Like Yelich, Zunino was rushed to the majors mid-season; and in an injury shortened season, Zunino hit only .214/.290/.329 in 52 games. And in December 2013, there were three sales of the same card graded BGS 9.5/10 in roughly the $30-$40 range, while Zunino's newly released (ungraded) 2013 Topps Chrome RC Gold Refractor autos #'d/50 could be had in the $40-$50 range.

Meanwhile, Profar had two sets of Bowman Chrome RC autos issued – one in the spring 2013 Bowman release as a redemption, and another inserted into packs in the fall 2013 Bowman Chrome release – providing a double whammy. Baseball America's No. 1 prospect entering the 2013 season, Profar hit only .234/.308/.336 while playing four different defensive positions in 85 games. Where his 2013 Bowman Chrome Gold Refractor auto redemptions were selling for $150-$200 in May-June 2013, both sets of live Bowman Chrome RC Gold Refractor autos were in the $50-$100 range by the end of 2013, with an unused redemption from the spring release selling for $81 on eBay on October 19. At the same time, Profar's 2013 Topps Chrome RC Gold Refractor autos #'d/50 were selling for $50-$60, while his 2013 Finest RC Gold Refractor autos were down in the $30-$40 range.

These are examples of players who may not have been buyable when their prospect status was the highest and their prices were bubbling. But depending on what you think of their potential from this point forward, you could make an argument that upon release, the going prices of the RCs released in the second half of 2013 – Topps Chrome, Finest, Bowman Chrome, Bowman Draft and Bowman Chrome Draft, and Bowman Sterling – may have undervalued the prospects of these players, and that these players might look more like Giancarlo Stanton (previously known as Mike Stanton) with an ungraded 2010 Topps Chrome RC Gold Refractor auto #/50 book value of $200 than Jason Heyward with an ungraded 2010 Topps Chrome RC Gold Refractor auto #/50 book value of $100, or Chicago Cubs SS Starlin Castro at $60.

Or, on the other hand, you might argue that they don't, and that they look more like Toronto Blue Jays 3B Brett Lawrie, with a 2012 Topps Chrome RC Gold Refractor auto #/50 ungraded book value of $40.

Injury RC Turnaround Plays

Other top prospects, rookies, or other RC-year players might see their card values decline due to injury. Baltimore Orioles RHP Dylan Bundy – Baseball America's No. 2 prospect entering the 2013 season – lost the entirety of what was to be his 2013 rookie campaign to Tommy John surgery, but nevertheless had a full slate of 2013-year RCs. When Bundy's 2013 Bowman Chrome RC auto was issued in the spring 2013 Bowman release, his 2013 Bowman Chrome RC Gold Refractor autos #'d/50 were trading in the $130-$150 range. By the time 2013 Topps Chrome was released in September 2013, his 2013 Topps Chrome RC Gold Refractor autos #'d/50 were trading in the $40-$50 range. And by the time 2013 Finest rolled out two weeks later, his 2013 Finest RC Gold Refractor autos #'d/50 were in the $30-$40 range.

At the same time, Baltimore Orioles 3B Manny Machado hit .283/.314/.432 with a league-leading 51 doubles in 156 games before tearing a knee ligament on September 23, ending his season, and requiring surgery. Still, Machado won a Gold Glove award with his defense, which helped him post an impressive 6.2 FanGraphs WAR. And the baseball media still viewed Machado as one of the top young talents in the game, if perhaps a notch below Mike Trout and Bryce Harper.

According to data from Terapeak.com, ungraded prices of Machado's 2013 Bowman Chrome RC Gold Refractor autos #'d/50 – issued in the spring 2013 Bowman release – began at $202.50 on May 9, 2013, steadily rising until it reached a high of $316 on June 1; a graded BGS 9.5/10 copy sold for $530 on June 14, while a graded PSA 9 Mint copy sold for $515 on August 12.

2013 Topps Chrome had an official September 25 release date, just after the date of Machado's injury. By this time, the redemptions for his Topps Chrome Gold Refractor autos #'d/50 ran in a range of $100-$120, with one outlier sale of $150 on October 20. Meanwhile, his 2013 Finest RC Gold Refractor autos #'d/50 – released two weeks later – sold at prices ranging generally from $50-$110 through the end of 2013, with one outlier sale at $150; those sales included three sales roughly in the $90-$110 range or so, and seven others in the $50-$70 range.

Meanwhile, sales of Machado's 2013 Bowman Chrome and Bowman Chrome Draft Gold Refractors #'d/50 (non-autos) were in the $40-$60 range – or not materially different than sales of the 2012 Bowman Chrome and Bowman Chrome Draft Yoenis Cespedes RC Gold Refractors #'d/50 upon their 2012 releases.

The question you have to ask is, how badly do these injuries affect the long-term outlook for Bundy and Machado? Has the market on these players gone too far south, such that these players might look attractive at these prices?

Overlooked Prospects

Be on the hunt for prospects who may be getting overlooked. In an article on its website, Dailywax.com presented a table showing the average first week sales for each of the players in the 2010 Bowman Chrome Draft Prospects Autographs set from December 2010.[87] A portion of the table is presented below, including the Low, High, and Avg. sales prices for the base autos of some of the more notable players in the set, along with their ungraded and graded BGS 9.5 book values from Beckett.com from December 2013.

2010 Bowman Chrome Draft Prospect Autos: Notable 1st Week Sales, Dec. 2010

Player	#	Low	High	Avg.	Ungraded BV Dec. 2013	BGS 9.5
Manny Machado	BDPP80	$40.22	$76.00	$53.20	$150	$400
Matt Harvey	BDPP84	$3.75	$14.99	$8.19	$120	$250
Noah Syndergaard	BDPP75	$0.99	$6.00	$3.31	$60	$100
Christian Yelich	BDPP78	$3.25	$13.10	$7.07	$40	$80
Jameson Taillon	BDPP79	$11.99	$38.00	$23.81	$40	$60
Aaron Sanchez	BDPP74	$2.79	$10.50	$5.50	$25	–
Chris Sale	BDPP92	$10.50	$18.01	$14.44	$25	$80
Michael Choice	BDPP61	$12.61	$22.50	$16.81	$15	–
Mike Olt	BDPP65	$4.75	$11.10	$7.49	$15	–

Sources: dailywax.com, Beckett.com

Manny Machado, the 3rd overall pick in the 2010 MLB First Year Player Draft, was the top prospect in the set, and has turned out well thus far. Pittsburgh Pirates prospect RHP Jameson Taillon was the 2nd overall pick behind Bryce Harper, and remains a top prospect, though his value hasn't changed much in three years.

But New York Mets RHP Matt Harvey (7th overall) rose from overlooked prospect to being widely regarded as one of the best pitchers in baseball in 2013, posting a 2.27 ERA in 178.1 innings over 26 starts before going down with a partially torn UCL, which would ultimately require Tommy John surgery. Toronto draftee RHP

---

[87] www.dailywax.com/2010/12/breakdown-of-2010-bowman-chrome-draft-auto-sales

Noah Syndergaard (3rd round) went from a certified common to a key prospect in the deal that sent Syndergaard and fellow prospect C Travis d'Arnaud to the New York Mets for 2012 NL Cy Young Award winner RHP R.A. Dickey prior to the 2013 season, and enters the 2014 season as one of the top pitching prospects in the game.

And similarly – if not quite as dramatically – then-Florida Marlins draft pick Christian Yelich (23rd overall) went from being of secondary prospect value into developing into one of the best prospects in the game entering the 2013 season.

Other players who started as less-heralded prospects before reaching elite prospect status (and valuations) include Mike Trout, Jurickson Profar, Jose Fernandez, and Wil Myers. These players are out there, and the best places to find them are in sources heavy in prospect coverage, including Baseball America, FanGraphs, and Baseball Prospectus.

Buying Strategies

Another one of the key differences between buying ungraded cards and graded cards – aside from the need to understand the BGS grading system and to be able to gauge quality to a reasonable extent – is that the sheer volume of cards that hit the market with each new release means that the value of good buying strategies is further enhanced.

The Price Ceiling Game

As we've discussed, the flood of new supply upon release means that premium color will often be plentiful. This plentiful supply of otherwise rare cards creates a unique window of opportunity where high-end cards may be under pricing pressure from the presence of other rare cards. Some will be listed at reasonable or unreasonable Buy It Now (BIN) prices, while others will be listed with the BIN or Best Offer feature; still others will be straight auctions.

We can use the presence of BIN listings – particularly the reasonable ones – to our advantage, by using them as price ceilings to put pressure on other listings.

Scenario #1

Let's say there are two Topps Chrome RC Gold Refractor #'d/50 auto redemptions on eBay for a top RC-year player we'll call Mike Trout 2. One is listed at a BIN price of $150, while the other listing is a straight auction ending in three days, with a current price of $80.

You think the card is fairly valued at $150 – not cheap – but you're willing to pay fair value to acquire premium color for a player of Mike Trout 2's caliber.

You want both cards. What's your strategy?

Card	Auction Type	Price	Duration
Mike Trout 2 Gold Refractor Auto Redemption	BIN	$150	–
Mike Trout 2 Gold Refractor Auto Redemption	Auction	$80	3 Days

While we are willing to pay the $150, the game here is to leave the BIN listing up until the 3-day auction is complete. By leaving the $150 BIN card on the market, we are keeping pricing pressure on the card up for straight auction; with the $150 BIN card still available, it is less likely that the card up for straight auction will run past $150.

283

After all, if you know you can buy a card BIN for $150, why would you bid more than $150 for an identical card at auction?

That said, by leaving the $150 BIN card up, we should be able to acquire the card at auction for less than $150. Once the auction is complete, we can take the $150 BIN card as well.

Scenario #2

Let's say that once again there are two Topps Chrome RC Gold Refractor #'d/50 auto redemptions on eBay. This time, one is listed at a BIN price of $150, while the other is listed at $250 BIN or Best Offer.

You still think the card is fairly valued at $150, and you want both cards. What's your strategy?

Card	Auction Type	Price	Duration
Mike Trout 2 Gold Refractor Auto Redemption	BIN or Best Offer	$250	–
Mike Trout 2 Gold Refractor Auto Redemption	BIN	$150	–

The game here is to use pricing pressure from the card listed at $150 BIN in order to try to get a better price on the card listed at $250 BIN or Best Offer, in effect using the $150 BIN card as a price ceiling. The play is to offer less than $150 on the card listed at $250 BIN or Best Offer, and try to cut a deal at $150 or less; once you've made a deal on that card (or determine that the seller is not willing to deal), you can take the other one at $150 as well.

Scenario #3

Let's say instead that there are four such cards. One is up for straight auction ending in three days with a current price of $80, while another is up for auction ending in five days with a current price of $30. A third card is listed at a BIN price of $150, and a fourth card is listed with a BIN or Best Offer price of $250.

What's your play?

Card	Auction Type	Price	Duration
Mike Trout 2 Gold Refractor Auto Redemption	BIN or Best Offer	$250	–
Mike Trout 2 Gold Refractor Auto Redemption	BIN	$150	–

Card	Auction Type	Price	Duration
Mike Trout 2 Gold Refractor Auto Redemption	Auction	$80	3 Days
Mike Trout 2 Gold Refractor Auto Redemption	Auction	$30	5 Days

This is a quite common scenario, and one that represents our bread-and-butter for finding good values in top RCs and prospects, and sometimes extraordinary values in lesser stars or secondary prospects.

Our strategy in this scenario depends slightly on the quality of player in question. For second-tier or long-shot talents that you are interested in taking a flyer on (but are not necessarily interested in betting the crap out of), this is a spot where you would leave all of the BIN and BIN or Best Offer listings up, and pick at the straight auctions in an effort to get extreme value.

But for a player of Mike Trout 2's caliber – where we want all four cards, if we can get them for fair value or better – we might play this a number of ways.

For starters, we can use the presence of the $150 BIN and two auctions to try to get even better deal on the $250 BIN or Best Offer card, as the seller with the $250 BIN or Best Offer card knows he needs to beat more than just the $150 BIN price in order to sell within the next five days (when the second auction ends). If the seller is motivated to sell, we might get a steal; if he isn't, then we'll forget about him, and use the presence of his card to keep pricing pressure on the two straight auction listings.

We still want to leave the $150 BIN card up in order to keep the prices of the two auctions down. Once those auctions clear – hopefully with favorable prices for us as buyers – we can click BIN on the $150 card.

That said, while this strategy makes sense in theory and generally works in practice, for a player like Mike Trout (or Mike Trout 2), the safer play in this scenario may be to simply take the $150 BIN card and leave the $250 BIN or Best Offer card – otherwise, you risk losing the $150 BIN card at a reasonable price, while you will lose pricing pressure on the auctions anyway if somebody else comes in and snatches up the $150 BIN card before the auctions end.

Combined Shipping Strategy: The Cost Advantage Play

When cases get broken, case breakers will put many, many player lots and singles out of those breaks up for auction, which might take place seconds or minutes apart. Typically, when you win one of these auctions, the shipping cost will be $2 or $3; but when you win two or more auctions from the same seller, the seller will combine shipping costs, such that the shipping fee for each additional auction won will be generally be between free (generally for singles) and $1 (usually for lots or graded cards) per auction won.

This is potentially a major advantage if you're interested in multiple lower-priced auctions from a given seller, because you will effectively be able to bid more than competing bidders who are only interested in the one auction.

Here's a simple example. Let's say you win an auction for $17.95 + $2.95 shipping = $20.90, and the seller has another card up for auction with a single current bid of $0.99 + $2.95 shipping; this seller will combine shipping, with additional singles at no additional cost (free).

You think this card is worth $4. In this case, because the shipping cost is free due to combined shipping, you can bid $4 (and obviously hope to win the auction for less), where a $4 bid would cost someone else only interested in the one card $4 + $2.95 = $6.95.

Combined shipping can be a major advantage that may allow you to pick up a lot of lower priced singles and lots on the cheap. It is particularly handy where if a case breaker has a multi-card lot or a #'d refractor for a certain player you are interested in, he is likely to have lots or other #'d refractors up for auction for other players you are interested in as well.

Corner the Market

The flood of new, high-end supply may also provide opportunities to corner the market on high-end cards for a given player. It's not uncommon for a collector to buy the crap out of the premium color refractors for a given player, or for a group of collectors to pool together funds to do it. By cornering the market, you gain pricing power by eliminating competition or potential competition when the time comes to sell.

Obviously you'd prefer to be able to do this at reasonable – if not steal – prices.

Player Case Breaks

Most case breaks are pre-sold in lots ahead of the break. Case breaks can be divided any number of ways – some case breakers do it by team, while others do it by player, or by type of card (autos vs. non-autos, paper vs. chrome, inserts vs. base + refractors, or refractors vs. base, etc.). Some case breakers sell lots at fixed prices on their websites, while others sell lots at auction on eBay.

For the most part, case breaks are bad bets value wise, and often attract two basic types of bidders/buyers:

1. Bidders/buyers who are looking to gamble for high-end hits, and are willing to pay a premium to do so, and/or

2. Bidders/buyers who are looking to gamble for high-end hits, but either don't know the odds of actually drawing certain high-end hits, or otherwise fundamentally overvalue the prospects of doing so.

But while the prices of many of these auctions – usually those including top prospects and autos – are often wildly overpriced, sometimes extreme values can be found by avoiding the "hottest" names in player-specific case breaks.

2013 Bowman Draft was officially released on November 13, 2013. The table on the next page shows the RC-logo player prices from auctions for a pair of 2013 Bowman Draft Hobby 10-case breaks – one dated Nov. 14, and the other dated Nov. 27, 2013. The auctions were for all base chrome and refractors pulled for a given player (no paper), including all of the regular colored refractors including 1/1 Superfractors, Red Refractors #'d/5, Orange Refractors #'d/25, Black Refractors #'d/35, Gold Refractors #'d/50, Green Refractors #'d/75, Blue Refractors #'d/99, and regular Refractors (but excluding the Blue Wave Refractors, Black Wave Refractors, Red Wave Refractors #'d/25, and Silver Wave Refractors #'d/25).

None of the RC auctions included autos, except for the Yasiel Puig auctions, which we'll discuss in a minute.

2013 Bowman Draft 10-Case Breaks: Chrome RCs

Player	#	Nov. 14	Nov. 27
Yasiel Puig + Auto	1	$204.00	$217.94
Tyler Skaggs	2	$10.26	$8.26
Nathan Karns	3	–	$7.23
Manny Machado	4	–	$71.00

287

Player	#	Nov. 14	Nov. 27
Anthony Rendon	5	–	$8.38
Gerrit Cole	6	$22.03	$38.00
Sonny Gray	7	–	$6.49
Henry Urietta	8	$11.50	$17.50
Zoilo Almonte	9	$8.49	$6.01
Jose Fernandez	10	$10.50	$26.00
Danny Salazar	11	$7.26	$9.53
Nick Franklin	12	–	$6.11
Mike Kickham	13	–	$4.99
Alex Colome	14	–	$8.00
Josh Phegley	15	$4.99	$6.61
Drake Britton	16	$4.99	$4.99
Marcell Ozuna	17	–	$6.82
Oswaldo Arcia	18	–	$7.55
Didi Gregorious	19	–	$7.25
Zack Wheeler	20	$7.50	$19.50
Michael Wacha	21	–	$38.00
Kyle Gibson	22	–	$6.61
Johnny Hellweg	23	$4.99	$4.99
Dylan Bundy	24	$13.01	$23.50
Tony Cingrani	25	–	$17.15
Jurickson Profar	26	$36.00	$21.50
Scooter Gennett	27	–	$9.72
Grant Green	28	–	$4.99
Brad Miller	29	–	$10.01
Hyun-Jin Ryu	30	$9.00	$6.75
Jedd Gyorko	31	$4.99	–
Shelby Miller	32	–	$13.05
Sean Nolin	33	–	$6.48
Allen Webster	34	–	$4.99
Corey Dickerson	35	$4.99	$7.50
Jarred Cosart	36	$4.99	–
Evan Gattis	37	$8.50	$33.00
Kevin Gausman	38	$7.00	$12.50
Christian Yelich	40	$10.50	$10.50

Player	#	Nov. 14	Nov. 27
Nolan Arenado	41	–	$13.50
Matt Magill	42	–	$6.45
Jackie Bradley, Jr.	43	$5.50	$11.62
Mike Zunino	44	–	$15.65
Wil Myers	45	$31.00	$36.00

Source: eBay

First, a couple of items of note. Not all players appeared in both sets of case breaks; this could be because the case breaker had sold these lots through other methods, or because these were lots he intended to keep for himself. Also, there were in some cases wide discrepancies in price even for the same player between the two case breaks, even though the expectation for what comes out of 10 cases was identical. For example, Evan Gattis sold for $8.50 in the first 10-case break, but for $33.00 in the second 10-case break, while Jose Fernandez sold for $10.50 in the first break but $26 in the second. On the other hand, Jurickson Profar sold for $36.00 in the first break, but only $21.50 in the second.

Puig vs. Everybody Else

The first things that stand out are the two Puig auctions at $204.00 and $217.94. These auctions included a shot at his super short-printed (SSP) Bowman Chrome Draft RC auto, for which there are no refractor variations. And so, the first thing we need to sort out is what that shot at the auto is worth.

The stated odds on the Puig auto redemptions were one every 38,000 packs, or approximately one every 131.9 cases (at 24 packs per box, and 12 boxes per case); as such, the odds of pulling a Puig auto in a 10-case break are worse than one in 13. And from the mid-November release date through the end of 2013, prices on the redemptions ranged from $315 to $480.

Thus, this chance to hit a $315-$480 redemption card one in 13.2 times was worth roughly between $23.88 and $36.39 per 10-case break. Backing these values out pegs the price paid for the non-autos between $167.61 and $194.06.

At $167.61 to $194.06 for the chrome non-autos, the people who won the Puig auctions paid about 2.4x-2.7x the amount paid for the Manny Machado auction at $71, and more than 5x Wil Myers at $31-$36. At least comparatively speaking, Jose Fernandez – who for my money is the best player with a 2013-year RC – looks like a super steal at $10.50 and $26, while Los Angeles Dodgers LHP Hyun-Jin Ryu looks like larceny at $9 and $6.75.

But whether those guys turned out to be steals depends largely on what one gets in a 10-case break. And so the next question is, what does one get in a 10-case break?

10-Case Partial Breakdown

I can tell you at least part of what comes out of a 10-case break, as I won the Gerrit Cole auction in the Nov. 14 break, saw what came out of that, and won 17 auctions in the Nov. 27 break.

Below is a list of the player lot with the price paid, along with the breakdown of the lot, including the gradability of the lot.

1. **Gerrit Cole ($22.03):** Gold Refractor #50/50, 21 base RCs, and 4 Refractors
   - **Notes:** Seven base cards and three Refractors have scratch issues
   - **Gradable:** Gold Refractor #/50, 14 base RCs, 1 Refractor
   - **Assessment:** Excellent return for the No. 1 overall pick in the 2011 MLB First-Year Player Draft. The Gold Refractor by itself paid for the lot, while the 21 base RCs and 4 Refractors also justify the $22 price themselves.

2. **Tyler Skaggs ($8.26):** 23 base RCs, 7 Refractors
   - **Notes:** All Refractors look good, but all of the base cards are off-center, half of them more so than the others
   - **Gradable:** 7 Refractors, zero base RCs
   - **Assessment:** Nothing spectacular, and disappointing centering issues on the base RCs, but still a passable return for the price.

3. **Anthony Rendon ($8.38):** Blue Refractor #'d/99, 20 base RCs, 4 Refractors
   - **Notes:** The Blue Refractor is well-centered but with a good-sized scratch down middle; one Refractor is off-center, another well-centered with a scratch; 17 base RCs are way off-center, while one is well-centered but with a large scratch; two base RCs are gradable – one definite, one with borderline 9-centering
   - **Gradable:** 2 base RCs, 2 Refractors
   - **Assessment:** Not a great lot condition-wise, but it's really hard to complain given the price.

4. **Sonny Gray ($6.49):** Gold Refractor #'d/50, 19 base RCs, 6 Refractors

   - **Notes:** The Gold Refractor is off-center with a scratch; one Refractor is centered with slight surface scratching, while the others are off-center; all but three base RCs are too off-center to grade; three gradable base, one of which has borderline centering

   - **Gradable:** 3 base RCs, 1 Refractor

   - **Assessment:** Not pretty condition-wise, but a clear win for a potential ace. $6.49 justifies the cost of the Gold Refractor *or* the 19 base RCs *or* the 6 refractors. Deep value investing at its finest.

5. **Jose Fernandez ($26.00):** 19 base RCs, 6 Refractors

   - **Notes:** 4 well-centered Refractors and two others with borderline 9-centering, though one of the centered ones has a slightly raised edge; 18 borderline 9-9.5 centering base RCs, and one probable 9-centering with a scratch

   - **Gradable:** 18 base RCs, 5 Refractors

   - **Assessment:** No color, but still good value on raw value alone – for reference, the ungraded BV of the base RC is $5, and Refractors are $10. If the Refractors grade out or even half the base cards grade out BGS 9.5, I'll see a decent return on investment.

6. **Marcell Ozuna ($6.82):** Green Refractor #'d/75, 24 base RCs, 7 Refractors

   - **Notes:** Green Refractor is a borderline 9-center, but otherwise clean; Refractors – one off-center with a scratch, one centered with a scratch, and five centered with minor potential surface issues; eight base RCs are off-center, one centered but scratched, and one centered but with what looks like a surface stain; 14 base RCs are gradable, with a couple of probable 9-centers

   - **Gradable:** Green Refractor #/75, 14 base RCs, 5 Refractors

   - **Assessment:** Deep value play. Qualitatively excellent return with a lot of potential upside should Ozuna reach power potential, but a longshot to realize any graded value in base RCs or Refractors given the player and team (Marlins), though cards theoretically could be flipped ungraded at a profit. The Green Refractor is a plus, even if hideous in color.

7. **Oswaldo Arcia ($7.55):** 24 base RCs, 7 Refractors

   - **Notes:** Refractors – one way off-center, one centered with multiple surface scratches, five gradable; three base RCs off-center, and three others with combination of center/surface issues; 18 base RCs gradable

   - **Gradable:** 18 base RCs, 5 Refractors

   - **Assessment:** No color. Like Ozuna, a good qualitative return, but also a longshot to realize any graded value where graded BGS 9.5/10 2013 Bowman Chrome RC *autos* run $20-$25; still, a good value, as cards theoretically could probably be flipped ungraded at profit.

8. **Zack Wheeler ($19.50):** 25 base RCs, 3 Refractors

   - **Notes:** Refractors – two borderline 9-centering, one off-center; three solid base RCs, two borderline 9-centering, and the rest probably 8.5-centering

   - **Gradable:** 5 base RCs, 2 Refractors

   - **Assessment:** Playable. No color, and a very poor return qualitatively speaking. But still a decent overall value at $19.50 for a top young pitcher on a playable team (Mets), if any of the gradables grade out.

9. **Kyle Gibson ($6.61):** Orange Refractor #'d/25, 21 base RCs, 7 Refractors

   - **Notes:** Orange Refractor looks like a slam dunk; Refractors – six off-center, one centered but with a scratch; 12 base RCs off-center, one scratched, eight base RCs borderline centered

   - **Gradable:** Orange Refractor #'d/25, 8 base RCs

   - **Assessment:** Home run. 8 borderline gradable base RCs have double longshot value in that Gibson may not pan out, while cards may not grade out. But the perfectly gradable Orange Refractor is a good value at $6.61, and makes the rest of the lot a freeroll.

10. **Dylan Bundy ($23.50):** 24 base RCs, 6 Refractors

    - **Notes:** One Refractor way off-center, another well off-center, and others have surface scratch issues; five base RCs are off-center and five others have scratches, but the other 14 are gradable, some with minor center or surface issues

    - **Gradable:** 14 base RCs

- **Assessment:** Playable, but not a good value. No color, and no gradable Refractors. Still, 14 potentially gradable base cards give the lot longshot value with upside should Bundy make it back from Tommy John surgery and reach potential.

11. **Tony Cingrani ($17.15):** 22 base RCs, 7 Refractors

  - **Notes:** Six Refractors gradable, one off-center; two gradable base, seven borderline 9-centering, with the other 13 off-center

  - **Gradable:** 9 base RCs, 6 Refractors

  - **Assessment:** No color, but fairly valued based on gradables alone. However, while I do think Cingrani has some upside, it's questionable whether the base RCs and regular Refractors are worth grading.

12. **Jurickson Profar ($21.50):** Gold Refractor #'d/50, Blue Refractor #'d/99, 21 base RCs, 5 Refractors

  - **Notes:** Gold and Blue Refractors are slam dunk gems; Refractors – 4 gradable, other is off-center with small stain; base RCs – 14 gradable, half borderline or probable 9-centers; four others off-center and three with scratching

  - **Gradable:** Gold Refractor #/50, Blue Refractor #/99, 14 base RCs, 4 Refractors

  - **Assessment:** Grand slam all around. Gradable Gold Refractor covers the cost of the lot alone, with a gradable Blue Refractor as a bonus. 14 gradable base RCs and 4 gradable Refractors also justify the cost of the lot alone. This is why we play the game.

13. **Shelby Miller ($13.05):** Green Refractor #'d/75, 25 base RCs, 7 Refractors

  - **Notes:** Green Refractor 9-9.5 centering, otherwise gradable; five Refractors are too off-center, one has a bad corner, and one has borderline centering; 12 base RCs are too off-center to grade, one has a bad corner, and another has a large surface scratch; 11 base RCs have mostly borderline centering and are borderline gradable

  - **Gradable:** Green Refractor #'d/75, 11 base RCs, 1 Refractor

  - **Assessment:** Spectacular value all around for $13, though not great condition-wise.

14. Christian Yelich ($10.50): 19 base RCs, 2 Refractors

- **Notes:** Both Refractors are centered, but one has a scratch; three base RCs are off-center, and two others have scratches; remaining 14 base RCs are gradable, through a couple have borderline centering

- **Gradable:** 14 base RCs, 1 Refractor

- **Assessment:** No color, and relatively thin return with only two Refractors and 19 base RCs – there must have been a few Blue Wave Refractors, Black Wave Refractors, Silver Wave Refractors #'d/25, or Red Wave Refractors #'d/25 in these cases. Otherwise, condition-wise a playable return with potential long-term graded value, thanks to the $10.50 price.

15. Nolan Arenado ($13.50): Blue Refractor #'d/99, 21 base RCs, 4 Refractors

- **Notes:** Blue Refractor is well centered, but has a large scratch down the center; four Refractors are very strong; one base RC has a scratch, but the other 20 are split 50-50 between 9 and 9.5 centering, and are all gradable

- **Gradable:** 20 base RCs, 4 Refractors

- **Assessment:** Unfortunate that the Blue Refractor won't play, but otherwise a very solid return at a very good price for a player who won a Gold Glove at third base as a rookie. As with Cingrani, the base and regular Refractors probably aren't worth grading at the moment, but may have long-term grade value.

16. Jackie Bradley, Jr. ($11.62): 23 base RCs, 7 Refractors

- **Notes:** Three Refractors are off-center, two are well-centered, and two have borderline 9 centering; 20 base RCs are way off-center, one is a very borderline 9-center, one a probable 9-center, and one is a probable 9.5 center

- **Gradable:** 2 base RCs, 4 Refractors

- **Assessment:** Not good, thanks to disastrous centering. But the benefit of paying a very good price is that it doesn't hurt much.

17. Mike Zunino ($15.65): Green Refractor #'d/75, 21 base RCs, 4 Refractors

- **Notes:** Green Refractor has borderline centering, but is otherwise clean; Refractors – one is a borderline 9-center with bad corners, but three are gradable, though one is a probable 9-center; 21 gradable base RCs, though a few are probable 9-centers

- **Gradable:** Green Refractor #'d/75, 21 base RCs, 3 Refractors
- **Assessment:** Good overall return with potential upside should Zunino figure out major league pitching.

18. Wil Myers ($36.00): 20 base RCs, 7 Refractors

- **Notes:** Refractors – one is a slam dunk and one has borderline 9 centering, while the others are not terrible but are not close enough on centering to grade; base RCs – two slam dunks and two probable 9 centering, while the other 16 are not close enough to grade
- **Gradable:** 4 base RCs, 2 Refractors
- **Assessment:** No color, and not a good return condition-wise, but a very good price on the lot generally speaking. Price works out to about $1 per base RC, and $2 per refractor (BV: $4 and $8). A few BGS 9.5 grades and this lot will work out just fine.

Conclusion: Thoughts on Value

I should warn that these results are probably atypical – these breaks came not long after the releases of 2013 Topps Chrome, Bowman Chrome, and Finest within a span of two weeks, which resulted in what at least appeared to be an unusually severe depression in the initial market values of these new issues. Moreover, 10-case breaks aren't necessarily typical now and may not be in the future; when fewer cases are broken, it may be harder to get such extreme values.

That said, if we can avoid the Puigs and other bubbly players, there may be potential bargains to be had in case breaks, but we can see that even in 10 cases there is a lot of variance in terms of color (though a big part is likely attributable to the exclusion of the Blue/Black/Silver/Red Wave Refractors from the lot in this particular case), and a lot of variance in terms of condition. This requires heavy discounting, as we don't get the chance to cherry pick the centered cards. Moreover, the 18 auctions produced only 10 colored refractors.

Now *that* said, our default play regarding premium color should be to pick off centered singles, rather than try to hit home runs in case breaks. And rather than try to estimate fair value and then apply a discount, our best approach to case breaks is often simply to look to pay prices that can't be wrong.

In these breaks, the most constant and reliable components were the base cards and regular (non-color) Refractors. On average, there were 21.8 base RCs and 5.6 Refractors per lot, with a low of 19 base RCs and 2 Refractors (both in the Yelich lot). For reference, the stated pack odds on refractors yield an expectation of 4.4 Refractors per player.[88]

Let's assume conservatively that we can expect 20 base RCs and 4 Refractors per player. Under these assumptions, a price of $28 for Jose Fernandez works out to $1 per base card and $2 per Refractor, with the colored refractor upside for free. This is a very good price on the base cards + Refractors alone, as $1 per base card works out to be 20%-33% of ungraded book, assuming we project ungraded book values between $3 and $5.

This is a price that can't be wrong.

But notice that we haven't even gotten around to figuring out what the expectation on a given lot is actually worth, factoring the expected value of the colored refractors. That is, at some point, we need to account for the odds of each colored refractor hitting and the value of each refractor, tally up the expected value of the colored refractors, and factor that into our expected valuation of each player lot. In this case, it wasn't particularly necessary, as I wasn't looking to gamble on the lots I acquired – for the most part, the lots I acquired were layups based strictly on base cards and Refractors alone.

But where we're not really looking to gamble, a lot of people are. And as we will see next with the Bowman Chrome Draft Prospects auto lots, the prospect for color in general, and prospects for autos in particular are often overvalued.

---

[88] One refractor every three packs and 288 packs per case works out to 960 refractors in 10 cases. 2013 Bowman Draft included 130 draft prospects, 45 base set RCs, and 45 top prospects for a total of 220 base cards with refractors; 960/220 = 4.36 refractors per player for every 10 cases.

Case Breaks Part II: Bowman Chrome Draft Prospect Autos

For many gambling-inclined collectors, the most attractive element of a case break is the prospect of hitting high-end refractor autos of rookies or prospects at a relatively low cost. But especially for the hottest prospects and RCs, this is often a double whammy – not only are these players often trading at bubble prices to begin with, but the prospects of hitting those high end cards are often wildly overvalued on top of that.

The fact of the matter is, in any auction, it only takes two bidders who either:

1. Don't know the odds of hitting a given card, or

2. Don't care.

And unfortunately, many of the guys bidding on these types of auctions are either superfractor hunting or are merely looking to gamble, driving up prices in either case. Still, it's worth examining the value of these auctions, if only for curiosity's sake.

The table on the next page lists the prices of Bowman Chrome Draft Prospect auto lots from the same 10-case 2013 Bowman Draft Hobby case breaks from the preceding discussion, dated 11/14/13 and 11/27/13. Each player lot includes all chrome prospect autos for each player, with the exception of the Blue Wave Refractors #'d/50 and Black Wave Refractors #'d/50. Included – should they hit – are the base autos, Refractors, Blue Refractors #'d/99, Green Refractors #'d/75, Gold Refractors #'d/50, Black Refractors #'d/35, Orange Refractors #'d/25, Purple Refractors #'d/10, Red Refractors #'d/5, Superfractors 1/1, and four 1/1 Printing Plates.

There were 47 prospects in the 2013 Bowman Chrome Draft Draft Picks Autographs set, but for simplicity, the table only includes the prospects who appeared in both 10-case breaks. This is a pretty representative group including the top prospects in the set, namely Cleveland Indians OF Clint Frazier (5th overall pick in the 2013 MLB First-Year Player Draft), Pittsburgh Pirates OF Austin Meadows (9th), Colorado Rockies RHP Jonathan Gray (3rd), Minnesota Twins RHP Kohl Stewart (4th), and Miami Marlins 3B Colin Moran (6th). It also includes two of the least valued prospects in the set in Miami Marlins RHP Trevor Williams (44th overall) and Detroit Tigers LHP Kevin Ziomek (58th).

10-Case Break: 2013 Bowman Chrome Draft Prospect Autos

Player	#	Nov. 14 Chrome Auto	Nov. 27 Chrome Auto
Aaron Blair	AB	$33.57	$26.00
Andrew Church	AC	$31.56	$36.27
Aaron Judge	AJ	$128.25	$133.50
Andrew Knapp	AK	$39.77	$22.72
Austin Meadows	AM	$455.00	$325.00
Chris Anderson	CA	$73.50	$69.00
Clint Frazier	CF	$441.00	$353.50
Colin Moran	CM	$147.71	$138.53
Chance Sisco	CS	$37.00	$40.75
Cord Sandberg	CSA	$81.00	$76.68
D.J. Peterson	DP	$130.49	$121.39
Dustin Peterson	DPE	$46.55	$45.27
Dominic Smith	DS	$256.11	$162.50
Eric Jagielo	EJ	$91.00	$72.51
Hunter Dozier	HD	$169.50	$132.50
Hunter Green	HG	$51.00	$41.00
Hunter Harvey	HH	$87.00	$72.00
Hunter Renfroe	HR	$107.28	$129.50
Ian Clarkin	IC	$70.00	$63.99
J.P. Crawford	JC	$115.38	$124.50
Jonathan Crawford	JCR	$46.00	$39.00
Jon Denney	JD	$43.98	$57.00
Jonathan Gray	JG	$202.50	$183.50
Josh Hart	JH	$42.00	$37.00
Justin Williams	JW	$59.75	$67.90
Kevin Franklin	KF	$26.87	$56.00
Kohl Stewart	KS	$197.50	$103.50
Kevin Ziomek	KZ	$27.56	$21.83
Trey Ball	TB	$142.38	$107.50
Travis Demeritte	TD	$71.00	$71.00
Tyler Danish	TDA	$27.88	$34.00
Trevor Williams	TW	$26.56	$28.51

Source: eBay

The Odds

The first thing we need to do is figure out how many and what kinds of autos we can expect to get for a given player in a 10-case break. For each type of auto, the table below lists the print run; the stated odds for each type of auto in 2013 Bowman Draft Hobby packs; the number of each type of auto that you can expect to pull in 10 cases (based on 24 packs per box and 12 boxes per case, which works out to 288 packs per 10 cases); the number of each type of auto per player in 10 cases (based on 47 prospects with chrome autos); and the percent of total chrome prospect autos that each type of auto represents (excluding Blue Wave Refractors #'d/50 and Black Wave Refractors #'d/50).

2013 Bowman Draft Hobby: Chrome Prospect Auto Breakdown

Color	Print Run	Pack Odds	Per 10 Cases	Per Player Per 10 Cases	Percent of Total
Base	–	1:35	82.29	1.75	69.4%
Refractor	–	1:132	21.82	0.46	18.4%
Blue	99	1:659	4.37	0.09	3.7%
Green	75	1:872	3.30	0.07	2.8%
Gold	50	1:1,309	2.20	0.05	1.9%
Black	35	1:1,097	2.63	0.06	2.2%
Orange	25	1:2,615	1.10	0.02	0.9%
Purple	10	1:6,555	0.44	0.01	0.4%
Red	5	1:13,065	0.22	0.00	0.2%
Superfractor	1	1:63,800	0.05	0.00	0.0%
Printing Plates	4	1:16,356	0.18	0.00	0.1%
Total	–	–	**118.58**	**2.52**	**100%**

It should be noted that despite the fact that the Black Refractors #'d/35 are rarer than the Gold Refractors #'d/50, the Black Refractors were easier to pull in 2013 Bowman Draft Hobby boxes because they were Hobby-only (they were inserted only into Hobby boxes, and not Jumbo), whereas the Gold Refractors were split between Hobby and Jumbo boxes.

That said, at 12 boxes per case and one chrome auto per box, there are 120 chrome autos per 10 cases. The stated odds yield *on average* a total of 118.58 chrome prospect autos per 10 cases excluding Blue Wave #/50 and Black Wave #/50 refractors, with the 1.42 auto difference attributable in part to 1/13th of a Puig RC auto; the Blue Wave Refractor autos #'d/50 and Black Wave Refractor autos #'d/50 that are not included in these lots; other insert autos; and rounding error.

Of these 118.58 chrome prospect autos per 10 cases, 82.29 will be base autos, and 21.82 will be Refractor autos. Only 14.48 colored, numbered refractor autos will appear per 10 cases (excluding Blue Wave and Black Wave Refractors).

For each player, you can expect to pull 2.52 autos per 10 cases (again excluding Blue Wave Refractors and Black Wave Refractors). And of these 2.52 autos per player, 2.21 or 87.8% will be either base autos (1.75 per player, or 69.4% of total) or non-colored Refractors (0.46 per player, or 18.4% of total), while you can expect to pull only 0.31 colored, numbered refractors (excluding Blue Wave and Black Wave Refractors) per 10-case break.

Valuation

Our next task is to figure out what these odds are worth. For any given player, this requires assigning values to each color parallel included in the lot.

The two lots for Cleveland Indians prospect Clint Frazier sold for $441.00 and $353.50 on Nov. 14 and Nov. 27, respectively. Let's be extra generous and value the lots by using the *highest price paid* for each variation of auto through early January 2014. Multiplying the highest price paid by the number of each variation we can expect to see in 10 cases yields the expected value of each variation; tallying up these numbers gives us the expected value for the entire lot.

The Superfractor value is estimated at $5,000, as there is no record of sale as of January 2014.

Clint Frazier: EV by Highest Price Paid Scenario

Color	Print Run	Card Value*	Per Player Per 10 Cases	Expected Value
Base	—	$90	1.75	$157.57
Refractor	—	$111	0.46	$51.53
Blue	99	$328	0.09	$30.50
Green	75	$310	0.07	$21.78
Gold	50	$500	0.05	$23.41
Black	35	$580	0.06	$32.40
Orange	25	$765	0.02	$17.93
Purple	10	$720	0.01	$6.73
Red	5	$2,225	0.00	$10.44
Superfractor	1	$5,000e	0.00	$4.80
Printing Plates	4	$250	0.00	$0.94
Total	—	—	**2.52**	**$358.01**

*Card prices from eBay and Terapeak.com; Superfractor value is estimated

The expected value of each lot in this scenario is $358.01. And so essentially, in terms of expectation, the guy who paid $353.50 paid an amount roughly equivalent to the *highest price anyone has paid* for each of the different variations, and the guy who paid $441.00 paid a whopping 23% *premium* to the highest price paid.

That is, even assuming they could turn around and sell whatever comes out of the break for the highest price yet sold – a completely unreasonable assumption to make – one guy broke even, and the other guy wildly overpaid.

Problem is, most of the base autos traded in a range more like $60-$80 over the first couple of months, while the Refractors were in the $80-$100 range. In fact, by the time graded BGS 9.5/10 copies appeared in January, multiple copies sold for as low as $90. At the same time, there were several Blue Refractor #/99 and Green Refractor #/75 sales in the $200-$240 range, with one outlier Blue Refractor sale at $175.

Meanwhile, the $2,225 paid for the Red Refractor #1/5 is in the same range as the 2013 Bowman Chrome Prospects Byron Buxton Red Refractor autos upon release, but does merit a premium as the #1/5. That said, based on his other sales, you would expect Frazier's other Red Refractors to trade more in the neighborhood of $1,500 (in which case the #1/5 sold at a relatively reasonable 50% premium).

On the other hand, there were some outliers in the other direction. Only one Purple Refractor auto #'d/10 sold in a fixed price listing (BIN or Best Offer), and at $720 sold at a price lower than two Orange Refractors #'d/25. Also, a 1/1 Printing Plate auto sold for $250 in another fixed price listing, which would be a very good price for the buyer under any assumption.

Let's examine the Clint Frazier case break auto lots under three more reasonable scenarios using market values over the first couple of months after initial release:

1. High Market Value
2. More Average Market Value
3. Low Market Value

The first scenario is the High Market Value scenario. We've adjusted the high end of base card value down to $80; Refractors down $100; and Blue and Green Refractors down to $300 each, while the Red Refractor #/5 value has been adjusted down to $1,500. Gold Refractors, Black Refractors, Orange Refractors, and the 1/1 Superfractor values remain the same. Purple Refractors #'d/10 have been adjusted upward to $1,000, while the value of the Printing Plates has been doubled to $500, in line with the Gold Refractor. Under this scenario, the value of the case break lots is $332.25.

Clint Frazier: High Market Value Scenario

Color	Print Run	Card Value	Per Player Per 10 Cases	Expected Value
Base	–	$80	1.75	$140.06
Refractor	–	$100	0.46	$46.42
Blue	99	$300	0.09	$27.90
Green	75	$300	0.07	$21.08
Gold	50	$500	0.05	$23.41
Black	35	$580	0.06	$32.40
Orange	25	$765	0.02	$17.93
Purple	10	$1,000	0.01	$9.35
Red	5	$1,500	0.00	$7.04
Superfractor	1	$5,000	0.00	$4.80
Printing Plates	4	$500	0.00	$1.87
Total	–	–	2.52	$332.25

In the More Average Market Value scenario, we drop the base auto value down to $70, and the Refractor value down to $90; the Blue and Green Refractors down to $250 each; the Gold Refractor value down to $50; the Black Refractor value down to $500; the Orange Refractor value down to $700; and the Purple Refractor value down to $900. This yields an expected value of $292.68.

Clint Frazier: More Average Market Value Scenario

Color	Print Run	Card Value	Per Player Per 10 Cases	Expected Value
Base	–	$70	1.75	$122.55
Refractor	–	$90	0.46	$41.78
Blue	99	$250	0.09	$23.25
Green	75	$250	0.07	$17.57
Gold	50	$450	0.05	$21.07
Black	35	$500	0.06	$27.93
Orange	25	$700	0.02	$16.40
Purple	10	$900	0.01	$8.41
Red	5	$1,500	0.00	$7.04
Superfractor	1	$5,000	0.00	$4.80
Printing Plates	4	$500	0.00	$1.87
Total	–	–	2.52	$292.68

In our Low Market Value scenario, we drop values to the lower end of reasonable price ranges (i.e. excluding outliers) for all variations. Base card value drops to $60, with Refractors dropping to $80; Blue and Green Refractors drop to $200 each; Gold Refractors drop to $400, while Black Refractors drop to $450; Orange Refractors drop to $600, with Purple Refractors dropping to $800 (still higher than the lone actual sale); Red Refractors drop to $1,200, with the projected Superfractor 1/1 value dropping to $4,000; lastly, the value of the 1/1 Printing Plate autos drops to $400.

In this scenario, the expected value of $251.20.

Clint Frazier: Low Market Value Scenario

Color	Print Run	Card Value	Per Player Per 10 Cases	Expected Value
Base	–	$60	1.75	$105.05
Refractor	–	$80	0.46	$37.14
Blue	99	$200	0.09	$18.60
Green	75	$200	0.07	$14.05
Gold	50	$400	0.05	$18.72
Black	35	$450	0.06	$25.14
Orange	25	$600	0.02	$14.06
Purple	10	$800	0.01	$7.48
Red	5	$1,200	0.00	$5.63
Superfractor	1	$4,000	0.00	$3.84
Printing Plates	4	$400	0.00	$1.50
Total	–	–	**2.52**	**$251.20**

And so, based on a reasonable range of *market* values, this yields a value range of $251.20 to $332.25 for each Clint Frazier auto 10-case break lot. Of course, these expected values still assume that Frazier is not being overvalued.

The Bubble Factor

Clint Frazier – the 2013 Baseball America High School Player of the Year – enters the 2014 season as the Indian's No. 2-ranked prospect according to Baseball America, with arguably his biggest tool being projected 70 power (on a 20-80 scouting scale, with 80 being the highest). And with initial ungraded sales of his base auto generally in the $60-$80 range and as high as $90, and initial BGS 9.5/10 sales in the $90-$125 range, he is already being valued higher than Atlanta Braves OF Jason Heyward (whose 2008 Bowman Chrome Prospects auto graded BGS

303

9.5/10 were trading down in the $50-$60 range by the end of 2013), and a notch under the 2013 AL Rookie of the Year in Tampa Bay Rays OF Wil Myers.

However, Frazier has also played all of 44 games in the Rookie-level Arizona League, where he hit a respectable .297/.362/.506 with 11 doubles, 5 triples, and 5 HRs, but also struck out 61 times in 172 ABs for a 35% strikeout rate.

Frazier may or may not be an elite prospect. But regardless, he is a long way away from the majors having yet to take a crack at even low-A ball, and the overwhelming probability is that he is being wildly overvalued. If it were my money, I would be more interested at prices like this:

Clint Frazier: If It Were My Money

Color	Print Run	Card Value	Per Player Per 10 Cases	Expected Value
Base	–	$30	1.75	$52.53
Refractor	–	$40	0.46	$18.57
Blue	99	$100	0.09	$9.30
Green	75	$100	0.07	$7.03
Gold	50	$200	0.05	$9.36
Black	35	$250	0.06	$13.96
Orange	25	$300	0.02	$7.03
Purple	10	$400	0.01	$3.74
Red	5	$600	0.00	$2.81
Superfractor	1	$1,500	0.00	$1.44
Printing Plates	4	$200	0.00	$0.75
Total	–	–	2.52	$126.52

Conclusion

Generally speaking, I would be cautious about jumping on hot prospects in general, but I would be doubly cautious about acquiring case break lots on such players. Because not only are the hot prospects often being wildly overvalued, but the odds of actually hitting these player's rare parallels are also often being wildly overvalued based even on the prevailing, wildly overvalued market prices, thus making case break auto lots a potentially double bad bet.

Your best bet with autos and premium color parallels in general is to pick off singles. And if you do choose to participate in player case breaks, you are better off looking for layups in terms of value, rather than looking for opportunities to gamble.

Submitting Cards for Grading

If you've never submitted cards for grading before, the prospect can be intimidating, particularly given the risk of spending a lot of money in an effort to build BGS 9.5 Gem Mint and BGS 10 Pristine cards, only to wind up with a bunch of BGS 9 Mint grades or worse. Meanwhile, no matter how well prepared you are, the nuances of BGS' grading standards will require experience in the form of at least two or three sets of submissions in order to get a good feel for them, and probably five or six sets of submissions to be able to more properly evaluate your own cards with any degree of confidence.

But have no fear, as we have options available which – along with a little bit of preparation – will help shade the odds in our favor.

The "No-Grade" or "Min-Grade" Option

For customers grading in sufficient bulk, BGS has a "no-grade" or "min-grade" option that is not advertised but is common knowledge. And with this option, for $1 or $2 per card – or more, depending on the size of your order and desired turnaround time – the grader will examine the card and only grade and slab the card if the grader determines that the card meets the standard for your desired minimum grade. For example, if you send in 200 cards and specify "min-grade BGS 9.5" and the grader deems only 100 cards to meet the minimum requirements to grade BGS 9.5 Gem Mint or BGS 10, then you will pay the $1 or $2 fee for all 200 cards, but only pay the grading fee on the 100 cards that grade BGS 9.5 Gem Mint or BGS 10.

With the "min-grade" option, the grading fee will also be slightly higher – for example, if your regular "grade all" fee based on your quantity and turnaround time is $7 per card + $1 per auto, the grading fee with the "min-grade" option might be $8 + $1 per auto, *in addition* to a $1 per card initial fee (note that prices are fluid). But particularly for novice graders, this is an extremely valuable option to have, as for the most part, you really don't want BGS 9s.

Group Submissions and Bulk Orders

The most cost effective way to grade cards is to do it in bulk (which may be north of 200 cards per submission) and with the longest turnaround time (a 30-day turnaround time is 30 *business* days, which works out to be about 7-8 weeks factoring shipping time in both directions). But unless you are planning on regularly submitting in bulk volume yourself, your best bet is to look for others in order to pool together cards so as to get the lowest bulk order rates.

The first place you should go to in order to do group submissions is your local brick-and-mortar card store, if it still exists. Some card stores pool together customer and store-owned cards for regular bulk submissions, allowing customers to benefit from the lowest grading fees. And if you still have a local card store in your area that doesn't do this, you should strongly suggest that they do, and see what the interest level of their other customers is.

That failing, another option is to find other collectors in online forums who pool cards for bulk submissions. Virtually all of the large online forums dedicated to sports cards will have members who host group submissions.

If, on the other hand, you are planning on submitting in sufficient bulk yourself, I would go online, contact BGS directly and ask about doing bulk submissions yourself.

Supplies

Before you submit cards, you should invest in the following supplies:

1. **A microfiber cloth.** Many cards you buy off the Internet are bound to have a fingerprint or two, if not worse. A microfiber cloth is often enough to wipe away fingerprints and other smudges.

2. **Card sleeves.** Standard size card sleeves are standard protection for any card of value. Among other things, they also allow for easy transfer between top loaders and graded card submission holders, etc. without fear of scratching or fingerprints. Most cards you submit will be in card sleeves inserted into graded card submission semi-rigid holders.

3. **Graded card submission semi-rigid holders.** Large semi-rigid holders are standard for submitting cards. The two most popular brands are Ultra PRO and Card Savers.

4. **One-Touch holders.** While I don't recommend buying ungraded super thick stock cards mostly because the people you buy from are apt not to handle them properly, they can still be highly collectible. But more to the point, if you open boxes you will inevitably wind up with a few worth grading. For 75 pt. memorabilia cards, you can probably get by with 130-pt. card sleeves and the graded card submission holders. But for 100-pt. and larger cards (generally memorabilia cards or other super thick high-end cards) I recommend using Ultra PRO One-Touch holders with magnetic closure (not screw-down), which come in various sizes. Often times, larger

stock cards will fit too tightly in card sleeves at the risk of damaging a corner or the edges; One-Touch (or similar) holders solve that problem. 130-pt. holders will fit most such cards, while other cards (like 2012 Topps Five Star Baseball) may require 180-pt. holders.

5. **Graded card sleeves.** Graded card sleeves are generally meant for use after cards have been graded and slabbed, and are designed to fit one card. However, they are also useful for helping store and organize cards in graded card submission holders that you intend to send off and grade. One sleeve can comfortably accommodate seven or eight chrome cards in graded card submission holders.

6. **Storage boxes.** Storage boxes can be useful both for storing and organizing cards you intend to grade, and also can be inserted into larger boxes when the time comes to ship off your cards. A 300-ct., single row cardboard storage box (from BCW, for example) that is normally intended for sets or commons or other cards is actually the perfect size for graded card submission holders, and can comfortably fit around 50 chrome cards in such holders. The box that the graded card submission holders came in also – quite naturally – can be used to store graded card submission holders with the cards you intend to grade. Another higher-volume storage option are small BCW graded card storage boxes designed to hold about 30 PSA graded cards, or about 25 BGS graded cards; again, while these boxes are intended for cards that have already been graded and slabbed, they can also comfortably accommodate about 130-140 chrome cards in graded card submission holders.

Which Cards to Grade?

For low-value cards with ungraded book values below $10 or so, it is generally value destructive to have cards grade BGS 9 Mint or worse, and generally not worth the cost of grading to have cards up to about $20 come back as BGS 9s. Meanwhile, for higher value cards in the short run (generally within six months of release, but certainly within a year of release, and especially for high value cards), well-centered ungraded cards are generally more valuable than BGS 9s, as people will pay more for a card which they perceive has a shot at grading BGS 9.5 than they will for a card that is a confirmed BGS 9.

With those things in mind, which cards you decide to grade will depend on the value of the card, your expertise level with grading, the grading options available to you, your cost of grading, and how long you intend to keep the card.

When the "no-grade/min-grade" option is available

If you have the "no-grade/min-grade" option available to you, you're willing to wait a couple of months for the cards to come back, and your cost of grading per card altogether (including the no-grade fee, grading fee, the auto grade fee when applicable, and shipping and insurance) is in the neighborhood of $10 or less per card, you can afford to take a shot at some borderline 9-9.5s. If it's your first time grading, I would start with only cards with ungraded book values of $10 or more. But once you've had a few submissions under your belt and start to have an idea of grading standards, you might go ahead and take a shot at some lower value cards.

Just be aware that cards with ungraded book values under $10 often won't be worth more than $15-$20 in immediately realizable value even if they grade BGS 9.5.

When the "no-grade/min-grade" option is not available

If you don't have the "no-grade/min-grade" option available to you, you should probably avoid sub-$10 value cards altogether until you've amassed enough experience to be able grade your own cards proficiently using BGS standards. And once you get to the point where you're dealing with low value base cards, you don't necessarily want to grade borderline cards; rather, you are probably better off sticking to slam dunks BGS 9.5s that may have a shot at BGS 10 Pristine grades.

Once you have a lot of experience such that you are an expert-level grader, at some point you might be better off going the "grade all" route and grading at lower prices. That said, if you are already an expert grader grading in bulk, don't need the "no-grade/min-grade" option and are able to grade at lower than advertised prices on your own, you probably don't need my advice.

Turnaround Time

If you are dealing primarily in high-value cards (say, $100 or greater) and want a quicker turnaround time at higher prices, this is OK, so long as the cost of grading isn't a substantial percentage of the card's value. For example, you generally don't want to be spending $15-$20 to grade cards with ungraded book values of $50 or less, but it's not as bad for cards worth $100 or more, where $15-$20 is 15%-20% of the ungraded book value of the card (or less, the higher the value of the card), rather than 30%-40% of the ungraded book value of the card or more.

How much you want to spend is up to you – obviously you should prefer to avoid the $15-$20 per card rates if you can avoid it, unless you're dealing with extremely high value cards you really don't want to wait on – but the one thing for certain is that you definitely do not want to spend $15-$20 or more grading cards worth $10 or less.

BGS 9 Mint Grades, High-Value Cards, and Holding Period

If you have high-value cards that are extremely unlikely to grade BGS 9.5 or better, and the player in question is likely trading at bubble valuations, your best bet is probably to sell the card raw (ungraded) rather than go for BGS 9 grades, as you are likely to get more value out of the ungraded card. But if the player is potentially being undervalued (which is often the reason you bought the card in the first place, unless you pulled it out of a pack) and has long term value as an established star (say, Manny Machado following his September 2013 injury, just before many of his key RC-logo cards appeared) – and especially if you are dealing with an auto or a premium color parallel – you might be better off holding onto the card if it will grade BGS 9 Mint.

Generally speaking, rare, high-value BGS 9s do better in the long run than in the short run (unless we're talking about prospects with high washout rates).

Prepping: Before You Submit

Before you send your cards in, you should double-check the condition of each card.

1. **Centering:** As usual, the first thing you should examine is the centering – if the card is unlikely to get a 9-centering grade, then it is extremely unlikely to grade BGS 9.5. Remember that a card with 8.5-centering cannot be BGS 9.5 Gem Mint.

2. **Corners and Edges:** If the card is sufficiently well-centered, the next step is to examine the corners. If a corner is bent, it's probably not a 9. Otherwise, you are allowed slight wear, which can be difficult to observe on cards with white borders, but should be easy to spot on cards with dark borders. On chrome cards with dark borders on the back, flip the card over and examine the corners – if the card's corners look clean on the front but you can see a speck of white on the back on one corner, there's a good chance the card will grade 9-corners.

    Edges can be more difficult to judge, unless there is something materially wrong with it – a lifted edge, or jagged edges from being miscut. If something is noticeably wrong, the edges are very unlikely to grade a 9, which should rule out grading the card.

3. **Surface:** Holding the card by its edges, slide the card out of its sleeve and examine the surface at an angle under sufficient light. While most people recommend using a magnifying glass (and of course it's a good idea), most

surface issues can be spotted with the naked eye. Fingerprints can, for the most part, be wiped away using a microfiber cloth. If you see a long, deep line that looks like somebody slashed the card with a box cutter, or if you see multiple smaller lines, you might reconsider submitting the card, as it is unlikely to attain a 9-surface grade.

If a card has two or more blemishes, it is extremely unlikely to grade out BGS 9.5, and more likely to grade BGS 9 Mint or worse. This should all but rule out low-value cards.

4. **Autos:** Autos are important to be able to judge, as if a card is likely to grade a 9 auto, you're probably going to need the card itself to grade BGS 9.5; or if a card is likely to grade with an 8 auto, you might rethink grading the card altogether.

   The default grade is a 10, so in order to grade less there generally must be something wrong with the signature. A bold signature with a slight smudge in one spot – perhaps you can see a speck of white in the signature – is likely to grade a 9. A streaky auto that looks like the signer was running out of ink is also likely to grade a 9 or less. A bold auto that runs off the card (or off the sticker, in the case of sticker autos) is also likely a 9. A super light auto or an auto that is somewhat streaky but runs off the card will likely grade 8 or less.

5. **Submission List:** Make sure you keep a detailed list of the cards you send in. Keep a spreadsheet with the card names, values, and serial numbers for serialized cards. This will help you keep track of your submissions, and help determine values for insurance purposes, as you will generally have to pay for shipping both to and from BGS.[89]

Submission

Now that your cards are ready to go, the final step is to actually submit your cards. This can be done at your local BGS submission center (card store), or a card show attended by BGS. Otherwise, you can mail the cards yourself from the post office; but prior to doing so, be sure to go online and contact BGS with any questions about the process.

---

[89] You can save shipping fees to BGS if you can submit directly to BGS at a card show or some other function.

Also be aware that as of early 2014, BGS' stated/promised turnaround times are listed in terms of *business* days rather than actual days. As such, a 10-day order may take about three weeks to come back, factoring shipping time in both directions, while a 20-day order will generally take about a month.

Part IX: Other Major League Sports

Football, Basketball, and Hockey.

Though the focus of this book has primarily been on baseball cards specifically, most everything we've discussed thus far also applies to cards from the other three major league sports – football, basketball, and hockey. That is, we should still focus on high-grade key cards, premium-color parallels, and on-card autos vs. sticker autos.

But there are a couple of key differences between baseball cards and other sports cards:

1. RC definitions and key cards

2. Key manufacturers

3. Position bias

RC Definitions and Key Cards

When Topps started including minor league prospects in its MLB-licensed 1992 Bowman set, these first cards of these prospects were considered official RCs by Beckett's definition. As we discussed in Part III, these prospect cards were treated as official RCs until the MLBPA changed the "official" definition of a rookie card in 2006, so that only players who actually play in a game at the major league level ultimately can have an officially-designated RC-logo card.

Topps was grandfathered into the practice of including cards of minor league prospects as "inserts" in its major league sets. And as we have observed – regardless of the "official" RC designation – the market still seems to converge on a player's first Bowman Chrome card as his key card.

In other sports, there is no such ambiguity. A player's rookie card in these other sports is his rookie card, and a player's key card and key RC are generally one and the same.

Key Manufacturers

While Topps has an exclusive MLB license which currently runs through 2020, the competition in the football trading card market is currently wide open between Topps and Panini. On the other hand, the competition for NBA basketball cards was wide open until Panini gained an exclusive multi-year agreement with the

NBA which started with the 2009-10 NBA season and currently extends through the 2016-17 season.[90]

Panini also joined the competition in the NHL market when it signed licensing deals with the NHL and NHLPA in 2010, though that market has long been dominated by Upper Deck; but then in February 2014, the NHL and NHLPA announced that Upper Deck would be the exclusive trading card licensee with a new multi-year agreement beginning with the 2014-15 season.[91]

Position Bias

Though there probably is a slight bias in baseball towards everyday position players over pitchers – and there is certainly a bias towards offensive talent over defensive talent, and against relief pitchers (particularly middle relievers) – superstar players and superstar values can and have come from any position. Football and hockey, on the other hand, are two sports that suffer greatly from position bias.

Football card values are dominated by quarterbacks (QBs), and to a lesser extent elite offensive skill position players (running backs and receivers). Defensive players are of secondary value, while offensive lineman are generally of inconsequential value.

Meanwhile, hockey card values are dominated by elite scoring forwards and elite goaltenders, while defenseman are generally of secondary value.

From an Investment Perspective

From an investment perspective, NFL, NBA, and NHL cards may be more attractive than baseball cards from the standpoint that RCs from these sports are far less speculative than minor league baseball prospects who often take several years to develop. Most NFL players enter the league after playing 3-4 years at the college level, while NBA players generally by rule have at least one year of experience playing at the college level before entering the NBA Draft; in stark contrast to baseball players, many NFL and NBA players often come out of the draft ready to play.

Basketball cards also benefit from relatively extreme star power and global appeal, which have helped to promote some of the most highly valued cards in the modern hobby.

---

[90] www.sportsbusinessdaily.com/Journal/Issues/2012/10/29/Marketing-and-Sponsorship/NBA-Panini.aspx

[91] www.nhl.com/ice/news.htm?id=706745

Hockey is slightly different in that only the top prospects generally come out of the NHL Draft ready to play at the NHL level. But the NHL's strict requirements regarding RCs means that only players who have played at the NHL level can be included in NHL-licensed sets, and thus have RCs. As such, hockey RCs are similar to NFL and NBA RCs in that they are significantly less speculative than baseball prospects.

Let's take a closer look at these sports individually.

NFL Football

Football RCs and RC classes are relatively easy to evaluate. The table below lists the top 13 Topps Chrome base RCs by ungraded book value from 2004-2013.

See if you notice anything.

Top Topps Chrome Football Base RCs by Ungraded BV, 2004-2013

Card	#	Pos.	Ungraded BV	BGS 9.5	Adj. Multiple
2004 Topps Chrome Ben Roethlisberger RC	166	QB	$40	$100	2.0x
2004 Topps Chrome Eli Manning RC	205	QB	$30	$80	2.0x
2004 Topps Chrome Phillip Rivers RC	230	QB	$12	$50	2.3x
2004 Topps Chrome Sean Taylor RC	202	S	$12	–	–
2005 Topps Chrome Aaron Rodgers RC	190	QB	$80	$250	2.8x
2007 Topps Chrome Adrian Peterson RC	TC181	RB	$30	$60	1.5x
2007 Topps Chrome Calvin Johnson RC	TC200	WR	$20	$50	1.7x
2008 Topps Chrome Joe Flacco RC	TC170	QB	$12	$30	1.4x
2009 Topps Chrome Matthew Stafford RC	TC210	QB	$15	$50	2.0x
2011 Topps Chrome Colin Kaepernick RC	25	QB	$15	$60	2.4x
2012 Topps Chrome Andrew Luck RC	1	QB	$20	$60	2.0x
2012 Topps Chrome Robert Griffin III RC	200	QB	$12	$50	2.5x
2012 Topps Chrome Russell Wilson	40	QB	$12	$40	1.8x

Source: Beckett.com, December 2013

This is very much a QB-driven game. Of the 13 most highly-valued players by ungraded book value from this period, 12 are players on the offensive side of the ball, and 10 of them are quarterbacks. The other two offensive players are both super elite skill position players in Minnesota Vikings RB Adrian Peterson and Detroit Lions WR Calvin Johnson. The only defensive player on this list is the late Sean Taylor.

As such, it's pretty clear that the evaluation of any draft class should start with the QBs and super elite skill position players. And for the most part, offensive lineman can safely be ignored, while defensive players in general are of secondary concern.

The 2012 NFL Draft Class

2012 was a banner year for football cards, highlighted by an unusually strong 2012 NFL rookie class. That rookie class featured what looks to be at least three elite quarterbacks, including Andrew Luck, who set single-season and single-game rookie passing yardage records, and led an Indianapolis Colts team that was the league's worst in 2011 to 11 wins and the playoffs in 2012 and then again in 2013; as well as Robert Griffin III of the Washington Redskins and Russell Wilson of the Seattle Seahawks, who both ranked in the top 5 in the NFL in passer rating and led their teams to the playoffs as rookies, while Wilson led the Seahawks to a Super Bowl victory in the 2013 season. That class also included Ryan Tannehill of the Miami Dolphins and Nick Foles of the Philadelphia Eagles, who look to join that group near the top after both QBs posted strong sophomore campaigns and narrowly missed the playoffs in 2013.

The 2012 draft class also had two running backs in the top 5 in the league in rushing yardage as rookies – Doug Martin of the Tampa Bay Buccaneers, and sixth-round pick Alfred Morris of the Washington Redskins – as well as LB Luke Kuechly of the Carolina Panthers who led the league in tackles as a rookie in 2012, and further established himself as one of the best linebackers in the game in 2013. In addition, that draft included two other highly rated prospects in RB Trent Richardson of the Cleveland Browns (later traded to the Colts during the 2013 season) and WR Justin Blackmon of the Jacksonville Jaguars – the 3rd and 5th overall picks in the 2012 NFL Draft, respectively – one of which at least appears to be a confirmed bust (Richardson), and the other which looked like a Pro Bowler but only appeared in 4 games in the 2013 after being suspended twice due to two separate violations of the NFL's substance abuse policy.

The strong rookie class made an immediate impact on cardboard prices. As demand increased while supply dried up, blaster boxes of 2012 Topps Chrome Football which sold for $19.99 at retail at Target and Wal-Mart were going for $30 to $35 a pop on eBay not long after the 2012 season ended; consider this against the fact that such retail blasters normally trade at a large discount to retail price on the open market. Meanwhile, 12-box hobby cases of the same set – which could be had for under $1,300 as recently as January 2013 – were pushing $1,700 to $1,800 per case by April 2013, and had broken the $2,100 barrier by the end of 2013.

Could more of the same be expected of the 2013 NFL draft class?

The 2013 NFL Draft Class

Entering the 2013 draft, dealers and collectors alike had expressed concern over what was perceived to be an exceptionally weak 2013 NFL draft class. On the other hand, at the March 2013 Industry Summit in Las Vegas, card manufacturers were quick to point out that players can emerge seemingly out of nowhere. After all, Russell Wilson was a 3rd-round pick, while Alfred Morris flew so under the radar as a sixth-round selection that he wasn't even included in the 2012 Topps Chrome set.

Were the card manufacturers right to be optimistic?

The short answer is no. Below is the position breakdown of the ESPN.com/Scouts Inc. Top 32 entering the 2013 NFL Draft.

2013 NFL Draft: Position Breakdown of ESPN.com/Scouts Inc. Top 32

Position	No. of Players
DT	6
OT	4
DE	4
LB	4
CB	4
OG	3
WR	3
QB	1
TE	1
S	1
RB	1

Source: ESPN.com

The 2013 NFL Draft appeared exceptionally weak where it counts. Only one QB – Geno Smith of West Virginia – even merited a first-round grade according to Scouts Inc. Moreover, Scouts Inc. had Smith as only the 20th-ranked player in the draft, and it might scare you to note that Blaine Gabbert of the Jacksonville Jaguars had a higher pre-draft rating in his 2011 draft year.

And if you were looking for offensive stars outside of the QB position, Scouts Inc. did not have a WR or RB in its top 15, either. As such, the odds were (and still are) strongly against a truly elite WR like Calvin Johnson or a RB like Adrian Peterson emerging from the 2013 draft.

Indeed, the top of the 2013 NFL Draft appeared to be strong on defense and strong on offensive linemen, but weak where it counts on cardboard. And while it is always possible that a Russell Wilson or an Alfred Morris – or a Colin Kaepernick, for that matter – could emerge (sometimes in Year 2 as in the case of Kaepernick and Nick Foles), it was apparent even before the draft that 2013 was going to be a good year for football card collector-investors to take it easy and sit on the sidelines, or otherwise take a wait-and-see approach.

As it turned out, the top-rated QB in Geno Smith was taken by the Jets in the second round (39th overall), and struggled through 16 games with 12 TD passes, 21 interceptions, and a 66.5 quarterback rating. And despite pulling out a few clutch wins, Smith finished his 2013 rookie season with questions regarding his status as a franchise quarterback. Meanwhile, with the 16th overall pick, the Buffalo Bills reached and made Florida State University QB E.J. Manuel the first quarterback taken in the draft; Manuel only played 10 games in 2013 due to various knee injuries, but threw for 11 TDs against 9 INTs while posting a respectable 77.7 rating, and appears to be the Bills' QB at least going into the 2014 season.

Following the 2013 season, the top two players with 2013 Topps Chrome RCs from the 2013 NFL Draft class were E.J. Manuel and Green Bay Packers RB Eddie Lacy (2nd round, 61st overall) with ungraded book values at $5 each, followed by Geno Smith, Tampa Bay Buccaneers QB Mike Glennon (3rd round, 73rd overall), Minnesota Vikings WR Cordarelle Patterson (1st round, 29th overall), and Cincinnati Bengals RB Giovanni Bernard (2nd round, 37th overall) at $4 each.

All six of these players play offensive skill positions.

In contrast, following the 2013 season, the 2012 Topps Chrome set already had five players – all QBs – with valuations of $6 or more, including Indianapolis Colts QB Andrew Luck, Seattle Seahawks QB Russell Wilson, Washington Redskins QB Robert Griffin III, Miami Dolphins QB Ryan Tannehill, and Philadelphia Eagles QB Nick Foles. Washington Redskins RB Alfred Morris – a 2012 6th-round pick who finished second in the league in rushing yardage as a rookie in 2012 – would also likely be above $6 if he had a Topps Chrome RC (his 2012 Panini Prizm RC is valued at $8; Panini Prizm and Topps Chrome RCs in 2012 generally carry equivalent book values).

And given the lack of high-end offensive talent in general and QB talent in particular, it is perhaps not surprising that 12-box Hobby cases of 2013 Topps Chrome Football were selling as low as $600 shipped on eBay by January 2014.

That said, with three QBs with first-round grades entering the 2014 NFL Draft – Louisville QB Teddy Bridgewater, UCF QB Blake Bortles, and Texas A&M QB

Johnny Manziel – plus four WRs in Scouts Inc.'s Top 32 as of January 2014, the 2014 NFL Draft class already looks materially better than in 2013, though perhaps without the depth and upside of the 2012 class.

Key Brands

In stark contrast to baseball, there are no exclusive licensing deals with regard to NFL trading cards. As a result, competition in this space is wide open, though currently dominated by the two biggest players in Topps and Panini. A third major player – Upper Deck – announced that it had lost its license to produce NFL trading cards in April 2010.[92]

Topps

The key Topps Chrome brand is essentially to football what the Bowman Chrome brand is to baseball, in that a player's Topps Chrome RC – and especially its parallels – is generally identifiable as a player's key non-auto, with a player's 1/1 Superfractor being the boss parallel. In 2011, Topps introduced the chrome on-card RC autographs to its Topps Chrome Football product (previously sticker autographs), inserted at a rate of one per Hobby box, or similar to Bowman Chrome Baseball (in contrast, Topps Chrome Baseball includes two autos per box). And so at least since 2011, a player's Topps Chrome RC auto has been generally identifiable as at least one of a player's key autos, with his 1/1 Superfractor auto being generally identifiable as a player's most desirable auto.

Other secondary chrome brands include the staple Finest brand which features a colored refractor lineup and on-cards autos (though its patch autos are sticker autos, as they are in baseball as well); Topps Platinum; and Bowman Sterling, which unfortunately has been a sticker auto-only brand (in contrast to Bowman Sterling Baseball, which in 2012 became primarily on-card autos, though in 2013 the prospect autos were primarily on-card autos while the RC autos were sticker autos). In addition, the high-end non-chrome Topps Five Star Baseball and Bowman Inception Baseball products introduced in 2012 and 2013, respectively, originated with Topps Five Star Football (2010) and Topps Inception Football (2011).

Panini

The Italian collectibles publisher Panini Group entered the football card market with its acquisition of Donruss Playoff in March 2009, immediately renaming its new subsidiary Panini America. Panini America later acquired NFL/NFLPA

---

[92] www.beckett.com/news/2010/04/upper-deck-loses-nfl-card-license

licenses under its own name, and then renewed its licenses in April 2012 for as many as 18 sets per year.[93]

The company's Panini Prizm product was introduced in 2012, and is Panini's answer to Topps Chrome. The Panini Prizm RC non-autos are generally equivalent in value to their Topps Chrome counterparts, with the key parallels being the Gold Prizms #'d/10. The autos, however, are not quite as comparable as sticker autos.

But while the Prizm sticker autos leave something to be desired, Panini is very strong on high end non-chromes.

In 2006, Donruss Playoff introduced Playoff National Treasures, later renamed Panini National Treasures starting in 2012. National Treasures are short-printed high end, memorabilia rich sets including rookies, current stars, and legends. Boxes generally run in the neighborhood of $500 per box (give or take $100), and in 2012 included one pack per box with eight cards per box.

Notable for RC auto collectors are the RC patch autos with a standard print run of 99 copies; these were sticker autos in the initial 2006 debut release, but became standard on-card autos with the 2007 release.

Top Panini/Playoff National Treasures RC Patch Autos: 2006-2012

Card	#	Pos.	Ungraded BV	BGS 9.5	Adj. Multiple
2007 Adrian Peterson RC Jsy Auto #/99	101	RB	$500	–	–
2007 Calvin Johnson RC Jsy Auto #/99	107	WR	$400	–	–
2008 Matt Ryan RC Jsy Auto #/99	111	QB	$350	$500	1.4x
2008 Joe Flacco RC Jsy Auto #/99	112	QB	$350	–	–
2008 Chris Johnson RC Jsy Auto #/99	105	RB	$200	–	–
2009 Matthew Stafford RC Jsy Auto #/99	121	QB	$400	$600	1.5x
2010 Sam Bradford RC Jsy Auto #/99	332	QB	$600	–	–
2010 Tim Tebow RC Jsy Auto #/99	334	QB	$300	–	–
2010 Dez Bryant RC Jsy Auto #/99	311	WR	$300	–	–
2010 Rob Gronkowski RC Jsy Auto #/99	329	TE	$250	–	–
2010 Demaryius Thomas RC Jsy Auto #/99	309	WR	$200	–	–
2011 Colin Kaepernick RC Jsy Auto #/99	327	QB	$900	$1,500	1.6x
2011 Cam Newton RC Jsy Auto #/99	328	QB	$800	$1,200	1.5x

---

[93] www.beckett.com/news/2012/04/nfl-nflpa-renew-card-license-with-panini-america

Card	#	Pos.	Ungraded BV	BGS 9.5	Adj. Multiple
2011 Andy Dalton RC Jsy Auto #/99	326	QB	$300	$500	1.6x
2011 Jake Locker RC Jsy Auto #/99	325	QB	$300	–	–
2011 Julio Jones RC Jsy Auto #/99	323	WR	$300	–	–
2011 A.J. Green RC Jsy Auto #/99	329	WR	$300	$500	1.6x
2012 Andrew Luck RC Jsy Auto #/99	301	QB	$2,000	–	–
2012 Russell Wilson RC Jsy Auto #/99	325	QB	$1,000	–	–
2012 Robert Griffin RC Jsy Auto #/99	302	QB	$1,000	–	–
2012 Nick Foles RC Jsy Auto #/99	318	QB	$400	–	–
2012 Ryan Tannehill RC Jsy Auto #/99	304	QB	$400	–	–
2012 Doug Martin RC Jsy Auto #/99	311	RB	$250	–	–
2012 Brock Osweiler RC Jsy Auto #/99	307	QB	$250	–	–

Source: Beckett.com, January 2014
*2006-2011 Playoff National Treasure, and 2012 Panini National Treasures

Meanwhile, the staple RC auto in football has long been the Playoff Contenders Rookie Ticket. These autos were first introduced in the 1998 Playoff Contenders set, showcasing the Peyton Manning Rookie Ticket RC Auto with an announced print run of only 200 copies, an ungraded book value of $3,800 and graded BGS 9.5 Gem Mint book value of $5,500. In contrast to National Treasures, Playoff Contenders – renamed Panini Contenders in 2012 – is a more standard issue with recent Hobby boxes containing 24 packs per box and 5 cards per pack. The Rookie Ticket autos are deliberately short-printed RC autos with varying print runs; the base cards are not serialized, but print runs for key players have generally been announced.

Top Panini/Playoff Contenders Rookie Ticket RC Autos: 1998-2012

Card	#	Pos.	Ungraded BV	BGS 9.5	Adj. Multiple
1998 Peyton Manning RC Auto /200	87	QB	$3,800	$5,500	1.4x
1998 Randy Moss RC Auto /300	92	WR	$350	$1,000	2.8x
1998 Hines Ward RC Auto /500	94	WR	$250	–	–
1999 SSD Kurt Warner RC Auto /1,825	146	QB	$175	$400	2.2x
2000 Tom Brady RC Auto	144	QB	$1,000	$4,000	4.0x
2001 Drew Brees RC Auto /500	124	QB	$800	$1,500	1.9x
2001 Michael Vick RC Auto /327	157	QB	$200	$700	3.3x

Card	#	Pos.	Ungraded BV	BGS 9.5	Adj. Multiple
2001 LaDainian Tomlinson RC Auto /600	150	RB	$250	$600	2.3x
2001 Reggie Wayne RC Auto /400	166	WR	$150	$400	2.5x
2001 Steve Smith RC Auto /300	190	WR	$120	$450	3.5x
2002 Julius Peppers RC Auto /40	142	DE	$600	–	–
2002 Ed Reed RC Auto /550	129	S	$100	–	–
2003 Tony Romo RC Auto /999	156	QB	$300	$600	1.9x
2003 Troy Polamalu RC Auto /989	190	S	$300	–	–
2003 Carson Palmer Blue RC Auto /158	136	QB	$250	$600	2.3x
2003 Andre Johnson RC Auto /199	141	WR	$250	–	–
2003 Jason Witten RC Auto /599	117	TE	$175	$400	2.2x
2004 Larry Fitzgerald RC Auto /50	151	WR	$800	–	–
2004 Eli Manning RC Auto /372	131	QB	$400	$1,600	3.9x
2004 Ben Roethlisberger RC Auto /541	106	QB	$300	$800	2.6x
2004 Philip Rivers RC Auto /556	162	QB	$150	$400	2.5x
2004 Wes Welker RC Auto	193	WR	$125	–	–
2005 Aaron Rodgers RC Auto /530	101	QB	$1,000	$2,500	2.5x
2005 Alex Smith RC Auto /401	106	QB	$150	$250	1.6x
2006 Jay Cutler RC Auto /501	152	QB	$100	$200	1.8x
2007 Adrian Peterson RC Auto /355	104	RB	$400	$700	1.7x
2007 Calvin Johnson RC Auto /525	123	WR	$225	$400	1.7x
2007 Patrick Willis RC Auto /239	205	LB	$100	–	–
2008 Matt Ryan RC Auto /246	179	QB	$300	$500	1.6x
2008 Joe Flacco RC Auto /220	151	QB	$250	$500	1.9x
2009 Matthew Stafford RC Auto /540	101	QB	$200	$350	1.7x
2009 Clay Matthews RC Auto	156	LB	$100	–	–
2010 Jimmy Graham RC Auto /358	151	TE	$125	$225	1.7x
2010 Sam Bradford RC Auto /377	232	QB	$100	$250	2.3x
2011 Colin Kaepernick RC Auto	227	QB	$250	$600	2.3x
2011 Cam Newton RC Auto	228	QB	$175	$400	2.2x
2012 Andrew Luck RC Auto /550	201	QB	$600	$850	1.4x
2012 Russell Wilson RC Auto /550	225	QB	$400	$700	1.7x
2012 Robert Griffin RC Auto /238	202	QB	$300	$600	1.9x

Card	#	Pos.	Ungraded BV	BGS 9.5	Adj. Multiple
2012 Nick Foles RC Auto /550	218	QB	$135	–	–
2012 Ryan Tannehill RC Auto /550	204	QB	$100	$200	1.8x

Source: Beckett.com, January 2014; print numbers are announced, and not serialized
*1998-2011 Playoff Contenders, and 2012 Panini Contenders

The Panini/Playoff Contenders Rookie Ticket RC autos are safe bets as key autos. In 2012 and 2013, Panini Contenders Rookie Ticket autos included Playoff Contenders parallels #'d/99, Cracked Ice parallels #'d/20 in 2012 and #'d/21 in 2013, and 1/1 Championship Ticket parallels.

Upper Deck

As noted, Upper Deck lost its licenses to produce NFL cards in 2010, but the company has a long track record of producing highly valued mid- to high-end products including SP Authentic and SPx, as well as high-end auto memorabilia-heavy products in Ultimate Collection and Exquisite Collection. Notably, the 1998 SP Authentic Peyton Manning RC with a serialized print run of 2,000 copies is Manning's most highly valued base RC non-auto, with an ungraded book value of $600 and graded BGS 9.5 book value of $1,600.

But the most prized of Upper Deck products is Exquisite Collection. Exquisite Collection made its football debut in 2005, and included six cards per pack/box at $500 per box. The initial 2005 set was serialized with a print run of only 150 sets, except for the patch autos which had a print run of 199 copies. The 2005 set included cut signature autos (autos cut from another source – typically a photograph – and then placed onto the card, as opposed to a sticker auto or on-card auto), before switching to on-card autos in 2006.

Exquisite Collection Football preceded and then dominated Playoff National Treasures Football on the high end through 2011, with its key highlights being the 2005 Aaron Rodgers RC patch auto #'d/199 (BV: $2,500; BGS 9.5: $3,800), the extremely short-printed 2006 Jay Cutler RC patch auto #'d/20 (BV: $3,000), and the 2007 Adrian Peterson RC patch auto #'d/99 (BV: $1,250) and Calvin Johnson RC patch auto #'d/99 (BV: $800).

By 2011, Upper Deck had lost its NFL license, and had begun relying on its exclusive NCAA license to produce cards of players in their college uniforms. As a result, the rookies included in the 2011 and 2012 Exquisite Collection Football sets are not considered to be official RCs.

Top Exquisite Collection RC Autos: 2005-2012

Card	#	Pos.	Ungraded BV	BGS 9.5	Adj. Multiple
2005 Aaron Rodgers RC Jsy Auto #/199	106	QB	$2,500	$3,800	1.5x
2005 Alex Smith RC Jsy Auto #/99	118	QB	$750	–	–
2006 Jay Cutler RC Jsy Auto #/20	134	QB	$3,000	–	–
2006 Marques Colston RC Jsy Auto #/99	135	WR	$350	–	–
2006 Reggie Bush RC Jsy Auto #/99	105	RB	$300	–	–
2007 Adrian Peterson RC Jsy Auto #/99	133	RB	$1,250	–	–
2007 Calvin Johnson RC Jsy Auto #/99	130	WR	$800	–	–
2008 Matt Ryan RC Jsy Auto #/99	168	QB	$800	–	–
2008 Joe Flacco RC Jsy Auto #/99	170	QB	$750	–	–
2009 Matthew Stafford RC Jsy Auto #/99	183	QB	$800	–	–
2009 Josh Freeman RC Jsy Auto #/99	190	QB	$300	–	–
2010 Sam Bradford RC Jsy Auto #/75	109	QB	$800	–	–
2010 Tim Tebow RC Jsy Auto #/75	110	QB	$300	–	–
2010 Jimmy Graham RC Auto #/65	158	TE	$300	–	–
2011 Colin Kaepernick Jsy Auto #/135	146	QB	$1,000	$1,200	1.2x
2011 Cam Newton Jsy Auto #/99	152	QB	$900	–	–
2011 A.J. Green Jsy Auto #/99	151	WR	$450	–	–
2011 Julio Jones Jsy Auto #/99	154	WR	$400	–	–
2011 Ryan Mallett Jsy Auto #/135	142	QB	$350	–	–
2011 Andy Dalton Jsy Auto #/135	145	QB	$350	–	–
2011 Jake Locker Jsy Auto #/99	156	QB	$300	–	–
2012 Andrew Luck Auto EXCH #/99	QB2	QB	$1,200	–	–
2012 Russell Wilson Jsy Auto #/150	127	QB	$700	–	–
2012 Robert Griffin Jsy Auto #/99	144	QB	$700	–	–
2012 Nick Foles Jsy Auto #/150	123	QB	$350	–	–
2012 Ryan Tannehill Jsy Auto #/99	145	QB	$300	–	–

Source: Beckett.com, January 2014

NBA Basketball

From a collector-investor standpoint, basketball cards may present the best all-around package, and for several reasons:

1. **No position bias.** In contrast to the QB-dominated football game and the forward/goalie-dominated hockey game, there is no position bias in basketball cards. Though the point guard position has been strong in recent years, elite-valued players come from all positions. Consequently, basketball cards do not have default dead weight by virtue of position.

2. **Star power.** Basketball benefits by being a star-driven sport, where relatively few players suit up for game, fewer play, and only a handful dominate the outcome of the game. This is a game dominated by stars, which enhances star value.

3. **Global appeal.** More so than any other major American sport, basketball benefits from global appeal across all continents – including Asia.

Thus, it should come as no surprise that many of the most highly valued cards produced in modern times are basketball cards.

Through the Early '90s

As far as sports cards are concerned, basketball was a late bloomer. Before the 1970s, literally only three sets of note were produced: The 1948 Bowman set including the George Mikan RC (BV: $2,250; PSA 9: $43,000), 1957-58 Topps with the Bill Russell RC (BV: $1,100; PSA 9: $26,500), and 1961-62 Fleer including the Wilt Chamberlain RC (BV: $800; PSA 9: $8,350) and Jerry West RC (BV: $600; PSA 9: $5,750).

None of these sets had follow-up issues.

Topps returned to the market and produced sets from 1969-70 through 1981-82, with such notable cards as the 1969-70 Topps Lew Alcindor RC (BV: $250; PSA 9: $5,700), 1970-71 Topps Pete Maravich RC (BV: $300; PSA 9: $2,300), 1972-73 Julius Erving RC (BV: $150; PSA 9: $950), and the 1980-81 Larry Bird RC/Julius Erving/Magic Johnson RC (BV: $250; PSA 10: $5,500).

No cards were produced in 1982-83. And for the next three seasons, the only sets produced were the rare and condition-sensitive Star issues sold in team bags at hobby shops.[94] The most notable card from these sets was, of course, the 1984-85 Star Michael Jordan XRC (BV: $2,200; BGS 8.5 NM-MT+: $3,000).

Fleer returned with the landmark 1986-87 Fleer set, the first pack-issued release to hit the market since 1981-82 Topps. The 1986-87 Fleer set included the only official RCs of Charles Barkley, Hakeem Olajuwon, Clyde Drexler, Patrick Ewing, Karl Malone, Dominique Wilkins, and James Worthy. It also included the iconic – and likely the most widely recognizable basketball card of all – 1986-87 Fleer Michael Jordan RC (BV: $700; BGS 9.5: $6,000).

As we noted earlier, as of early 2014, there were a total of five BGS 10 Pristine copies of the 1986-87 Fleer Michael Jordan RC in existence. The last copy sold in a June 5, 2011 Memory Lane, Inc. auction for $100,000 (when the BGS 10 population was three).[95]

Through the end of the 1980s, Fleer was the dominant brand, though card values would deteriorate with every new issue. Competition arrived with 1989-90 Hoops, which included the short-printed David Robinson RC (BV: $12; BGS 9.5: $120). With heightened supply levels along with the arrival of 1990-91 SkyBox, 1991-92 Upper Deck, and then 1992-93 Topps and Stadium Club, basketball card values went the way of baseball card values, with the exception of the 1992-93 Shaquille O'Neal RCs.

The Early Modern Era: Finest, Topps Chrome, and the Refractor

Like its iconic 1993 Finest Baseball counterpart, the initial 1993-94 Finest Basketball set introduced the chromium-stock card and refractor parallel to the basketball card market, marking the new high end of the market and ushering in the Modern Era. For three years from 1993-94 through 1995-96, Finest produced the game's key RCs for players including Chris Webber, Anfernee Hardaway, Grant Hill, Jason Kidd, and Kevin Garnett.

Also evident in the values is the star power of Michael Jordan.

Finest Basketball: 1993-94 through 1995-96

Card	#	Ungraded BV	BGS 9.5	Adj. Multiple
1993-94 Finest Chris Webber RC	212	$15	$60	2.4x
1993-94 Finest Anfernee Hardaway RC	189	$12	$50	2.3x

---

[94] www.sportscollectorsdaily.com/a-brief-history-of-basketball-card-sets
[95] www.beckett.com/news/2011/06/perfect-michael-jordan-rookie-card-sells-for-100000

Card	#	Ungraded BV	BGS 9.5	Adj. Multiple
1993-94 Finest Michael Jordan	1	$20	$80	2.7x
1994-95 Finest Grant Hill RC	240	$15	$50	2.0x
1994-95 Finest Jason Kidd RC	286	$15	$60	2.4x
1994-95 Finest Michael Jordan	331	$20	$60	2.0x
1995-96 Finest Kevin Garnett RC	115	$40	$100	2.0x
1995-96 Finest Michael Jordan	229	$15	$60	2.4x

Source: Beckett.com, January 2014

The values for the refractors of these key cards are listed in the table below. It should be noted that the 1995-96 Finest set inexplicably did not include refractors for the rookies.

Finest Basketball Refractors: 1993-94 through 1995-96

Card	#	Ungraded BV	BGS 9.5	Adj. Multiple
1993-94 Finest Chris Webber RC Refractor	212	$80	$150	1.7x
1993-94 Finest Anfernee Hardaway RC Refractor	189	$60	–	–
1993-94 Finest Michael Jordan Refractor	1	$300	$800	2.6x
1994-95 Finest Grant Hill RC	240	$150	$300	1.9x
1994-95 Finest Jason Kidd RC	286	$120	$300	2.3x
1994-95 Finest Michael Jordan	331	$200	$400	1.9x
1995-96 Finest Michael Jordan	229	$250	–	–

Source: Beckett.com, January 2014

Though the Finest product line would continue, Topps Chrome and its refractors were introduced in 1996-97 to take the game to the next level – and just in time for Kobe Bryant. As noted earlier in this book, a BGS 10 Pristine copy of the 1996-97 Topps Chrome Kobe Bryant Refractor sold for $16,250 in August 2013.

Topps Chrome and its refractor parallels would represent the key non-auto RCs for players through its last season in 2009-10.

Topps Chrome: Top RCs 1996-97 through 2002-03

Card	#	Ungraded BV	BGS 9.5	Adj. Multiple
1996-97 Kobe Bryant RC	138	$300	$800	2.6x
1996-97 Steve Nash RC	182	$25	$80	2.3x
1996-97 Allen Iverson RC	171	$30	$80	2.0x
1996-97 Ray Allen RC	217	$25	$125	3.6x
1997-98 Tim Duncan RC	115	$30	$100	2.5x
1998-99 Dirk Nowitzki RC	154	$15	$50	2.0x
1998-99 Vince Carter RC	199	$15	$30	1.2x
1998-99 Paul Pierce RC	135	$12	$40	1.8x
2001-02 Tony Parker RC	155	$12	$35	1.6x
2002-03 Manu Ginobili RC	124	$10	$30	1.5x
2002-03 Amare Stoudemire RC	126	$10	$25	1.3x
2002-03 Yao Ming RC	146	$12	$30	1.4x

Source: Beckett.com, January 2014

Through the end of the century, Topps Chrome only included a regular refractor parallel. The base refractor parallel would start to lose value in 2001-02 as rarer, serialized parallels would appear higher in the Topps Chrome hierarchy (more on this in a minute).

Topps Chrome: Top RC Refractors 1996-97 through 2002-03

Card	#	Ungraded BV	BGS 9.5	Adj. Multiple
1996-97 Kobe Bryant RC Refractor	138	$2,500	$4,000	1.6x
1996-97 Steve Nash RC Refractor	182	$200	–	–
1996-97 Allen Iverson RC Refractor	171	$200	$600	2.9x
1996-97 Ray Allen RC Refractor	217	$100	–	–
1997-98 Tim Duncan RC Refractor	115	$200	$500	2.4x
1998-99 Dirk Nowitzki RC Refractor	154	$80	$225	2.5x
1998-99 Vince Carter RC Refractor	199	$80	$200	2.2x
1998-99 Paul Pierce RC Refractor	135	$50	$200	3.3x
2001-02 Tony Parker RC Refractor	155	$60	$100	1.4x
2002-03 Manu Ginobili RC Refractor	124	$25	–	–
2002-03 Amare Stoudemire RC Refractor	126	$25	$50	1.4x
2002-03 Yao Ming RC Refractor	146	$30	–	–

Source: Beckett.com, January 2014

1997-98: Super High-End Parallels

In addition to the Topps Chrome refractor, the mid-to-late 1990s also saw the emergence of rare and often serialized parallels, which have achieved relatively absurd prices.

Fleer's 1996-97 E-X2000 Kobe Bryant RC has a Credentials parallel #'d/499, which carries an ungraded book value of $1,250, vs. $60 for the base RC. The 1997-98 E-X2001 Jambalaya insert set includes a Michael Jordan card with an ungraded value of $3,000, and a BGS 9.5 copy of the card sold on eBay for nearly $5,200 in January 2014.

The 1997-98 SkyBox Premium Michael Jordan Star Rubies parallel #'d/50 carries an ungraded book value of $8,000 vs. a measly $5 for the base card, while Kobe Bryant's Star Rubies card #'d/50 carries an ungraded book value of $4,000, compared to a base card value of $5. The 1997-98 SPx Michael Jordan Grand Finale parallel #'d/50 books for $5,000, while the base card books for $15.

But perhaps the biggest of these sets was the 1997-98 SkyBox Metal Universe Precious Metal Gems parallels to the Metal Universe set. The Precious Metal Gems were #'d/100, though the first 10 of each set had green backgrounds, and the other 90 had red backgrounds. A red version of the Michael Jordan card #'d/100 carries an ungraded book value of $6,500, while one of two BGS 9.5 Gem Mint copies in existence sold for $17,410 in November 2013.

The base card carries an ungraded book value of $8.

The LeBron James Era

The emergence of LeBron James and the now-legendary 2003 NBA Draft class came with many changes to the game. One such change was the addition of the new Topps Chrome Gold Refractors.

The first table below lists the key Topps Chrome RCs from 2003-04 through the final 2009-10 set. Note that the 2009-10 RCs are short-printed and #'d/999.

Topps Chrome Basketball: Top RCs 2003-04 through 2009-10

Card	#	Position	Ungraded BV	BGS 9.5	Adj. Multiple
2003-04 LeBron James RC	111	SF	$150	$400	2.5x
2003-04 Dwyane Wade RC	115	SG	$20	$50	1.7x
2003-04 Carmelo Anthony RC	113	SF	$15	$40	1.6x

Card	#	Position	Ungraded BV	BGS 9.5	Adj. Multiple
2003-04 Chris Bosh RC	114	PF	$10	$25	1.3x
2004-05 Dwight Howard RC	166	C	$20	$40	1.3x
2005-06 Chris Paul RC	168	PG	$20	$50	1.7x
2005-06 Deron Williams RC	200	PG	$10	$35	1.8x
2006-07 Rajon Rondo RC	201	PG	$15	$40	1.6x
2007-08 Kevin Durant RC	131	SF	$50	$125	2.1x
2008-09 Derrick Rose RC	181	PG	$50	$120	2.0x
2008-09 Russell Westbrook RC	184	PG	$15	$60	2.4x
2008-09 Kevin Love RC	185	PF	$15	–	–
2009-10 Blake Griffin RC #/999	96	PF	$125	$150	1.1x
2009-10 Ricky Rubio RC #/999	97	PG	$60	$100	1.4x
2009-10 James Harden RC #/999	99	SG	$50	$80	1.3x
2009-10 Stephen Curry RC #/999	101	PG	$60	$150	2.1x

Source: Beckett.com, December 2013

This table of Gold Refractors is not very comparable. Topps Chrome Gold Refractors were #'d/50 in 2003-04, 2008-09, and 2010, but were #'d/99 in 2004-05 and 2005-06 and #'d/25 in 2006-07. In 2007-08, the X-Factors were #'d/50.

Topps Chrome Basketball Gold Refractors: 2003-04 through 2009-10

Card	#	Base	Gold	Gold-Base Multiple
2003-04 LeBron James RC	111	$150	$1,500	10.0x
2003-04 Dwyane Wade RC	115	$20	$700	35.0x
2003-04 Carmelo Anthony RC	113	$15	$200	13.3x
2003-04 Chris Bosh RC	114	$10	$150	15.0x
2004-05 Dwight Howard RC	166	$20	$200*	10.0x
2005-06 Chris Paul RC	168	$20	$200*	10.0x
2005-06 Deron Williams RC	200	$10	$60*	6.0x
2006-07 Rajon Rondo RC	201	$15	$300**	20.0x
2007-08 Kevin Durant RC	131	$50	$600***	12.0x
2008-09 Derrick Rose RC	181	$50	$600	12.0x
2008-09 Russell Westbrook RC	184	$15	$400	26.7x
2008-09 Kevin Love RC	185	$15	$350	23.3x
2009-10 Blake Griffin RC #/999	96	$125	$1,200	9.6x
2009-10 Ricky Rubio RC #/999	97	$60	$400	6.7x

Card	#	Base	Gold	Gold-Base Multiple
2009-10 James Harden RC #/999	99	$50	$300	6.0x
2009-10 Stephen Curry RC #/999	101	$60	$300	5.0x

Source: Beckett.com, December 2013
*Gold Refractors #'d/99
**Gold Refractors #'d/25
***X-Fractors #'d/50

The staple Topps Chrome RCs and parallels are good bets as key RC non-autos. But the biggest changes in 2003-04 would come on the higher end.

The New High End: Exquisite Collection and National Treasures

Before there was National Treasures or Exquisite Collection Football, there was Exquisite Collection Basketball.

Upper Deck redefined the term "high-end" when it introduced Exquisite Collection Basketball in 2003-04 at $500 per box, with one five-card pack per box. Like the football version that would come later, Exquisite Collection basketball was a memorabilia-driven set with a variety of limited print, serialized patches and patch autos of rookies and stars – such as Michael Jordan – alike.

The 2003-04 Exquisite Collection is perhaps quite easily the most valuable modern set ever produced. It includes RC patch autos of LeBron James, Dwyane Wade, Carmelo Anthony, and Chris Bosh all #'d/99; the LeBron James RC patch auto #'d/99 has an ungraded book value of $12,000 and a graded BGS 9.5 book value of $15,000. These RC patches also have Rookie Patch Parallels #'d to each player's jersey number – which in the case of LeBron James means that there are only 23 such copies, while Carmelo Anthony only has 15 such cards.

An *ungraded* copy of the LeBron James Rookie Patch Parallels #12/23 sold for just under $25,000 in November 2013.

Among the other patch autographs are a variety of LeBron James, Michael Jordan, and Kobe Bryant patch autos, most of which have book values of $4,000 or more. The Michael Jordan Limited Logos patch auto #'d/75 has a book value of $8,500, while a Number Piece auto #'d/23 (Jordan's jersey number) books for $6,500.

Though the follow-up sets as a whole can't match the value of the original 2003-04 Exquisite Collection, the short-printed RC patch autos remain comparable, and generally represent a player's very best RC auto through the 2008-09 set – the last year the Exquisite Collection included NBA-licensed RC patch autos.

Exquisite Collection RC Patch Autos: 2003-04 through 2008-09

Card	#	Ungraded BV	BGS 9.5	Adj. Multiple
2003-04 LeBron James RC Jsy Auto #/99	78	$12,000	$15,000	1.2x
2003-04 Dwyane Wade RC Jsy Auto #/99	74	$4,000	–	–
2003-04 Carmelo Anthony RC Jsy Auto #/99	76	$3,000	–	–
2003-04 Chris Bosh RC Jsy Auto #/99	75	$1,900	$2,500	1.3x
2004-05 Dwight Howard RC Jsy Auto #/99	90	$2,600	$3,200	1.2x
2005-06 Chris Paul RC Jsy Auto #/99	46	$2,000	$3,500	1.7x
2005-06 Deron Williams RC Jsy Auto #/99	45	$750	$1,300	1.7x
2006-07 Rajon Rondo RC Jsy Auto #/225	60	$500	–	–
2007-08 Kevin Durant RC Jsy Auto #/99	94	$4,500	–	–
2008-09 Derrick Rose RC Jsy Auto #/99	92	$3,800	–	–
2008-09 Russell Westbrook RC Jsy Auto #/225	93	$1,100	–	–
2008-09 Kevin Love RC Jsy Auto #/225	61	$700	–	–

Source: Beckett.com, January 2014

In January 2009, Panini America entered into an exclusive agreement with the NBA. Panini's 2009-10 Playoff National Treasures RC patch autos more or less pick up where Exquisite had left off (the 2009-10 Exquisite set would feature regular non-patch RC autos of players in their college uniforms). National Treasures would become Panini National Treasures in 2012-13.

Panini/Playoff National Treasures RC Patch Autos: 2009-10 through 2012-13

Card	#	Ungraded BV	BGS 9.5	Adj. Multiple
2009-10 Blake Griffin RC Jsy Auto #/99	201	$2,800	–	–
2009-10 Stephen Curry RC Jsy Auto #/99	206	$1,000	–	–
2009-10 James Harden RC Jsy Auto #/99	203	$800	$2,000	2.5x
2009-10 Tyreke Evans RC Jsy Auto #/99	204	$600	–	–
2009-10 Jrue Holiday RC Jsy Auto #/99	216	$400	–	–
2010-11 John Wall RC Jsy Auto #/99	201	$2,000	$2,600	1.3x
2010-11 DeMarcus Cousins RC Jsy Auto #/99	205	$750	–	–
2010-11 Paul George RC Jsy Auto #/99	210	$500	–	–
2010-11 Derrick Favors RC Jsy Auto #/99	203	$400	–	–

Card	#	Ungraded BV	BGS 9.5	Adj. Multiple
2012-13 Kyrie Irving RC Jsy Auto #/199	101	$1,500	–	–
2012-13 Anthony Davis RC Jsy Auto #/199	151	$1,200	–	–
2012-13 Bradley Beal RC Jsy Auto #/199	153	$500	–	–
2012-13 Harrison Barnes RC Jsy Auto #/199	157	$400	–	–
2012-13 Andre Drummond RC Jsy Auto #/199	159	$400	–	–
2012-13 Klay Thompson RC Jsy Auto #/199	110	$400	–	–
2012-13 Kawhi Leonard RC Jsy Auto #/199	114	$400	–	–

Source: Beckett.com, January 2014
*2009-10 and 2010-11 Playoff National Treasures, and 2012-13 Panini National Treasures

SP Authentic RC Autos

Though there were Topps Chrome, Bowman Chrome, and Finest RC autos, there wasn't a standard line of RC autos in the way that there are Bowman Chrome prospect autos or Topps Chrome RC autos in baseball. And high-end patch autos aside, the closest thing there is to a standard on-card auto line are the SP Authentic RC autos (though patch autos appeared in 2007-08 and 2008-09).

SP Authentic RC Autos: 2002-03 through 2008-09

Card	#	Ungraded BV	BGS 9.5	Adj. Multiple
2002-03 Yao Ming RC Auto #/1,500	143	$50	$100	1.7x
2002-03 Manu Ginobili RC Auto #/1,500	172	$50	$100	1.7x
2003-04 LeBron James RC Auto #/500	148	$1,000	$1,500	1.5x
2003-04 Dwyane Wade RC Auto #/500	152	$250	$400	1.5x
2003-04 Carmelo Anthony RC Auto #/500	150	$150	$200	1.3x
2003-04 Chris Bosh RC Auto #/500	151	$80	$125	1.4x
2004-05 Dwight Howard RC Auto #/999	186	$150	$300	1.9x
2005-06 Chris Paul RC Auto #/1,299	94	$100	$250	2.3x
2005-06 Deron Williams RC Auto #/1,299	93	$40	$100	2.0x
2006-07 Rajon Rondo RC Auto #/999	111	$80	$125	1.4x
2007-08 Kevin Durant RC Jsy Auto #/299	152	$1,000	–	–
2008-09 Derrick Rose RC Jsy Auto #/299	130	$700	$1,000	1.4x
2008-09 Russell Westbrook RC Jsy Auto #/299	139	$300	–	–
2008-09 Kevin Love RC Jsy Auto #/299	126	$250	–	–

Source: Beckett.com, January 2014

Panini

In October 2012, Panini extended its exclusive licensing agreement with the NBA through the 2016-17 season, which will allow for up to 25 different sets per year.[96] These sets run the complete range, from Panini and NBA Hoops on the lower end, to more mid-level products like Prestige, Contenders, Threads, and the chromium Prizm and Select brands. And then there is the super high-end stuff like National Treasures, Immaculate, and Flawless.

So far, so good on the secondary markets.

As we mentioned earlier in the book, Panini Flawless was released in October 2013, and came in a *briefcase* at a suggested retail price of $1,250 per 10-card pack/box, thus taking the term "high end" to yet another level. By November 2013, prices had broken $2,000 per briefcase/box, with two-box cases reaching $4,500 by January 2014, perhaps helped by the fact that a Kyrie Irving RC patch auto 1/1 broke $10,000 in December 2013, after another Kyrie Irving RC auto 1/1 sold for $9,200 in November 2013. A Damian Lillard RC 1/1 non-patch non-auto also sold for $6,500 in November 2013.

Among other notable sales, a 2012-13 Panini Prizm Kyrie Irving RC Gold Prizm #'d/10 and graded BGS 10 Pristine sold for $8,600 at auction in January 2014. And in November 2013, a 2012-13 Panini Immaculate Scottie Pippen NBA Logoman patch auto 1/1 sold for $9,500, while another Anthony Davis NBA Logoman RC patch auto 1/1 sold for $6,999.

And none of that even compares to the 2009-10 Playoff National Treasures Blake Griffin RC patch auto 1/1 that reportedly sold for $38,000 in January 2012.[97,98]

---

[96] www.sportsbusinessdaily.com/Journal/Issues/2012/10/29/Marketing-and-Sponsorship/NBA-Panini.aspx

[97] www.sportscollectorsdigest.com/infield-dirt/blake-griffin-card-sells-for-38000

[98] paniniamerica.wordpress.com/2012/10/29/the-panini-group-extends-nba-partnership-with-new-multiyear-exclusive-agreement

NHL Hockey

Hockey presents relatively fertile ground in that this area of the hobby at present is quite Canadian-centric – a quick survey of the graded card supply, as well as the new ungraded supply with every new issue reveals an inordinate number of sellers from Canada. But as the sport continues to grow in popularity in the United States, the overwhelming probability is that there is a lot of potential upside in hockey cards.

Post-War Origins

The first post-war hockey card set was produced by a Toronto, Ontario-based confectionary manufacturer called Parkhurst. The inaugural 105-card 1951-52 Parkhurst set works out to be something of hockey's equivalent of the 1952 Topps Baseball set, and included the RCs of Detroit Red Wings RW Gordie Howe (BV: $3,000; PSA 9: $33,500), Montreal Canadiens RW Maurice "Rocket" Richard (BV: $1,500; PSA 9: $15,000), and Red Wings G Terry Sawchuk (BV: $1,200; PSA 9: $6,500). Topps soon joined with the 1954-55 Topps set, featuring cards of the four American teams of what was then a six-team National Hockey League; though the set included four RCs, the key card in the set was not an RC, but rather the card of Gordie Howe (BV: $1,800, PSA 9: $8,500).

From 1955-56 through 1959-60, Parkhurst only produced cards of the two Canadian NHL teams – the Toronto Maple Leafs and Montreal Canadians. Topps, meanwhile, did not produce cards for 1955-56 or 1956-67, but returned to the market in 1957-58 after entering an agreement with Canadian confectionary manufacturer O-Pee-Chee which saw production of NHL cards move to London, Ontario. The O-Pee-Chee-produced Topps sets still only included cards of the four American teams – the Detroit Red Wings, Chicago Blackhawks, New York Rangers, and Boston Bruins – but now with French translations along with the English text on the back.

In 1960-61, Parkhurst added the Detroit Red Wings – and thus Gordie Howe – to its lineup, leaving Topps/O-Pee-Chee with just three teams. But following the 1963-64 set, Parkhurst left the market, leaving Topps/O-Pee-Chee with a monopoly and all six NHL teams beginning in 1964-65.[99][100]

The NHL expanded for the 1967-68 season, doubling in size to 12 teams with the addition of the Los Angeles Kings, Minnesota North Stars, Philadelphia Flyers,

---

[99] http://en.wikipedia.org/wiki/Parkhurst_Products
[100] http://en.wikipedia.org/wiki/O-Pee-Chee

Pittsburgh Penguins, California Seals, and St. Louis Blues.[101] In anticipation, Topps produced a 1966-67 "USA Test" set that paralleled the design of the O-Pee-Chee-produced 1966-67 Topps set. In contrast to the bilingual O-Pee-Chee-made set, this "USA Test" set is English-only on the back, and is rarer and more valuable than the original Topps set; its key card is the Bobby Orr RC (BV: $8,000; PSA 9: $80,000).

Starting with the 1968-69 season, Topps and O-Pee-Chee began producing two sets of NHL hockey cards: A smaller Topps set for the U.S. market, and a larger set of cards using the same design under the O-Pee-Chee brand for the Canadian market. And from 1968-69 through 1989-90 – through further expansion, including the challenge from the World Hockey Association (WHA) beginning in 1972-73 through the 1979 merger agreement, which resulted in four WHA teams joining the NHL (the Edmonton Oilers, Quebec Nordiques, Hartford Whalers, and Winnipeg Jets) – a player's truest key RC is the O-Pee-Chee version of his RC.

Some of the most notable cards from this period are the 1979-80 O-Pee-Chee Wayne Gretzky RC (BV: $800; PSA 10: $94,000) and the 1985-86 O-Pee-Chee Mario Lemieux RC (BV: $200; PSA 10: $2,750).

The Modern Landscape

The modern NHL hockey card landscape is dominated by Upper Deck. The 1990s was mostly dead space until Upper Deck's 1996-97 Black Diamond set appeared, featuring the key RC of Boston Bruins C Joe Thornton (BV: $300; BGS 9 Mint: $400), the #1 overall pick in the 1997 NHL Entry Draft.

The company would introduce its SP Authentic and SPx mid-high end product lines in the 1999-00 season. And with much competition but nobody else really producing anything of value, and with the lockout eliminating the 2004-05 NHL season, Upper Deck emerged from the lockout with exclusive NHL/NHLPA licenses starting with the 2005-06 season.

Upper Deck's exclusive license lasted until the NHL granted Panini a license in March 2010.[102] But after four years of competition, Upper Deck later regained its exclusivity in February 2014.

---

[101] http://en.wikipedia.org/wiki/National_Hockey_League

[102] www.beckett.com/news/2010/03/breaking-news-panini-to-join-upper-deck-in-the-hockey-card-market-beginning-next-season

And despite the brief entry of Panini into the hockey card market, a player's most identifiable key RC since the turn of the century has been his short-printed Upper Deck Young Guns RC.

Upper Deck Young Guns RCs (2000-01 to Present) and Position Bias

Though the Young Guns moniker goes back to the inaugural 1990-91 Upper Deck set, Upper Deck began deliberately short-printing Young Guns rookie cards with the 2000-01 set. Ever since, Young Guns RCs (YGs) have been inserted into Upper Deck packs generally at a rate of one every four packs (six per 24-pack box), though with some exceptions – 2000-01 Upper Deck Series 2 included YGs at a rate of one every 23 packs, for example, while 2002-03 Upper Deck Series 1 included YGs at a rate of one per box, lending the YGs from 2002-03 Upper Deck Series 1 in particular unusually high values.

The top Upper Deck Young Guns from 2000-01 through 2013-14 are listed below.

Upper Deck Hockey Young Guns: Top RCs 2000-01 through 2013-14

Card	#	Pos.	Ungraded BV	BGS 9.5	Adj. Multiple
2000-01 Upper Deck Marian Gaborik YG RC	381	RW	$25	$150	4.3x
2001-02 Upper Deck Pavel Datsyuk YG RC	422	C	$80	$200	2.2x
2001-02 Upper Deck Ilya Kovalchuk YG RC	211	LW	$50	$200	3.3x
2002-03 Upper Deck Rick Nash YG RC	232	RW	$200	$400	1.9x
2002-03 Upper Deck Henrik Zetterberg YG RC	234	C	$200	$250	1.2x
2002-03 Upper Deck Tim Thomas YG RC	429	G	$40	$100	2.0x
2002-03 Upper Deck Jason Spezza YG RC	443	C	$40	$80	1.6x
2003-04 Upper Deck Marc-Andre Fleury YG RC	234	G	$50	$175	2.9x
2003-04 Upper Deck Eric Staal YG RC	206	C	$40	$100	2.0x
2003-04 Upper Deck Patrice Bergeron YG RC	204	C	$40	$80	1.6x
2005-06 Upper Deck Sidney Crosby YG RC	201	C	$300	$600	1.9x
2005-06 Upper Deck Alexander Ovechkin YG RC	443	LW	$100	$150	1.4x
2006-07 Upper Deck Evgeni Malkin YG RC	486	C	$120	$175	1.3x
2007-08 Upper Deck Jonathan Toews YG RC	462	C	$80	$150	1.7x
2007-08 Upper Deck Patrick Kane YG RC	210	RW	$50	$100	1.7x
2007-08 Upper Deck Carey Price YG RC	227	G	$50	$100	1.7x

Card	#	Pos.	Ungraded BV	BGS 9.5	Adj. Multiple
2008-09 Upper Deck Steven Stamkos YG RC	245	C	$80	$150	1.7x
2009-10 Upper Deck John Tavares YG RC	201	C	$60	$150	2.1x
2010-11 Upper Deck Tyler Seguin YG RC	456	C	$80	$120	1.3x
2010-11 Upper Deck Taylor Hall YG RC	219	LW	$60	$100	1.4x
2010-11 Upper Deck Jordan Eberle YG RC	220	RW	$50	$100	1.7x
2011-12 Upper Deck Ryan Nugent-Hopkins YG RC	214	C	$60	$120	1.7x
2013-14 Upper Deck Nathan MacKinnon YG RC	238	C	$60	–	–

Source: Beckett.com, January 2014

Notice that there is strong position bias – the market strongly favors elite offensive forwards and elite goaltenders. In fact, of the 23 players on this list, *there is not a single defenseman.*

Also note that most of the super elite forwards have been identified at the very top of the NHL Entry Draft. Ilya Kovalchuk, Rick Nash, Sidney Crosby, Alexander Ovechkin, Patrick Kane, Steven Stamkos, John Tavares, Taylor Hall, Ryan Nugent-Hopkins, and Nathan MacKinnon were all No. 1 overall draft choices, as was Pittsburgh Penguins goalie Marc-Andre Fleury. Meanwhile, Marian Gaborik, Jason Spezza, Evgeni Malkin, Jonathan Toews, and Tyler Seguin were all Top 3 choices.

RC Autos: SP Authentic Future Watch

The closest thing that hockey has to a standard RC auto are the SP Authentic Future Watch autos which date back to the 2001-02 SP Authentic release. The base autos were #'d/900 in 2001-02 and 2003-04, but have been #'d/999 in every other year. It should also be noted that while these are standard on-card autos, they were sticker autos from 2006-07 through 2008-09.

Several defenseman do crack the $50 ungraded book value mark in Pittsburgh Penguins D Kris Letang, Los Angeles Kings D Drew Doughty, Ottawa Senators D Erik Karlsson, and Montreal Canadiens D P.K. Subban.

SP Authentic Future Watch RC Autos: 2001-02 through 2011-12

Card	#	Pos.	Ungraded BV	BGS 9.5	Adj. Multiple
2001-02 SP Authentic Ilya Kovalchuk RC Auto #/900	175	LW	$150	$300	1.9x
2002-03 SP Authentic Rick Nash RC Auto #/999	184	LW	$100	–	–
2002-03 SP Authentic Henrik Zetterberg RC Auto #/999	186	C	$100	–	–
2002-03 SP Authentic Jason Spezza RC Auto #/999	191	C	$80	$140	1.6x
2003-04 SP Authentic Marc-Andre Fleury RC Auto #/900	153	G	$80	$200	2.2x
2003-04 SP Authentic Eric Staal RC Auto #/900	137	C	$50	$150	2.5x
2003-04 SP Authentic Patrice Bergeron RC Auto #/900	146	C	$50	$120	2.0x
2005-06 SP Authentic Sidney Crosby RC Auto #/999	181	C	$800	$1,000	1.2x
2005-06 SP Authentic Alexander Ovechkin RC Auto #/999	190	LW	$400	$550	1.3x
2005-06 SP Authentic Henrik Lundqvist RC Auto #/999	171	G	$80	$150	1.7x
2006-07 SP Authentic Evgeni Malkin RC Auto #/999	196	C	$200	$300	1.4x
2006-07 SP Authentic Anze Kopitar RC Auto #/999	184	C	$60	$125	1.8x
2006-07 SP Authentic Kristopher Letang RC Auto #/999	200	D	$50	–	–
2007-08 SP Authentic Jonathan Toews RC Auto #/999	203	C	$200	$300	1.4x
2007-08 SP Authentic Patrick Kane RC Auto #/999	204	RW	$150	$250	1.6x
2007-08 SP Authentic Carey Price RC Auto #/999	225	G	$120	–	–
2007-08 SP Authentic Tuuka Rask RC Auto #/999	201	G	$120	–	–
2007-08 SP Authentic Nicklas Backstrom RC Auto #/999	250	C	$50	–	–
2007-08 SP Authentic Jonathan Bernier RC Auto #/999	219	G	$50	–	–

Card	#	Pos.	Ungraded BV	BGS 9.5	Adj. Multiple
2008-09 SP Authentic Steven Stamkos RC Auto #/999	247	C	$250	$400	1.5x
2008-09 SP Authentic Claude Giroux RC Auto #/999	237	C	$120	$200	1.5x
2008-09 SP Authentic Drew Doughty RC Auto #/999	244	D	$50	$100	1.7x
2008-09 SP Authentic Brandon Sutter RC Auto #/999	195	C	$50	–	–
2009-10 SP Authentic John Tavares RC Auto #/999	201	C	$135	$300	2.1x
2009-10 SP Authentic Matt Duchene RC Auto #/999	203	C	$60	$120	1.7x
2009-10 SP Authentic Erik Karlsson RC Auto #/999	209	D	$80	$150	1.7x
2010-11 SP Authentic Tyler Seguin RC Auto #/999	301	C	$100	$225	2.0x
2010-11 SP Authentic Taylor Hall RC Auto #/999	280	LW	$100	$200	1.8x
2010-11 SP Authentic Jordan Eberle RC Auto #/999	281	RW	$80	$200	2.2x
2010-11 SP Authentic P.K. Subban RC Auto #/999	271	D	$60	$150	2.1x
2010-11 SP Authentic Jeff Skinner RC Auto #/999	295	C	$50	–	–
2010-11 SP Authentic Jacob Markstrom RC Auto #/999	310	G	$50	–	–
2010-11 SP Authentic Nazem Kadri RC Auto #/999	250	C	$50	–	–
2011-12 SP Authentic Ryan Nugent-Hopkins RC Auto #/999	248	C	$175	$300	1.6x
2011-12 SP Authentic Gabriel Landeskog RC Auto #/999	247	LW	$60	$120	1.7x

Source: Beckett.com, January 2014

Closing Thoughts

When everybody *knows* something to be true, exceptions are bound to occur, and markets will correct in one direction or the other.

In the late 1980s, everybody *knew* that baseball cards had value; investor/speculator confidence was sky high, and the bubble ultimately burst. But right now in early 2014, everybody *knows* that modern baseball cards are worthless, and collector/ investor confidence is comparatively low. And yet, it's pretty remarkable to think that many of the most valuable sports cards of the last 50 years have been printed in the last five to ten years.

And if cards printed in the last five to ten years can trade at prices like $10,000 or $18,000 when overall collector/investor confidence is relatively low, what do you think will happen when the general populace catches on, the collector base grows, and collector/investor confidence rises?

I think – at the very least – that the case for high-grade, premium color key cards of legitimate Hall of Fame-caliber players is very strong. Consider for a moment two things:

1. Four separate 1909-11 T206 Honus Wagner cards have now recorded a total of seven sales for over $1 million, while two of them have sold for over $2 million on three occasions.

2. If you were to be generous and assumed that the entire print run of 2009 Bowman Chrome Draft Mike Trout Gold Refractor autos #'d/50 were valued at $10,000 each; the Orange Refractor autos #'d/25 at $20,000; the Red Refractor autos #'d/5 at $50,000; and the 1/1 Superfractor at $100,000, the total value would be $1,350,000.

When viewed this way, it becomes pretty clear that the market for certain modern baseball cards printed in these quantities can be very sensitive to changes in demand, and could change very fast. In the same way that the T206 Honus Wagner has generated seven separate million dollar sales pretty much on a whim – setting the market for vintage baseball cards in the process – the same thing could happen to modern baseball cards. Whether it turns out to be a Wall Street banker or a professional high stakes gambler or whoever, the fact is that it might only take one or two people with cash to play with to completely change the market for any given player.

Moreover, given the quantities that we are talking about, they could do this on a whim.

And I don't know that it's one or two people, but as I write this in April 2014, the market for Mike Trout has completely changed even just in the past few months. Recall from Part I that in January 2013, a 2009 Bowman Chrome Draft Mike Trout Orange Refractor auto #/25 graded BGS 10 Pristine with a 10 Auto sold for $8,500. Based on early 2014 sales of other 2009 Bowman Chrome Draft Mike Trout autos, the implied value of the BGS 10/10 Orange Refractor has at least tripled.

2009 Bowman Chrome Draft Mike Trout Auto Sales: Early 2014

Card/Grade	Price	Date
Orange Refractor #/25 BGS 9.5/10	$15,995	2/28/14
Gold Refractor #/50 BGS 9.5/10	$15,000	3/29/14
Gold Refractor #/50 BGS 9.5/10	$10,000	3/1/14
Gold Refractor #/50 BGS 9.5/10	$8,908	3/24/14
Gold Refractor #/50 PSA 10	$8,050	2/28/14
Gold Refractor #/50 PSA 10	$6,500	1/18/14
X-Fractor #/225 BGS 10/10	$4,145	2/6/14
Blue Refractor #/150 BGS 9.5/10	$4,103	4/9/14
Blue Refractor #/150 BGS 9.5/10	$3,753	3/20/14
Blue Refractor #/150 BGS 9.5/10	$3,706	3/31/14
Gold Refractor #/50 BGS 8/10	$3,553	3/22/14
Blue Refractor #/150 BGS 9.5/10	$3,425	3/2/14

Sources: eBay, Terapeak.com

I'm not saying these values are reasonable – only that the market for modern baseball cards can change very quickly, such that at some point we could be staring at a new reality not just for Mike Trout, but for modern baseball cards in general.

That said, while I think the case for modern baseball cards is strong particularly on the high end, this is not a perfect game. This book is not intended to be a blanket vote of confidence for cards issued in 2014 and beyond, and is certainly not to be taken as a vote of confidence in the card manufacturers, chiefly Topps.

I have many concerns about this industry moving forward, starting at the top.

Managing Supply Growth

It's the natural inclination for any business to want to grow. The problem with baseball cards is that growth in supply is **never** a good thing; on the other hand, it's not necessarily disastrous so long as collector demand is growing with it. That said, if collector demand does in fact grow, this will require a concerted effort on the part of the manufacturer to manage supply growth such that:

1. Secondary market values can persist for new issues, and

2. We don't see wild swings in supply.

However, as we discussed in Part VI: The Supply Chain and the Value Cycle, Topps' policy of printing to pre-order demand ("print to order") has serious shortcomings as a default.

Topps Five Star Baseball is a perfect example of this.

With an initial release price of about $500 per box with five cards per box, 2012 Topps Five Star Baseball was an exclusive release printed on super thick stock, and clearly aiming to become the baseball equivalent of Upper Deck's Exquisite Collection. The 80-card base set was a mix of active players and retired legends such as Mickey Mantle and Babe Ruth; this base set was #'d/80, and included only two RCs in Bryce Harper and Yu Darvish, who both made the All Star game as rookies in 2012.

The base autograph checklist included 42 retired players and 43 active players. None of the active player autographs – which included several RC-year players (including Yoenis Cespedes, Will Middle brooks, Trevor Bauer, and Jesus Montero in addition to Harper and Darvish) – were #'d higher than 150.

2013 Topps Five Star Baseball was a different story. The base set now included 100 players #'d/75, including 10 RCs; among those RCs was Dylan Bundy, who never threw a pitch at any level in 2013, and pitched all of 1.2 innings at the major league level in 2012. But more troublesome was the autograph print run – most of the base RC autographs in 2013 Topps Five Star Baseball were #'d/*386*, while the Manny Machado RC auto was issued as a redemption and turned out to be #'d/353.

In other words, by Year 2, these "exclusive" cards were no longer very exclusive by any measure. And it's not surprising that by April 2014, sealed boxes of the new 2013 Topps Five Star Baseball product were selling down in the $250-$300 range.

This is a disaster. And there are two problems here:

1. Any devaluation in a brand devalues the brand.

2. Volatility in supply creates risk.

To the first point, even Upper Deck knew better than to gut the value of its top-end product. Throughout Exquisite Collection's run as the dominant high end basketball brand from 2003-04 through 2008-09, the top RC patch autos *every single year* were #'d/99, while the remainder were never #'d higher than 225. Meanwhile, Upper Deck's SP Authentic Hockey Future Watch RC autos have been #'d/999 or #'d/900 every year since its initial 2001-02 run.

Topps, on the other hand, doesn't seem to have had any awareness that more than doubling the print run of its RC autos in Topps Five Star would render the brand impotent. Instead, Topps essentially chose to sacrifice long-term brand value in exchange for pre-order profits in 2013.

The fact is, 1989 Upper Deck was a big deal, but 1990 Upper Deck is mostly worthless. 1990 Leaf was a big deal, but you can't give away boxes of 1991 Leaf. 1993 Finest Baseball was a big deal, but 1994 Finest Baseball is an afterthought. And in actuality, even 2012 Topps Five Star Baseball was a bigger deal in theory than it has been in reality – even sealed boxes of the initial 2012 release were selling down in the $250-$300 range by April 2014.

Meanwhile, volatility in print numbers also creates risk in the marketplace. After all, if you can't count on a limited print size, why would you ever pre-order Five Star Baseball, much less *any* Topps product? If the Topps Five Star RC autos are #'d/99 in 2014, does it give you any more confidence about the print size of the Topps Five Star RC autos in 2015?

That said, unless Topps figures out how to manage its print numbers beyond simply printing to pre-order demand, this is a game that could end very quickly. And this goes not just for Topps Five Star Baseball, but for *all* trading card products of value.

Playing Against the Collector

Every year at the Global Gaming Expo (G2E) in Las Vegas, table game creators from all corners of the earth bring new games aimed at capturing real estate on the casino floor. The games may vary – and some are both arcane and completely unnecessary (like one game I came across at the 2011 show in which a dealer deals cards from a shoe in order to simulate a horse race, which is then displayed on an LCD monitor[103]) – but invariably the game makers always tout their games' house advantage, which are often higher than usual. However, aside from the established table game makers who already control floor space – chiefly Shuffle Master, acquired by **Bally Technologies** (NYSE: BYI) in 2013 – these new game makers inevitably fail to make a dent on casino floors.

Why? Because the question they always seem to forget to ask is: "Where's the value for the gambler, and why would anybody play this game?"

It's an annual double insult, really: Not only are these companies designing games that the gambler has no hope of beating, but they are forcing the gambler to take the time to learn how to play games they know are designed to beat them – and with odds that are often materially worse than staple games like blackjack, baccarat, or craps.

The underlying assumption must be that the gambler is an idiot.

And make no mistake – card manufacturers are game makers who sell unregulated gambling products in the form of sealed packs of cards, boxes, and cases. Every year with every product, card manufacturers determine the odds of the game – setting payout rates in the form of hits and checklist composition, while to an extent dictating the value of newly published collectibles by setting print run sizes.

And while Topps is not responsible for what happens on the secondary market, the company should not be playing against the collector, either.

We talked about "multiple chromes risk" in Part VI. Short-printing the 2012 Bowman Chrome Yu Darvish RC autos (#209) in the spring 2012 Bowman release was a great idea; but coming back and printing two more sets of short-printed Bowman Chrome Yu Darvish RC autos (both #RA-YD) to help sell the 2012 Bowman Chrome and 2012 Bowman Draft releases later that year was not a good idea. Printing a set of 2013 Bowman Chrome Jurickson Profar RC autos (#RA-JP) for the fall 2013 Bowman Chrome after issuing a set of Bowman Chrome Jurickson Profar RC autos (also #RA-JP) in the spring 2013 Bowman release was also a terrible idea.

If Topps can come back and simply print more Bowman Chrome RC autos later in the year in Bowman Chrome and Bowman Draft – and thus gut the value of any Bowman Chrome RC auto issued in the spring Bowman release in the process –

---

[103] www.fool.com/investing/general/2011/10/17/g2e-racing-card-derby.aspx

then why would anybody buy a Bowman Chrome RC auto issued in the spring Bowman release upon initial release?

Either Topps does not understand the value of its own cards, or the company is assuming that collectors are stupid. Because what's happened is that Topps is creating risk in the marketplace, which (unless collectors are, in fact, stupid) will ultimately impact the initial value of every Bowman Chrome RC auto issued in its spring Bowman releases until the day that Topps promises to quit the practice.

And if Topps can print three sets of 2012 Bowman Chrome Yu Darvish RC autos, what's to stop the company from printing three sets of 2014 Bowman Chrome Kris Bryant prospect autos?[104]

eBay

For the most part, I've had a pretty good experience dealing – mostly buying, but some selling – on eBay. But I've also engaged in several thousand transactions over the past couple of years,[105] and when you deal with enough people, you are bound to run into a few bad apples.

In November 2012, I bought a 2012 Bowman Chrome Bryce Harper RC Gold Refractor auto redemption in a Buy It Now listing for $473, from a seller with 99 100% positive feedback. A week later, I hadn't received the card, and sent a message to the seller. He didn't respond, but later that evening, eBay marked the item as shipped, as it does automatically whenever the seller purchases a shipping label directly from eBay.

I did get a package a few days later – only instead of a $473 redemption card, I got a part of a $3 socket wrench.

I immediately opened a case with eBay, and eventually got my money back. And sure enough, within a span of five weeks from December 2012 through January 2013, the seller picked up nine negative feedback for failing to ship; he is no longer a registered user on eBay under this account.

I had another guy try to sell me a card he apparently didn't have. I paid $230 for an ungraded 2009 Bowman Sterling Mike Trout auto back in September 2012, from a seller with a couple hundred feedback, included one neutral and two negative feedback for "forgetting" to ship items. The seller left tracking information, but

---

[104] For some reason, the answer "because they haven't done it before" inspires little confidence in my mind.
[105] With, I might add, a feedback score of nearly 2,400 100% positive feedback as of April 2014!

never shipped the card. Two weeks and two messages later, I still had neither received the card, nor gotten a response from the seller. But I did see that the seller had time to list other items, including a 2012 Finest Andrew Luck RC Red Refractor #/25, and two more 2009 Bowman Sterling Mike Trout autos.

Finally, after 17 days and three messages, the seller responded. He swore he had shipped the card; but upon request, he insta-refunded my payment anyway without even bothering to contact USPS about the package. And sure enough, within a span of six weeks, the seller picked up 28 negative feedback for failing to ship high-value cards, including various Mike Trout and Bryce Harper autos.

He's probably in jail by now, for one reason or another.

Transactions like these are certainly the exception rather than the norm, and in my experience, eBay has been very good about buyer protection (I can't speak for seller protection). It's also important to realize that sellers sometimes do make honest mistakes. But unfortunately, these things do happen; and whether correctable or not, these are some of the hazards of dealing on eBay.

Retail Blasters and Packs

There are three major problems with buying the retail packs and boxes you might find at Walmart and Target:

1. **Retail product is rarely worth the full retail price.** Except in rare circumstances – such as 2012 Topps Chrome Football blaster boxes – retail product is very rarely worth full retail. Unopened packs are basically never worth retail price, while sealed retail blaster boxes often trade on the open market at significant discounts to retail price, even long after a given product is no longer available at Walmart or Target.

2. **Packs are vulnerable to pack searching.** The odds of pulling key hits – such as autos, memorabilia cards, or other inserts – out of retail packs are slim to begin with, but your true odds are often materially worse due to a practice known as pack searching, in which somebody goes through the packs and tries to identify packs containing hits by differences in weight, feel, or shape. Though the practice is generally discouraged, it is not illegal and may even be rampant.[106][107] And unfortunately, until the practice is

---

[106] www.sportscollectorsdaily.com/responsibility-pack-searching-retailers-manufacturers
[107] dingedcorners.com/2008/12/interview-with-pack-searcher.html

eliminated by manufacturer and retailer countermeasures, all you can really do as a collector is avoid buying retail packs, period.

3. **Packs and even blaster boxes are not tamper proof.** Perhaps an even bigger problem is that packs and blaster boxes are vulnerable to being purchased, opened, and then resealed and returned, before winding up back on the shelf or rack at the retailer.

It was early 2013. I had walked into a local Target in Las Vegas, and was surprised to find a couple of the $20 2012 Topps Chrome Football blasters, at a time when they were selling for $30-$35 on eBay. I picked them up. And then I thought it'd be fun to make a day (or two) out of it, and wound up spending parts of a couple of days driving around to every Target and Walmart in Las Vegas in search of 2012 Topps Chrome Football.

I made out with a couple dozen blaster boxes – a pretty good haul – all of them from a handful of Target stores. In addition, one of the Targets also had maybe half a dozen rack packs total – each containing three retail packs, plus a pack of orange refractors – while one of the Walmarts had a stray one; I bought all of those as well.

As far as I could tell, the blasters were OK. But the rack packs were not.

Aside from being apparently the only rack packs in Las Vegas, the unusual thing about them were the contents – at least to my (untrained) eye, all of the rack packs had seemed perfectly ordinary. The first rack pack I opened was the Walmart one, which seemed to be devoid of rookie cards (which should have been in every pack) and refractors (which were easy to pull); at first, I chalked this up to bad luck, as I didn't really have a basis for comparison other than the blasters.

But then I got around to opening the rack packs from Target. The first was similar to the one from Walmart, but it was the second rack pack that was a dead giveaway – the first pack out of it only had three cards instead of four, while the other two packs were perfectly (re)sealed, but were unquestionably short a card as well. I did not open those.

To Target's credit, they did take these and the other sealed rack packs back. I didn't bother with Walmart, as there was no way I could prove that the one pack I bought from them had been tampered with.

Later in November 2013, the online wholesaler Blowout Cards was having its annual Black Friday sale, and were selling the Walmart version of the 2012 Topps

Chrome Football blaster boxes for $30 (these boxes are now $50). Along with the (many) other things I bought, I picked up six of these.

The Walmart version of the 2012 Topps Chrome Football blasters included 7 packs and a relic, whereas the Target version included 8 packs. But the first perfectly sealed box in this batch contained *no packs of any kind* – only a *stack* of Topps Prime Football commons.

The other five boxes were perfectly sealed, but I didn't even bother opening them. I contacted Blowout, who took the six boxes back for a full refund and offered $25 in store credit.

Not knowing anything about how Blowout acquires its inventory, I think it's a safe bet that the box in question was resealed and "returned" to a Walmart, which then returned the box to the distributor from which Blowout likely acquired it.

For the record, I didn't have any problems with the other $2,000+ in boxes I bought from Blowout on Black Friday (in fact, I pulled a Yasiel Puig Printing Plate Auto 1/1 out of a 2013 Bowman Chrome Jumbo box),[108] and had not had any previous problems buying from Blowout in the past. And I do want to give them credit for their excellent customer service response, which is more than I can say for Topps (next).

That said, the integrity of even the retail blaster boxes is a real concern. I don't know how common an issue it is – and I haven't bought much retail product – but I have had enough *questionable* experiences to put doubt in my mind (not so much with newly released product, but mostly with older boxes that say "Extreme Value" and "$11.99"), such that it might even be beneficial for Walmart and Target to consider a no-return policy on sealed packs and boxes.

---

[108] This was an expensive book to write.

Damaged Topps Redemptions and $10k+ "Customer Service"

On the evening of Friday, February 28, 2014 – just as I was completing a draft of the manuscript for this book – I received a good-sized, nearly cube-shaped box from Topps, and delivered by FedEx. I signed for it.

Now this was completely unusual. To this point, every redemption card I had gotten back from Topps was shipped one-by-one, in a sleeve and top loader, and either in a stiff, flat, yellow mailer (for lower value cards), or wrapped in bubble wrap and placed in a larger white mailer (for higher value cards). I thought to myself, *This must be good.*

Except when I went to open the box – a perfectly intact box – I found what turned out to be 103 cards (all autos) with a combined value well over $10k, just stacked loosely in the box with some pieces of foam.[109] There were no sleeves or top loaders, and the cards were not secured in any sort of way. Moreover, one of the corners of all of the cards was damaged by some kind of oily liquid, most of the cards were stuck together, and some of the autos were smeared.

At least in terms of this condition sensitive game, the value of all 103 cards was essentially destroyed.

---

[109] When I first opened the box, I couldn't look. I took pictures, and finally worked up the courage to take the cards out of the box to take inventory that Sunday.

Among the cards that were damaged were (all autos):

2013 Topps Chrome Yasiel Puig Sepia Refractor #/75

2013 Topps Chrome Manny Machado
- Atomic Refractor #/10
- (3) Camo Refractors #/15
- (2) Red Refractors #/25
- Silver and Black Refractor #/25
- Red Hot Rookie #/25
- (2) Gold Refractors #/50
- (2) Sepia Refractors #/75

2013 Topps Chrome Jose Fernandez
- Atomic Refractor #/10
- Camo Refractor #/15
- (3) Red Refractors #/25
- (7) Gold Refractors #/50
- (6) Sepia Refractors #/75, including #16/75 (jersey #) and #75/75
- (7) Black Refractors #/100
- (2) Blue Refractors #/199
- Refractor
- Base

2013 Finest Jose Fernandez
- (2) Red Refractors #/25
- (9) Gold Refractors #/50
- (12) X-Fractors #/149
- (5) Orange Refractors #/99
- (6) Green Refractors #/125
- (4) Refractors
- Gold Refractor Patch Auto #16/50 (jersey #)

2012 Bowman Sterling Gerrit Cole Sterling Auto Showcase #1/25
2013 Topps Chrome Shelby Miller Silver and Black Auto Refractor #1/25
2013 Topps Chrome Jurickson Profar Silver and Black Auto Refractor #/25
(2) 2013 Topps Chrome Anthony Rendon Atomic Auto Refractors #/10
2013 Topps Chrome Anthony Rendon Camo Auto Refractor #/15
...and several others.

Many thoughts ran through my head, including:

1. Holy shit.

2. This is unbelievable.

3. There's no way I can prove this.

4. Nobody will ever believe me.

5. It's only money.

6. Thanks, Topps!

Luckily, I turned out to be wrong about the third and fourth lines.

The first thing I did was go to Topps.com to contact customer service, which it turns out conveniently is only available Monday through Friday from 9 a.m. to 4 p.m. ET – hours clearly geared towards serving business-to-business customers, rather than the collectors who actually buy the cards. I left them a message, took a picture of the box, and posted it on Twitter to make sure I had their attention.

By Sunday, Topps still hadn't responded, though their Twitter account definitely works weekends. At this point, the only thing I knew was that the weight of the package listed on the label was 2.2 lbs., which should not be enough to put 103 cards (one of them a sterling silver card from 2012 Bowman Sterling) in top loaders.

I posted about the incident on the Blowout Cards forums (knowing that this is unbelievable, and that it would draw at least a few skeptics).[110] Somebody suggested that the original package must have been damaged in FedEx's possession, and that a FedEx employee must have picked up the cards and threw them in another box. This turned out to be the case, as there was another label on the box, confirming a FedEx relabel:

02:37 02/25/2014
FedEx Relabel

---

[110] www.blowoutcards.com/forums/baseball/676463-topps-destroys-10k-redemptions.html

So mystery solved – it's FedEx's fault – and this should be a piece of cake. Right? Moreover, among the other things that emerged from the Blowout thread was that it is apparently common practice for Topps to ship multiple cards – even high value cards up to at least $400 or $500 in value – in *snap cases* (the same ones you might use to store a handful of commons).

When this happened, I *desperately* wanted to be able to say that Topps dealt with this in a fair, professional, and timely manner. But that's not at all what's happened.

On Monday morning, a Topps Customer Service Manager sent me an e-mail first thing in the morning, and followed up with a phone call. I sent her pics of the cards and the perfectly intact carton, along with the label detailing the "relabel." On the phone call, she said that she would get back to me later that afternoon or the next day with a pre-paid shipping label so that I could send the cards back to Topps; she followed up with an e-mail later that afternoon saying she was still waiting on the shipping label.

By Wednesday, I still had not received the shipping label, and sent the customer service (CS) manager an e-mail to no response. On Thursday, I followed up with another e-mail to no response. I went to Twitter; Topps did not respond, but FedEx responded immediately, and within a couple of hours confirmed via e-mail that the original package had been damaged in their possession:

> **FedEx:** "It is my understanding that your package was damaged while in transit." *(via e-mail, 3/6/14)*

I posted my findings in the Blowout thread. On Friday, the Topps CS manager finally responded to my e-mail(s), saying that she had sent the FedEx label on Tuesday (which I didn't get, but whatever), and that she was traveling and hadn't had access to her e-mail (which might have made sense in 1994).

At this point, I suspected that Topps hadn't insured the package, and was looking for a way out; otherwise, you would think they would want the evidence back in this open-and-shut case so that they could make their case with FedEx to recover the insurance. At any rate, I immediately mailed out the package using the pre-paid overnight shipping label (the "overnight" part being of no value because Topps Customer Service/Support, conveniently, does not work weekends), and e-mailed the Topps CS manager informing that I had done so.

FedEx tracking confirmed that Topps received the package on Monday morning. But I did not hear from Topps until Wednesday, when the CS manager finally e-mailed to confirm that they had received the package. She said that she was trying to secure inventory to replace the damaged cards; that she would "advise value and available substitution" for the cards she could not replace; and that she would "be in touch no later than Monday."

On Monday (of course), March 17, the CS manager e-mailed back saying that she had found replacements for 96 cards, but would need to replace 7 cards *they* valued at $1,060 (Topps' ascribed valuations in parenthesis):

- 2013 Topps Chrome Atomic Refractor Manny Machado #/10 ($300)
- (2) 2013 Topps Chrome Atomic Refractor Anthony Rendon #/10 ($155)
- 2013 Topps Chrome Red Refractor Jose Fernandez #/25 ($150)
- (3) 2013 Topps Chrome Gold Refractor Jose Fernandez #/50 ($100)

I asked how they came up with the valuations; she said they used eBay completed auctions.

I said wait a minute. The last 2013 Topps Chrome Manny Machado Atomic Refractor auto #/10 sold for $420 on 2/28/14, while a Camo Refractor #/15 sold for $367.50 on 2/9/14. Regarding the Jose Fernandez Topps Chrome autos, three Atomic Refractors #/10 sold for $1,300 (12/18/13), $600 (1/5/14), and $475 (2/8/14); the last Red Refractor #/25 sold for $250 (3/13/14) (albeit the #25/25); and two Gold Refractors #/50 sold for $165 (3/6/14 and 1/19/14). Meanwhile, the last Anthony Rendon Atomic Refractor #/10 sold for $175 on 3/1/14.

In addition, among the cards damaged were key serial numbers, including:

- 2013 Topps Chrome Shelby Miller Black and Silver Auto Refractor #1/25
- 2012 Bowman Sterling Gerrit Cole Sterling Showcase Auto #1/25
- 2013 Finest Jose Fernandez Gold Refractor Jersey Auto #16/50 (Fernandez's jersey #)
- 2013 Topps Chrome Jose Fernandez Sepia Autos #16/75 and #75/75 (jersey # and #75/75)

These cards are worth about a 50% premium to whatever they are replacing them with. Consequently, the value of my cards to be replaced should be more like $1,700-$1,750 rather than $1,060.

On Friday, March 21, the Topps CS manager e-mailed back with:

> Here is what I am able to offer you:
>
> $420 on Machado
>
> $200 on Fernandez
>
> Premium numbers are not a guarantee...luck of the draw.

$200 presumably for the Fernandez Red Refractor is reasonable, considering that the one that sold for $250 was the #25/25. But what about the Gold Refractors?

Moreover, the argument about premium numbers being "luck of the draw" is incorrect. I already won that draw. Topps is not replacing the draw – they are replacing the cards that were damaged during delivery. Moreover, I now have a **zero** percent chance of hitting those key numbers, which means that whatever cards Topps replaces them with has a **100% chance** of being worth materially less.

At this point, I told her that their customer service response was "third world" – what I really meant to say is that it is a shit show. For a $10k+ customer service issue, Topps should be looking to rectify it in a fair, professional, and timely manner; instead, they are dragging their feet and lowballing me.

Having not heard from Topps, I e-mailed FedEx to inquire about whether Topps insured the package, and if so for what amount. In an e-mail dated Thursday, March 27, the FedEx representative responded:

> **FedEx:** I looked up your tracking number and do not see that additional declared value was purchased.

In other words, Topps shipped my $10k+ in cards in snap cases, and did not insure the package for *any* amount.

Finally on Tuesday, April 1, the Topps CS manager e-mailed back saying that they could "offer individual cards or product for the value ($1,830)."

I don't know about the math they used to get to that number, but I'm not going to complain. I said $1,830 works, and asked what my options were.

The Topps CS manager responded (italics mine): "I can send product (box/case) or individual cards (*random*) for the value."

Well first of all, it shouldn't even be legal for Topps to be able to offer "random" cards at values they assign to them. The fact is that if Topps were regulated by a state gambling commission, this practice would never be allowed – that would be the equivalent of a casino being allowed to say "We can't pay the $100,000 in cash we owe you, but we can offer this $30,000 car we value at $100,000."

I said I prefer individual cards, but not "random." And besides, other customers have been allowed to pick their cards.

She says I can make her a list of players and teams I like, and she'll see what she has and get back to me. I did so.

That was Thursday, April 3. A week later, on April 10, the Topps CS manager apologized for the delayed response, said she was "working on the cards I have available to complete this," and would "be in touch by Monday with what is available."

Well, as I write this, it is now Friday, April 18, 2014. It's been seven weeks since I received the package of damaged cards, and over two weeks since we have settled on a value for the cards that need to be replaced. And Topps hasn't even gotten around to actually offering replacements.

The State of the Industry

This is my fifth book, and fourth time writing Closing Thoughts. Usually, this would be my favorite part of the book – the part where I would get to reminisce about my experiences over the past couple of years, revisiting one of my favorite childhood hobbies, and the development of the ideas that would make me sit down and write a nearly 400-page book. But unfortunately, there are bigger issues to deal with.

On the one hand, I feel pretty strongly that the modern baseball card is underappreciated and potentially ripe for a revaluation, at least on the higher end. On the other hand, this is an industry that could destroy itself pretty easily.

For starters, we have an effective monopoly baseball card manufacturer which has demonstrated no ability to manage supply, and instead has shown that it will print whatever it can sell in the short run, at the expense of the long-term health of card values – the very card values which make it possible for them to even print cards to begin with. That same company has also demonstrated a willingness to take its best brand – Bowman Chrome – and print three sets of potentially identically valued

RC autos for the same player in order to help sell its late-year Bowman Chrome and Bowman Draft products, and at the expense of anybody who had purchased its earlier year Bowman product.

Though I think eBay has been stellar as far as buyer protection and generally being a safe place to be a buyer, the fact is that anywhere there is money, there will be scumbags. At best, the hassle of having to deal with scumbags is a persistent threat, even if any issues may potentially be rectified.

The integrity of retail product is also a major concern. Putting aside the fact that retail product is rarely worth its value, nobody should have to walk into a Walmart or Target and have to question whether or not the product they are buying has been searched or otherwise tampered with.

And finally, we have an effective monopoly baseball card manufacturer which is printing IOUs which apparently are not worth face value, and seems to approach customer service issues like an insurance company ("We're not going to insure your $10k+ shipment, and if it doesn't arrive intact, we will try to replace it for less!").

The fact is that when I began writing this book, I wanted to be able to be Topps' biggest supporter. I wanted to be able to say that this is a great game that's completely underappreciated, and look what these card manufacturers are doing now. When the $10k+ shipment of redemptions arrived, I was extremely disappointed. I wished that it hadn't happened, but hoped that Topps would make it right and make this easy.

For the sake of this book – and for the sake of this game – I *desperately* wanted to be able to say that Topps handled the matter in a professional, fair, and timely manner; instead, Topps Customer Support has dragged their feet and lowballed me on the value of my cards, such that it's been seven weeks and they haven't even offered replacements yet.

After Topps took four days to get me the shipping label, I didn't pester them at any point. But I figure that's not really my responsibility, either – if you screw up a $10k+ customer order (or any order for that matter), you should be at the customer's feet.

I suppose I also could have mentioned the book in order to effect a quick and positive outcome, but:

1. **That would be letting Topps off the hook.** Which Topps has done nothing to deserve. I figure if you screw up a $10k+ shipment, drag your feet and lowball me on the value of my cards, you can feel free to dig as big a hole as you'd like.

2. **It wouldn't have been fair to anyone else who doesn't have that option.** For me to let Topps off the hook now would be to condemn anybody else with legitimate customer service issues to be treated by Topps in the same manner.

I never really understood those movies where the victim or the victim's family says it feels pity rather than anger towards the culprit. But I get it now, because that's the way that I feel.

What I've come to realize is that, from top to bottom, Topps is one of the dumbest companies in America. Right now, they are flying under the radar because the sports card industry is not one that anybody outside the industry really cares about at the moment. As a consequence, their attitude seems to be that customer service issues – $10k+ or otherwise – aren't a big deal, because the worst that can happen is that somebody complains about it on an online discussion forum, where all anyone does is complain about them anyway.

What they don't seem to grasp is that by demonstrating an unwillingness to deal with even a $10k+ issue in a fair, professional, and timely manner, Topps is creating risk in the marketplace – the risk that their redemptions are not worth face value, and that the threat of even having to deal with Topps is in itself a risk. These risks fundamentally devalue the value of a Topps redemption/IOU.

They also don't seem to grasp that while the collectors holding the redemptions aren't buying from Topps directly, these collectors are in fact Topps customers by virtue of the supply chain. The fact is, without the guys spending $10k on redemptions, there are no case breakers to sell them. And without the case breakers – who appear to already be squeezing themselves out of the market anyway – pre-order demand drops.

Moreover, this is not a hobby that I or anyone else *needs*.

I went nearly 20 years without buying a baseball card. This is a hobby that I have enjoyed coming back to, but one I can certainly live without. And unless something drastically changes, I am content to take the collection that I have and call it a day.

I can't speak for or against Panini or Upper Deck having not really dealt with them. But the one thing I will say is that Panini strikes me as a company that is very interested in what's happening with both the supply chain and the collector. At the March 2013 Industry Summit in Las Vegas, I sat in on a conference session involving the emergence of the case breaker segment. We went around the room, and everybody introduced themselves; among those in attendance were a couple of guys from Topps and a couple of guys from Upper Deck, but about a half a dozen guys announcing themselves as representing Panini America.

And at the 2014 Industry Summit, Panini announced a new Panini Rewards system designed to eliminate player-specific redemptions. Starting with the May 2014 release of 2014 Score Football, collectors will now get cards with a point value for which the collector can redeem for existing inventory on Panini's website or app, instead of getting a redemption for a specific card which may take years to fulfill.[111] Whether this is the best solution regarding redemptions is debatable and remains to be seen, but I'll at least give Panini points for trying to make changes for the better.

Be a Collector First, Everything Else Second

Despite all that, this has very much been a hobby that I've enjoyed coming back to. The fact is, you don't write 120,000 words and nearly 400 pages on anything without enjoying it.

My journey back to baseball cards actually started with modern, limited edition, serialized guitar effects pedals, which is another story in itself. But from that, I learned about the pricing power of rare, serialized collectibles, and that this principle is not limited to vintage issues.

That got me to thinking about the baseball cards I used to collect as a kid. Like many other former collectors my age, what I found was that, not only could I afford to buy unopened boxes of all of the 1980s and early 1990s card issues I wanted as a kid but couldn't afford, but that I could also buy more than could ever be practical, and at a fraction of what they cost even back then. I started by buying a few boxes of various issues for kicks – 1987 Donruss, 1989 Upper Deck, 1992 Bowman. I bought a new issue of Beckett Baseball magazine, and eventually got a subscription to the Beckett online price guide.

One of the first things that caught my eye were the book values of graded cards. How is it that a BGS 9.5 1987 Donruss Greg Maddux RC is worth $100, when

---

[111] www.beckett.com/news/2014/03/panini-to-eliminate-player-specific-redemptions-and-add-patch-database

brand new boxes can be had for $20-$30 each (I would figure this out later)? I then set out to buy boxes of pretty much everything from the 1980s, plus 1990 Leaf, 1992 Bowman, and 1994 Fleer Flair in an attempt to build gems. My goal was to build one each of all of the key RCs from these sets.

While I had a fun time trying to do this, I figured out later that if you really just want a Gem Mint copy of a card from these sets, and you don't really care about opening boxes and trying to build it, you're probably better off just going on eBay and trying to buy a graded one on the cheap.

Eventually, I got around to looking at more modern card issues, more out of curiosity than anything else.

It was the spring of 2012, and I had walked into one of the remaining local card stores to pick up supplies to store all of the stuff from the '80s I had bought. I asked the owner about the new stuff. "What's good? And which one has the rookie card of this Harper kid?" I walked out with a jumbo pack of 2012 Topps, and a pack of 2011 Bowman.

Now at this point I am thoroughly confused. For starters, this one pack of Bowman included parts of three different sets listed in the Beckett Baseball magazine price guide – Bowman, Bowman Prospects, and Bowman Chrome Prospects. Why? And why is this 2011 Bowman Bryce Harper (the one that I didn't pull in this pack) not listed as a rookie card in the Beckett price guide?

I figured this out, and eventually started picking at graded RC and prospect cards – mostly established stars at first, and then eventually prospects – but mostly base cards, adding to my modest collection. But then I looked at the relatively expensive, serialized cards and realized that I was wasting my time – what I saw in the premium-color, serialized parallels was what I saw in the rare, serialized guitar pedals: Pricing power.

What followed from there is what you see in this book.

This is a game that makes good use of principles from a variety of disciplines, including retail, economics, stocks investing, real estate, gambling in general, and poker. And despite any negative experiences I've had, this is very much a game that I've enjoyed playing, and one I anticipate that many, many, others will enjoy as well.

That said, I will leave you with two pieces of advice:

1. **Don't spend your life savings on baseball cards.** While I think the case I've made for modern high-grade, limited print baseball cards is a very good one, it can always be logically argued that the fundamental value of a baseball card is zero, particularly in the event of a zombie apocalypse. If you are going to spend more than a token amount of money on baseball cards – for investment purposes or otherwise – make sure your house is in order first. Pick (undervalued) stocks before baseball cards.

2. **Be a collector first, and an investor and everything else second.** If you approach this game as a way to make money above all else, you are setting yourself up for disappointment. Instead, be a collector first, and think of it as a way to have your collection, and one that may potentially pay for itself – and maybe more.

Jeff Hwang
April 18, 2014

Glossary

Absolute scarcity: Scarcity in the truest sense, generally relating to the highest quality (best condition) of the scarce.

Adjusted multiple: The graded book value multiple to ungraded book value, adjusted for the cost of getting a card graded, which for our purposes is assumed to be $10.

Auto: A card which has been autographed; generally refers to certified autos.

BGS: Beckett Grading Services, a third-party card grading and authenticating service established in 1999.

Book value (BV): A card's value according to Beckett price guides; now termed by Beckett as "Beckett Value."

Book value replacement cost: A measure of replacement cost, defined as book value plus the cost of grading.

Case breaker: A new breed of service provider which performs commercialized group breaks.

Card removal effect: When the highest-quality copies of a given card become graded and thus removed from the pool of ungraded cards, resulting in a lower average quality and thus lower average value of the remaining pool of ungraded cards.

Chromes: Chromium stock card.

Collectors Universe (Nasdaq: CLCT): Parent company of PSA.

Condition sensitive: When relatively few high-grade examples exist compared to the total print run, thus placing an extra premium on the highest-quality examples.

Cost approach: Valuation approach in real estate appraisal which uses replacement cost as a value ceiling.

Cut signature: When the manufacturer cuts a signature from another source – typically a photo or some other document – and places it on the card. Often used when the autograph subject is not available to sign a card or sticker (often because the subject is deceased).

Distributor: A firm which distributes product from manufacturer to retailers, hobby dealers, and case breakers.

Expected Value Comp Approach (EV Comp): Valuation approach used to compare values of current prospects to comparable but more established players.

Equilibrium collectible value: Underlying value of a collectible good.

Freeroll: When you can't lose, and thus have risk-free upside.

Gem Mint: A basically perfect card. The highest grade under the PSA grading system, and the second-highest grade under the BGS grading system.

Gem Mint frequency: For a given card, the number of copies graded Gem Mint as a percentage of all cards graded and slabbed.

Grade scarcity: For a given card, the scarcity of cards of a given grade.

Group break: When multiple collectors pool together resources to acquire unopened cases or boxes that an individual otherwise might not be able to acquire.

The Greater Fool Theory: The theory that you can justify buying anything at any price if you think someone else will pay more for it; generally refers to overvalued assets.

Hobby dealer: Your local card shop, or other online dealer that deals in Hobby-only product.

Intrinsic value: An asset's underlying, fundamental value.

Key card: The card that trumps all other cards of a given player in terms of both recognition and value.

Leverage: Sensitivity to changes in demand, or the ability for card values to rise (or fall) and multiples to expand (or contract) along with changes in demand.

Liquidity: The degree to which a card can be sold within a given time frame at prevailing market equilibrium prices.

Manufacturer: Company that makes cards.

Margin of safety: The discount between an asset's underlying value and its current price.

Margin of safety principle: Principle ascribed by Benjamin Graham dictating that an investor should look to acquire assets at a sufficient discount to estimated fair value to account for errors in projection or adverse outcome.

Maximum leverage: The highest possible leverage, achieved when Gem Mint+ quality cards no longer exist in the pool of ungraded cards, and thus the supply of Gem Mint+ cards stops growing.

Memorabilia card: A card which includes some piece of game-worn or player-used artifact, such as a jersey or bat knob.

Multiple contraction: The thinning spread in value between BGS 9.5 Gem Mint and lesser graded or ungraded copies of the same card – and between premium color parallels and base versions of the same cards – due to a bursting bubble or generally declining demand.

Multiple expansion: The widening spread in value between BGS 9.5 Gem Mint and lesser graded or ungraded copies of the same card – and between premium color parallels and base versions of the same cards – generally as a function of increasing demand, card removal, and/or grade scarcity.

On-card auto: Autographed card on which the autograph subject signs the card directly.

Paper card: Standard issue non-chrome card.

Patch card: A card featuring a piece of game-used jersey; though sometimes loosely used to refer to any card with a piece of game-used jersey, it is a term which is often meant to describe an actual patch, such as a piece of a player's jersey number, team name, sleeve, or other logo.

Position bias: When certain positions in a given sport are more highly valued than other positions.

Premium color: Generally Gold Refractors #'d/50 (or equivalent) or better.

Pricing power: The ability to raise prices that comes with having the best available version of a given card on the market at a given time.

Pricing pressure: Loss of pricing power due to the availability of like or superior (scarcer) versions of the same card on the market at the same time.

Pristine: A BGS 10 Pristine grade is the highest possible grade under the BGS grading system.

PSA: Professional Sports Authenticator, a third-party card grading and authenticating service established in 1991.

Quad 10s: When a BGS 10 Pristine card has all four subgrades graded a perfect 10.

Redemption card: An IOU, inserted into packs by the manufacturer to be redeemed for autographed cards or other memorabilia.

Relative scarcity: The scarcity of one card compared to another.

Replacement cost: The cost to build like asset in a given condition (e.g. BGS 9.5 Gem Mint).

Retailer: Refers to non-hobby sellers of card products, primarily Target and Walmart.

Rookie card (RC): Through 1988, a player's first card issued in a pack-issued, MLB-licensed set; from 1989-2005, a player's first card issued in an MLB-licensed set. From 2006-present, a player's first card issued as part of the base set (excluding prospect inserts) in an MLB-licensed set. Officially-designated rookie cards carry "Rookie Card" logo from 2006-2009, and "RC" logo from 2010-present.

Sales comparison approach: Valuation approach use in real estate appraisal which uses recent sales of comparable assets as a proxy for value.

Secondary color: Colored, serialized refractors or other parallels more common than Gold Refractors #'d/50 (or equivalent).

Shill bidding: When a seller or cohort bids up the price of his own auction. A strictly forbidden practice on eBay, though one which still does occur.

Slab: A card that has been graded and placed into a sealed holder by a third-party grading company.

Sticker auto: Autographed card where the subject signs a sticker, which is subsequently placed onto the card by the manufacturer.

Tell: A clue a seller may provide as to the condition of an ungraded card for sale.

Value investing: General approach to investing in which the practitioner seeks to acquire assets at prices lower than the assets' intrinsic value.

XRC: Extended rookie card. Designation used by Beckett from 1982-1988 for rookie cards issued as part of extended sets.

53927378R00204

Made in the USA
Columbia, SC
22 March 2019